The Philosophers of the Ancient World

An A to Z Guide

The Philosophers of the Ancient World

An A to Z Guide

Trevor Curnow

Duckworth

First published in 2006 by
Gerald Duckworth & Co. Ltd.
90-93 Cowcross Street, London EC1M 6BF
Tel: 020 7490 7300
Fax: 020 7490 0080
inquiries@duckworth-publishers.co.uk
www.ducknet.co.uk

A catalogue record for this book is available
from the British Library

ISBN 0 7156 3497 6
EAN 9780715634974

Typeset by Ray Davies
Printed and bound in Great Britain by
CPI Bath

Contents

For Howard, Alan and Vivian
the best of brothers

Acknowledgements

My greatest debt is to the people who produced all the books I have drawn on in putting this book together, especially the major reference works that appear in the Bibliographical Essay. Their efforts have made mine much easier in tracking down the less familiar characters who appear in the following pages. I am also grateful to Lancaster University library for its admirable collection of useful and relevant items. As with my previous book on *The Oracles of the Ancient World*, Deborah Blake of Duckworth has been a supportive editor and has once again produced the excellent maps.

Lancaster, April 2006   T.C.

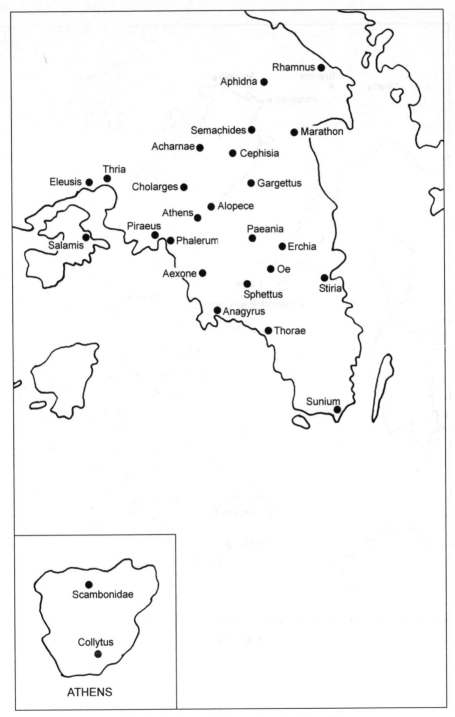

Map 1. Attica and Athens (see also Map 5).

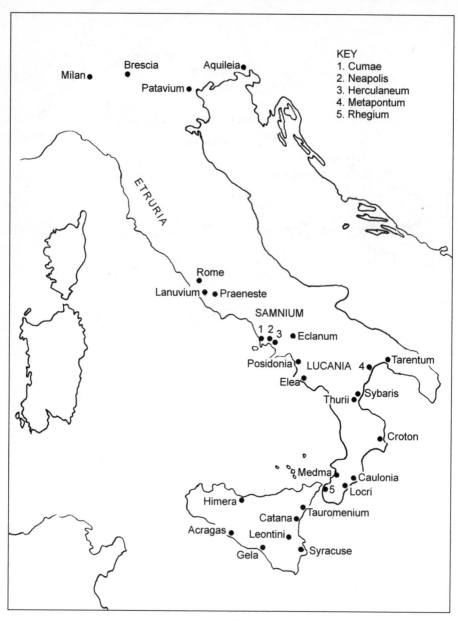

KEY
1. Cumae
2. Neapolis
3. Herculaneum
4. Metapontum
5. Rhegium

Milan

Brescia

Aquileia

Patavium

ETRURIA

Rome

Lanuvium • Praeneste

SAMNIUM

1 2 3 • Eclanum

Posidonia LUCANIA 4 • Tarentum

Elea

Thurii • Sybaris

Croton

Medma • Caulonia

5 • Locri

Himera

Catana • Tauromenium

Acragas • Leontini

Gela • Syracuse

Map 2. Italy.

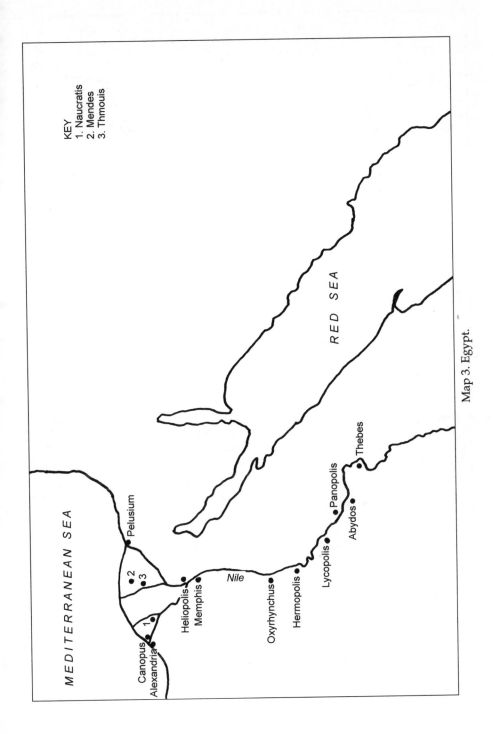

KEY
1. Naucratis
2. Mendes
3. Thmouis

MEDITERRANEAN SEA

RED SEA

Pelusium

Canopus
Alexandria

Heliopolis
Memphis

Nile

Oxyrhynchus

Hermopolis

Lycopolis

Panopolis

Abydos

Thebes

Map 3. Egypt.

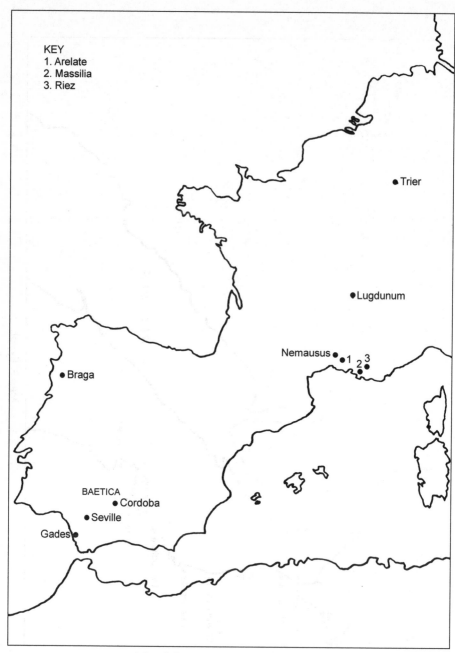

KEY
1. Arelate
2. Massilia
3. Riez

● Trier

●Lugdunum

Nemausus ● ●1 ₂3●

● Braga

BAETICA
● Cordoba
● Seville
Gades ●

Map 4. Spain, France and Germany.

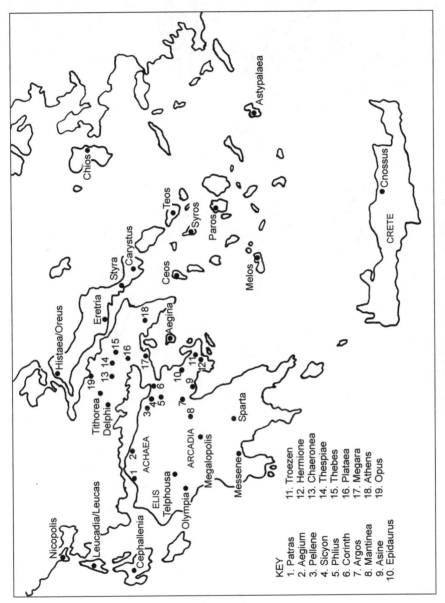

Map 5. Southern Greece (see also Map 1).

KEY
1. Patras
2. Aegium
3. Pellene
4. Sicyon
5. Phlius
6. Corinth
7. Argos
8. Mantinea
9. Asine
10. Epidaurus
11. Troezen
12. Hermione
13. Chaeronea
14. Thespiae
15. Thebes
16. Plataea
17. Megara
18. Athens
19. Opus

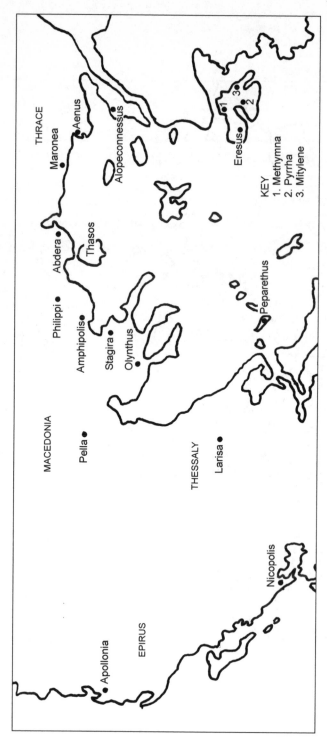

Map 6. Northern Greece.

Map 7. North Africa.

Map 8. The Black Sea, Asia Minor and the Near East.

Map 9. Asia Minor (detail).

KEY
1. Byzantium
2. Parium
3. Lampsacus
4. Abydos
5. Alexandria Troas
6. Assus
7. Atarneus
8. Apollonia
9. Erythrae
10. Samos
11. Magnesia on the Maeander
12. Tralles
13. Miletus
14. Myndus
15. Halicarnassus

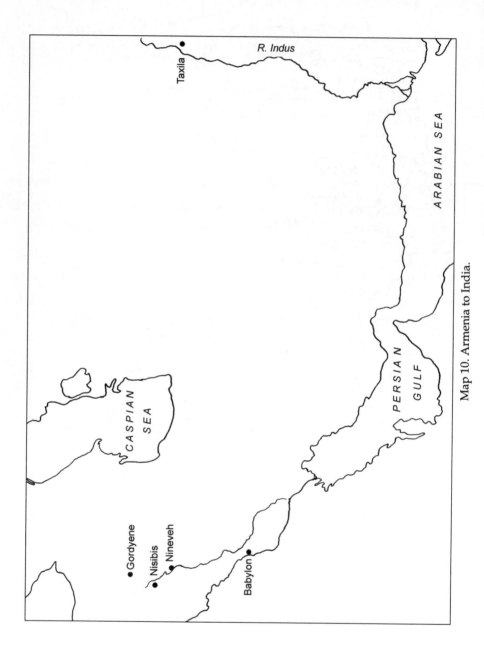

Map 10. Armenia to India.

Introduction

The aim of this book is to provide within the scope of a single volume an A to Z guide to the philosophers of the ancient world. The names of over 2,300 people appear here, some very well-known, some barely remembered and many somewhere in between. The part of the ancient world covered comprises Europe, North Africa and West Asia, with very occasional exceptions. I have made no attempt to include the ancient philosophers from areas further east as that would require a different and much larger book. The exceptions are those who had a direct influence on or contact with those further west.

The history of Western philosophy traditionally begins around 600 BC with Thales of Miletus, and few names appear here from before his time. Those that do are often semi-legendary. I have taken the year AD 641 as marking the end of the ancient world for present purposes. It was chosen for the simple reason that this is the year at which the last volume of the *Prosopography of the Later Roman Empire* ends and there seemed to be a certain logic in following suit.

Establishing geographical and chronological boundaries was easier than deciding who was and who was not to count as a philosopher. Philosophy overlapped with many other activities in antiquity, such as mathematics and medicine. I have operated on the basis that those using this book will primarily be interested in what counts as philosophy today and that those mainly interested in ancient Greek mathematicians, for example, will look for information on them elsewhere. However, some of the most important mathematicians, physicians and others have been included in order to give some sense of what the areas of overlap were.

Given that the historical scope of this book encompasses a significant proportion of the Christian era, it has also been necessary to decide which theologians to admit and which to exclude. Decisions have generally been made on the basis of the extent to which they engaged in philosophical debates, whether contemporary or historical, that extended beyond Christian circles.

There was also the problem of the ancient conception of philosophy according to which it might comprise a certain kind of life. This was especially the case with Stoics and Epicureans, many of whom pursued careers in public office, but were guided by the values of the schools. These have had to be decided on a case by case basis, with attention paid to the centrality of these values in their lives and the extent to which they were clearly identified with them.

All the decisions taken with regard to all of these problems are disputable and doubtless many will be disputed. I should also point out that while the

1

length of a particular entry may be a rough guide to the perceived importance of an individual, it is no more than a rough guide. While the shortest entries tend to say all that is known about someone, the longest entries could all have been considerably longer. While longer works have the luxury of setting out alternative interpretations of the available material, whether philosophical or historical, I have often had to be more ruthless and make decisions. Although I think those decisions are all defensible, unfortunately that is not the same as being able to guarantee that they are all correct.

It is hoped that the book will be valuable to newcomers and experts in the field alike. Newcomers will find it a wide-ranging introduction to ancient philosophy while experts should find it a useful and convenient source of reference to hundreds of minor figures. For those less familiar with the field, 'A Brief Overview of the History of Ancient Philosophy' is a good place to start and should help to explain the very limited specialist vocabulary of the book. 'Conventions and Format' provides the little explanation needed to make sense of the entries. The 'Bibliographical Essay' provides information on sources and further reading. Finally the 'Index of Places' provides a guide to the maps.

It goes without saying that there are bound to be mistakes in the book, whether borrowed or original, and I would be grateful to hear about them. I can be contacted via the publisher or by email at TCurnow@ucsm.ac.uk.

A Brief Overview of the History of Ancient Philosophy

The first relatively firm date in the history of Western philosophy is 28 May 585 BC. Thales of Miletus, usually regarded as the first philosopher, correctly predicted that there would be a total eclipse of the sun on that day. Miletus lay in the area of Asia Minor known as Ionia and Thales and his immediate philosophical successors from the same region are often known as the Ionians. (In modern terms, they may have been as much scientists as philosophers.) Quite why Western philosophy began there and then is a mystery, as is the extent to which Thales and those who came after him drew on non-Greek sources of inspiration such as Egypt and Phoenicia.

Thales was regarded as one of the Seven Sages of ancient Greece. There was never a definitive list of these, and among the many names that cropped up on the alternative versions were poets and politicians as well as individuals who belong as much to legend as to history. However, in some way or other they were all supposed to have demonstrated a special capacity for wisdom.

Following the Ionians came an altogether more varied and dispersed group of philosophers including Pythagoras, Parmenides of Elea, and Empedocles of Acragas. With Pythagoras in particular, philosophy opens up from being speculation about the nature of the world to a distinctive way of life within it. Among this group were also Anaxagoras of Clazomenae, who is said to have been the first philosopher to teach in Athens, and Leucippus of Miletus and Democritus of Abdera who were the first to develop atomism. Pythagoras is said to have been the first to use the term 'philosopher', meaning 'lover of wisdom', to describe himself.

The philosophical world of the last part of the fifth century BC is dominated by the figure of Socrates, to the extent that those who came before him are collectively known as the Presocratics. Socrates was often credited with making ethics the most important part of philosophy. Following his death in 399 BC, a long period of philosophy began that was dominated by a group of institutions known as the schools.

The first of these was the Academy in Athens, founded by Plato, who had been a pupil of Socrates. For obvious reasons, its members became known as Academics or Platonists. The history of the Academy and Platonism is often divided into a number of different phases. First there was the Old Academy or Early Platonism dominated by Plato's immediate successors. Then came the Middle Academy, dominated by Arcesilaus of Pitane and Carneades of

Cyrene. During this period (roughly 260 to 80 BC) the Academy took a strongly sceptical line. The New Academy was inaugurated when Antiochus of Ascalon rejected the sceptical approach in favour of a more dogmatic one. Confusingly, this is called Middle Platonism, which lasted until the advent of Neoplatonism under Plotinus in the third century AD. Neoplatonism remained dominant during the rest of the period covered by this book.

The Lyceum was founded by Aristotle, a pupil of Plato. His followers were often known as Peripatetics after the the *peripatos* (covered walkway) at the Lyceum, which was a grove sacred to Apollo at Athens, where members of the school met. After Aristotle's time the school became a major centre for scientific research. When Andronicus of Rhodes became head of the Lyceum in the first century BC he inaugurated a long period in which writing commentaries on the works of Aristotle became the school's predominant activity.

The Stoa, named after the colonnade in Athens where he taught, was founded by Zeno of Citium. Its history is usually divided into three stages. The early Stoa was the period of Zeno and his immediate successors during the third century BC. The Middle Stoa was inaugurated in the second century BC and dominated by Panaetius of Rhodes and Posidonius of Apamea, who made the school's teachings rather less severe. The later Stoa is associated with the names of Seneca, Epictetus and Marcus Aurelius who belong to the first and second centuries AD. During this time Stoicism became highly influential in the Roman world.

The fourth of the main schools was known as The Garden, founded by Epicurus at the end of the fourth century BC. In many ways it was the most conservative of them all. Because its teachings changed less, there are no obvious periods into which to divide the school's history. It too became influential for a while in Italy.

These four schools were all initially established in Athens and remained based there for a substantial period. However, by the time of Posidonius the centre of gravity of the Stoics at least seems to have shifted away from Athens and later Alexandria would become an important centre of Platonism. They may all have migrated by AD 176 when Marcus Aurelius sponsored new professorships for each of them in Athens. There was also a tendency, less pronounced in Epicureanism, for the schools to become increasingly reconciled with each other over time. Each came to endorse a degree of eclecticism with the result that sometimes made it difficult to distinguish one from the other.

There were two more major schools and a number of minor ones. The two major ones were the Sceptics and the Cynics, although it is somewhat misleading to call either movement a school. Founded by Pyrrho of Elis in the fourth century BC, the Sceptics were also sometimes called Pyrrhonists. In the third century BC, thanks to Philinus and Serapion, Scepticism found its way into the Empiricist school of medicine, while in the same century it also dominated the Middle Academy. However, there seems to have been no sceptical school as such until the revival led by Aenesidemus of Cnossus, probably in the first century BC, and it is unclear how much this genuinely owed to Pyrrho.

The original Cynics were far too independent and anti-social to have their own school, although Antisthenes of Athens and Diogenes of Sinope certainly attracted followers in the fourth century BC. Over time, the Cynics evolved an unofficial uniform comprising a cloak and a satchel, which in turn became almost an official uniform for philosophers in general. In the fourth century AD the emperor Julian was concerned about people who pretended to be Cynics simply by adopting this uniform.

The minor schools all seem to have had direct connections with Socrates. Euclides of Megara was a friend, and is usually regarded as the founder of the Megaran school. He was probably succeeded by Eubulides of Miletus, under whom the school's followers became known as Eristics. They were later named Dialecticians by Dionysius of Chalcedon. The Elean school was founded by Phaedo of Elis, another friend of Socrates. When Menedemus of Eretria took it over, probably late in the fourth century BC, he removed the school to Eretria from which it took its name thereafter. Aristippus of Cyrene also knew Socrates and the school of Cyrene was founded either by him or a grandson who shared his name.

As a cautionary note, it is important to be aware that under the influence of authors such as Sotion and Hippobotus it became popular to structure the history of philosophy by dividing philosophers into schools and then identifying the schools' successive heads. This approach was substantially adopted by Diogenes Laertius, the author of a major source of our knowledge about ancient philosophy. The extent to which the division into schools is philosophically justified or the successions historically accurate is always difficult to assess. Consequently it is entirely possible that the reality was far less tidy than is often suggested here. Nevertheless, this brief overview should provide some broad context, however sparse and imperfect, for understanding the more detailed information found elsewhere in the book.

As a postscript it is appropriate to add a few comments about gnosticism as a number of gnostic thinkers appear in this book. Opinions are divided as to whether gnosticism should be regarded as a deviant form of Christianity or a quite independent tradition of thought that made itself felt both in Christianity and elsewhere. Typically, gnostics tended to articulate, often in complex terms, an account of the universe that opposed matter and spirit and adopted a negative attitude towards earthly existence which was often portrayed as a kind of imprisonment or exile. Liberation came through knowledge, *gnosis*.

Conventions and Format

The conventions used in this book are few. Personal names are generally given in their Latinised forms. Exceptions are usually due to an alternative spelling being more familiar or commonly used. Consistency is doubtless a virtue but it is equally certain that it is not the only one. Place names are designed to be recognised, so sometimes ancient ones are used, sometimes modern ones and sometimes both. As many of them as possible appear on the maps. I have been sparing with dates because so few of them are truly firmly established. It may generally be assumed that when someone is identified as third century BC, they spent the whole or almost all of their life during that century. Third/second century BC usually indicates that a substantial number of years were lived in each century. The absence of any indication of dates indicates complete ignorance, while the presence of a question mark denotes significant uncertainty. Numbers in square brackets after names are there only to distinguish between individuals with the same name. Otherwise alphabetical order is maintained, with 'of' and 'the' treated as parts of names. Roman names are distributed according to where I think people are most likely to look for them, so Marcus Tullius Cicero comes under 'C' but Quintus Horatius Flaccus (Horace) comes under 'H'. When a name appears in bold within an entry, it indicates that it has a separate entry of its own.

References in round brackets at the end of entries are to works by the individual concerned that can be found in English translation, including in anthologies and on the internet. References in square brackets are to further reading, whether monographs or relatively substantial treatments in larger works or on internet sites. In order to avoid cluttering the text and secure more space for the entries, these references have been kept to a minimum, and preference has been given to the most accessible sources. The bibliographical essay lists many other works that contain further bibliographical information. References are to the most recent editions of a book unless otherwise stated. The only abbreviations used concern series of books. 'Loeb' refers to volumes in the Loeb Classical Library, originally published by Heinemann but now appearing under the imprint of Harvard University Press. Information on the *Ante-Nicene Fathers* and *Nicene and Post-Nicene Fathers* series appears in the bibliographical essay. A full bibliographical reference for the *Routledge Encyclopaedia of Philosophy* can also be found there.

❖ A ❖

ABAMMON
A pseudonym used by **Iamblichus of Chalcis** in the work usually known as *On the Mysteries of the Egyptians.*

ABARIS THE HYPERBOREAN (sixth century BC?)
It is extremely difficult to separate fact from legend where Abaris is concerned. He is meant to have written a number of works and to have possessed a magic arrow enabling him to fly. He seems to have been a priest and a prophet but his philosophical credentials are unclear. According to **Iamblichus of Chalcis**, he became a pupil of **Pythagoras** late in life.

ABNIMUS (second century AD)
Abnimus was a philosopher from Gadara. Some think he may have been a Cynic and possibly the same person as **Oenomaus of Gadara**.

ACAMATIUS OF HELIOPOLIS (fifth century AD)
Acamatius achieved a reputation in his home town (better known as Baalbek) as a philosopher, although his learning was apparently amateurish and shallow. It is said that **Damascius** exposed him as a fraud.

ACHAICUS (first or second century AD?)
According to **Diogenes Laertius** and **Clement of Alexandria**, Achaicus wrote a work on ethics. He also wrote commentaries on works of **Aristotle** [1] and was probably a Peripatetic.

ACHILLAS (third/fourth century AD)
Achillas was a leading Christian and theologian of Alexandria. According to **Eusebius of Caesarea**, he was an exceptionally gifted philosopher.

ACHILLES (third century AD?)
Achilles is best known for having written a commentary on the *Phaenomena* of **Aratus of Soli**. He was mainly interested in astronomy, and is thought to have been a Stoic.

ACILIUS, GAIUS (second century BC)
Acilius was a politician and historian. He was also fluent in Greek and served as interpreter for **Carneades of Cyrene**, **Diogenes of Seleucia** and **Critolaus** when they came to Rome in 155 BC to represent Athens before the Senate.

ACMONIDAS OF TARENTUM (fifth century BC?)
According to **Iamblichus of Chalcis**, Acmonidas was a Pythagorean.

ACRISIUS (first/second century AD)
The inscription on a bust of **Chrysippus of Soli** found in Athens indicates that its donor was someone called Acrisius, who is assumed to have been a Stoic.

ACULINUS or AQUILINUS (third century AD)
According to **Eunapius**, Aculinus was a Neoplatonist and a pupil of **Plotinus**. However, **Porphyry** describes him as one of the gnostics attacked by Plotinus in his lectures. As a contemporary of Aculinus, Porphyry is likely to be the more reliable source.

ACUSILADAS OF TARENTUM (fifth century BC?)
According to **Iamblichus of Chalcis**, Acusiladas was a Pythagorean.

ACUSILAUS OF ARGOS (sixth century BC)
Acusilaus was regarded by some as one of the Seven Sages of ancient Greece. His main interest was in history and he was renowned for the clarity of his style.

ADEIMANTUS (fourth century BC)
Adeimantus was a Platonist and pupil of **Xenocrates of Chalcedon**.

ADEIMANTUS OF COLLYTUS (fifth/fourth century BC)
Adeimantus is best known for his appearance as a character in the *Republic* of **Plato** [1] where he takes part in a debate with **Socrates** on the question of justice.

ADELPHIUS (third century AD)
Adelphius was a gnostic Christian who taught in Rome and attracted a number of followers. He seems to have been a critic of Platonism, and was one of those **Plotinus** had in mind when he made his attacks on gnosticism.

ADRASTUS (fifth century AD)
Adrastus taught philosophy in Aphrodisias. When **Asclepiodotus of Alexandria** claimed that his wife had miraculously given birth, Adrastus exposed him as a fraud.

ADRASTUS OF APHRODISIAS (second century AD)
Adrastus was a Peripatetic who wrote commentaries on the works of **Aristotle** [1] as well as one on the *Timaeus* of **Plato** [1]. Some fragments of his writings have survived in the later works of others.

ADRASTUS OF PHILIPPI (fourth century BC?)
Adrastus is said to have been a pupil of **Aristotle** [1].

AEDESIA (fifth century AD)
Aedesia was the wife of **Hermias**, the mother of **Ammonius** and **Heliodorus** [2], and a widely respected woman in Alexandria. She was convinced of the value of philosophy and after Hermias died took her sons to Athens so that they could study under **Proclus** [1], who had been a friend of her late husband. **Syrianus** [1], to whom she was related, wanted her to marry Proclus but he

declined (because one of the gods vetoed the idea, according to **Suda**). The author of Suda claimed to have known her in her old age and attended her funeral.

AEDESIUS (third/fourth century AD)
Aedesius came from Cappadocia. His father sent him away to learn something useful and was very disappointed when Aedesius returned as a convert to philosophy. However, he soon changed his mind and even encouraged his son in his new interest. Aedesius went on to study in Syria under **Iamblichus of Chalcis** and subsequently founded his own school at Pergamum. He had a great reputation for learning and the emperor **Julian** sought to become one of his students. However, by this time he was an old man and so he encouraged Julian to study with two of his former pupils, **Eusebius of Myndus** and **Chrysanthius of Sardis**, instead. He was a popular figure in Pergamum on account of his affable and modest character.

AEGIMIUS OF ELIS (fourth/third century BC?)
Aegimius was a physician and an atomist.

AELIAN [CLAUDIUS AELIANUS] (second/third century AD)
Aelian came from Praeneste and was a teacher of rhetoric. However, he was also a popular and prolific author, and some of his writings, mainly comprising collections of anecdotes, survive. In his more philosophical works he took a Stoic line.
(Aelian, *Historical Miscellany*, trans. N.G. Wilson, Loeb, 1997)

AELIUS ARISTIDES (second century AD)
Aelius came from Mysia and was a pupil of **Herodes Atticus**. Known best as a sophist, essayist and orator, he defended the sophists against the philosophers. Of his own oratory, it is said he once moved **Marcus Aurelius** to tears.

AELIUS STILO, LUCIUS (second/first century BC)
Aelius came from Lanuvium. He was a Stoic and a teacher of **Varro**.

AENEAS (fifth century AD)
Nothing is known about Aeneas except that **Nilus the Monk** sent him a letter in which it is apparent that he was a pagan philosopher.

AENEAS OF GAZA (fifth/sixth century AD)
Aeneas studied under **Hierocles of Alexandria**. However, as a Christian he rejected those elements of Neoplatonism that he regarded as incompatible with his faith, in particular the beliefs that souls existed before they came into the world and that the world itself had always existed. He wrote *Theophrastus*, a philosophical dialogue that still survives, in which he suggested that philosophy in Athens was in decline in his time.

AENEAS OF METAPONTUM (fifth century BC?)
According to **Iamblichus of Chalcis**, Aeneas was a Pythagorean.

AENESIAS OF MEGALOPOLIS (fourth/third century BC)
Aenesias was a Peripatetic and pupil of **Theophrastus of Eresus**.

AENESIDEMUS OF CNOSSUS (first century BC?)
Aenesidemus was a Sceptic. According to one view, Scepticism faded into obscurity after the time of **Timon of Phlius** only to be revived much later by Aenesidemus. However, **Diogenes Laertius** records another tradition whereby Aenesidemus was taught by **Heraclides** [2], who came at the end of a line of succession stretching back to Timon himself. There is also evidence that Aenesidemus had been a member of the Academy but left it when **Philo of Larisa** led it in a direction he found uncongenial. He then founded his own school called the Pyrrhonists. What is certain is that he wrote a book called *Pyrrhonist Discourses*, dedicated to Lucius Aelius **Tubero**, which became a central text in the Sceptical canon. As it has long since disappeared it is impossible to know how much it actually owed to **Pyrrho of Elis**. **Sextus Empiricus** explicitly acknowledged his debt to Aenesidemus and credited him with developing some of the 'modes' of scepticism. Aenesidemus took the view that there was no certain knowledge about anything as there were always reasons for doubt of one kind or another. He did not assert that knowledge was impossible (because that would have been a dogmatic claim) but rather argued that there appeared to be no better reasons for believing one thing rather than another.
[R.J. Hankinson, *The Sceptics*, London, Routledge, 1995; Richard Bett, *Pyrrho, his Antecedents and his Legacy*, Oxford, Oxford University Press, 2000]

AEPHICIANUS (second century AD)
Aephicianus was a Stoic and a physician who taught **Galen**. He helped to develop an approach to medicine based on both **Hippocrates of Cos** and Stoicism.

AESARA (fifth/fourth century BC?)
Aesara is said to have been a Pythagorean. He is probably to be identified with **Aresas**.

AESCHINES OF NEAPOLIS [Naples] (second/first century BC)
According to **Diogenes Laertius**, Aeschines was a Platonist and favourite pupil of **Melanthius of Rhodes**. He seems to be the same person as the Aeschines said by **Plutarch of Chaeronea** to have studied under **Carneades of Cyrene** when Carneades was an old man.

AESCHINES OF SPHETTUS (fifth/fourth century BC)
Aeschines came from Athens, was one of the circle of **Socrates**, and probably present at his death. He wrote a number of philosophical dialogues of which only a few fragments survive. **Diogenes Laertius** reports a tradition that Socrates, rather than Aeschines, was their true author, but it is unclear how widely this was believed.

AESCHRION (fourth century BC)
Aeschrion came from Mytilene. He was a favourite student of **Aristotle** [1], wrote poetry, and joined the army of Alexander the Great.

AESCHRION OF PERGAMUM (first/second century AD)
Aeschrion belonged to the empiricist school of medicine and was a teacher of **Galen.**

AESCHYLUS (fifth century BC)
Aeschylus was a pupil of **Hippocrates of Chios** and developed a theory about comets that was later criticised by **Aristotle** [1].

AESIMUS, CLAUDIUS (third century AD?)
An undated inscription found at Pergamum refers to Aesimus as a philosopher.

AETHALIDES
Aethalides is a legendary figure, a son of Hermes and one of the Argonauts. According to **Heraclides of Pontus, Pythagoras** claimed to have been Aethalides in an earlier life.

AETHIOPS (fourth century BC)
According to **Diogenes Laertius,** Aethiops was a follower of **Aristippus of Cyrene.** He is described as coming from Ptolemais, although there was probably no city of that name at the time he lived.

AETIUS (fourth century AD)
Aetius came from Antioch. He went to study in Alexandria where he became a keen Aristotelian. It is not clear at what stage in his career he became a Christian. The orthodox regarded him as a heretic because he allied himself with the supporters of **Arius** but he appears to have had his differences with them as well. According to **Suda,** he returned to Antioch and would enter into disputes with people there, seeking to resolve them according to the principles of Aristotelian logic.

AE... see also AI...

AGAMESTOR (third/second century BC)
Agamestor was a Platonist. He is probably the person referred to by **Plutarch of Chaeronea** as Agapestor, a Platonist who suffered from lameness.

AGAPIUS (fourth century AD)
Agapius was a Christian Platonist. His views, which seem to have constituted a mixture of gnosticism and asceticism, were condemned by the Church.

AGAPIUS OF ATHENS (fifth/sixth century AD)
Agapius studied under **Marinus of Neapolis,** and perhaps also under **Proclus** [1]. He achieved a reputation for being a man of learning, and it is said that he took particular delight in devising new and difficult dilemmas, presumably for

his own students to work on. He was arrested sometime during the reign of Zeno (AD 476-91). His subsequent fate is unknown, but someone of the same name taught **John of Lydia** in Constantinople in AD 511, and it may be the same person.

AGASICLES see AGATHOCLES OF TYRE

AGATHARCHIDES (second century BC)
Agatharchides was a philosopher who wrote books on many different subjects including history and geography. Opinions differ as to whether he came from Cnidus or Samos. He may have been an Aristotelian and his name sometimes appears as Agatharchus.

AGATHINUS, CLAUDIUS (first century AD)
Agathinus came from Sparta and studied medicine as well as philosophy. In medicine, he subscribed to the Pneumatist school of **Athenaeus of Attaleia**, under whom he studied. He was also a pupil of Lucius Annaeus **Cornutus**, and his general philosophical outlook was that of a Stoic.

AGATHION see SOSTRATUS HERACLES

AGATHOBULUS (fourth/third century BC?)
Plutarch of Chaeronea mentions an Epicurean called Agathobulus, but this may be a confused reference to **Aristobolus**, the brother of **Epicurus**.

AGATHOBULUS OF ALEXANDRIA (first/second century AD)
Agathobulus was a Cynic with a reputation for a strict asceticism. **Demonax** was one of his followers, and perhaps also **Peregrinus Proteus**.

AGATHOCLES [1] (third century BC?)
The name of Agathocles, a Stoic, appears in a work by **Lucian of Samosata**. Opinions are divided as to whether Lucian invented him or not.

AGATHOCLES [2] (second century AD)
Agathocles was a Peripatetic.

AGATHOCLES OF TYRE (second century BC)
Agathocles was a Platonist and pupil of **Carneades of Cyrene**. His name sometimes appears as Agasicles.

AGATHON (third century BC)
Chrysippus of Soli wrote a book on logic that seems to have been designed as a response to one by Agathon, who is otherwise unknown.

AGEAS OF CROTON (fifth century BC?)
According to **Iamblichus of Chalcis**, Ageas was a Pythagorean.

AGELAS OF CROTON (fifth century BC?)
According to **Iamblichus of Chalcis**, Agelas was a Pythagorean.

AGESARCHUS OF METAPONTUM (fifth century BC?)
According to **Iamblichus of Chalcis**, Agesarchus was a Pythagorean.

AGESIDAMUS OF METAPONTUM (fifth century BC?)
According to **Iamblichus of Chalcis**, Agesidamus was a Pythagorean.

AGESILAUS [1] (fourth century BC?)
Agesilaus was the supposed recipient of a letter falsely attributed to **Diogenes of Sinope**. He is assumed to have been a Cynic.

AGESILAUS [2] (second century AD)
Agesilaus was the father of the poet Oppian. He seems to have taught philosophy in his home town of Anazarbus in Cilicia. For some reason the emperor Septimius **Severus** objected to what he was doing and in AD 194 banished him to an island in the Adriatic.

AGLAOPHAMUS (sixth century BC)
According to **Iamblichus of Chalcis**, Aglaophamus was the priest who initiated **Pythagoras** into the mysteries of Orphism, revealing to him the importance of number in understanding the world.

AGRICOLA, CNAEUS JULIUS (AD 40-93)
Agricola made his name as a politician, and was the Roman governor of Britain AD 77-84. His son-in-law, the historian Tacitus, wrote a biography of him, claiming that in his youth Agricola had had a great passion for philosophy but that his mother had done her best to rid him of it. She was largely successful, but in his later years Agricola claimed to have acquired and retained a sense of proportion from his years of philosophical study.

AGRIPPA [1] (first/second century AD)
Agrippa was a Sceptic whose name is often linked with a set of five 'modes', or reasons for entertaining doubt, although his actual connection with them is unclear. The first says that there are many issues on which people disagree, and it is impossible to know who is right and who is wrong. The second says that every claim needs justification, but that each justification needs further justification, and so on ad infinitum. The third says that the appearance of a things is relative to the perceiver and the context in which the perception takes place. The fourth says that claims are frequently based on unproven assumptions. The fifth says that arguments are frequently circular. Together the modes amount to grounds for questioning any claim to certainty.
[Jonathan Barnes, *The Toils of Scepticism*, Cambridge, Cambridge University Press, 1990]

AGRIPPA [2] (third/fourth century AD)
All that is known of Agrippa is that **Iamblichus of Chalcis** dedicated a book to him, and he is assumed to have been a follower.

AGRIPPINUS, QUINTUS PACONIUS (first century AD)
Agrippinus was a member of the Stoic opposition to the emperor Nero and as a result was banished from Italy in AD 66. He was praised by **Epictetus** for his imperturbability.

AGYLUS OF CROTON (fifth century BC?)
According to **Iamblichus of Chalcis**, Agylus was a Pythagorean.

AIETIUS OF PAROS (fifth century BC?)
According to **Iamblichus of Chalcis**, Aietius was a Pythagorean.

AIGON OF CROTON (fifth century BC?)
According to **Iamblichus of Chalcis**, Aigon was a Pythagorean. Some identify him with **Aston of Croton**.

ALBINUS [1] (second century AD)
Albinus was a Platonist. He taught at Smyrna, where one of his pupils was **Galen**. He believed that only the rational part of the soul was immortal, and that the soul became entangled with the material world as a result of its ignorance. He wrote an introduction to the dialogues of **Plato** [1] in which he incorporated a number of ideas taken from Aristotelianism and Stoicism.
(*The Platonic Doctrines of Albinus*, trans. J. Reedy, York Beach, Phanes, 1992)
[John Dillon, *The Middle Platonists 80 BC to AD 220*, London, Duckworth, 1996]

ALBINUS [2] (fourth century AD)
Albinus wrote books on logic and geometry, none of which survive.

ALBINUS, CEIONIUS RUFIUS (fourth century AD)
According to an inscription found in Rome, Albinus, who held high public office, was also a philosopher.

ALBUCIUS, TITUS (second century BC)
Albucius was an Epicurean who studied in Athens as a young man. He pursued a political career but was sent into exile after being found guilty of extortion. He returned to Athens and found contentment in studying philosophy there again. **Cicero** suggests that he was not a particularly good Epicurean and something of a poser.

ALBUCIUS SILUS (first century AD)
Albucius was an orator and a pupil of Papirius **Fabianus**. He appears to have regularly included philosophical arguments and allusions in the speeches he made on behalf of clients.

ALCIAS OF METAPONTUM (fifth century BC?)
According to **Iamblichus of Chalcis**, Alcias was a Pythagorean.

ALCIDAMAS [1]
According to **Diogenes Laertius**, Alcidamas wrote a book in which he set out the teachings of various philosophers on the nature of the world.

ALCIDAMAS [2]
Alcidamas may have been an Epicurean and the subject of a lost essay by **Plutarch of Chaeronea**.

ALCIDAMAS OF ELAEA (fourth century BC)
Alcidamas came from Elaea in Aeolis. He studied under **Gorgias of Leontini** and his main interest was in rhetoric. He wrote a work on death that **Cicero** rated highly, although he hesitated to call it genuinely philosophical.

ALCIMACHUS OF PAROS (sixth/fifth century BC)
According to **Iamblichus of Chalcis**, Alcimachus was a pupil of **Pythagoras**. He was exiled from Croton when the local population rose against the Pythagoreans and his subsequent fate is unknown.

ALCIMUS (fourth/third century BC)
According to **Diogenes Laertius**, Alcimus was a celebrated orator who became a pupil of **Stilpo**. Elsewhere he quotes an Alcimus, who wrote a series of essays arguing that **Plato** [1] had borrowed a great deal from **Epicharmus**. Opinions are divided as to whether the author and the orator were the same person.

ALCINOUS (second century AD?)
Nothing is known about Alcinous. His name is attached to a surviving *Handbook of Platonism*, but some have identified its author with **Alcinous the Stoic** and others with **Albinus** [1]. The available evidence is too slight to make any such identification anything other than conjectural. Whoever wrote it, the book is a valuable text, being a systematic account of what is generally known as Middle Platonism, in which the philosophy of **Plato** [1] is substantially supplemented with ideas drawn from both Aristotelianism and Stoicism. After an initial introduction to the philosophical life, the author proceeds through the areas of logic, physics and ethics, before ending with a final flourish in which he compares the sophist unfavourably with the philosopher. Alcinous does not appear to have been a particularly original thinker, and there are substantial borrowings from the works of **Arius Didymus**.
(Alcinous, *The Handbook of Platonism*, trans. J. Dillon, Oxford, Clarendon Press, 1993)
[John Dillon, *The Middle Platonists 80 BC to AD 220*, London, Duckworth, 1996]

ALCINOUS THE STOIC (second century AD?)
Alcinous is mentioned by Flavius **Philostratus** who says that a speech attributed to him was really the work of the sophist Marcus of Byzantium.

ALCIPHRON (second century AD?)
According to **Suda**, Alciphron was a philosopher from Magnesia.

ALCIPPUS OF ERESUS (fourth century BC)
According to **Diogenes Laertius, Theophrastus of Eresus** was a pupil of Alcippus before moving to Athens.

ALCIUS (second century AD)
Alcius was one of two Epicureans (the other was **Philiscus**) expelled from Rome some time between AD 150 and 175.

ALCMAEON OF CROTON (sixth/fifth century BC)
According to **Iamblichus of Chalcis**, Alcmaeon was a pupil of **Pythagoras**. His main interest was in medicine, and he regarded health as a kind of internal balance. He studied perception and believed that the eye was connected with the brain, which was itself the centre of emotion and thought. According to **Diogenes Laertius**, he also wrote on physics, arguing that the soul is always in motion and the moon, planets and stars are eternal.
(Jonathan Barnes, *Early Greek Philosophy*, Harmondsworth, Penguin, 1987)
[W.K.C. Guthrie, *A History of Greek Philosophy* vol. 1, Cambridge, Cambridge University Press, 1962; Carl Huffman, 'Alcmaeon', *The Stanford Encyclopedia of Philosophy* (Summer 2004 Edition), Edward N. Zalta (ed.), plato.stanford.edu/archives/sum2004/entries/alcmaeon/]

ALEXAMENUS (fifth century BC?)
Diogenes Laertius relates a tradition that Alexamenus was the first to write philosophical dialogues. He is said to have come from either Styra or Teos.

ALEXANDER [1] (third century BC)
Chrysippus of Soli wrote a book on logic addressed to Alexander and **Sosigenes** [1]. They were almost certainly Stoics and probably colleagues or pupils of Chrysippus.

ALEXANDER [2] (second/first century BC)
Alexander was a Peripatetic, the friend and teacher of Marcus Licinius Crassus. According to **Plutarch of Chaeronea**, he lived a very modest life and showed a great indifference towards material possessions, behaving more like a Stoic than a Peripatetic.

ALEXANDER [3] (first/second century AD)
Alexander was an Epicurean and friend of **Plutarch of Chaeronea**. He may have been the same person as Titus Flavius Alexander, a sophist and father of another sophist, Titus Flavius Phoenix.

ALEXANDER, APPIUS (second/third century AD)
Alexander was a public official honoured as a philosopher at Ephesus.

ALEXANDER, TIBERIUS CLAUDIUS (first century AD?)
All that is known of Alexander is a funerary inscription found in Rome identifying him as a Stoic philosopher.

ALEXANDER, TIBERIUS JULIUS (first century AD)
Alexander was probably the nephew of **Philo of Alexandria** and features in some of his writings in which problems concerning providence and the nature of animals are discussed. The extent of his interest in philosophy is unclear, and he is better known for having pursued a career in public and military life.

ALEXANDER OF AEGAE (first century AD)
Alexander was a Peripatetic philosopher who was tutor to Nero for a time. He wrote a commentary on the *Categories* of **Aristotle** [1].

ALEXANDER OF ANTIOCH (fourth century AD)
Alexander was a Christian philosopher who became bishop of Antioch. He was admired for his wisdom and renowned for leading a simple life.

ALEXANDER OF APHRODISIAS (second/third century AD)
Alexander was a Peripatetic who wrote many commentaries on the works of **Aristotle** [1] and became head of the school in Athens. He used the occasion of his promotion to this post to launch a withering attack on the Stoics, accusing them of immorality and subversion. Most of his writings have a calmer tone. His commentaries, some of which survive, are generally undogmatic and he is often prepared to endorse unorthodox positions, while at the same time he is credited with making some of Aristotle's views clearer and more coherent than Aristotle managed to himself.
(Alexander of Aphrodisias, *On Aristotle Metaphysics, On Aristotle On Sense Perception, On Aristotle Prior Analytics, On Aristotle Topics, On Aristotle Meteorology, Quaestiones, Ethical Problems, On Fate*: various translators, London, Duckworth, 1989- ; A.P. Fotinis, *The 'De Anima' of Alexander of Aphrodisias*, Washington, University Press of America, 1979. R.B. Todd, *Alexander of Aphrodisias on Stoic Physics*, Leiden, Brill, 1976)
[Dorothea Frede, 'Alexander of Aphrodisias', *The Stanford Encyclopedia of Philosophy* (Winter 2003 Edition), Edward N. Zalta (ed.), plato.stanford.edu/archives/win2003/entries/alexander-aphrodisias/ *Routledge Encyclopaedia of Philosophy*, vol. 1]

ALEXANDER OF DAMASCUS (second century AD)
Alexander was a Peripatetic who taught in Athens. His pupils included Flavius **Boethus** and **Galen**.

ALEXANDER OF LIBYA (third century AD?)
According to **Porphyry**, Alexander was the author of some gnostic texts circulating in the time of **Plotinus**.

ALEXANDER OF LYCOPOLIS (third/fourth century AD)
Alexander was an Egyptian philosopher who wrote an attack on Manichaeism. It survives, and is a significant source of information on the object of his attack. He accuses Manichaeism of being unnecessarily complicated as well as contradictory. Opinions are divided as to whether Alexander was a Christian or a Platonist.
(*Ante-Nicene Fathers*, vol. XIV; P.W. van der Horst and J. Mansfield, *An Alexandrian Platonist against dualism: Alexander of Lycopolis' treatise 'Critique of the Doctrines of Manichaeus'*, Leiden, Brill, 1974)

ALEXANDER OF PENTAPOLIS (fourth/fifth century AD)
Alexander was a philosopher from Libya and a cousin of **Synesius of Ptolemais**.

ALEXANDER OF SELEUCIA (second century AD)
Alexander was a pupil of **Favorinus** and **Dionysius of Miletus**. He is said to have travelled widely, even visiting the 'naked philosophers' of Egypt, a group of ascetics originally from India. He impressed **Marcus Aurelius** sufficiently for him to be made a senior civil servant. However, although Marcus regarded him as a Platonist, his nickname of *Peloplaton* (literally 'Clay Plato') suggests that his philosophical accomplishments were limited.

ALEXANDER POLYHISTOR (second/first century BC)
Alexander came from Miletus and wrote *Successions of Philosophers*, a source used by **Diogenes Laertius**. He also wrote a separate book on Pythagoreanism. He was taken as a slave to Rome in 82 BC but was later freed and went on to teach there. An extract from his writings preserved by Diogenes sets out the basics of the Pythagorean worldview, which had absorbed significant elements of Platonism by his time.
(Diogenes Laertius, *Lives of Eminent Philosophers* (2 vols), trans. R.D. Hicks, Loeb; Eusebius, *Preparation for the Gospel* (2 vols), trans. E.H. Gifford, Eugene, Wipf and Stock, 2002)
[Oleg Romanov, 'Alexander Polyhistor', *Internet Encyclopaedia of Philosophy*, www.iep.utm.edu/a/alexpoly.htm]

ALEXICRATES (first/second century AD)
Alexicrates was a Pythagorean. According to **Plutarch of Chaeronea**, although the pupils of Alexicrates ate no fish, they did eat meat on occasions.

ALEXINUS OF ELIS (fourth/third century BC)
According to **Diogenes Laertius**, Alexinus studied under **Eubulides of Miletus** in Elis, then moved to Olympia to found his own school. One of those he taught was **Dionysius the Renegade**. However, the school fared badly and eventually all his pupils abandoned him. He died as the result of impaling himself on a reed whilst swimming. He appears to have enjoyed arguing about anything and kept up a long series of exchanges with **Zeno of Citium**.

ALOPECUS OF METAPONTUM (fifth century BC?)
According to **Iamblichus of Chalcis**, Alopecus was a Pythagorean.

ALYPIUS (fourth/fifth century AD)
Alypius was a friend and pupil of **Augustine**, from whom he may have acquired his knowledge of Platonism. They both converted to Christianity at the same time and Alypius went on to become bishop of Tagaste.

ALYPIUS OF ALEXANDRIA (third/fourth century AD)
Alypius was possessed of a short body and a sharp mind, and achieved renown for his skill in disputation. He became a friend of **Iamblichus of Chalcis**, who

thought highly of him. After the death of Alypius, Iamblichus wrote his biography, although according to **Eunapius** it was composed in an impenetrable style. Alypius himself wrote nothing, but was a popular teacher in his native Alexandria where he died an old man.

AMAFINIUS, CAIUS (second/first century BC)
Amafinius was an Epicurean. He was criticised by **Cicero** for his poor understanding of Epicurean teachings, his inadequate literary style, and for devoting his attention to relatively uneducated people. At least in part this was because Amafinius chose to teach and write about the philosophy of **Epicurus** in Latin, enabling him to reach a wider but often less sophisticated audience. The extent to which he genuinely misrepresented Epicureanism is impossible to tell as no texts survive, but he does seem to have helped to make the ideas of the school better known and appreciated.

AMBROSE (fourth century AD)
Originally from Trier, Ambrose is usually associated with Milan where he became bishop in AD 374 and died in AD 397. He wrote a major work on ethics, *On the Duties of Priests*, which relies heavily on the *On Duties* of **Cicero**. In it he discusses Christian ethics with special reference to the clergy.
(*Nicene and Post-Nicene Fathers* series II, vol. X)

AMEINIAS [1] (sixth/fifth century BC)
According to **Diogenes Laertius**, Ameinias was a Pythagorean and the teacher of **Parmenides of Elea**. On his death, Parmenides erected a shrine to him.

AMEINIAS [2] (third century BC)
Chrysippus of Soli wrote one of his books on logic as a reply to Ameinias.

AMELAXUS (fifth/sixth century AD?)
Three books are attributed to Amelaxus. One, a commentary on **Proclus** [1], identifies him as bishop of Athens. The others are commentaries on works of **Aristotle** [1]. Some suspect that 'Amelaxus' may be a corruption of another name, but there is no consensus as to what that other name might be.

AMELIUS GENTILIANUS (third century AD)
Amelius was a follower of **Plotinus**, who used to call him 'Amerius' (suggesting indivisibility). He came from Etruria where he studied with **Lysimachus** [3]. He arrived in Rome in AD 246 and studied with Plotinus for 24 years, becoming a close friend of **Porphyry** in the process. He wrote a great deal. He took copious notes of the lectures of Plotinus and wrote them up into a series of volumes for the benefit of his adopted son **Hostilianus Hesychius**. He wrote another series of volumes attacking the views of the gnostic **Zostrianus**, and he also produced a book defending Plotinus against charges of plagiarising the works of **Numenius of Apamea**. Given his output, there may be some truth in the suggestion of Cassius **Longinus** that Amelius tended to write at greater length than was necessary. He left Rome for Apamea in around AD 270.

AMMICARTUS

Nothing is known about Ammicartus except for a single reference to him by Proclus [1] in which he is commended for his skills in a style of dialectic associated with **Parmenides of Elea** and **Plato** [1].

AMMONIANUS (fifth century AD)

Ammonianus was best known as a grammarian. However, according to **Suda**, he was a friend of **Syrianus** [2] and both had philosophical interests, although Syrianus had the greater talent and accomplishments. It is said that an ass became so interested in the lectures Ammonianus gave on poetry that it would even go without food in order to listen to them!

AMMONIUS (fifth/sixth century AD)

Ammonius was the son of **Hermias** [2] and **Aedesia**. When his father died, his mother took him and his younger brother **Heliodorus of Alexandria** to Athens so that they could study under **Proclus** [1]. Ammonius later returned to Alexandria and taught philosophy there, although he was interested in astronomy and astrology as well. He gave lectures on **Aristotle** [1] and **Plato** [1], some of which have survived in the form of his students' published notes. A commentary he wrote on Aristotle's *Categories* has also survived. He had a number of notable pupils including **Damascius, Olympiodorus** [2] and **Simplicius**. He had a reputation for being a hard worker and fond of money. He is sometimes referred to as Ammonius Hermeiou ('son of Hermias'). (Ammonius, *On Aristotle Categories*, trans. S.M. Cohen and G.B. Matthews, 1991; *On Aristotle On Interpretation 1-8*, trans. D. Blank, 1996, *On Aristotle On Interpretation 9*, trans. D. Blank, 1998: all London, Duckworth)

AMMONIUS SACCAS (second/third century AD)

Ammonius taught philosophy in Alexandria. Amongst his pupils were **Herennius, Origen** and **Plotinus** who, according to **Porphyry**, solemnly undertook not to reveal their master's teachings. While Plotinus kept his word, the others did not. Unfortunately, whatever Herennius revealed has been totally lost and Porphyry refers to only two works by Origen as evidence of his guilt. On the other hand, as Plotinus studied with Ammonius for ten years, it seems inconceivable that his philosophy does not reflect the influence of his teacher. Consequently there are grounds for considering Ammonius to be the inspiration behind Neoplatonism. It is said that he was brought up as a Christian but when faced with a choice between his religion and his philosophy chose his philosophy.

AMMONIUS, MARCUS ANNIUS (first century AD)

Ammonius was the teacher of **Plutarch of Chaeronea** and appears as a character in a number of his works. He was a Platonist based in Athens, although he originally came from Egypt.

AMMONIUS THE PERIPATETIC (second/third century AD)

According to Flavius **Philostratus**, Ammonius was the most learned person he had ever met.

AMPHICLEIA (third/fourth century AD)
Amphicleia was a pupil of **Plotinus**. She married **Ariston** [2] the son of **Iamblichus of Chalcis**.

AMPHINOMUS (fourth century BC)
Amphinomus was a philosopher and mathematician, much admired by **Proclus** [1].

AMPHION (third century BC)
Amphion was a friend and probably pupil of **Lyco** [1]. He was one of those to whom Lyco left the Lyceum in his will.

AMYCLAS (fourth century BC)
According to **Diogenes Laertius**, Amyclas was both a Pythagorean and a pupil of **Plato** [1]. He was one of those who interceded when Plato sought to burn the works of **Democritus of Abdera**. He may be the same person as Amyclus of Heraclea and Amyntas of Heraclea, although it is also possible that they are three different people whose stories have become hopelessly confused with each other.

AMYCLUS OF HERACLEA see AMYCLAS

AMYNANDER (fourth century BC?)
Amynander was the supposed recipient of a letter falsely attributed to **Diogenes of Sinope**. He is assumed to have been a Cynic.

AMYNIAS OF SAMOS (first century BC/first century AD)
Amynias was an Epicurean and priest at the temple of Hera on Samos.

AMYNTAS OF HERACLEA see AMYCLAS

AMYNTIANUS (fourth/fifth century AD)
Amyntianus was a philosopher from Cyrene and a friend of **Synesius of Ptolemais**.

ANACHARSIS THE SCYTHIAN (sixth century BC)
Anacharsis was a semi-legendary figure renowned for his knowledge and wisdom. According to **Suda** he invented the anchor and the potter's wheel, while according to Herodotus he was the only exceptional figure to emerge from the whole area around the Black Sea. He goes on to say that Anacharsis was killed by his own people for becoming too Hellenised. The Greeks, however, came to adopt him as one of their own and he appears on some of the lists of their Seven Sages. The Cynics regarded him highly and a set of letters attributed to him appeared (probably during the third century BC) that portray him as an acute and outspoken commentator on Greek society. Like the Cynics, he speaks as an outsider.
(A. Malherbe, *The Cynic Epistles: a study edition*, Missoula, Society of Biblical Literature, 1977)
[Jan Fredrik Kindstrand, *Anacharsis*, Uppsala, Uppsala University Press, 1981]

ANATOLIUS (third century AD)
Iamblichus of Chalcis was a pupil of Anatolius before going on to study under **Porphyry**. He was highly regarded and probably a Neoplatonist.

ANATOLIUS OF ALEXANDRIA (third century AD)
Anatolius set up his own school of Aristotelianism in Alexandria and was active in politics. At some stage in his career he became a Christian and he ended it as bishop of Laodicea. He wrote a lengthy work on mathematics.

ANAXAGORAS OF CLAZOMENAE (fifth century BC)
Anaxagoras appears to have been the first philosopher to take up residence in Athens. Among his pupils were certainly **Pericles of Cholarges** and possibly **Euripides**. He was put on trial for impiety because he claimed that the sun and moon were nothing but physical objects. Pericles may have helped him to escape from Athens, and he made his way to Lampsacus. He probably founded his own school there, and after he died he was commemorated each year with a holiday for the children of the city.

His view of the world was that it was composed of an infinite number of infinitely small particles. There are many different kinds of particle, each with its own properties (rather like chemical elements). These properties manifest themselves when many particles of the same kind are joined together. Objects are composed of many different kinds of particle, and there is at least one particle of each kind in everything. However, one or more kind will predominate and this is what gives things their distinctive characters. Originally all the particles were randomly and chaotically distributed throughout the world, but the power of mind or intelligence brought order to them. Exactly what this mind or intelligence is is unclear, but it may have been material in nature and it made itself felt in all living things.

Anaxagoras set his views out in a book entitled *On Nature*. According to **Socrates** in the *Apology* of **Plato** [1], this was on sale in Athens at a modest price. (D. Sider, *The Fragments of Anaxagoras*, Meisenheim, Anton Hain, 1981; Jonathan Barnes, *Early Greek Philosophy*, Harmondsworth, Penguin, 1987) [Malcolm Schofield, *An Essay on Anaxagoras*, Cambridge, Cambridge University Press, 1980]

ANAXARCHUS (fourth/third century BC)
According to **Plutarch of Chaeronea**, Anaxarchus was the recipient of a letter from **Epicurus**. He is assumed to have been an Epicurean himself.

ANAXARCHUS OF ABDERA (fourth century BC)
Anaxarchus may have been a pupil of **Democritus of Abdera**, although **Diogenes Laertius** suggests his teacher was **Diogenes of Smyrna**. He was a friend, and perhaps teacher, of **Pyrrho of Elis**. He earned himself the nickname of 'the contented' because of his outlook on life. He attracted the admiration of Alexander the Great, and accompanied him on his conquest of Asia. After Alexander died he was captured by the king of Cyprus, whom

he had previously offended. It was said he was pounded to death in a stone mortar.

ANAXILAIDES or ANAXILIDES
Anaxilaides wrote a work entitled *On Philosophers*, used as a source by **Diogenes Laertius**.

ANAXILAUS (fourth century BC?)
Anaxilaus is unknown except as the supposed recipient of a letter falsely attributed to **Diogenes of Sinope**. He is assumed to have been a Cynic and is addressed in the letter as 'Anaxilaus the Wise'.

ANAXILAUS OF LARISA (first century BC/first century AD)
Anaxilaus was a Pythagorean who was expelled from Italy by Augustus. Pliny the Elder quoted his views on the uses of hemlock, which he believed could be rubbed on adolescent girls' breasts to make them permanently firm and on adolescent boys' testicles to lower their libido.

ANAXIMANDER (seventh/sixth century BC)
Anaximander came from Miletus, and may have been a pupil of **Thales of Miletus**. He appears to have been interested mainly in metaphysics, speculating on the origin of the world and life within it, although he also directed himself to more practical concerns such as producing maps of the world and the heavens. His metaphysical views are not easy to interpret because central to them is a term whose meaning is unclear. Literally it appears to mean 'the boundless' or 'the limitless' but opinions differ as to whether it should be interpreted in a spatial sense to mean 'the infinite' or whether it is better understood as something more like 'the indefinite' or 'the indeterminate'. The latter is perhaps more coherent as it would suggest that the origin of the world lay in the formless taking on form. Anaximander seems to have thought that life on Earth began with a mixture of heat and damp and that the earliest living creatures were fish-like. Human beings first emerged as the offspring of these creatures. The interaction of basic principles such as hot and cold, dry and damp appears to have constituted a fundamental aspect of his metaphysics.
(Jonathan Barnes, *Early Greek Philosophy*, Harmondsworth, Penguin, 1987)
[Charles H. Kahn, *Anaximander and the Origins of Greek Cosmology*, Indianapolis, Hackett, 1994; Dirk Couprie, 'Anaximander', *Internet Encyclopaedia of Philosophy*, www.iep.utm.edu/a/anaximan.htm]

ANAXIMENES OF LAMPSACUS (fourth century BC)
Anaximenes was an historian and teacher. Alexander the Great was one of his pupils and Anaximenes wrote a work on rhetoric for him. He may at one time have been a pupil of **Diogenes of Sinope**.

ANAXIMENES OF MILETUS (sixth century BC)
Anaximenes appears to have been a younger contemporary of **Anaximander**,

but otherwise nothing is known about his life. Unlike Anaximander, he believed that everything derived from a single basic element, which he identified as air, although his understanding of air was different from the modern one. For example, he and his contemporaries believed that mist was condensed air. According to Anaximenes, air could exist in various degrees of density, and this made it possible for it to take on a variety of forms. As the source of all being and, as breath, the source of all life, air was regarded as divine.

(Jonathan Barnes, *Early Greek Philosophy*, Harmondsworth, Penguin, 1987)
[Charles H. Kahn, *Anaximander and the Origins of Greek Cosmology*, Indianapolis, Hackett, 1994]

ANAXIPPUS (third century BC)
Anaxippus was not a philosopher but a comic writer who poured scorn on philosophers, criticising them for being wise in what they said and foolish in what they did.

ANCHIPYLUS (fourth century BC)
According to **Diogenes Laertius**, Anchipylus was a pupil of **Phaedo of Elis**. He may have headed the school of Elis for a time, perhaps with **Moschus**, after the death of **Plistanus of Elis**.

ANDRAGATHIUS (fourth century AD)
Andragathius was a teacher of philosophy in Antioch. **John Chrysostom** was one of his pupils.

ANDROCYDES (second century BC?)
According to **Iamblichus of Chalcis**, Androcydes wrote a book entitled *On the Pythagorean Symbols*.

ANDROMENIDES (second century AD?)
Andromenides is unknown apart from a few passing references to him that are sufficiently ambiguous for some to regard him as a Stoic and some to regard him as a Peripatetic.

ANDRON OF EPHESUS
Andron was the author of a work called *The Tripod* that told about the Seven Sages of ancient Greece. It was used as a source by **Diogenes Laertius**.

ANDRON OF GARGETTUS (fifth century BC)
According to **Plato** [1] in *Gorgias*, Andron used to meet to discuss philosophical matters with **Callicles, Tisander** and **Naucicydes**. They agreed that while the study of philosophy was valuable, it should not be taken too far. He may have been a student of **Hippias of Elis**.

ANDRONICIANUS (fourth century AD)
Andronicianus was a Christian philosopher who wrote some works that were critical of **Eunomius**.

ANDRONICUS (fourth century AD)
Andronicus was a philosopher from Caria who was executed for treason in Antioch in AD 371.

ANDRONICUS, MARCUS POMPILIUS (first century BC)
Andronicus was an Epicurean from Syria. He was the author of a work on grammar, a subject he taught in Rome for some time. Later he moved to Cumae where he devoted himself to writing.

ANDRONICUS OF EGYPT (fourth century AD)
Andronicus was a pupil of **Themistius** [2] before making a name for himself as a writer.

ANDRONICUS OF RHODES (first century BC)
Andronicus is generally credited with reviving interest in the works of **Aristotle** [1]. He edited, published and wrote commentaries on Aristotle's lecture notes. By an accident of history, these are virtually the only works of Aristotle we now possess. As head of the Lyceum for around twenty years, he sought to refocus the attention of the school on the actual writings of Aristotle rather than on the further development of his ideas. He was succeeded by **Boethus of Sidon**.

ANDROSTHENES OF AEGINA (fourth century BC)
Androsthenes was the son of **Onesicritus of Aegina** and brother of **Philiscus of Aegina**. Androsthenes was sent to Athens by his father and there became a follower of **Diogenes of Sinope**. Later his brother and father followed suit.

ANEBO (third century AD?)
Porphyry wrote a famous letter to Anebo in which he raised a number of issues about the gods and popular religion. Anebo was supposed to be an Egyptian priest, but he may have been Porphyry's own invention.

ANNICERIS (fourth century BC?)
Anniceris was the supposed a recipient of a letter falsely attributed to **Diogenes of Sinope** in which he is portrayed as a Cynic. In it Diogenes bemoans being banned from Sparta.

ANNICERIS OF CYRENE (fourth/third century BC)
Anniceris was the brother of **Nicoteles of Cyrene** and led an offshoot or branch of the Cyrenaic school. He was a pupil of **Paraebates** and later taught **Theodorus the Atheist**. While he shared the general principles of **Aristippus of Cyrene**, he seems to have taken a slightly more altruistic line, acknowledging that we may sometimes act out of patriotic motives or make sacrifices for friends.

ANNIUS (third century AD)
Annius was a Stoic, a contemporary of **Plotinus**. According to **Porphyry** he wrote a number of books, but nothing is known about their contents.

ANTALCYDES (fourth century BC?)
Anatalcydes was the supposed recipient of a letter falsely attributed to **Diogenes of Sinope**. In it Diogenes berates him for being more interested in talking about virtue than in living virtuously.

ANTHEMIUS [1] (fourth/fifth century AD)
Anthemius was a pagan priest and philosopher in Athens renowned for his wisdom. It is said that **John Chrysostom**, who may have studied with him, converted him to Christianity.

ANTHEMIUS [2] (fifth century AD)
Anthemius was one of the last of the Western Roman emperors, although he was born in Constantinople. It was presumably there that he studied philosophy and became acquainted with a number of Neoplatonists. He was made emperor in AD 467 and died five years later when trying to defend Rome from attack.

ANTHES OF CARTHAGE (fifth century BC?)
According to **Iamblichus of Chalcis**, Anthes was a Pythagorean.

ANTIBIUS OF ASCALON
Antibius was a Stoic.

ANTIDORUS (fourth century BC)
Antidorus was an opponent of **Epicurus**, who wrote two books attacking him in return.

ANTIGENES (first century BC)
Antigenes was a friend of **Philodemus of Gadara** and probably also an Epicurean.

ANTIGONUS GONATAS (fourth/third century BC)
Antigonus was king of Macedonia. He was a friend, student or patron of a number of philosophers. **Euphantus of Olynthus** was one of his teachers. He was close to **Zeno of Citium** and attended his lectures in Athens. **Timon of Phlius** was another friend, while he helped to support **Bion of Borysthenes** when he was ill and **Menedemus of Eretria** died at his court. He died himself in 239 BC, by then an old man.

ANTIGONUS OF CARYSTUS (third century BC)
Antigonus wrote a number of philosophical biographies that were drawn on by **Diogenes Laertius**.

ANTILOCHUS
According to **Clement of Alexandria**, Antilochus wrote a history of philosophy from the time of **Pythagoras** to that of **Epicurus**.

ANTIMEDON OF CROTON (fifth century BC?)
According to **Iamblichus of Chalcis**, Antimedon was a Pythagorean.

ANTIMENES OF METAPONTUM (fifth century BC?)
According to **Iamblichus of Chalcis**, Antimenes was a Pythagorean.

ANTIOCHUS EPIPHANES (third/second century BC)
Antiochus IV ruled Syria from 175 BC to 164 BC. He was an Epicurean, the pupil of **Philonides**, although how much this affected his political judgment is a matter of dispute.

ANTIOCHUS OF AEGAE (second/third century AD)
Antiochus came from Cilicia and achieved a reputation as a sophist and man of learning. He was evidently well informed on matters of science and religion and wrote a major work of history. He was a critic of **Alexander of Seleucia** and may have been the author of some cutting epigrams.

ANTIOCHUS OF ASCALON (second/first century BC)
Antiochus is generally credited with bringing the Academy's extended flirtation with Scepticism to an end and returning it to a more dogmatic outlook. He studied under **Philo of Larisa**, but they subsequently fell out, with Philo continuing to embrace Scepticism. However, the dogmatism of Antiochus had a distinctly eclectic dimension and he claimed that the teachings of Platonism, the Stoa and the Peripatetics were fundamentally compatible and in harmony with each other, differing sometimes only in terminology. He even suggested that **Zeno of Citium** had borrowed a lot of his ideas from the Academy in the first place. He was particularly interested in moral philosophy, and in this area the gaps between the schools were perhaps easier to bridge than they were in others. **Cicero** was one of his students and his *On Moral Ends* contains an account of Antiochus' approach to ethics. When he died, he was succeeded by his younger brother **Aristus of Ascalon**.
[John Dillon, *The Middle Platonists 80 BC to AD 220*, London, Duckworth, 1996; J. Glucker, *Antiochus and the Late Academy*, Gottingen, Vandenhoeck and Ruprecht, 1978; James Allen, 'Antiochus of Ascalon', *The Stanford Encyclopedia of Philosophy* (Spring 2005 Edition), Edward N. Zalta (ed.), plato.stanford.edu/archives/spr2005/entries/antiochus-ascalon/]

ANTIOCHUS OF CILICIA (second/third century AD)
Antiochus was, or at least pretended to be, a Cynic. He joined the army and during the war with the Parthians helped soldiers cope with the cold by demonstrating his indifference to it, rolling himself in the snow in front of them. He was generously rewarded for his efforts, but then swapped sides, earning himself the nickname of 'the Deserter'.

ANTIOCHUS OF LAODICEA (first century BC/first century AD?)
According to **Diogenes Laertius**, Antiochus was a Sceptic and the pupil of **Zeuxis**. **Menodotus of Nicomedia** was his pupil.

ANTIPATER (first century AD?)
Antipater was an Epicurean and a friend of **Diogenes of Oenoanda**.

ANTIPATER OF ALEXANDRIA (second century BC)
Antipater was a Platonist and a pupil of **Carneades of Cyrene**.

ANTIPATER OF CYRENE (fourth century BC)
Antipater was a pupil of **Aristippus of Cyrene**.

ANTIPATER OF TARSUS (second century BC)
Antipater headed the Stoic school at Athens from around 152 BC to around 130 BC, succeeding **Diogenes of Babylon** and being succeeded in turn by **Panaetius of Rhodes**. He seems to have emphasised the similarities between Stoicism and Platonism, in particular in the area of ethics. He also made contributions to logic, and wrote a book defending divination. He committed suicide by taking poison.

ANTIPATER OF TYRE (first century BC)
Antipater taught philosophy and was responsible for introducing **Cato the Younger** to Stoicism. He wrote a book on physics in which he portrayed the whole world as a single living rational being, with its intelligence located in the aether.

ANTIPHANES (third/second century BC)
Antiphanes was an Epicurean who for unknown reasons fell out with the school.

ANTIPHON OF ATHENS (fifth/fourth century BC)
Antiphon was the half-brother of **Plato** [1]. In *Parmenides*, Antiphon recounts philosophical conversations that had taken place between **Socrates**, **Parmenides** and **Zeno of Elea** many years earlier. However, by the time he is asked to talk about them, he has become more interested in horses than in philosophy.

ANTIPHON OF RHAMNUS (fifth century BC)
The sources concerning Antiphon have sometimes been regarded as too difficult to reconcile with each other for them all to be about a single person. He was a contemporary of **Socrates** and one of the best known sophists of his time, particularly noted for his speechwriting. He developed the idea that personal problems could be resolved through philosophical discussion and established what was effectively the first philosophical counselling practice in Corinth. However, it did not pay very well and he turned to more lucrative enterprises. He also wrote a work called *On Truth* in which he argued for a kind of empiricism. He claimed that knowledge should have its basis in concrete experience while words were merely conventional labels attached to things. Consequently, purely conceptual knowledge had no substance.
(Rosemary Kent Sprague (ed.), *The Older Sophists*, Indianapolis, Hackett, 2001)
[*Routledge Encyclopaedia of Philosophy*, vol. 1]

ANTISTHENES [1] (fourth century BC?)
According to **Diogenes Laertius**, there was an Antisthenes who was a follower of **Heraclitus of Ephesus**.

ANTISTHENES [2] (second century AD)
Antisthenes was a Platonist and a friend of **Galen**.

ANTISTHENES OF ATHENS (fifth/fourth century BC)
Antisthenes became a close friend of **Socrates** after previously studying with **Gorgias of Leontini**. Some view him as the founder of Cynicism and believe that the word itself derives from 'Cynosarges', the name of the gymnasium where he taught. The Cynosarges was set aside for those who were less than full citizens of Athens, and there is a tradition that the mother of Antisthenes was a Thracian slave. It is possible to interpret his philosophy as that of the outsider, the person rejected by society in turn rejecting society itself. What he took from Socrates were the values of independence and self-sufficiency, although it is not clear exactly how far he took them. Certainly he developed a passive indifference towards social values and material goods, but the extent to which he actively opposed or challenged them is another matter. The essence of his teaching was that virtue alone is sufficient for happiness and that strength of character is the key to virtue. His unusually positive attitude towards pain should be understood in terms of the asceticism required to build up strength of character. He is said to have been the teacher of **Diogenes of Sinope**, although this is widely doubted. Even if the story is untrue, he was nevertheless an inspirational figure for those who came later and who certainly were regarded as Cynics. He wrote a great deal but only fragments survive.
[Luis E. Navia, *Antisthenes of Athens: setting the world aright*, Westport, Greenwood Press, 2001]

ANTISTHENES OF PAROS (first century AD)
According to Flavius **Philostratus**, Antisthenes was of Trojan ancestry and spent a short time as a follower of **Apollonius of Tyana**.

ANTISTHENES OF RHODES (third/second century BC?)
Antisthenes wrote a history of philosophy that was used as a source by **Diogenes Laertius**. He may have been a Peripatetic.

ANTITHEUS (fourth century BC)
According to **Suda**, Antitheus was a student of **Plato** [1] and assassin of **Clearchus of Heraclea**.

ANTONINUS [1] (third century AD)
Antoninus was a pupil of **Ammonius Saccas**. He appears to have been familiar with Persian philosophy.

ANTONINUS [2] (fourth century AD)
Born in Alexandria, Antoninus was the son of **Sosipatra** and **Eustathius** [2]. He studied under **Aedesius** at Pergamum and then returned to Egypt where he settled at Canopus. There he achieved considerable fame as a philosopher, while also dedicating himself to the cult of Serapis at the city's temple. He had a reputation as a prophet and predicted that the temple would not long outlast

him. It was destroyed in AD 389, and he appears to have died not long before, although some claim the prophecy related to the great temple of Serapis in Alexandria, which was destroyed in AD 391.

ANTONIUS (second century AD)
Antonius was an Epicurean who exchanged views with **Galen** on medical matters.

ANTONIUS OF ALEXANDRIA (fifth century AD)
According to **Suda**, Antonius was a pious man dedicated to the truth. He withdrew from public life in order to study philosophy and be with others like himself.

ANTONIUS OF RHODES (third century AD)
Antonius was a friend of **Porphyry**, and they arrived in Rome together in AD 263. It is assumed that he shared his friend's interest in philosophy and perhaps also became a student of **Plotinus**.

APATOURIUS (second century AD)
Apatourius studied at the Academy and died young.

APELLAS (first/second century AD?)
According to **Diogenes Laertius**, Apellas was a Sceptic who wrote a book entitled *Agrippa*.

APELLES [1] (fourth/third century BC)
Apelles was a follower of **Epicurus**.

APELLES [2] (third century BC)
Apelles was a pupil of **Chrysippus of Soli**. Some identify him with **Apollas**.

APELLES [3] (second century AD)
Apelles was a gnostic from Alexandria who advanced a complicated theology claimed by **Hippolytus of Rome** to postulate five gods.

APELLES [4] (fifth century AD)
Apelles was said to have been one of a group of philosophers who accompanied **Eudocia** on her journey from Athens to Constantinople.

APELLES OF CHIOS (third century BC)
Apelles was a Platonist and a friend of **Arcesilaus of Pitane**.

APELLICON (second/first century BC)
Apellicon was a Peripatetic from Teos. He acquired an extensive collection of the works of **Aristotle** [1] and **Theophrastus of Eresus** that had once belonged to **Neleus of Scepsis**. Sulla took it away from him in 84 BC and transported it to Rome where **Tyrannio** was put in charge of sorting it out and looking after it.

APER (fourth/third century BC?)
Aper was the supposed recipient of a letter purporting to be written by **Crates**

of Thebes. In it Crates suggests Aper should spend less time reading poetry and more time trying to emulate people like **Socrates** and **Diogenes of Sinope**.

APHRODISIUS (fifth century AD)
Aphrodisius was mainly interested in astrology and astronomy, but **Nilus the Monk** wrote a letter to him referring to him as a philosopher.

APOLAUSTUS OF MEMPHIS (second century AD)
Apolaustus was a celebrated dancer who may also have been a philosopher.

APOLEXIS (fourth century BC?)
Apolexis is unknown except as the supposed recipient of some letters falsely attributed to **Diogenes of Sinope**. He is assumed to have been a Cynic.

APOLLAS (third century BC)
Chrysippus of Soli addressed two of his books on logic to Apollas, suggesting he was a pupil or colleague. Some identify him with **Apelles** [2].

APOLLINARIUS OF HIERAPOLIS (second century AD)
Apollinarius was a Christian who became bishop of Hierapolis. He wrote a number of apologetical works, all lost, but their titles include one *On Truth*.

APOLLINARIUS OF LAODICEA (fourth century AD)
Apollinarius came from Berytus (Beirut) and was appointed bishop of Laodicea in around AD 360. He wrote extensively, including many theological commentaries and a long attack on **Porphyry**, but little survives. He believed that human nature consisted of body, soul and spirit. The implications of this led him to the position that Christ could not have been fully human. This in turn led to him leaving the church and having his teachings condemned.

APOLLODORUS [1] (fourth century BC)
Apollodorus was an Epicurean and a brother of **Leontius of Lampsacus**.

APOLLODORUS [2] (third century BC)
Apollodorus was an Epicurean, perhaps a pupil of **Polystratus**.

APOLLODORUS [3] (second/first century BC)
Apollodorus was a Platonist and a pupil of **Charmadas**.

APOLLODORUS [4] (second century BC)
Apollodorus was an Epicurean, heading the school for most of the second half of the second century BC. His long tenure earned him the nickname of 'Tyrant of the Garden'. He wrote many books, including a life of **Epicurus**, and was the teacher of **Zeno of Sidon** [2].

APOLLODORUS OF ATHENS [1] (second century BC)
Apollodorus studied under **Diogenes of Babylon**. He wrote a theological work *On the Gods* and a history beginning with the fall of Troy, which earned him the nickname of 'the Chronologist'. He also wrote a book on different philosophical

sects. The *Library*, a collection of myths long attributed to him, is now thought to be the work of another, later author.

APOLLODORUS OF ATHENS [2] (second/first century BC)
Apollodorus was a Stoic and a pupil of **Antipater of Tarsus**.

APOLLODORUS OF CYZICUS (fifth/fourth century BC?)
Apollodorus was a source used by **Diogenes Laertius**. He wrote about **Democritus of Abdera** and may have been his pupil. He may be the same person as **Apollodotus of Cyzicus**.

APOLLODORUS OF PHALERUM (fifth/fourth century BC)
Apollodorus was a successful businessman who became a follower of **Socrates**. From what is said about him by **Plato** [1] in *Symposium*, it appears he may have been mentally unstable.

APOLLODORUS OF SELEUCIA (second century BC)
Apollodorus was a Stoic who wrote an introduction to Stoicism drawn on by **Diogenes Laertius**. In most respects his writings appear to have conformed to Stoic orthodoxy, although in his account of moral philosophy he made the surprising observation that Cynicism was a short cut to virtue.

APOLLODOTUS OF CYZICUS (fifth/fourth century BC?)
According to **Clement of Alexandria**, Apollodotus believed that the end of life was simple gratification. He may be the same person as **Apollodorus of Cyzicus**.

APOLLONIDES [1] (third century BC)
Chrysippus of Soli dedicated a work on logic to Apollonides, making it likely he was a colleague or pupil.

APOLLONIDES [2] (third century BC)
Apollonides was an Epicurean.

APOLLONIDES [3] (first century BC)
Apollonides was a Stoic philosopher and a friend and companion of **Cato the Younger**. He was present at the latter's death.

APOLLONIDES OF CAESAREA (first century AD)
Apollonides was a pupil of **Apollonius of Tyana**.

APOLLONIDES OF NICAEA (first century BC/first century AD)
Apollonides wrote commentaries on lampoons composed by **Timon of Phlius** and dedicated them to the emperor **Tiberius**. Apollonides was presumably a Sceptic himself.

APOLLONIDES OF SMYRNA (second century BC)
Apollonides was a Stoic and a pupil of either **Diogenes of Babylon** or **Antipater of Tyre**.

APOLLONIUS [1] (second century BC)
Apollonius was a Platonist, a pupil of **Carneades of Cyrene**.

APOLLONIUS [2] (second century BC)
Apollonius was a Platonist and a pupil of **Telecles of Phocaea**. He probably came from Cyrene.

APOLLONIUS [3] (first century BC)
Apollonius was a Stoic, a friend of **Cicero** and, like him, had studied with **Diodotus** [2].

APOLLONIUS [4] (second century AD)
Apollonius was a Christian philosopher who was martyred in around AD 180.

APOLLONIUS CRONUS (fourth century BC)
Apollonius came from Cyrene. He was a pupil of **Eubulides of Miletus** and became a teacher of philosophy at Megara. One of his pupils was **Diodorus Cronus**, who acquired his master's nickname. The name seems to have been coined in recognition of the fact that Apollonius was as crafty in argument as the god Cronus had been in other ways.

APOLLONIUS MOLON (second/first century BC)
Apollonius came from Alabanda and became a celebrated teacher of rhetoric in Rhodes. **Cicero** and Julius **Caesar** were among his pupils. He wrote a book on philosophy in which he argued that the oracle at Delphi had not declared **Socrates** to be the wisest person alive because the pronouncement in question did not conform to the correct format of Delphic utterances.

APOLLONIUS OF ALEXANDRIA (first century AD?)
Apollonius was a Peripatetic who wrote a commentary on the *Categories* of **Aristotle** [1]. He may have been the same Apollonius who was the elder brother of **Sotion of Alexandria** [2].

APOLLONIUS OF CHALCEDON (second century AD)
Apollonius was a Stoic who taught two Roman emperors, Commodus and **Marcus Aurelius**. He was regarded with some suspicion by Antoninus Pius, who thought he charged rather too much, but Marcus came to admire him greatly. In his *Meditations* he describes Apollonius as someone full of energy who knew how to relax, as someone who taught him how to deal with pain and rely on reason, and as someone whose teachings were a model of clarity.

APOLLONIUS OF CYRENE (second century BC)
Apollonius was a Platonist and a pupil of **Carneades of Cyrene**.

APOLLONIUS OF HADRIANOPOLIS (second/third century AD)
Apollonius was a friend of **Bassus Polyaenus**. It is not clear whether he was a Stoic like Bassus or belonged to a different school.

APOLLONIUS OF MEGALOPOLIS (third century BC)
Apollonius was a Platonist and a pupil of **Arcesilaus of Pitane**.

APOLLONIUS OF NYSA (second/first century BC)
Strabo of Amaseia mentions Apollonius as being not only a Stoic but also the best pupil of **Panaetius of Rhodes**.

APOLLONIUS OF PERGE (first/second century AD?)
Apollonius was a Stoic who probably taught in Rome. He is not to be confused with another Apollonius from Perge who was a famous mathematician of the third century BC.

APOLLONIUS OF PTOLEMAIS (second/first century BC)
Apollonius was a Stoic who studied with **Dardanus** and **Mnesarchus of Athens**.

APOLLONIUS OF SYRIA (first/second century AD)
Apollonius was said to have been a Platonist in the time of Hadrian who predicted his ascendancy to power on the basis of an oracle. However, there are doubts over his historicity.

APOLLONIUS OF TYANA (first century AD)
That Apollonius was a genuine historical figure seems certain, but little else about him is. He is known now primarily from a life of him written by Flavius **Philostratus** for **Julia Domna**. It is illuminating but regarded as frequently unreliable, and some of the sources he cites may even be his own invention. Apollonius is usually regarded as a neo-Pythagorean, and is said to have studied with **Euxenus** and travelled to meet with wise men as far afield as Egypt and India. He is also said to have possessed supernatural powers, including the ability to disappear in one place and reappear in another. However, if only a fraction of what Philostratus says about him is true, he was evidently a remarkable and charismatic figure, and even **Augustine** acknowledged his eminence amongst pagans. He claimed to be able to see into the future, leading him to sometimes fall foul of the authorities, who tended to take a dim view of such activities. It is not clear that he ever established his own school anywhere, but he appears to have spent several years in the area around Smyrna and Ephesus.
[Philostratus, *Life of Apollonius of Tyana* (2 vols), trans. C.P. Jones, Loeb, 2005; Philostratus, *Life of Apollonius*, trans. C.P. Jones, Harmondsworth, Penguin 1970 (an abridged edition)]

APOLLONIUS OF TYANA THE YOUNGER (second century AD)
Suda tells of a second Apollonius of Tyana, but the claim is not corroborated and many doubt its authenticity.

APOLLONIUS OF TYRE (first century BC)
Apollonius wrote at least two books about the life of **Zeno of Citium** that were used by **Diogenes Laertius**. He was probably a Stoic himself and may have written other works on the history of the school.

APOLLOPHANES [1] (third century BC)
Apollophanes came from Antioch. He was a Stoic, although not a very orthodox one, and a pupil of **Ariston of Chios**. He wrote a book on the nature of the world and held that practical wisdom was the only virtue.

APOLLOPHANES [2] (second/third century AD?)
According to **Porphyry**, **Origen** studied the works of Apollophanes. It seems likely he was a Platonist or Pythagorean or a mixture of the two, as many were at that time.

APOLLOPHANES OF PERGAMUM (first century BC)
Apollophanes was an Epicurean and a leading citizen of Pergamum, sent on a mission to Rome on his city's behalf.

APULEIUS, LUCIUS (second century AD)
Apuleius was a Platonist best known for his novel *Metamorphoses*, more commonly referred to as *The Golden Ass*. From Madaura in North Africa, Apuleius studied in Carthage, Athens and Rome, where he practised as a lawyer for some years. He was also interested in religion and the occult. He later returned to Carthage where he took up writing. In addition to *The Golden Ass*, a few short philosophical works attributed to him survive, including an exposition of Platonism and a short piece on logic that was highly regarded well into the Middle Ages.
(Apuleius, *Metamorphoses* (2 vols), trans. J.A. Hanson, Loeb, 1989; Apuleius, *The Golden Ass*, trans. R. Graves, Harmondsworth, Penguin, 1950)
[John Dillon, *The Middle Platonists 80 BC to AD 220*, London, Duckworth, 1996]

AQUILA (third/fourth century AD)
Aquila was a Neoplatonist. He appears to have written mainly on rhetoric but also, perhaps, on logic. His work was much admired by **Syrianus** [1].

AQUILINUS see ACULINUS

AQUILINUS, JULIUS (second century AD)
Aquilinus was a man of considerable learning and eloquence. In Rome, he debated with the Platonists of his day, although it is unclear what his own philosophical views were. He was a friend of Marcus Cornelius **Fronto**.

ARATUS OF SOLI (fourth/third century BC)
Aratus achieved fame as a dramatic poet, but he was also a student of **Zeno of Citium**. He wrote a celebrated surviving poem, *Phaenomena*, dealing with astronomy and meteorology. It was widely read, **Cicero** translated it into Latin, and it may have been used by **Lucretius**. Aratus depicted the universe as a rational and organised system bearing the hallmark of its divine creator.
(Aratus, *Phaenomena*, ed. D. Kidd, Cambridge, Cambridge University Press, 2004)

ARCEAS OF TARENTUM (fifth century BC?)
According to **Iamblichus of Chalcis**, Arceas was a Pythagorean.

ARCEPHON [1] (fourth/third century BC)
Arcephon was an Epicurean and the recipient of a letter from **Epicurus** himself.

ARCEPHON [2] (third century BC)
Arcephon was a Stoic and a pupil of **Chrysippus of Soli.**

ARCESILAUS OF PITANE (fourth/third century BC)
Arcesilaus became head of the Academy in around 266 BC after the death of **Crates of Thria** and the brief tenure of **Socratides.** He inaugurated the period some call the Middle Academy and others call the New Academy, and famously declared that he was certain of nothing, not even that he was certain of nothing! Before joining the Academy he had studied mathematics under Autolycus in his native Pitane, and had subsequently become a pupil of **Theophrastus of Eresus.** At the Academy he was taught by his friend **Crantor.** His belief in suspending judgment on every issue indicates a clear affinity with Scepticism, but he may also have been influenced by **Diodorus Cronus** and the Eretrian school. He was very keen and precise in argumentation and much admired by his pupils. He also attracted a certain amount of scandal, living openly with two prostitutes while pursuing male lovers as well, but this did not affect his popularity. He died in around 240 BC as the result of excessive drinking.
[R.J. Hankinson, *The Sceptics*, London, Routledge, 1995; Charles Brittain, 'Arcesilaus', *The Stanford Encyclopedia of Philosophy* (Spring 2005 Edition), Edward N. Zalta (ed.),
plato.stanford.edu/archives/spr2005/entries/arcesilaus/]

ARCHAGORAS (fifth century BC)
According to **Diogenes Laertius,** Archagoras was a follower of **Protagoras of Abdera.**

ARCHAENETUS (first century AD?)
Syrianus [1] refers to an Archaenetus who was a Pythagorean. Some think this may be a confused reference to **Archytas of Tarentum.**

ARCHEDEMUS (second century BC)
Archedemus came from Tarsus, studied in Athens and founded his own school of Stoicism in Babylon. He was a pupil of **Diogenes of Seleucia** at the same time as **Antipater of Tarsus.** They both acquired reputations as being skilled in argument, but they disagreed on many points of substance. **Crinis** was probably one of his pupils. Exactly why he decided to move to Babylon after many years in Athens is unclear, but it may have been connected with his rivalry with Antipater who became the head of the school. Archemedus is known to have written a number of books, but they do not seem to have been of any significant originality.

ARCHEDEMUS OF SYRACUSE (fourth century BC)
Archedemus was a Pythagorean and a pupil of **Archytas of Tarentum.** He

became a friend of **Plato** [1] and accommodated him for a while at his home in Sicily. **Xenocrates of Chalcedon** wrote a book entitled *Archedemus or On Justice*, which may have referred to him.

ARCHELAUS OF ATHENS (fifth century BC)
Archelaus probably came from Athens, although **Diogenes Laertius** and **Suda** both mention traditions associating him with Miletus. He is said to have been a pupil of **Anaxagoras of Clazomenae** and a teacher of **Socrates**. The little that is known of his thought suggests that he developed a very eclectic approach to metaphysics, borrowing ideas from not only Anaxagoras but also **Anaximander, Anaximenes of Miletus** and **Empedocles of Acragas**. The actions of heat and cold were central to the system he developed from these sources. He believed that all animals had minds, and that moral values were matters of convention. Pliny the Elder ascribed to Archelaus the belief that goats breathed through their ears rather than through their noses, but it is possible another Archelaus is meant.
(Jonathan Barnes, *Early Greek Philosophy*, Harmondsworth, Penguin, 1987)

ARCHEMACHUS OF TARENTUM (fifth century BC?)
According to **Iamblichus of Chalcis**, Archemachus was a Pythagorean.

ARCHETIMUS (fourth century AD)
Forgotten now, in his time Archetimus was reckoned to be nearly the equal of **Aristotle** [1].

ARCHIADAS [1] (fifth century AD)
Archiadas was the grandson of **Plutarch of Athens** and became a close friend of **Proclus** [1]. While Proclus became the philosophical head of the Neoplatonist school, Archiadas became the person who looked after its external affairs.

ARCHIADAS [2] (fifth/sixth century AD)
Archiadas was the son of **Hegias** and the brother of **Eupeithius**. He took an interest in philosophy, but a greater one in more material things.

ARCHIPPUS, FLAVIUS (first/second century AD)
Archippus was a citizen of Prusa with whom Pliny the Younger had some professional dealings. Archippus pleaded exemption from jury service on the grounds that he was a philosopher and produced letters from the emperor Domitian testifying to that fact and to his good character. It emerged that he had previously been sentenced to hard labour in the mines for forgery, which might cast some doubt on the authenticity of the letters. Although some of his fellow citizens were keen to see him back in the mines, he was generally popular.

ARCHIPPUS OF SAMOS (fifth century BC)
According to **Iamblichus of Chalcis**, Archippus was a Pythagorean.

ARCHIPPUS OF TARENTUM (fifth century BC)

Archippus was a follower of **Pythagoras**. While living in Croton he nearly lost his life when those opposed to the Pythagoreans set fire to a house in which he was attending a meeting.

ARCHYTAS OF TARENTUM (fifth/fourth century BC)

Archytas was a Pythagorean and a friend of **Plato** [1]. When Plato got into trouble in Syracuse, Archytas sent **Lamiscus of Tarentum** to go and rescue him. His interests were wide-ranging, but lay primarily in pure and applied mathematics. It is thought that Plato acquired a great deal of what he knew about mathematics from Archytas. He made advances in geometry and contributed to musical theory. According to **Iamblichus of Chalcis**, he took the view that parts could only be understood properly in the context of the wholes to which they belonged. However, it is not clear whether this view should properly be attributed to him as his name became attached to a number of later Pythagorean writings long after his death.

(Carl A. Huffman, *Archytas of Tarentum: Pythagorean, Philosopher and Mathematician King*, Cambridge, Cambridge University Press, 2005)
[Carl Huffman, 'Archytas', *The Stanford Encyclopedia of Philosophy* (Fall 2003 Edition), Edward N. Zalta (ed.),
plato.stanford.edu/archives/fall2003/entries/archytas/]

ARCHYTAS THE ELDER (sixth/fifth century BC)

According to **Iamblichus of Chalcis**, Archytas was a pupil of **Pythagoras**. According to **Suda**, **Archytas of Tarentum** taught **Empedocles of Acragas**, which is impossible, but the reference may be to this Archytas who also seems to have come from Tarentum, although some question whether such an individual ever existed.

ARESANDRUS OF LUCANIA (fifth/fourth century BC?)

According to **Iamblichus of Chalcis**, Aresandrus was a Pythagorean. Many think he is to be identified with **Aresas**.

ARESAS (fifth/fourth century BC?)

Aresas was a Pythagorean. According to **Iamblichus of Chalcis**, he re-established the school of **Pythagoras**, and **Diodorus of Aspendus** became one of his students or companions. He is also said to have previously fled from Croton when it was attacked by enemies of the Pythagoreans and sought safety with friends at a distance, but he would have had to have lived an extraordinarily long time for both stories to be true. Although many identify Aresas with **Aresandrus of Lucania**, it may be that two separate stories and people have been confused, with the earlier history belonging to Aresandrus and the later one to Aresas.

ARETE (fourth century AD)

Arete was a philosopher to whom **Iamblichus of Chalcis** dedicated one of his books. It seems likely that she was one of his pupils. Her neighbours (presumably Christians) tried to get her thrown out of her home in AD 351 or 352, but the emperor **Julian** himself went to Phrygia to help her.

ARETE OF CYRENE (fourth century BC)
Arete was the daughter and pupil of **Aristippus of Cyrene**, and went on to teach her own son, **Aristippus Metrodidactus**.

ARGIA (fourth/third century BC)
According to **Clement of Alexandria**, Argia was a daughter of **Diodorus Cronus** and accomplished in philosophy.

ARIDICAS or ARIDICES (third century BC)
Aridicas was a Platonist from Rhodes who studied under **Arcesilaus of Pitane**. Some believe Aridicas and Aridices may have been two different people, although if they were they seem to have lived at the same time.

ARIGNOTE (sixth/fifth century BC)
According to **Suda**, Arignote was a Pythagorean. She came from Samos and studied with **Pythagoras** and his wife **Theano**. It is possible she was their daughter. It is said that she wrote a number of philosophical and mystical works, but nothing survives except the titles of a handful them.

ARIMNESTUS (sixth/fifth century BC)
According to **Porphyry**, Arimnestus was a son and follower of **Pythagoras**.

ARION OF LOCRI (fifth/fourth century BC)
Arion was a Pythagorean visited by **Plato** [1].

ARIPHRADES (fifth century BC)
Ariphrades is said to have been a pupil of **Anaxagoras of Clazomenae**, although not one of good character.

ARISTAENETUS (fourth century AD)
Aristaenetus was a friend of **Libanius** [1] and died in an earthquake in Nicomedia in AD 358. He is said to have been the author of a number of letters on various topics, including philosophical ones, but this is widely questioned.

ARISTAENETUS OF NICAEA (first/second century AD)
Aristaenetus was a pupil of **Plutarch of Charonea**.

ARISTAEUS OF CROTON (sixth/fifth century BC)
According to **Iamblichus of Chalcis**, Aristaeus was a pupil of **Pythagoras**. When Pythagoras died, Aristaeus became his successor and married his widow, **Theano**. Fragments of a later work on harmony were attributed to him.

ARISTAGORAS (third century BC)
According to **Diogenes Laertius**, **Chrysippus of Soli** dedicated a number of books on logic to Aristagoras. He was probably a colleague or a pupil.

ARISTAGORAS OF SALAMIS (second century BC)
Aristagoras was a Platonist and a pupil of **Telecles of Phocaea**.

ARISTANAX (second century BC)
Aristanax was a Platonist and pupil of **Carneades of Cyrene**.

ARISTANDER (first/second century AD?)
Proclus [1] mentions an Aristander who had written a commentary on the *Timaeus* of **Plato** [1]. He believed there was a world-soul that mediated between the material world and the realm of Forms. Mathematical in nature, it converted the singularity of the Forms into the multiplicity of material objects.

ARISTANGELUS OF CYRENE (fifth century BC?)
According to **Iamblichus of Chalcis**, Aristangelus was a Pythagorean.

ARISTARCHUS OF SAMOS (fourth/third century BC)
Aristarchus was a pupil of **Strato of Lampsacus** and may also have been influenced by **Heraclides of Pontus**. However, he made his name in science rather than in philosophy and may have been the first to argue that the Sun rather than the Earth lay at the centre of the universe.

ARISTEAS OF METAPONTUM (fifth century BC?)
According to **Iamblichus of Chalcis**, Aristeas was a Pythagorean.

ARISTEAS OF PROCONNESSUS (seventh century BC?)
Aristeas was revered by the Pythagoreans. Interpretations of the stories attached to him vary widely, but many thought he had come back from the dead or at least travelled outside his body. Some identify him with **Aristeas of Metapontum**.

ARISTIDES [1] (fourth/third century BC)
Aristides was a teacher of **Paeonius**, who left him to study under **Stilpo**. He probably taught in Megara.

ARISTIDES [2] (third century BC)
Aristides was a Peripatetic and one of the executors of the will of **Strato of Lampsacus**.

ARISTIDES, AELIUS (second century AD)
Aristides came from Mysia and was principally known as a sophist and hypochondriac. The son of **Eudaimon of Hadriani**, he studied under Titus Claudius **Aristocles**. He took a particular interest in the works of **Plato** [1], but sought to defend rhetoric against Plato's attacks on it.

ARISTIDES, MARCIANUS (first/second century AD)
Aristides was a philosopher from Athens who became a Christian. He wrote a book that set out arguments for the existence of God and the superiority of Christianity over other religions. Long lost, a Syriac version of it was discovered in 1889.
(*Ante-Nicene Fathers*, vol. X)

ARISTIDES, QUINTILIANUS (third century AD?)
Aristides wrote a surviving theoretical work on music that incorporated Pythagorean ideas.
(A. Barker, *Greek Musical Writings*, vol. II: *Harmonic and Acoustic Theory*, Cambridge: Cambridge University Press, 1989)

ARISTIDES OF RHEGIUM (fifth century BC?)
According to **Iamblichus of Chalcis**, Aristides was a Pythagorean.

ARISTILLUS (third century BC)
Aristillus was a philosopher from Alexandria whose main interest lay in astronomy. A crater on the Moon is named after him.

ARISTIPPUS (first century BC)
Aristippus came from Cyrene. He was a Platonist and a pupil of **Lacydes of Cyrene**.

ARISTIPPUS METRODIDACTUS (fourth century BC)
Aristippus was the grandson of **Aristippus of Cyrene** and the son of **Arete of Cyrene**. His mother was also his teacher, leading to his nickname of Metrodidactus meaning 'mother-taught'. There is some dispute as to whether he or his mother or his grandfather actually or formally founded the Cyrenaic school, but as they all apparently espoused the same philosophy the question is of limited importance.

ARISTIPPUS OF CYRENE (fifth/fourth century BC)
Aristippus is widely regarded as the founder of the Cyrenaic school, although some accord that honour to his daughter **Arete of Cyrene** or his grandson **Aristippus Metrodidactus**. However, at the very least it is evident that Aristippus was a philosopher with his own distinctive views. The influence of others on the formation of his views is unclear, although he was certainly familiar with the thought of **Socrates** and **Plato** [1], amongst others. He took the view that the only reliable sources of knowledge were the senses, but that the only reliable knowledge we can have is of our actual sensations. We are not entitled to draw conclusions from them about the nature of anything else. Sensation itself he believed to be a kind of movement, pleasurable sensations were smooth movements and pains were rough ones. The aim of life was to maximise pleasurable sensations. **Diogenes Laertius** relates a number of anecdotes concerning Aristippus that suggest he took his pleasures seriously. When asked to choose between three prostitutes, he took them all, remarking that choosing between three women had brought Paris of Troy nothing but grief. He is said to have written a number of works but nothing survives of them.

ARISTIPPUS OF TARENTUM (fifth century BC?)
According to **Iamblichus of Chalcis**, Aristippus was a Pythagorean.

ARISTO, TITIUS (first/second century AD)
Aristo was a legal scholar. However, Pliny the Younger also describes him as a man of wisdom, superior in virtue to all the philosophers of his time.

ARISTO see ARISTON

ARISTOBOLUS [1] (fourth/third century BC)
Aristobolus was a brother of **Epicurus**, apparently persuaded by him to take up philosophy.

ARISTOBOLUS [2] (third century BC)
Chrysippus of Soli wrote a book on logical fallacies addressed to Aristobolus, suggesting he was a logician himself and probably a Stoic one.

ARISTOBOLUS THE PERIPATETIC (second century BC?)
Aristobolus claimed that Jewish philosophy was both older than Greek philosophy and the source of a great deal of it. Although traditionally referred to as a Peripatetic, he may have been more of an eclectic.

ARISTOCLEIDAS OF TARENTUM (fifth century BC?)
According to **Iamblichus of Chalcis**, Aristocleidas was a Pythagorean.

ARISTOCLES (fifth century AD)
Aristocles was the recipient of a letter from **Proclus** [1] on the subject of the Chaldaean Oracles.

ARISTOCLES, TITUS CLAUDIUS (second century AD)
Aristocles came from Pergamum. As a young man he was a Peripatetic, but later he travelled to Rome to study with **Herodes Atticus**, and subsequently abandoned philosophy for a career as a sophist. According to Flavius **Philostratus**, when Aristocles had been a philosopher he took no interest in his personal appearance and led an austere life. When he became a sophist he began to dress well and indulge himself. He returned to Pergamum where he became so successful that Herodes himself went to hear him speak.

ARISTOCLES OF LAMPSACUS (third century BC?)
According to **Suda**, Aristocles was a Stoic who wrote a commentary on a work by **Chrysippus of Soli**. As **Diogenes Laertius** mentions an Aristocles who had a book on similes dedicated to him by Chrysippus, it seems likely both references are to the same person.

ARISTOCLES OF MESSENE (first century AD?)
Aristocles was a Peripatetic philosopher who wrote a work entitled *On Philosophy*, an account of the different philosophical schools and their beliefs. Substantial fragments of this are quoted by **Eusebius of Caesarea**, in particular the arguments Aristocles put against the Sceptics, the Cyrenaics and the Epicureans. However, **Plato** [1] is exempted from these criticisms and Aristocles appears to see little difference between the Peripatetics and the

Academy. He was once thought to have been the teacher of **Alexander of Aphrodisias** but is now generally believed to have lived significantly earlier. (Eusebius, *Preparation for the Gospel* (2 vols), trans. E.H. Gifford, Eugene, Wipf and Stock, 2002)

ARISTOCLES OF RHODES (first century AD)
Aristocles was probably a Platonist. **Proclus** [1] refers to him in a discussion of the *Timaeus*.

ARISTOCRATES, PETRONIUS (first century AD)
Aristocrates came from Magnesia. He was regarded as an accomplished philosopher, a man of great learning and someone who lead a pious life. He was a pupil of Lucius Annaeus **Cornutus** and a friend of both the poet **Persius** and **Agathinus**.

ARISTOCRATES OF RHEGIUM (fifth century BC?)
According to **Iamblichus of Chalcis**, Aristocrates was a Pythagorean.

ARISTOCREON (third/second century BC)
Aristocreon was the nephew and pupil of **Chrysippus of Soli**, and brother of **Philocrates**. Chrysippus dedicated several of his books to him. Like his uncle, he came from Soli but settled in Athens where he became both prominent and affluent.

ARISTOCRITUS [1] (first century BC?)
According to **Clement of Alexandria**, Aristocritus wrote a book attacking the work of **Heracleodorus** [2].

ARISTOCRITUS [2] (fifth century AD)
Aristocritus is an elusive figure whose name is connected with a work entitled *Theosophy* that discussed oracles of various kinds. He appears to have been a Platonist and a Christian who was condemned for suggesting that Judaism, Christianity and Manichaeism were all fundamentally the same religion.

ARISTODEMUS OF SPARTA (sixth century BC)
According to **Dicaearchus of Messene**, Aristodemus was one of the Seven Sages of ancient Greece. It is said that he was awarded a prize for being the wisest Greek of his time, but refused to accept it. As his one preserved saying identifies people's worth with their wealth, he was probably right to refuse.

ARISTODEMUS OF AEGIUM (second/third century AD)
Aristodemus was a pupil of **Plutarch of Charonea** and appears as a character in some of his writings.

ARISTODORUS OF SYRACUSE (fourth century BC)
Aristodorus was the recipient of the tenth letter of **Plato** [1] in which he is credited with being a philosopher himself.

ARISTOMACHUS (third century BC)
Aristomachus was one of those to whom **Lyco** [1] bequeathed the Lyceum on his death. He had presumably been a pupil there for some time.

ARISTOMBROTUS
The name of Aristombrotus is attached to surviving fragments of a work on vision. The name is thought to be that of a Pythagorean.

ARISTOMENES OF METAPONTUM (fifth century BC?)
According to **Iamblichus of Chalcis**, Aristomenes was a Pythagorean.

ARISTON [1] (third/second century BC)
Ariston studied at the Academy under **Lacydes of Cyrene**.

ARISTON [2] (third/second century BC)
Ariston studied at the Academy under **Telecles of Phocaea**.

ARISTON [3] (second century BC)
Ariston was a Platonist. He taught **Boethus of Marathon** and may be the same person as **Ariston of Ephesus**.

ARISTON [4] (second century BC)
Ariston was a Peripatetic and a pupil of **Critolaus of Phaselis**.

ARISTON [5] (first century BC/first century AD)
Aristo was a philosopher in Rome, attached to the household of Marcus Lepidus. According to **Seneca**, he used to engage in philosophical discussions when travelling around in a carriage, leading a wit to observe that he was obviously not a 'peripatetic'.

ARISTON [6] (third/fourth century AD)
Ariston was the son of **Iamblichus of Chalcis**. He married **Amphicleia**, a follower of **Plotinus**.

ARISTON OF ALEXANDRIA (second/first century BC)
Ariston studied under both **Antiochus of Ascalon** and **Aristus of Ascalon** before leaving their school to become a Peripatetic.

ARISTON OF CARTHAGE (third/second century BC)
Ariston was a Platonist who seems to have studied at the Academy under either **Lacydes of Cyrene** or **Telecles of Phocaea**.

ARISTON OF CEOS (third/second century BC)
Sometimes known as Ariston of Julii after the town on Ceos where he was born, Ariston was one of those to whom **Lyco** [1] bequeathed the Lyceum on his death and was probably his successor as head of the school. It is not known exactly what he wrote but some biographical works by him appear to have been used by **Diogenes Laertius**. Diogenes notes out that some books commonly attributed to **Ariston of Chios** may have been by Ariston of Ceos.

ARISTON OF CHIOS (fourth/third century BC)
Ariston was a pupil of **Zeno of Citium** and was known as both 'the Bald' and 'the Siren'. Although a Stoic, he was far from being an orthodox one and was regarded by some as the founder of his own school. He was a philosophical radical, arguing that only ethics was important and that logic and physics could be dispensed with. He believed that there was only one virtue, practical wisdom, and that all other so-called virtues were simply so many different manifestations of it. He further held that apart from virtue (and its opposite), everything should be treated with complete indifference. He argued that the wise person would reject all opinion and be content with nothing less than knowledge. However, he rejected the extreme Scepticism of **Arcesilaus of Pitane**, with whom he had many exchanges. His influence was ultimately slight. **Chrysippus of Soli** opposed his unorthodox ideas and went on to become head of the school. Ariston died of sunstroke, having taken insufficient care to protect his bald head.
[James I. Porter, 'The Philosophy of Aristo of Chios', in R. Bracht Branham and Marie-Odile Goulet-Cazé (eds), *The Cynics: the Cynic movement in antiquity and its legacy*, Berkeley, University of California Press, 1996]

ARISTON OF COS (second/first century BC)
Ariston was a Peripatetic who may have been the pupil and successor of **Ariston of Ceos**.

ARISTON OF EPHESUS (third/second century BC)
Ariston was a Platonist who seems to have studied at the Academy under either **Lacydes of Cyrene** or **Telecles of Phocaea** and subsequently taught there. One of his pupils was **Boethus of Marathon**.

ARISTON OF JULII see ARISTON OF CEOS

ARISTONYMUS [1] (fourth century BC)
Aristonymus was a pupil of **Plato** [1]. He may have come from Arcadia and helped to reform the laws there.

ARISTONYMUS [2] (third/second century BC)
Aristonymus was an Epicurean and a friend of **Dionysius** [3].

ARISTOPHANES OF BYZANTIUM (third/second century BC)
Aristophanes became head of the library at Alexandria. He appears to have produced an edition of the works of **Plato** [1] in which the dialogues were divided into groups of three.

ARISTOTLE [1] (384-322 BC)
Aristotle came from Stagira. He was still a teenager when his father, who was a doctor, died and his guardian decided to send him to Athens to study with **Plato** [1]. When Plato died in around 347 BC, **Speusippus** succeeded him as head of the school and Aristotle moved to Assus where he became close to **Hermias of Atarneus**. The death of Hermias at the hands of the Persians

obliged Aristotle to move again, and he seems to have settled in Lesbos before being invited to become the tutor of the future Alexander the Great. After Speusippus died he returned to Athens and founded the Lyceum or Peripatos. The death of Alexander made it dangerous for those associated with the Macedonians to stay in Athens, so Aristotle moved again, to Chalcis in Euboea, but died the following year.

For reasons that are unclear, the works of Aristotle that have survived are those that remained unpublished in his lifetime. They are generally thought to come from notes he prepared for his lectures. The first attempt to put them into some kind of order for others to read seems to have been the work of his son **Nicomachus** along with **Eudemus of Rhodes**. After their time the history of these works is somewhat obscure until they were edited and published by **Andronicus of Rhodes** in the first century BC.

Aristotle took an interest in a wide range of subjects and was a keen scientist as well as a philosopher. His writings reflect this and they cover many different topics. He wrote about meteorology and cosmology, while a significant proportion of his works deals with biology in one way or another. Most of these contain relatively little to detain the reader whose primary interest is in philosophy. However the *Physics* and what is in some ways its companion volume the *Metaphysics* move into more philosophical territory, setting out his more general views on the way the world works. These include an influential analysis of causation in which he distinguishes between four aspects, what he terms the material, formal, final and efficient causes. The material and the formal are characteristics of any object, that of which the object is made (for example, wood) and the form it possesses that makes it a particular object or one kind of object rather than another (for example, a table). The final and efficient causes are specifically concerned with processes, the final cause is what the process aims at and the efficient cause is what brings the process about. His speculations on the problem of causation also lead him to posit the existence of a necessary being, the 'unmoved mover', on which the whole universe ultimately depends.

His works dealing with logic became collectively known as the Organon. These comprise the *Prior Analytics, Posterior Analytics, Categories, On Interpretation* and *Topics*. In them he set out the principles of the syllogism, analysing the different kinds of relationship between propositions of the form 'All As are Bs', 'No As are Bs', 'Some As are Bs', and 'Some As are not Bs'. He also analysed language into its constituent parts and considered problems of meaning.

On the Soul is an early work in human psychology, but it is also far more than that as Aristotle believed that all living things had souls. *Rhetoric* discusses what one would expect it to, while *Poetics* is an early work of literary theory dealing with epic poetry and tragedy, in which a template for tragedy is worked out.

Finally there are the works of Aristotle that are the most often read today, the *Politics* and the *Ethics*. In fact there are two works with the title *Ethics*, known more fully as the *Eudemian Ethics* and the *Nicomachean Ethics*, but it is the latter, the more substantial one, that is usually meant. *Politics* and *Ethics* are best read together as they deal with the good life and the good society, and these are seen as intrinsically connected because the good society is the best environment in which to pursue and achieve the good life. *Politics* examines the origins of human society and the best forms of government while *Ethics* deals with virtue and happiness. For Aristotle, the best, most fulfilling life is the life of study and contemplation because the rational mind is the highest element in human nature. However, if our minds in some ways make us like gods, our bodies are a constant reminder that we are not gods and so the best life must also recognise and address this fact. Material comforts also have their place.

In *Ethics* Aristotle recapitulates in a human developmental context the idea of potentiality that can be found in other areas of his work. The good life is one in which we fulfil our potential. In *Ethics* he also expounds his theory of the doctrine of the mean, arguing that virtuous behaviour is that which avoids excess. To behave virtuously is to behave appropriately, neither going beyond nor falling short of what the situation demands. It is also in *Ethics* where he makes clear his disagreements with Plato's Theory of Forms.

In *Politics*, on the other hand, it is possible to see Aristotle at work as both scientist and philosopher. It is only after studying actual societies, organising and categorising them, that he moves on to the question of which forms of social organisation are the best. During his lifetime and for some time afterwards the Lyceum had a reputation for being in the forefront of scientific research. When he had to leave Athens, **Theophrastus of Eresus**, another accomplished scientist, succeeded him as its head.

(*The Complete Works of Aristotle: the revised Oxford translation* (ed. J. Barnes), Princeton, Princeton University Press, 1984; *The Basic Works of Aristotle* (ed. R. McKeon), New York, Random House, 1941; *A New Aristotle Reader* (ed. J.L. Ackrill), Princeton, Princeton University Press, 1987; also many editions and translations of individual works, especially *Ethics*; classics.mit.edu/Browse/browse-Aristotle.html)
[W.D. Ross, *Aristotle*, London, Methuen 1964; D.J. Allan, *The Philosophy of Aristotle*, Oxford, Oxford University Press, 1970; Abraham Edel, *Aristotle and his Philosophy*, Chapel Hill, University of North Carolina Press, 1982; J.L. Ackrill, *Aristotle the Philosopher*, Oxford, Oxford University Press, 1981]

ARISTOTLE [2] (fourth century BC)
According to **Diogenes Laertius**, Aristotle was a pupil of **Aeschines of Sphettus**.

ARISTOTLE [3] (fourth/third century BC)
The will of **Theophrastus of Eresus** mentions an Aristotle who was to be allowed to study at the Lyceum. He was the son of **Medius** [1] and **Pythias**, and so the grandson of **Aristotle** [1].

ARISTOTLE OF CYRENE (fourth/third century BC)
Aristotle was the teacher of **Clitarchus** and **Simmias** before they became pupils of **Stilpo**.

ARISTOTLE OF MYTILENE (second century AD)
Aristotle was a Peripatetic, and perhaps the teacher of **Alexander of Aphrodisias**.

ARISTOTLE OF THORAE (fifth century BC)
Aristotle was a young follower of **Socrates** and appears as a character in the *Parmenides* of **Plato** [1].

ARISTOTLE THE DIALECTICIAN (third century BC)
Aristotle, in collaboration with **Deinias**, assassinated the tyrant Abantidas of Sicyon. Abantidas took an interest in philosophical matters and this enabled them to lure him to his death.

ARISTOXENUS (fourth century AD)
Aristoxenus was a philosopher from Cappadocia. The emperor **Julian** summoned him to Tyana in AD 362 to help with the pagan revival there.

ARISTOXENUS OF CYRENE
Aristoxenus was a Peripatetic philosopher who wrote a number of works used or referred to by **Diogenes Laertius**. These included *On Pythagoras and his School* and a life of **Plato** [1].

ARISTOXENUS OF TARENTUM (fourth century BC)
Aristoxenus left his native Tarentum for Mantinea where he studied philosophy. He was taught by **Xenophilus of Chalcis**, and then by **Aristotle** [1]. Although he proved a more than able pupil, Aristotle made **Theophrastus of Eresus** rather than Aristoxenus his successor, and this led to a great deal of bitterness. He wrote a great deal, including works about **Pythagoras** and his followers that were very influential even if not wholly reliable. However, it was as a theoretician of music that he achieved the highest reputation. Taking a fundamentally materialist and Aristotelian approach, he focused on music as it was heard by the human ear rather than on its physical or metaphysical properties. His *Elements of Harmonics* became one of the most influential works on music that the ancient world produced. Some of his supposed sayings have also been preserved.
(A. Barker, *Greek Musical Writings*, vol. II: *Harmonic and Acoustic Theory*, Cambridge: Cambridge University Press, 1989)

ARISTUS OF ASCALON (first century BC)
Aristus was the brother of **Antiochus of Ascalon** and a friend of **Brutus**. Aristus was said to have been an inferior philosopher to his brother, but a wholly admirable individual. When Antiochus died he succeeded him as head of the school. **Cratippus of Pergamum** and **Ariston of Alexandria** were two of his pupils, but it was **Theomnestus** [2] who probably succeeded him.

ARIUS (third/fourth century AD)
Arius probably came from Libya. He was ordained a priest in Alexandria but became a leading advocate of views later judged to be heretical. Named after him, Arianism claimed that Christ had been created by God and was less than fully divine. Although condemned more than once, his views continued to be influential in one place or another until the sixth century.

ARIUS DIDYMUS or AREIUS (first century BC)
When Augustus marched into Alexandria in 30 BC following the defeat of Antony and Cleopatra, he declared that one of the reasons he had spared the city was because his friend the philosopher Areius had been born there. It is generally thought that this Areius and Arius Didymus are one and the same person. He remained close to the imperial family for many years, and composed a message of consolation (much admired by **Seneca**) for the empress Livia when her son Drusus died in 9 BC. He also wrote at least one substantial work, the *Epitome*, that set out and summarised the teachings of the major philosophical schools. His writings are known only through fragments preserved in the writings of others, in particular **Stobaeus**, and it is not always clear exactly what is to be attributed to Arius Didymus himself. The best known of these fragments deal with Stoic and Peripatetic ethics, with the material on Stoic ethics being particularly valuable.
(B. Inwood and L.P. Gerson (eds), *Hellenistic Philosophy: introductory readings*, Indianapolis, Hackett, 1997)
[William W. Fortenbaugh (ed.), *On Stoic and Peripatetic Ethics: the work of Arius Didymus*, New Brunswick, Transaction, 1983]

ARNOBIUS OF SICCA (third/fourth century AD)
Arnobius came from Numidia where he began a career as a teacher of rhetoric. After his conversion to Christianity in around AD 295 he began writing works in defence of his new faith. In *Against the Pagans*, which still survives, he draws on both Platonism and Stoicism in articulating his views on God and the soul. (*Ante-Nicene Fathers*, vol. VI)

ARNOUPHIS (second century AD)
According to **Suda**, Arnouphis was a philosopher from Egypt. However, his talents appear to have been magical rather than philosophical as he was said to have conjured up a storm for the Romans at a time when they were short of water.

ARRIA (second century AD)
Arria was a Platonist and a friend of **Galen**. She was admired by the emperors Septimus **Severus** and Caracalla for her devotion to philosophy.

ARRIA PAETUS THE ELDER (first century AD)
Arria was the wife of **Caecina Paetus** and, like her husband, a Stoic. He became involved in a conspiracy against the emperor Claudius, and was ordered to commit suicide in AD 42. Arria decided to encourage her husband in the act and

stabbed herself, handing him the dagger with the words, 'It doesn't hurt, Paetus.' They were the parents of **Arria Paetus the Younger**.

ARRIA PAETUS THE YOUNGER (first century AD)
Arria was the daughter of **Arria Paetus the Elder** and **Caecina Paetus** and the wife of **Thrasea Paetus**. Like her parents, she was a Stoic, and like her mother, in AD 66 she was faced with the situation of her husband being condemned to death for his political activities. Although she wanted to die with him, he instructed her to stay alive and look after their daughter.

ARRIAN [LUCIUS FLAVIUS ARRIANUS] (first/second century AD)
Arrian came from Nicomedia. He is best known as an historian, but he also studied under his friend **Epictetus**. The *Handbook* and *Discourses* of Epictetus were both produced by Arrian from the notes he took when Epictetus was teaching. He had a career in public life and was honoured as a philosopher in his own right by the time he died in AD 160.

ARTEMIDORUS (first/second century AD)
Artemidorus was a close friend of Pliny the Younger who admired him greatly and supported him after he was one of the philosophers expelled from Rome in AD 93. Pliny described him as a man of sincerity and integrity, as someone who lived a frugal and disciplined life, and as someone who faced physical hardship with indifference.

ARTEMIDORUS OF AMBLADA
Artemidorus was a philosopher in his home town of Amblada, where a statue was set up in his honour.

ARTEMIDORUS OF DALDIS (second century AD)
Artemidorus is famous for having written a book on dream interpretation that still survives. Although the book is primarily a manual, he discusses different philosophical outlooks on dreams including those of the Stoics and Epicureans, while he also refers to a range of other philosophers such as **Plato** [1], **Aristotle** [1] and **Pythagoras** in his exposition.
(Artemidorus, *The Interpretation of Dreams*, trans. R. White, Park Ridge, Noyes Press, 1975)

ARTEMIDORUS OF PARIUM (first century BC/first century AD?)
Artemidorus wrote a book on celestial phenomena with which **Seneca** entirely disagreed. He may have been an Epicurean.

ARTEMIDORUS THE DIALECTICIAN (third century BC)
Artemidorus wrote a book addressed to **Chrysippus of Soli** that detailed the accomplishments of **Protagoras of Abdera**.

ARTEMISIA (fourth/third century BC)
According to **Clement of Alexandria**, Artemisia was a daughter of **Diodorus Cronus** and accomplished in philosophy.

ARTEMON [1] (third/second century BC)
Artemon was an Epicurean and the teacher of **Philonides of Laodicea**.

ARTEMON [2] (third or second century BC?)
Artemon produced an edition of the letters of **Aristotle** [1]. He was presumably himself a Peripatetic.

ARUECAS (fourth century BC?)
Aruecas was the supposed recipient of a letter falsely attributed to **Diogenes of Sinope** in which he is encouraged to pursue the philosophical life.

ARULENUS RUSTICUS, QUINTUS JUNIUS (first century AD)
Arulenus was originally from Patavium (Padua). He became a politician and a Stoic. He actively supported the Stoic opposition and was eventually condemned to death by the emperor Domitian in around AD 93 for publicly defending the activities of **Thrasea Paetus** and **Helvidius Priscus**.

ASCANIUS OF ABDERA
Ascanius wrote about the philosophy of **Pyrrho of Elis** and was a source used by **Diogenes Laertius**. His evident admiration for Pyrrho suggests he was probably a Sceptic himself.

ASCLEPIACUS (second century AD?)
An inscription found in Bursa (ancient Prusa) came from the grave of Asclepiacus and identified him as Pythagorean.

ASCLEPIADES [1] (second century AD)
Asclepiades seems to have been a Pythagorean and a friend of **Damophilus of Bithynia**.

ASCLEPIADES [2] (second/third century AD)
Asclepiades was both a philosopher and a physician based in Rome. A Platonist, he wrote a work on the immortality of the soul based on his interpretation of certain pronouncements of the oracle of Apollo at Delphi.

ASCLEPIADES [3] (third/fourth century AD)
Asclepiades was a friend of **Lactantius** and wrote a book on providence.

ASCLEPIADES, JULIUS (first/second century AD)
Asclepiades was a philosopher from Alexandria who left some land to the city.

ASCLEPIADES OF ALEXANDRIA (fifth century AD)
Asclepiades was the brother of **Heraiscus** and father of **Horapollon**. He was both a philosopher and a scholar of Egyptian history and culture. He spent his career teaching in Alexandria where his pupils included **Isidore of Alexandria** as well as his own son.

ASCLEPIADES OF APAMEA (second century BC)
Asclepiades was a pupil of **Carneades of Cyrene**.

ASCLEPIADES OF MENDES (first century BC/first century AD)
Asclepiades lived in the time of Augustus and wrote works on pagan theology.

ASCLEPIADES OF PERGAMUM (first/second century AD)
Two lost works by **Plutarch of Chaeronea** were dedicated to Asclepiades, one a letter of consolation and the other an exhortation to philosophy.

ASCLEPIADES OF PHLIUS (fourth/third century BC)
Asclepiades was originally a pupil of **Stilpo**, but later transferred his allegiance to the school of Elis, which he headed for a time with his friend **Menedemus of Eretria**. He was a friend of Menedemus for many years and they shared a house together. Although he was older than Menedemus, it is said that Asclepiades became his son-in-law when he married a woman at the same time Menedemus married her mother. He lived to a considerable age and died in Eretria.

ASCLEPIADES OF PRUSA or OF BITHYNIA (second/first century BC)
Asclepiades was a doctor who practised medicine in Rome. He developed a new approach to his chosen discipline by introducing ideas based on atomism.

ASCLEPIADES THE CYNIC (fourth century AD)
Asclepiades was a wandering Cynic who visited the emperor **Julian** in Antioch in AD 362. It is said that he accidentally set fire to the temple of Apollo in nearby Daphne, although the accusation may be unjust.

ASCLEPIGENIA (fifth/sixth century AD)
Asclepigenia was the daughter of **Plutarch of Athens** and for a time the teacher of **Proclus** [1] in matters of religion.

ASCLEPIODORUS (fifth/sixth century AD)
Asclepiodorus was a philosopher at Constantinople.

ASCLEPIODOTUS (first century BC)
Asclepiodotus was a Stoic and a pupil of **Posidonius of Apamea**. He wrote a book on military matters.
(Aeneias Tacticus, Asclepiodotus, Onasander, trans. Illinois Greek Club, Loeb, 1923)

ASCLEPIODOTUS OF ALEXANDRIA (fifth century AD)
From an early age Asclepiodotus displayed a keen mind and great curiosity. At first he studied medicine, then he went to Athens to study philosophy under **Proclus** [1]. He later taught in Aphrodisias and Alexandria, and seems to have played a prominent role in attempts to revive paganism in those places and elsewhere. He was interested in esoteric matters and tried to develop a scientific understanding of Egyptian mysticism. Unfortunately, he also appears to have had a weakness for making disputed claims. One of these was that he could see in the dark. Another was that his wife, **Damianes of Aphrodisias**, had miraculously given birth (a claim **Adrastus** successfully disproved). Despite this, he enjoyed a high reputation. **Damascius** was a friend of his for

many years, **Isidore of Alexandria** was one of his students, and **Simplicius** became a great admirer of his work.

ASCLEPIODOTUS OF NICAEA (second/first century BC)
Asclepiodotus was a Stoic and a pupil of **Panaetius of Rhodes**.

ASCLEPIUS (fifth/sixth century AD)
Confusingly, Asclepius studied under **Ammonius** at the same time as **Asclepius of Tralles** did. He went on to specialise in medicine.

ASCLEPIUS OF TRALLES (fifth/sixth century AD)
Asclepius of Tralles studied under **Ammonius** and wrote commentaries on the works of **Nicomachus** and **Aristotle** [1].

ASPASIA (fifth century BC)
Aspasia came from Miletus. In Athens she taught rhetoric to **Socrates** and became the lover and companion of **Pericles of Cholarges** for twenty years.

ASPASIUS (second century AD)
Aspasius was a Peripatetic who wrote the earliest commentary on **Aristotle** [1] that still survives in its entirety. It concerns the *Nicomachean Ethics*, now generally regarded as Aristotle's most important work of moral philosophy. Before that time, however, the work known as the *Eudemian Ethics* was the more often studied. It appears that the influence of Aspasius was a significant factor in this shift of emphasis.
(Michael of Ephesus/Aspasius/Anonymous: *On Aristotle Nicomachean Ethics*, trans. D. Konstan, London, Duckworth, 2001)

ASPHALIUS (third/fourth century AD)
Asphalius had a book dedicated to him by **Iamblichus of Chalcis** and is assumed to have been one of his followers.

ASTEAS OF TARENTUM (fifth century BC?)
According to **Iamblichus of Chalcis**, Asteas was a Pythagorean.

ASTERIUS (fourth century AD)
Asterius was a sophist who converted to Christianity and became bishop of Amaseia. He wrote theological works defending the position of **Arius** that show the influence of Cynicism.

ASTON OF CROTON (sixth/fifth century BC?)
Aston was a Pythagorean. According to **Diogenes Laertius**, there was a view that he was the true author of some works attributed to **Pythagoras**.

ASTYLUS OF METAPONTUM (fifth century BC)
According to **Iamblichus of Chalcis**, Astylus was a Pythagorean.

ATEINIANUS, MARCUS
Ateinianus was a philosopher from Nicaea.

ATHAMAS OF POSIDONIA (fifth century BC?)
According to **Clement of Alexandria,** Athamas was a Pythagorean who believed that everything was composed of the four elements, earth, fire, air and water.

ATHANASIUS [1] (fourth century AD)
Athanasius came from Alexandria, where he studied and became bishop. He had a turbulent career, being deposed and exiled more than once, during which time he helped to introduce monasticism to Western Europe. He led the opposition to the views of **Arius** and wrote a number of works criticising them. (*Nicene and Post-Nicene Fathers* series II, vol. IV)

ATHANASIUS [2] (fourth/fifth century AD)
Athanasius was a friend of **Synesius of Ptolemais** and a philosophical acquaintance of **Hypatia of Alexandria.** He appears to have studied philosophy but made a living as a sophist.

ATHANES (third century BC)
Athanes was a Peripatetic and one of the executors of the will of **Strato of Lampsacus.**

ATHENADES (third century BC)
Chrysippus of Soli dedicated some of his works on logic to Athenades, suggesting he was a fellow Stoic and perhaps a pupil.

ATHENAEUS [1] (third century BC)
Athenaeus was an Epicurean, a pupil of **Polyaenus of Lampsacus.**

ATHENAEUS [2] (third century AD)
According to **Porphyry,** Athenaeus was one of those philosophers who dedicated himself to teaching and wrote little. He was a Stoic, probably based in Athens.

ATHENAEUS OF ATTALEIA (first/second century AD)
Athenaeus achieved fame as a physician, founding the Pneumatist school of medicine. His philosophical importance derives from his analysis of causation in the context of illness, which was much admired by **Galen.** In particular, he distinguished between preceding causes (internal dispositions) and antecedent causes (external influences). This idea is sometimes associated with the Stoics, and Athenaeus may have been one himself.

ATHENAEUS OF NAUCRATIS (second/third century AD)
Athenaeus is known as the author of a work, *The Deipnosophists* or *Scholars at Dinner.* In it a variety of scholars meet to discuss a variety of subjects. Athenaeus includes quotations from or references to a wide range of sources. Some of those taking part in the discussion are philosophers, but opinions are divided as to their historicity.
(Athenaeus, *The Deipnosophists* (7 vols), trans. C.B. Gulick, Loeb, 1927-41)

ATHENAEUS OF SELEUCIA (first century BC)
Athenaeus was a Peripatetic and a statesman. Accused of involvement in a plot against Augustus, he was found to be innocent and released. Not long afterwards he died when his house collapsed while he was inside it.

ATHENAGORAS [1] (second/first century BC)
Athenagoras was an Epicurean.

ATHENAGORAS [2] (second century AD)
Athenagoras was an Athenian who wrote a long essay to the emperor **Marcus Aurelius** defending Christianity from some of the accusations made against it. He appeals to the emperor as a philosopher to recognise Christianity as a philosophy and to treat Christians with the same tolerance extended to members of other philosophical schools. Much of the work is a defence against charges of atheism, in which he develops a rationalist justification of monotheism, drawing on a wide range of philosophical sources.
(*Ante-Nicene Fathers*, vol. II)

ATHENAGORAS [3]
Athenagoras had a work on **Plato** [1] dedicated to him and was probably a Platonist himself.

ATHENION THE ELDER (second/first century BC)
Athenion was a Peripatetic and a pupil of **Erymneus**.

ATHENION THE YOUNGER (second/first century BC)
Athenion was the acknowledged illegitimate son of **Athenion the Elder** and his Egyptian servant. Like his father he appears to have studied with **Erymneus**, but he also seems to have had some acquaintance with Pythagoreanism. The culmination of a colourful career was when he became virtual dictator of Athens in around 88 BC.

ATHENODORUS [1]
Diogenes Laertius refers on a number of occasions to a book called *Walks* by Athenodorus that appears to have dealt with the lives of a number of philosophers.

ATHENODORUS [2] (third century BC)
Chrysippus of Soli dedicated one of his books on logic to Athenodorus, suggesting that he was a fellow Stoic and perhaps a pupil.

ATHENODORUS [3] (first century BC?)
Athenodorus was a Peripatetic who theorised about the connections between language and music.

ATHENODORUS [4] (first century BC/first century AD?)
Pliny the Younger tells the story of a philosopher called Athenodorus who bought a haunted house in Athens. There appear to have been a number of philosophers called Athenodorus around in the first centuries BC and AD, most

of them being either Stoics or Peripatetics, and it is often impossible to know which fact to assign to which philosopher. Some think the Athenodorus referred to by Pliny was **Athenodorus of Tarsus**.

ATHENODORUS [5] (first century AD?)
Suda mentions an Athenodorus who was a pupil of **Dionysius the Areopagite** and wrote several books. He presumably lived at the time of the original Dionysius and not at the time when the works written under his name actually appeared centuries later.

ATHENODORUS [6] (third century AD)
Athenodorus came from Neocaesarea and was a brother of **Gregory Thaumaturgus**. Like Gregory, he was a keen student of philosophy. They both studied under **Origen** and both became bishops.

ATHENODORUS [7] (fifth century AD)
Athenodorus was a philosopher in Athens at the same time as **Proclus** [1]. He had a reputation for the clarity of his writing. **Sallustius of Syria** admired his work, but tried to persuade him to give up philosophy.

ATHENODORUS CORDYLION (second/first century BC)
Athenodorus was a Stoic philosopher from Tarsus. He moved to Pergamum to take charge of the library there. Later, **Cato the Younger** took him to Rome where he supported him until he died in around 47 BC.

ATHENODORUS OF ATHENS (first century AD)
Athenodorus was an Epicurean.

ATHENODORUS OF RHODES (second/first century BC?)
Athenodorus objected to rhetoric being regarded as an art. He may have been a Peripatetic and a pupil of **Critolaus of Phaselis**.

ATHENODORUS OF SOLI (third century BC)
Athenodorus was a Stoic and pupil of **Zeno of Citium**. He may have been the brother of **Aratus of Soli**.

ATHENODORUS OF TARSUS (first century BC)
Athenodorus studied Stoicism in Rhodes under **Posidonius of Apamea**, and went on to become a teacher in Apollonia, Epirus, where the young Augustus (then Octavian) was one of his pupils. The two remained close and Augustus later sent him back to Tarsus to take charge of the government of the city. He was also a friend of **Cicero**. He is sometimes known as Athenodorus Calvus, Athenodorus of Cana and the son of Sandon.

ATHENODOTUS (first/second century AD)
Athenodotus was a Stoic, a pupil of **Musonius Rufus** and teacher of Marcus Cornelius **Fronto**.

ATTALUS (first century BC/first century AD)
Attalus was a Stoic and a teacher of **Seneca**. He taught that self-improvement was the aim of philosophy, and that it brought happiness because it was in accordance with nature. He cautioned against all luxuries and riches, and believed that it was necessary to eliminate or moderate all desires, including the desire to learn.

ATTICUS [1] (second century AD)
Atticus taught Platonism in Athens. He held that **Plato** [1] was the first person to produce a systematic philosophy, bringing together ideas and disciplines previously developed separately by others such as **Pythagoras, Parmenides of Elea** and **Thales of Miletus** and their followers. He opposed the incorporation of Aristotelian ideas into Platonism, maintaining a more orthodox position than some of his contemporaries. However, he also regarded the Forms of Plato as ideas in the mind of God rather than as free-standing entities.
(Eusebius, *Preparation for the Gospel* (2 vols), trans. E.H. Gifford, Eugene, Wipf and Stock, 2002)
[John Dillon, *The Middle Platonists 80 BC to AD 220*, London, Duckworth, 1996]

ATTICUS [2] (fourth/fifth century AD)
Atticus came from Sebasteia where he studied philosophy with a Christian monk. He moved to Constantinople where he eventually became patriarch. He produced a number of writings attacking the heresies of his times.

ATTICUS, TITUS POMPONIUS (110-32 BC)
Atticus was a great friend of **Cicero** for many years. They regularly corresponded with each other, and many of the letters Cicero wrote to him still survive. It is likely that Atticus himself was responsible for publishing them. In 85 BC, fearing the onset of civil war, he moved to Athens and studied Epicureanism. On returning to Rome in around 65 BC he decided his principles would not permit him to become involved in politics, but they did not stop him making a lot of money. When he found he was incurably ill, he starved himself to death.

AUGUSTINE [AURELIUS AUGUSTIUS] (AD 354-430)
Augustine was born in Tagaste and died as the bishop of nearby Hippo. His introduction to philosophy probably came when he was a student in Carthage, where he became acquainted with the logic of **Aristotle** [1] and some of the works of **Cicero**. Later he acquired a knowledge of Platonism, and for several years he was a follower of **Mani**. Although raised by a Christian mother, it was not until AD 386 that he made his final and decisive choice to be a Christian, thanks in large part to the influence of **Ambrose**.

The writings of Augustine are substantial rather than systematic and many are as much polemical as philosophical. From being an admirer of Mani he became an implacable opponent, while **Pelagius** became a particular target within the Christian community. As a polemicist he drew support from wherever he could find it, invoking the words and ideas of a variety of philosophers as and when occasion demanded. *The City of God*, written over a long period, reads in part like an encyclopaedia of ancient philosophy. Nevertheless, Augustine makes it clear that his sympathies lie firmly with **Plato** [1], disagreeing with him only when his philosophy is clearly contradicted by Christianity. However, because he came to Plato primarily through the works of the Neoplatonists, he subscribed to a particularly mystical interpretation of his philosophy. *The City of God* is also important as a seminal work in the Christian philosophy of history. Other writings range over a variety of philosophical issues and areas including determinism, language and epistemology.

Written at a time when the Western Roman Empire was breaking up, the works of Augustine, and through him Platonism, were to have an enormous influence on the theology of the Latin-speaking church centred on Rome.

(*Nicene and Post-Nicene Fathers* series I, vols I-VIII; various editions of *The City of God* including Loeb, Penguin and Everyman, and other individual works) [Vernon J. Bourke, *Augustine's Quest of Wisdom*, Albany, Magi, 1993; Peter Brown, *Augustine of Hippo*, Berkeley, University of California Press, 1967; Michael Mendelson, 'Saint Augustine', *The Stanford Encyclopedia of Philosophy* (Winter 2000 Edition), Edward N. Zalta (ed.), plato.stanford.edu/archives/win2000/entries/augustine/]

AULUS GELLIUS (second century AD)
Aulus Gellius was a pupil of both Lucius Calvenus **Taurus** and **Peregrinus Proteus**. He was also a friend of **Herodes Atticus** and **Favorinus**. He is best known for his *Attic Nights*, a collection of essays in which he talks about books he has read, lectures he has heard and various other bits and pieces in which he took an interest for one reason or another.
(Aulus Gellius, *Attic Nights* (3 vols), trans. J.C. Rolfe, Loeb, 1927-30)

AURELIAN OF SMYRNA (second/third century AD?)
Aurelian was a Pythagorean honoured at Delphi.

AUSONIUS (fourth century AD)
Ausonius was a Christian poet whose works reveal an eclectic approach to philosophy. His pupils included the emperor Gratian and **Paulinus of Nola**.
(Ausonius (2 vols), trans. H.G.E. White, Loeb 1919, 1921)

AUTOBOULUS, MESTRIUS (first/second century AD)
Autoboulus was a Platonist and related to **Plutarch of Chaeronea**, perhaps his son. He was noted for his dedication to philosophy.

AUTOBOULUS, SEXTUS CLAUDIUS (third century BC)
Autoboulus was a Platonist and a descendant of **Plutarch of Chaeronea**.

AUTOCHARIDAS OF SPARTA (fifth century BC?)
According to **Iamblichus of Chalcis**, Autocharidas was a Pythagorean, as was his sister **Cleaichma of Sparta**.

AUTODORUS (third century BC?)
According to **Diogenes Laertius**, Autodorus was an Epicurean and critic of **Heraclides of Pontus**.

AVIDIENUS (first century BC)
Avidienus was a Cynic. According to **Horace** he lived on a diet of old olives, wild fruit, sour wine, rancid oil, cabbage and vinegar.

AVIDIUS ARCHESTRATUS (second century AD)
Avidius Archestratus was a philosopher from Thespiae and something of a local philanthropist. His father, **Avidius Parmenides**, was also a philosopher.

AVIDIUS PARMENIDES (first/second century AD)
Avidius Parmenides was a philosopher from Thespiae. His son, **Avidius Archestratus**, was also a philosopher.

AVIENUS, RUFIUS FESTUS (fourth century AD)
Avienus was a poet who translated the *Phaenomena* of **Aratus of Soli** into Latin. He was also a Stoic and distant descendant of **Musonius Rufus**.

AXIONICUS (second century AD)
Axionicus was a gnostic, a follower of **Valentinus**.

AXIOPISTUS OF LOCRI
Axiopistus is thought to have been the author of some of the works attributed to **Epicharmus**.

AXIOTHEA OF PHLIUS (fourth century BC)
Axiothea is one of two women said to have been students of both **Plato** [1] and **Speusippus**. (The other was **Lasthenia of Mantinea**.) According to **Diogenes Laertius**, she may have been in the habit of wearing men's clothes, although this may indicate nothing more than a preference for wearing the cloak often favoured by philosophers.

❖ **B** ❖

BABELYCA OF ARGOS
According to **Iamblichus of Chalcis**, Babelyca was a Pythagorean.

BACCHIUS (first century BC)
Bacchius was a friend of **Philodemus of Gadara** and probably also an Epicurean.

BACCHIUS OF PAPHOS (second century AD)
Bacchius was a Platonist. **Marcus Aurelius** attended his lectures as a young

man. He was honoured at Delphi at the same time as **Zosimus of Athens, Nicostratus of Athens** and **Cornelianus of Mallus**. He may have been the adopted son of **Gaius**.

BAGOAS (second/third century AD)
It is said that Bagoas was a eunuch and a Peripatetic. In AD 178, he was one of those considered as a candidate for the chair of Peripatetic philosophy in Athens. However, there were objections to his candidacy on the grounds that he did not have a beard. The story comes from **Lucian of Samosata** and how much truth it contains is questionable.

BALBILLUS, TIBERIUS CLAUDIUS (first century AD)
Balbillus was a man of learning, much admired by **Seneca**, who became head of the library of Alexandria. He was the personal astrologer of Nero and wrote a long book on astrology.

BALBUS, LUCIUS CORNELIUS (first century BC)
Balbus came from Gades (Cadiz) in Spain and went on to become the first foreign-born consul of Rome in 40 BC. He became a friend of **Cicero**, who successfully defended him in a legal action. Comments made by Cicero suggest he was an Epicurean.

BALBUS, QUINTUS LUCILIUS (first century BC)
Balbus was a Stoic. **Cicero** uses him as a spokesman for Stoicism in *On the Nature of the Gods*.

BARACHUS (fourth century AD)
Barachus was a philosopher and friend of **Symmachus**, who admired him greatly.

BARDESANES (second/third century AD)
Bardesanes came from Edessa, his original Syriac name being Bar-Daisan. He seems to have been a Christian, although the extent to which he was an orthodox one is questionable. He believed that the world was composed of five eternal elements: fire, wind, water, light and dark. They had originally co-existed in a chaotic way, but God imposed order on them. Bardesanes also composed a work entitled *The Book of the Laws of the Countries* in which he challenges the astrologers' belief in fate. According to Bardesanes, because of their free will, human beings' lives are dictated only to a certain degree by their nature and not at all by the stars. Their nature is what they all have in common with each other. Although a familiarity with both Platonism and Stoicism is evidenced in his work, it seems doubtful that Bardesanes belonged to any particular school. It was long thought that he was a gnostic, but this is now regarded as unlikely.
(H.J.W. Drijvers, *The Book of the Laws of the Countries. Dialogue on Fate of Bardaisan of Edessa*, Assen, Van Gorcum, 1966; Eusebius, *Preparation for the Gospel* (2 vols), trans. E.H. Gifford, Eugene, Wipf and Stock, 2002)

BARSAUMA (sixth century AD)
Barsauma was a philosopher from Gordyene and taught **Chosroes I** when the king visited there. He was later chosen by Chosroes as a member of a delegation he sent to Constantinople.

BASIL OF CAESAREA (fourth century AD)
Basil was the brother of **Gregory of Nysa** and became bishop of Caesarea in Cappadocia, succeeding **Eusebius of Caesarea** in that post in AD 370. As a young man he had studied philosophy in Athens alongside the future emperor **Julian**.
(*Nicene and Post-Nicene Fathers*, vol. VIII)

BASILIDES (second century AD)
Basilides was a leading gnostic and a prolific author. He probably came from Syria but became a teacher in Alexandria where he founded his own sect that seems to have lasted for at least two hundred years. He taught that the highest God is beyond human knowledge and that our world was created by the last in a series of emanated spiritual beings. The material human body, intrinsically corrupt, is of no importance in his system and therefore its behaviour is a matter of complete indifference, resulting in a profound principled antinomianism.
(Arland J. Hultgren and Steven A. Haggmark (eds), *The Earliest Christian Heretics*, Minneapolis, Fortress Press, 1996)

BASILIDES OF PIRAEUS (second century BC)
Basilides was a Stoic at the school in Athens.

BASILIDES OF SCYTHOPOLIS (second century AD)
Basilides was probably a Stoic and may have been a teacher of **Marcus Aurelius**.

BASILIDES OF SYRIA (third/second century BC)
Basilides succeeded **Dionysius** [3] as head of the Epicurean school. He was particularly interested in mathematics.

BASSUS, LUCIUS AUFIDIUS (first century AD)
According to **Seneca**, Bassus was an Epicurean who bore witness to his school's teachings in the way he coped with prolonged ill health. He was an historian but none of his writings have survived.

BASSUS POLYAENUS, TITUS AVIANIUS (second century AD)
Bassus was a Stoic. A statue was erected in his honour in his home town of Hadriani.

BASSUS OF CORINTH (first century AD)
Bassus is said to have crossed philosophical swords with **Apollonius of Tyana**, who subsequently accused him of killing his own father and trying to kill Apollonius.

BATACES (second century BC)
Bataces came from Nicaea and was a pupil of **Carneades of Cyrene**.

BATHYLAUS OF POSIDONIA (sixth/fifth century BC)
According to **Iamblichus of Chalcis**, Bathylaus was a Pythagorean. He is probably the same person as the Bathyllus to whom **Alcmaeon of Croton** dedicated a book.

BATIS (fourth/third century BC)
Batis was the sister of the Epicurean **Metrodorus of Lampsacus** [2] and married **Idomeneus of Lampsacus**. She appears to have been an Epicurean herself.

BERONICIANUS OF SARDIS (fourth/fifth century AD)
Beronicianus was a pupil of **Chrysanthius of Sardis** and highly regarded as a philosopher by **Eunapius**.

BESAS (fourth century AD)
Besas was a Cynic. He visited the tomb of Ramesses VI in the Valley of the Kings and left an inscription there.

BESAS OF PANOPOLIS (fourth century AD)
Besas was an Egyptian Platonist and teacher of philosophy. He was a friend of **Bouriccius of Ascalon**.

BETION (fourth/third century BC)
Betion was a friend and lover of **Bion of Borysthenes**, and probably a Cynic.

BIAS OF PRIENE (sixth century BC)
Bias was usually reckoned as one of the Seven Sages of ancient Greece. The stories about him are few and confused, but he was evidently held in high esteem in his home town and **Heraclitus of Ephesus** admired him. His personal motto is said to have been 'Most men are bad!'

BINDACUS or RHYNDACUS (fifth century BC?)
According to **Iamblichus of Chalcis**, Bindacus was a Pythagorean and the brother of **Philtys**. Some suspect this is a mistake on the part of Iamblichus and that Bindacus was female and the sister of **Eccelus of Lucania** and **Occelus of Lucania**.

BION (fifth/fourth century BC?)
According to **Diogenes Laertius**, there was a Bion who studied under **Democritus of Abdera**. Whether on the basis of experience or conjecture, he claimed that there were places in the world where night and day could last six months.

BION OF BORYSTHENES (fourth/third century BC)
Bion's father was a fish merchant and his mother was a prostitute. The family was sold into slavery because of financial difficulties. Bion was fortunate to be bought by a teacher of rhetoric who died leaving him all his property. Bion sold

everything and went to Athens to study philosophy. First he attended the Academy, but he was critical of Platonism. Then he became a Cynic. Later he attached himself to **Theodorus the Atheist**, and seems to have become an atheist himself. Later again he spent time at the Lyceum studying under **Theophrastus of Eresus**. He appears to have travelled a great deal and lived lavishly. While he attracted admirers, according to **Diogenes Laertius** he had no real followers. He died in 245 BC.
[Jan Fredrik Kindstrand, *Bion of Borysthenes*, Uppsala, Uppsala University Press, 1977]

BITALE (sixth/fifth century BC?)
According to **Iamblichus of Chalcis**, Bitale was both the grand-daughter and daughter-in-law of **Pythagoras**, being the daughter of **Damo** and the wife of **Telauges**. It is said that Damo passed on her father's teachings to Bitale. The historical existence of Bitale is widely doubted.

BITON OF SOLI (second century BC)
Biton was a Platonist and pupil of **Carneades of Cyrene**.

BITYS
According to **Iamblichus of Chalcis**, Bitys was an Egyptian who discovered and translated important mystical texts. However, it is widely supposed that Iamblichus invented her.

BLOSSIUS, GAIUS (second century BC)
Blossius was a Stoic from Cumae who is thought to have had an influence on the reforms introduced in Rome by Tiberius Gracchus.

BOETHIUS, ANICIUS MANLIUS SEVERINUS (fifth/sixth century AD)
Boethius studied philosophy from an early age. He is best known for translating many important works, including those on logic by **Aristotle** [1], from Greek into Latin, and for his own *Consolation of Philosophy*, written while he was in prison. As a Christian, he also wrote a number of theological works. He followed a successful political career before being outmanoeuvred by his enemies and subsequently executed. He may have been a Neoplatonist, but the *Consolation* is full of references to a wide variety of earlier thinkers. In it, Philosophy personified visits him in his cell to bring him comfort in his time of trial. **Cassiodorus** was his pupil.
(Boethius, *Consolation of Philosophy*, trans. J.C. Relihan, Indianapolis, Hackett, 2001, and many other editions and translations; ccat.sas.upenn.edu/jod/boethius/boetrans.html)
[Henry Chadwick, *Boethius, the Consolations of Music, Logic, Theology and Philosophy*, Oxford, Clarendon Press, 1981; John Marenbon, 'Anicius Manlius Severinus Boethius', *The Stanford Encyclopedia of Philosophy* (Summer 2005 Edition), Edward N. Zalta (ed.), plato.stanford.edu/archives/sum2005/entries/boethius/]

BOETHUS [1]

Boethus was the author of a guide to the works of **Plato** [1] dedicated to **Melantas**.

BOETHUS [2] (first/second century AD)

Boethus was an Epicurean and a friend of **Plutarch of Chaeronea**. He came from Athens and was particularly interested in geometry.

BOETHUS, FLAVIUS (second century AD)

Flavius Boethus came from Ptolemais in Phoenicia, the city later known as Acre. He was a Peripatetic and a pupil of **Alexander of Damascus**. **Galen** and **Eudemus** were amongst his friends. He pursued a political career, rising to the rank of consul.

BOETHUS OF MARATHON (second century BC)

Boethus was a Platonist, studying under **Ariston of Ephesus** and **Eubulus of Ephesus**.

BOETHUS OF PAROS (second century BC)

Boethus was a Platonist and pupil of **Carneades of Cyrene**.

BOETHUS OF SIDON [1] (second century BC)

Boethus was a Stoic and pupil of **Diogenes of Babylon**. He allowed a wider range of reliable sources of knowledge than did most Stoics, and he rejected the traditional Stoic view that the world was periodically consumed by flames in favour of asserting its indestructibility.

BOETHUS OF SIDON [2] (first century BC)

Boethus was a Peripatetic and the brother of **Diodotus of Sidon**. He was the pupil of **Andronicus of Rhodes** and his successor as head of the school. **Strabo of Amaseia** was one of his pupils. He believed that philosophy should begin with the study of nature, although most of his known writings (of which only fragments survive) dealt with the logic of **Aristotle** [1]. He criticised the arguments advanced by **Plato** [1] for the immortality of the soul. He argued that time was something independent of motion, and that emotions were internal movements that reached a certain strength.

BOIDAS (fifth/fourth century BC?)

Boidas was a philosopher criticised and insulted in a poem by a Diphilus of uncertain time and place.

BOIDION (fourth/third century BC)

According to **Plutarch of Chaeronea**, Boidion was a pupil of **Epicurus**. She may have been a prostitute.

BOIO OF ARGOS

According to **Iamblichus of Chalcis**, Boio was one of the most famous Pythagorean women.

BOLUS OF MENDES (third century BC?)
Suda refers to two people called Bolus, one a Pythagorean and the other a Democritean. It is now thought that they may have been one and the same person, despite the important differences between the two schools. However, **Democritus of Abdera** is said to have studied with **Philolaus of Croton** and written on **Pythagoras**. The works attributed to Bolus indicate an interest in strange natural phenomena and the medicinal use of drugs.

BOTON OF ATHENS (sixth century BC)
According to **Diogenes Laertius**, Boton was a teacher of **Xenophanes of Colophon**.

BOULAGORAS (fifth century BC)
According to **Iamblichus of Chalcis**, Boulagoras was a Pythagorean, and the fourth leader of the school. He succeeded **Mnesarchus**, the son of **Pythagoras**, and was in turn succeeded by **Gartydas of Croton**. It was during the leadership of Boulagoras that the Pythagoreans were expelled from Croton, in around 450 BC.

BOULO or BULO (third century BC)
Boulo was one of those to whom **Lyco** [1] bequeathed the Lyceum on his death. He had presumably been a pupil there for some time.

BOURICCIUS OF ASCALON (fourth century AD)
Bouriccius was a Platonist. He visited the tomb on Ramesses VI with **Besas of Panopolis** and left an inscription there.

BOUTHERUS OF CYZICUS (fourth century BC?)
According to **Iamblichus of Chalcis**, Boutherus was a Pythagorean. Surviving fragments of a work on numbers are attributed to him.

BOUTHUS OF CROTON (fifth century BC?)
According to **Iamblichus of Chalcis**, Bouthus was a Pythagorean. Some identify him with **Xuthus**.

BROMIUS (second/first century BC?)
Bromius was an Epicurean.

BRONTINUS or BROTINUS OF METAPONTUM or OF CROTON (sixth/fifth century BC)
The name of Brontinus crops up more than once in stories about **Pythagoras**. Some say he was his father-in-law, others his son-in-law. He is also said to have been a pupil of **Alcmaeon of Croton**. **Clement of Alexandria** says he wrote a book on the nature of the world. It is possible that a father and son sharing the same name have been confused with each other.

BRUTUS, MARCUS (first century BC)
Brutus is best known as the assassin of Julius **Caesar**, but he took a keen interest in philosophy for many years. Although he was familiar with the teachings of all the main schools, his personal preference was for Platonism, and he was

particularly attracted to the teachings of **Antiochus of Ascalon** whose brother, **Aristus of Ascalon**, spent some time in his house. After the assassination of Caesar in 44 BC, he spent some time in Athens where he attended the lectures of **Theomnestus** and **Cratippus of Pergamum**. He died in 42 BC.

BRYAS OF CROTON (fifth century BC?)
According to **Iamblichus of Chalcis**, Bryas was a Pythagorean.

BRYAS OF TARENTUM (fifth century BC?)
According to **Iamblichus of Chalcis**, Bryas was a Pythagorean.

BRYSON (sixth/fifth century BC)
According to **Iamblichus of Chalcis**, as a young man Bryson studied with **Pythagoras** who was by then an old man.

BRYSON OF ACHAEA (fourth century BC)
Bryson is said to have been the teacher of **Crates of Thebes**.

BRYSON OF HERACLEA (fourth century BC)
Bryson was best known for suggesting a way of squaring the circle (i.e. producing a square with the same area as a given circle), although he failed to produce an actual method for doing so. He is also said to have argued that 'bad' language was no worse than any other kind since the relation between a word and that to which it refers is of a simple one-to-one kind, admitting no variation in quality. He may have influenced **Plato** [1], but the extent to which he did so is unclear and disputed.

BRYSON OF MEGARA (fourth/third century BC?)
The stories surrounding Bryson are extremely complicated, confusing and to a large extent incoherent. He is said to have been the son of **Stilpo** and the teacher of **Pyrrho of Elis**, while also finding time to be taught by **Polyxenus** and teach **Clinomachus of Thurii**, perhaps. Some identify him with **Bryson of Heraclea** while others believe that there was a Bryson attached to the school of Megara who was quite distinct from the mathematician.

❖ **C** ❖

CAECINA, AULUS (first century BC)
Caecina was a friend of **Cicero** and an expert on divination. According to **Seneca**, he wrote a book about lightning.

CAECINA PAETUS (first century AD)
Caecina Paetus was the husband of **Arria Paetus the Elder** and both were Stoics. Caecina became involved in a plot against the emperor Claudius. He

was condemned to commit suicide, and his wife encouraged him to go through with it by committing suicide first.

CAELIUS AURELIANUS (fifth century AD)
Caelius was a physician with an interest in philosophy. He wrote on the history of medical thought and translated some of the works of **Soranus of Ephesus**.

CAERELLIA (first century BC)
Caerellia was a friend of **Cicero** and they often corresponded. His letters testify to her keen interest in philosophy.

CAESAR, GAIUS JULIUS (100-44 BC)
Caesar had many friends who were Epicureans and it is clear that he had some leanings towards Epicureanism himself. Exactly how far these went is unclear and whether he ever actually became an Epicurean is a matter of dispute.

CAILIANUS, TITUS VARIUS (first/second century AD)
Cailianus taught philosophy in Athens.

CAINIAS OF TARENTUM (fifth century BC?)
According to **Iamblichus of Chalcis**, Cainias was a Pythagorean.

CALAIS OF RHEGIUM (fifth century BC?)
According to **Iamblichus of Chalcis**, Calais was a Pythagorean.

CALANUS (fourth century BC)
Calanus was the name given by the Greeks to a Hindu philosopher they met in Taxila. He joined the entourage of Alexander the Great and eventually committed suicide in Persia by climbing onto his own funeral pyre.

CALCIDIUS or CHALCIDIUS (fourth century AD)
Calcidius translated the *Timaeus* of **Plato** [1] into Latin and also produced a commentary on it that still survives. In his understanding of matter and form, he appears to have borrowed substantially from **Aristotle** [1]. His commentary is also a valuable source of information on Stoic physics as he makes several references to what **Zeno of Citium, Chrysippus of Soli** and **Cleanthes of Assus** thought about such issues as fate and substance. He may also have been familiar with the works of **Iamblichus of Chalcis** and **Porphyry**. Opinions are divided as to whether or not he was a Christian.
(J. den Boeft, *Calcidius on Fate: his doctrine and sources*, Leiden, Philosophia Antiqua, 1970, and *Calcidius on Demons*, Leiden, Philosophia Antiqua, 1977. These are translations of and commentaries on parts of Calcidius' work)
[John Dillon, *The Middle Platonists 80 BC to AD 220*, London, Duckworth, 1996]

CALLAESCHRUS, TITUS FLAVIUS (second/third century AD)
Callaeschrus was a Platonist based at Athens. He was the uncle of Titus Flavius **Glaucus**.

CALLIAS OF AEXONE (fifth century BC)
Callias was a pupil of **Zeno of Elea**.

CALLIAS OF ALOPECE (fifth/fourth century BC)
Callias was a rich Athenian who appears in some of the dialogues of **Plato** [1] and who studied with **Protagoras of Abderra, Hippias of Elis** and **Prodicus of Ceos**.

CALLICLES OF ACHARNAE (fifth century BC)
Callicles appears as a character in the *Gorgias* of **Plato** [1]. In that dialogue he takes a dim view of sophists and argues for the superiority of nature over law. Some have questioned his historicity.

CALLICLES OF LARISA (second century BC)
Callicles was a Platonist and a pupil of **Carneades of Cyrene**.

CALLICRATIDAS
The name of Callicratidas is attached to some fragments of Pythagorean writing preserved by **Stobaeus** and thought to date from the third century BC. For no obvious reason the supposed author was sometimes identified with the Callicratidas who was a Spartan admiral in the fifth century BC, while others see a connection or confusion with the Callicratides who was a brother of **Empedocles of Acragas**.
(David Fideler (ed.), *The Pythagorean Sourcebook*, Grand Rapids, Phanes, 1987)

CALLIETES (third century AD)
Callietes was a Stoic in Athens and an acquaintance of **Porphyry** and Cassius **Longinus**.

CALLIGENES (fourth/third century BC)
Calligenes was a pupil of **Plato** [1].

CALLIMACHUS (fourth/third century BC)
Callimachus was a poet and grammarian. His name is sometimes linked with that of the Peripatetic philosopher **Praxiphanes**, but it is unclear whether Callimachus was his pupil or a critic.
(Callimachus, *Aetius, Iambu, Lyric Poems*, trans. C.A. Tryanis, Loeb, 1958)

CALLIMBROTUS OF CAULONIA (fifth century BC?)
According to **Iamblichus of Chalcis**, Callimbrotus was a Pythagorean.

CALLINICUS OF PETRA (third century AD)
Callinicus was mainly known as a sophist. According to **Suda** he wrote many works including *Against the Philosophical Sects*. He was also known as Suetorius or Suctorius, and may have been murdered.

CALLINUS (fourth/third century BC)
Callinus was a pupil of **Theophrastus of Eresus**, and one of those to whom Theophrastus bequeathed the Lyceum when he died.

CALLINUS OF HERMIONE (third century BC)
Callinus was one of those to whom **Lyco** [1] bequeathed the Lyceum on his death. He had presumably been a pupil there for some time.

CALLIPHON (third century BC?)
Calliphon attempted to reconcile the teachings of Stoicism and Epicureanism by claiming that the greatest good in life consisted of virtue combined with pleasure. Initially, virtue is sought for the pleasure it brings but, once experienced, becomes valued in its own right.

CALLIPHON OF CROTON (sixth century BC)
Calliphon was a pupil of **Pythagoras**.

CALLIPPUS OF ATHENS or **OF AEXONE** (fourth century BC)
Despite the claims of both **Diogenes Laertius** and **Suda** that Callippus was a pupil of **Plato** [1], this is not now generally held to be true, although they were certainly contemporaries and quite probably acquaintances.

CALLIPPUS OF CORINTH (third century BC)
Callippus was a pupil of **Zeno of Citium**.

CALLIPPUS OF CYZICUS (fourth century BC)
Callippus was the pupil of **Polemarchus**. Best known as an astronomer and mathematician, he was one of those from whom **Aristotle** [1] adopted the idea of the universe being formed of revolving spheres.

CALLISTHENES (fourth/third century BC)
Callisthenes was a pupil of **Theophrastus of Eresus** and one of those to whom Theophrastus bequeathed the Lyceum on his death.

CALLISTHENES OF OLBIA (second/third century AD)
Callisthenes was a rich and prominent citizen of Olbia who appears to have been philosophically self-taught and honoured by his fellow citizens for his accomplishments.

CALLISTHENES OF OLYNTHUS (fourth century BC)
Callisthenes was a pupil of **Aristotle** [1], to whom he was related. He joined the army of Alexander the Great, and became Alexander's historian. He had a sharp mind and was admired for his simple and disciplined life, although he also had a reputation as a sycophant. In the end he fell out with Alexander and died in unclear but almost certainly unpleasant circumstances.

CALLISTRATUS (third century BC?)
Callistratus was an Epicurean.

CANTHARUS (second century AD)
Cantharus came from Sinope. He was a Cynic and friend of **Peregrinus Proteus**. Cantharus means 'scarab' and so was presumably a nickname.

CANUS or CANIUS see KANUS

CAPITO (second century AD)
Capito was a Platonist and a friend of Aelius **Aristides**.

CARNEADES (first century AD)
Carneades was a Cynic and a contemporary of **Apollonius of Tyana**, according to **Eunapius**.

CARNEADES OF ATHENS (fifth century BC)
According to **Suda**, Carneades was a pupil of **Anaxagoras of Clazomenae**.

CARNEADES OF CYRENE (third/second century BC)
Carneades was a Platonist who succeeded **Hegesinus of Pergamum** as head of the Academy. According to **Diogenes Laertius**, his devotion to philosophy was such that he would let his hair and nails grow long rather than leave his studies. In 155 BC he was sent to Rome along with **Diogenes of Babylon** and **Critolaus** to protest against a fine that had been imposed on Athens. However, the Romans did not take to his brand of philosophising and he was soon asked to leave. He resigned his position as head of the Academy in 137 BC and was succeeded by his namesake, **Carneades the Younger**. He died a few years later.

Some regard Carneades as the founder of the New Academy in succession to the Middle Academy of **Arcesilaus of Pitane**, while others take the New Academy to begin with Arcesilaus himself and regard the idea of a Middle Academy as an unnecessary complication. What is certain is that whatever differences there were between the two, both were Sceptics. Some have argued that Carneades modified his sceptical approach to knowledge by admitting the notion of probability while others maintain that he advocated nothing more than following normal custom and practice without in any way judging it to be superior to the available alternatives. He seems to have been particularly interested in ethics and so with the necessity of making choices in the absence of knowledge. He had studied the works of **Chrysippus of Soli** in some detail and was a persistent and acute critic of Stoicism. He appears not to have written anything himself, but his pupil **Clitomachus of Carthage** recorded many of his teachings for posterity.
[R.J. Hankinson, *The Sceptics*, London, Routledge, 1995; *Routledge Encyclopaedia of Philosophy*, vol. 2; James Allen, 'Carneades', *The Stanford Encyclopedia of Philosophy* (Fall 2004 Edition), Edward N. Zalta (ed.), plato.stanford.edu/archives/fall2004/entries/carneades/]

CARNEADES THE YOUNGER (second/first century BC)
Carneades was the successor of **Carneades of Cyrene** as the head of the Academy, but led it for only a few years. He was succeeded by **Crates of Tarsus**.

CARNEISCUS (fourth/third century BC)
Carneiscus was a pupil of **Epicurus**. He wrote a book on friendship arguing against the views taken on the subject by **Praxiphanes**.

CARNEIUS OF MEGARA (first century AD?)
Carneius was a Cynic who appears in *Banquet of the Cynics* by **Parmeniscus** [2].

CAROPHANTIDAS OF TARENTUM (fifth century BC?)
According to **Iamblichus of Chalcis**, Carophantidas was a Pythagorean.

CARPOCRATES (second century AD)
Carpocrates was a gnostic from Alexandria who founded his own sect. He taught that the world had been created by angels, and that souls were endlessly reincarnated until they achieved release. This was done by experiencing everything life had to offer, including those things conventionally frowned upon. Not surprisingly, this gained the sect a reputation for licentiousness.
(Arland J. Hultgren and Steven A. Haggmark (eds), *The Earliest Christian Heretics*, Minneapolis, Fortress Press, 1996)

CARUS (fifth century AD)
Carus was said to have been one of a group of philosophers who accompanied **Eudocia** on her journey from Athens to Constantinople. The story is doubted, and he may never have existed.

CASSIAN, JOHN (fourth/fifth century AD)
Cassian was a monk and scholar. He wrote two major works, *Institutions* and *Conferences*, both of which were designed to be used by monks. *Institutions* is primarily concerned with ethics and borrows heavily from Stoicism, while *Conferences* is more wide-ranging and cautions against excessive reliance on philosophy.
(*Nicene and Post-Nicene Fathers*, vol. XI)

CASSIODORUS, FLAVIUS MAGNUS AURELIUS (fifth/sixth century AD)
Cassiodorus was a pupil and colleague of **Boethius**. He made a career in politics before a combination of conviction and expediency encouraged him to turn to the religious life. Taking his library with him, he founded a monastery. In so doing, he helped to establish the foundations of medieval scholarship by making the monastery a centre of learning. He wrote a number of works, some of which are philosophical in nature, in particular a metaphysical work on the nature of the soul.

CASSIUS LONGINUS, CAIUS (first century BC)
Cassius, one of those who assassinated Julius **Caesar**, was an Epicurean. He converted to Epicureanism after an earlier interest in Stoicism, and defended his new philosophy in correspondence with his friend **Cicero**.

CASSIUS THE SCEPTIC (first/second century AD?)
Little is known about Cassius. **Galen** makes a passing reference to him as someone arguing against developments within the Empiricist school of medicine, which suggests he was a physician. **Diogenes Laertius** mentions him as a critic of *Republic* by **Zeno of Citium**. Cassius accuses Zeno of coming to a number of conclusions that are either morally repugnant or highly impractical.

However, none of the criticisms has a particularly Sceptical ring to it. Diogenes indicates that Cassius had followers, implying that he was a figure of some significance in his time. It is possible that Galen and Diogenes were referring to different people of the same name.

CATIUS (first century BC)
Catius is presented by **Horace** as something of a philosophical dilettante obsessed with food. He may be the same person as **Catius Insuber**.

CATIUS INSUBER (first century BC)
Catius was an Epicurean who wrote four books in which he set out the school's teachings on the nature of the universe and the most important things in life. The books were aimed at making the teachings available and accessible to a wide audience.

CATO THE YOUNGER [MARCUS PORCIUS CATO OF UTICA] (95-46 BC)
A statesman and philosopher, Cato studied Stoicism as a young man before taking up a political career. He was a pupil of **Antipater of Tyre** and later befriended **Apollonides** [3] and **Demetrius the Peripatetic**, and looked after **Athenodorus Cordylion** in his old age. A staunch republican, Cato committed suicide when he believed the ultimate victory of Julius **Caesar** in the civil war was inevitable. He was much admired by **Cicero** and many regarded him as an embodiment of traditional Roman values, just as his great-grandfather, Cato the Censor, had been before him.

CATULUS, CINNA (second century AD)
Catulus was a Stoic and a teacher of **Marcus Aurelius**.

CEBES OF CYZICUS (first century AD?)
Cebes appears as the host in *Banquet of the Cynics* by **Parmeniscus** [2].

CEBES OF THEBES (fifth/fourth century BC)
Cebes was a Pythagorean and a friend of **Socrates** who features in some dialogues of **Plato** [1]. **Diogenes Laertius** says Cebes wrote three dialogues himself.

CELER, CAIUS ARTORIUS (first or second century AD?)
Celer was an Epicurean philosopher from North Africa.

CELER, PUBLIUS EGNATIUS (first century AD)
Celer came from Berytus (Beirut) but probably studied in Tarsus. He claimed to be a Stoic, but in AD 70 was prosecuted by another one, **Musonius Rufus**, for giving false testimony against yet another one, Barea **Soranus**, while **Demetrius** [3] the Cynic defended him.

CELESTIUS (fourth/fifth century AD)
Celestius came from Britain. He became an ally of **Pelagius** and argued that because sin was an act of free will, the existence of sin proved the existence of free will. His views were condemned as heretical in AD 431.

CELSINUS OF CASTABALA (fourth century AD)
Celsinus was probably a Neoplatonist, and the author of an encyclopaedic work on philosophy. **Augustine** may have acquired some of his knowledge of Neoplatonism from him. He was also a correspondent of **Libanius** [1].

CELSUS [1] (first century AD)
Celsus was an Epicurean who lived during the time of Nero.

CELSUS [2] (second century AD)
Celsus was an Epicurean and a friend of **Lucian of Samosata**.

CELSUS [3] (second/third century AD)
Celsus wrote a work entitled *On the True Doctrine* that prompted a sustained response from **Origen** many years later. It used to be thought that it was written by an Epicurean Celsus of the time, but it is now generally regarded as the work of another Celsus who was a Platonist. In it, Celsus praises Christians for their morals but criticises them for their lack of tolerance.
(Celsus, *On the True Doctrine*, trans. R.J. Hoffmann, Oxford, Oxford University Press, 1987)
[John Dillon, *The Middle Platonists 80 BC to AD 220*, London, Duckworth, 1996]

CELSUS [4] (fourth/fifth century AD)
Celsus was the son of **Archetimus** and a friend of **Symmachus**. Originally from Athens, he taught philosophy in Rome.

CELSUS, CORNELIUS (first century AD)
Celsus was a follower of Quintus **Sextius**. He wrote an encyclopaedic work that dealt with a variety of disciplines including philosophy, but only the section on medicine has survived.

CELSUS OF ANTIOCH (fourth century AD)
Celsus studied philosophy in Sicyon and Athens and later under **Themistius** [2] in Constantinople. In Athens he befriended the future emperor **Julian**, who later appointed him to high office. He was probably a Platonist.

CENSORINUS (second century AD)
Censorinus came from Athens and wrote about philosophy. He may have been a Platonist.

CEPHALUS OF CLAZOMENAE (fifth/fourth century BC)
Cephalus appears in the *Parmenides* of **Plato** as someone with an interest in philosophy.

CEPHALUS OF SYRACUSE (fifth century BC)
Cephalus was a rich friend of **Socrates** who enjoyed philosophical discussions in later life.

CEPHISODORUS (fourth century BC)
Cephisodorus was an orator who wrote a lengthy criticism of **Aristotle** [1] that in part sought to defend the status of rhetoric.

CEPHISOPHON (second century BC?)
Cephisophon was an Epicurean.

CERAMBUS OF LUCANIA (fifth century BC?)
According to **Iamblichus of Chalcis**, Cerambus was a Pythagorean.

CERCIDAS OF MEGALOPOLIS (third century BC)
Cercidas was a politician who also wrote poetry. **Diogenes Laertius** quotes a verse he wrote on **Diogenes of Sinope**. He is thought to have been a Cynic, although his surviving works suggest a variety of philosophical influences. It is said that on his death bed he announced he was looking forward to meeting **Pythagoras**.
(Theophrastus, Herodas, Cercidas and the Choliambic Poets, trans. J. Rusten, I.C. Cunningham and A.D. Knox, Loeb, 1993)
[Donald R. Dudley, *A History of Cynicism from Diogenes to the Sixth Century AD*, 2nd edn, London, Bristol Classical Press, 1998]

CERCOPS (sixth/fifth century BC?)
Cercops was a Pythagorean, said by some to have been the true author of *Sacred Discourses*, a work attributed to Orpheus.

CERDO (second century AD)
Cerdo came from Syria but established himself as a teacher in Rome. He taught a version of Christian gnosticism, radically distinguishing between the God of the Old Testament and that of the New Testament, and claiming that only the soul, and not the body, will be resurrected.
(Arland J. Hultgren and Steven A. Haggmark (eds), *The Earliest Christian Heretics*, Minneapolis, Fortress Press, 1996)

CERINTHUS (first/second century AD)
Cerinthus was a gnostic, perhaps educated in Alexandria. He founded his own sect which believed that creation was the work of a power remote from, and ignorant of, God.
(Arland J. Hultgren and Steven A. Haggmark (eds), *The Earliest Christian Heretics*, Minneapolis, Fortress Press, 1996)

CHABRIAS OF AEXONE (fifth/fourth century BC)
Chabrias was an Athenian friend of **Plato** [1] who studied at the Academy. He went on to have a successful military and political career.

CHAEREAS OF ALEXANDRIA (third or second century BC?)
According to **Philo of Alexandria**, Chaereas was a highly educated person who admired and emulated the way in which **Diogenes of Sinope** spoke his mind. He may have been a Cynic.

CHAERECRATES OF SPHETTUS (fifth century BC)
Chaerecrates was the brother of **Chaerephon of Sphettus** and, like him, a friend and follower of **Socrates**.

CHAEREDEMUS OF GARGETTUS (fourth/third century BC)
Chaeredemus was a brother of **Epicurus** and converted to philosophy by him.

CHAEREMON OF ALEXANDRIA (first century AD)
Chaeremon was a Stoic and a teacher of Nero. He was an authority on Egyptian history and religion. He took a materialist view of the world, claiming that the gods should be identified with the planets, and that everything in the world could be explained in physical terms.
(P.W. van der Horst, *Chaeremon, Egyptian Priest and Stoic Philosopher*, Leiden, Brill, 1984)

CHAEREPHON OF SPHETTUS (fifth century BC)
Chaerephon was a friend of **Socrates**, and the one who enquired of the oracle at Delphi whether Socrates was the wisest person alive. He appears in some of the dialogues of **Plato** [1] where he is mentioned as also being a friend of **Gorgias of Leontini**. He evidently took a keen interest in philosophy, but was an object of fun for many Athenians because they thought he looked like a corpse. His brother was **Chaerecrates of Sphettus**.

CHAERON OF PELLENE (fourth century BC)
Chaeron studied under **Plato** [1] and **Xenocrates of Chalcedon** before giving up philosophy for politics and becoming the ruler of Pellene.

CHAMAELION OF HERACLEA (fourth/third century BC)
Chamaelion was a Peripatetic who wrote works on moral philosophy.

CHARAX, CLAUDIUS (second century AD)
Charax came from Pergamum and was a priest as well as a philosopher. According to **Suda**, he wrote many books on Greek history. **Marcus Aurelius** admired his intellect.

CHARIDEMUS OF MESSENE (first/second century AD)
Charidemus may have been a pupil of **Dion Cocceianus**.

CHARILAMPIANES OLYMPIAS, AURELIA (third century AD)
Charilampianes came from Heraclea in Pontus. Her husband had an epitaph carved on her tombstone identifying her as a philosopher.

CHARMADAS (second/first century BC)
Charmadas was a pupil of **Carneades of Cyrene**. He was strongly opposed to the use of rhetoric. Lucius Lucinius **Crassus** was one of his pupils.

CHARMANDER (first century BC/first century AD?)
According to **Seneca**, Charmander wrote a book on comets.

CHARMIDES [1] (fourth century BC?)
Charmides was the supposed recipient of a letter falsely attributed to **Diogenes of Sinope**. In it Diogenes reproaches him with teaching his pupil **Euremon** a philosophy that was more interested in argument than in virtue.

CHARMIDES [2] (fourth/third century BC)
Charmides was an Epicurean and a friend of **Arcesilaus of Pitane**.

CHARMIDES OF ATHENS (fifth century BC)
Charmides was an uncle of **Plato** [1] and appears in the dialogue named after him where he discusses the virtue of moderation with **Socrates**.

CHARONDAS OF CATANA (sixth/fifth century BC)
According to **Iamblichus of Chalcis**, Charondas was a Pythagorean, one of those who studied with **Pythagoras** himself during his later years. He achieved a reputation as a legislator, although Iamblichus suggests that all he did was act as a vehicle for the ideas of Pythagoras in this regard. It is said that when he found out he had accidentally broken one of his own laws, he committed suicide. Whether he was ever a Pythagorean at all is now widely questioned. Substantial portions of a work on laws attributed to him survive.
(David Fideler (ed.), *The Pythagorean Sourcebook*, Grand Rapids, Phanes, 1987)

CHEILAS OF METAPONTUM (fifth century BC?)
According to **Iamblichus of Chalcis**, Cheilas was a Pythagorean.

CHEILONIS (sixth century BC?)
Cheilonis was probably the daughter of **Chilon** and according to **Iamblichus of Chalcis** was one of the most famous Pythagorean women.

CHILON (sixth century BC)
Chilon came from Sparta and appears on some lists of the Seven Sages of ancient Greece. According to **Diogenes Laertius** he taught that knowledge of the future based on reason was the greatest human accomplishment. 'Do not speak ill of the dead' was one of his sayings and **Cheilonis** was probably his daughter.

CHION (fourth century BC)
Chion came from Heraclea in Pontus. He was the son of **Matris**, a student of **Plato** [1] and assassin of **Clearchus of Heraclea**.

CHONUPHIS (fifth/fourth century BC)
Chonuphis was an Egyptian priest. **Plato** [1] and **Ellopion of Peparethus** are said to have visited him, and **Eudoxus of Cnidus** was one of his pupils.

CHOSROES I (sixth century AD)
Chosroes ruled Persia AD 531-79. He took a great interest in Greek philosophy and arranged for a number of works to be translated into Persian. He received visits from a number of philosophers including **Damascius** and **Uranius** and studied briefly with **Barsauma**.

CHREMONIDES OF ATHENS (third century BC)
Chremonides was a Stoic and a pupil of **Zeno of Citium** at the same time as **Cleanthes of Assus**. However, he made his career in politics rather than in philosophy.

CHRYSANTHIUS OF SARDIS (fourth century AD)
Chrysanthius was a Neoplatonist. He became a student of **Aedesius** in Pergamum before going on to study the works of the other schools by himself. He had a number of celebrated pupils including the emperor **Julian** and **Eunapius** as well as **Beronicianus of Sardis** and **Epigonus of Sparta** who were his successors. Despite coming from one of the aristocratic families of Sardis, he led a plain and simple life. He attracted many students and continued to teach and write into old age.

CHRYSAORIUS (third century AD)
Chrysaorius was a pupil of **Porphyry**, who dedicated several books to him.

CHRYSERMUS OF ALEXANDRIA (second century BC)
Chrysermus was a Stoic, probably a pupil of **Diogenes of Babylon**.

CHRYSIPPUS (fourth/third century BC)
Chrysippus was a grandson of **Eudoxus of Cnidus**. According to **Diogenes Laertius** he spent a great deal of time trying to understand the workings of nature, and wrote a book on the treatment of eye problems.

CHRYSIPPUS OF CNIDUS (fourth century BC)
According to **Diogenes Laertius**, Chrysippus was a pupil of **Eudoxus of Cnidus**, attending his lectures on physics and metaphysics. He also studied medicine and became a physician. His son shared both his name and his occupation.

CHRYSIPPUS OF CORINTH
According to **Iamblichus of Chalcis**, Chrysippus was a Pythagorean.

CHRYSIPPUS OF SOLI (third century BC)
Chrysippus was a runner before taking up philosophy. He became a pupil of **Cleanthes of Assus** and eventually succeeded him as head of the Stoa. However, he disagreed with both Cleanthes and **Zeno of Citium** on numerous points, and spent some years outside the school. He also studied at the Academy under **Arcesilaus of Pitane** and **Lacydes of Cyrene**. He wrote an enormous number of works (reputedly more than 700) setting out his ideas and seeking to make Stoic teachings more systematic. For this, he is sometimes regarded as the second founder of the school. According to **Diogenes Laertius**, some of his writings were found offensive as he had little taste for delicacy. He was also inclined to repeat himself and quote at length from others. Diogenes makes it clear that most of his writings were on logic. Because few of the titles attributed to either Zeno or Cleanthes deal with this area, Stoic logic is often regarded as primarily the work of Chrysippus. He explored various kinds of

paradox and fallacy, the nature of language and the origins of knowledge. Later Stoic writers routinely refer back to Chrysippus when discussing such matters. There are two stories about his death, one that he died laughing, the other that he died as the result of drinking. It is possible both are true.

[J.B. Gould, *The Philosophy of Chrysippus*, Albany, SUNY, 1970; Brad Inwood (ed.), *The Cambridge Companion to the Stoics*, Cambridge, Cambridge University Press, 2003]

CHYTRON (fourth century AD)

Chytron was a Cynic and an acquaintance of the emperor **Julian**.

CICERO, MARCUS TULLIUS (106-43 BC)

Scholar, statesman, lawyer and orator, both intellectually and politically Cicero was one of the towering figures of the late Roman republic. A staunch republican himself, he was killed in the civil war that followed the assassination of Julius **Caesar**. Between 79 and 77 BC he spent most of his time outside Rome and studied philosophy in Athens and Rhodes. His teachers included **Posidonius of Apamea, Apollonius Molon** and **Antiochus of Ascalon**. Although sometimes thought of as a Stoic, Cicero identified himself with the teachings of the Academy, although his Platonism was of the eclectic kind advanced by Antiochus. However, since many of his works are written in the form of dialogues, he is a valuable source of information on all the major schools of his time. Most of his philosophical output comes from the last few years of his life when he was no longer active in public affairs. Cicero made little claim to originality as a philosopher. His major contribution was to make Latin a language in which serious philosophical issues could be discussed. Before his time, Romans were virtually obliged to learn Greek in order to learn philosophy. After his time they were not. He left behind him a substantial body of philosophical writings and the firm foundations of a technical philosophical vocabulary.

His most important surviving works are probably those on ethics, *On Duties* and *On Moral Ends*, reflecting the importance Cicero himself attached to this area of philosophy. *On the Republic* and *On Laws*, closely based on the works of **Plato** [1], deal with political philosophy. *On the Nature of the Gods* is a work of comparative theology, while *Tusculan Disputations* is an extended reflection on the value of philosophy. Other works include *On Old Age, On Friendship* and *On Divination*, which features a debate between Cicero and his brother Quintus Tullius Cicero. In it, Quintus is made to defend divination on broadly Stoic lines and he may have been a Stoic himself.

(Volumes XVI to XX of the Loeb edition of Ciero contain his philosophical works: various translations of individual texts including *On the Nature of the Gods, On Duties* and *On Moral Ends*)

[Paul MacKendrick, *The Philosophical Books of Cicero*, London, Duckworth, 1989]

CINCIUS (first century BC?)

Cincius was a Stoic, perhaps from Etruria.

CINEAS (third century BC)
Cineas was an adviser to Pyrrhus, the king of Epirus. He was clearly well-versed in philosophy and may have been an Epicurean.

CINNA CATULUS (second century AD)
Cinna was a Stoic and a teacher of **Marcus Aurelius**. The emperor claimed to have learnt from him the value of friendship, children and praise.

CLARANUS (first century BC/first century AD)
Claranus was a friend of **Seneca** from the time they studied philosophy together, perhaps under **Attalus**. In a letter to **Lucilius the Younger**, Seneca contrasted the ugliness of his body with the beauty of his soul.

CLAUDIANUS OF SMYRNA (fourth century AD)
Claudianus was the brother of **Maximus of Ephesus** and **Nymphidianus of Smyrna**. He became a teacher of philosophy in Alexandria.

CLAUDIANUS MAMERTUS (fifth century AD)
Claudianus was a poet, theologian and philosopher. After a career in rhetoric, he became a monk. His main philosophical work was a treatise on the soul in which he defended the Neoplatonist position that the soul was immaterial. It was written primarily as a response to the position of **Faustus of Riez**.

CLAUDIUS, APPIUS (fourth/third century BC)
Claudius lost his sight and was thereafter commonly known as Caecus ('blind'). He was a reforming politician who, according to **Cicero**, was at least influenced by Pythagoreanism.

CLAUDIUS ATTALUS, PUBLIUS (second century AD)
Claudius was the son of the sophist Marcus Antonius Polemo. Primarily known as a sophist himself, he was also a logician.

CLAUDIUS ANTONINUS (second century AD)
Claudius was a philosopher highly regarded for his moral virtue.

CLAUDIUS MAXIMUS (second century AD)
Claudius was a Stoic and a friend of **Marcus Aurelius**. He had a career in public life and was highly respected. Marcus Aurelius says he learnt the value of self-control from him and admired him for his cheerfulness, modesty, imperturbability and generosity of spirit. He spent some time in Africa where he presided over a trial involving Lucius **Apuleius**.

CLAUDIUS NICOSTRATUS (second century AD)
Claudius was a Platonist honoured at Delphi.

CLAUDIUS SEVERUS (second century AD)
Claudius was a Peripatetic and friend of **Marcus Aurelius**. The emperor admired him for his kindness, warmth and honesty, as well as for his dedication to philosophy.

CLEA (first/second century AD)
Clea was a friend of **Plutarch of Chaeronea**. She evidently took an interest in philosophical matters and he dedicated two books to her. She was a priestess at Delphi.

CLEAICHMA OF SPARTA (fifth century BC?)
According to **Iamblichus of Chalcis**, Cleaichma was one of the most famous Pythagorean women. She was the sister of **Autocharidas of Sparta**.

CLEANOR OF SPARTA (fifth century BC?)
According to **Iamblichus of Chalcis**, Cleanor was a Pythagorean and married to **Cratesicleia of Sparta**.

CLEANTHES OF ASSUS (fourth/third century BC)
Cleanthes was a pupil of **Zeno of Citium** and his successor as head of the Stoa. Before taking up philosophy when he was aged around 50, he was a boxer. He was admired for his industry and dedication, but his critics questioned the depth of his intelligence. However, he was apparently intelligent enough to write over 50 books, although only a few fragments of them survive. He was known more for loyalty to the teachings of Zeno than for innovation, which was perhaps one of the reasons why he succeeded him as head of the school. When he himself died in around 230 BC, supposedly at the age of a hundred, he was succeeded by **Chrysippus of Soli**.
[*Routledge Encyclopaedia of Philosophy*, vol. 2]

CLEARATUS OF TARENTUM (fifth century BC?)
According to **Iamblichus of Chalcis**, Clearatus was a Pythagorean.

CLEARCHUS OF HERACLEA (fourth century BC)
As a young man, Clearchus travelled to Athens where he studied with **Plato** [1]. He later left Athens and became something of an adventurer, eventually being invited by the people of Heraclea in Pontus to help them resolve their civil strife. He became their dictator, lost his initial popular support, and was assassinated in 353 BC by **Chion**, **Leonides** and **Antitheus**. Some have identified or confused him with **Clearchus of Soli**.

CLEARCHUS OF SOLI (fourth/third century BC)
Clearchus was a pupil of **Aristotle** [1]. He wrote a number of works including a biography of **Plato** [1] in which he suggested that Apollo played a role in his conception. His other writings covered a range of topics such as education, love and friendship.

CLEEMPORUS
According to Pliny the Elder, some attributed to Cleemporus a book on the properties of herbs that others attributed to **Pythagoras**. He seems to have been a physician.

CLEMENS [1] (fourth/fifth century BC)
Clemens was a philosopher and a friend of **Libanius** [1].

CLEMENS [2]
Clemens wrote a guide to the works of **Plato** [1].

CLEMENS, ATTIUS (first/second century AD)
Clemens was a friend of Pliny the Younger and may have studied with **Euphrates**.

CLEMENT OF ALEXANDRIA (second/third century AD)
Clement may have come from Athens. He seems to have both travelled and studied widely, spending several years in Alexandria with **Pantaenus**. Whether he actually succeeded him as head of the Catechetical School there is a matter of some dispute. **Origen** was probably one of his students. He devoted a great deal of time to writing and editing works designed to convince people of the merits of Christianity. His wide reading permitted him to draw upon and cite an enormous array of texts, making his works a valuable source of information on ancient philosophy. Through his use of allegorical and other kinds of interpretation, he was able to find support for Christianity in the most unlikely of areas. His own philosophical preference appears to have been for Platonism, although he also shows an appreciation of Stoic ethics.
(*Ante-Nicene Fathers*, vol. II)
[S.R.C. Lilla, *Clement of Alexandria: a study in Christian Platonism and Gnosticism*, Oxford, Oxford University Press, 1971]

CLEOBULUS (seventh/sixth century BC)
Cleobulus was regarded by some as one of the Seven Sages of ancient Greece. He was said to have known something of Egyptian philosophy. **Diogenes Laertius** records a number of sayings attributed to him. While they often embody common sense, they suggest nothing more profound.

CLEOCRITUS (third century BC)
Cleocritus was a Platonist, perhaps a pupil of **Telecles of Phocaea**.

CLEODAMUS (third century AD)
According to **Porphyry**, Cleodamus was a follower of **Plotinus**.

CLEOMBROTUS OF AMBRACIA (fifth/fourth century BC)
Cleombrotus was one of the circle of **Socrates** and a friend of **Aristippus of Cyrene**. He seems to be the person referred to by **Cicero** as **Theombrotus** [2].

CLEOMEDES (second century AD?)
Cleomedes was a Stoic who wrote a book explaining the school's philosophy. A section of it, dealing with astronomy, survives.
[*Routledge Encyclopaedia of Philosophy*, vol. 2]

CLEOMENES [1] (fourth/third century BC)
Cleomenes was a Cynic and a pupil of either **Metrocles of Maronea** or **Crates of Thebes**. He taught **Timarchus of Alexandria** and **Echecles of Ephesus**.

CLEOMENES [2] (third century AD)
Cleomenes was a gnostic who founded his own sect in Rome. He had originally been a pupil of **Epigonus**.

CLEOMENES OF CONSTANTINOPLE (fourth century AD)
Cleomenes was a Cynic. **Libanius** [1] regarded him as a schemer and treated him with suspicion.

CLEON (third century BC)
Chrysippus of Soli dedicated a work on ethics to Cleon who was probably a colleague or pupil.

CLEON OF TARENTUM (fifth century BC?)
According to **Iamblichus of Chalcis**, Cleon was a Pythagorean.

CLEOPATRA see QUEEN CLEOPATRA

CLEOPHON (fourth century BC)
According to **Clement of Alexandria**, **Speusippus** wrote a book criticising the views of Cleophon. Unfortunately, he does not say what the views of Cleophon were or what they were about.

CLEOPHRON OF CROTON (fifth century BC?)
According to **Iamblichus of Chalcis**, Cleophron was a Pythagorean.

CLEOSTHENES OF CROTON (fifth century BC?)
According to **Iamblichus of Chalcis**, Cleosthenes was a Pythagorean.

CLINAGORAS OF TARENTUM (fifth century BC?)
According to **Iamblichus of Chalcis**, Clinagoras was a Pythagorean.

CLINIAS OF SCAMBONIDAE (fifth/fourth century BC)
Clinias was a close contemporary of **Plato** [1] and a follower of **Socrates**. He appears as a character in Plato's *Euthydemus*.

CLINIAS OF TARENTUM (fifth/fourth century BC?)
The information about Clinias is confusing, but running through it all is the constant theme that he was a Pythagorean. **Iamblichus of Chalcis** associates him with both Tarentum and Heraclea, and **Diogenes Laertius** associates him with **Amyclus of Heraclea**. Clinias and Amyclus are said to have prevailed upon **Plato** [1] not to burn the works of **Democritus of Abdera**. Iamblichus mentions Clinias in an illustration of Pythagorean friendship, claiming he went to the financial aid of **Prorus of Cyrene** at considerable cost and risk to himself. Although neither story is possible to date with any precision, if both are true, Clinias would appear to have lived a very long time. A confusion of two people with the same name is perhaps more likely.

CLINOMACHUS OF THURII (fourth century BC)
Clinomachus belonged to the school of Megara and was probably a pupil of **Euclides of Megara** himself. According to **Diogenes Laertius** he was the first to write about propositions and predicates. He was interested in logic and attached great value to the use of argument. Opinions are divided as to whether he took the school in a significant new direction or set up a new school of his own. Some regard him as the initiator of the Dialectical school, although others attribute this to **Dionysius of Chalcedon**.

CLITARCHUS (fourth/third century BC)
Clitarchus was a pupil of **Stilpo**, having previously studied with **Aristotle of Cyrene**.

CLITOMACHUS OF CARTHAGE (second century BC)
Clitomachus was originally called Hasdrubal and taught philosophy in Carthage. When he was forty he went to Athens and became a pupil of **Carneades of Cyrene**. However, he broke with the Academy for a time and set up his own school. He returned when **Crates of Tarsus** was its head and eventually succeeded him. He was a prolific author. He claimed that doctrines attributed to Carneades were misinterpretations of arguments he used against his opponents, and that he never actually endorsed them as true.

CLITUS (third century BC)
Chrysipus of Soli dedicated one of his works on logic to Clitus, suggesting he was a pupil or a colleague.

CLITUS OF MILETUS (fourth/third century BC)
Clitus was a pupil of **Aristotle** [1] who wrote a book about his native Miletus.

CLODIUS OF NEAPOLIS [Naples?] (first century BC?)
According to **Porphyry**, Clodius wrote a book arguing against vegetarianism. He may be the same person as Clodius Sextus, a teacher of rhetoric originally from Sicily.

COERANIUS (fourth century AD)
Coeranius was a respected philosopher from Egypt, tortured and executed in AD 372 along with **Maximus of Ephesus**.

COERANUS (first century AD)
Coeranus was a Greek philosopher living in Rome in the time of Nero.

COLARBASUS (second/third century AD)
According to **Hippolytus**, Colarbasus advocated a form of gnosticism derived from that of **Valentinus** but which also incorporated an emphasis on numbers that came from Pythagoreanism.

COLOTES OF LAMPSACUS (fourth/third century BC)
Colotes was a pupil of **Epicurus**, who taught in Lampsacus before moving to Athens. He became a teacher himself, and **Menedemus of Lampsacus** was one

of his pupils before becoming a Cynic. Colotes wrote a great deal, arguing for the superiority of Epicureanism over all other philosophies. Platonism seems to have been his favourite target. He particularly opposed any form of Scepticism with regard to the reliability of the senses, arguing that if they could not be trusted, life would be practically impossible. Several centuries later, **Plutarch of Chaeronea** wrote a long essay in reply.

COMMODIAN (third century AD?)
Commodian was a Christian poet, two of whose works have survived. The *Song of Apology*, despite its title, is an apocalyptic work, while *Instructions* mainly concerns ethics. Although he is critical of pagans, there is evidence of the influence of Stoicism.
(*Ante-Nicene Fathers*, vol. IV)

COMOSICUS (first century BC/first century AD)
Comosicus was a philosopher who served as an adviser to the Gothic king in succession to **Dicineus**.

COPONIUS MAXIMUS, TITUS (first/second century AD)
Coponius was a leading Stoic in Athens.

CORINTHUS (second century AD)
Corinthus taught in Argos. He is referred to by **Justin Martyr** as a Socratic philosopher, but it is not entirely clear what that is intended to signify so long after the time of **Socrates** himself.

CORISCUS OF SCEPSIS (fourth century BC)
Coriscus was the brother of **Erastus of Scepsis** and father of **Neleus of Scepsis**. He studied under **Plato** [1] and became a friend of **Aristotle** [1]. He and his brother set up their own school in Assus.

CORNELIANUS OF MALLUS (second century AD)
Marcus Sextus Cornelianus was a Platonist honoured at Delphi at the same time as **Bacchius of Paphos**, **Nicostratus of Athens** and **Zosimus of Athens**.

CORNIFICIUS LONGUS (first century BC/first century AD)
Cornificius wrote a work on etymology. He was probably a Stoic.

CORNUTUS, LUCIUS ANNAEUS (first century AD)
Cornutus was a Stoic from Leptis Magna in Libya. He moved to Rome, perhaps initially as a slave, and became one of the city's leading intellectuals. The name Annaeus seems to have been acquired after his arrival and points to a connection of some kind with the family of **Seneca**. He taught rhetoric and philosophy, his students including **Agathinus**, Petronius **Aristocrates**, **Lucan** and **Persius**. In his will, Persius left Cornutus his books, which he accepted, and his money, which he rejected. He seems to have been sent into exile by Nero in around AD 64. He wrote an influential commentary on the *Categories* of **Aristotle** [1] in which he argued that the categories reflected divisions within

language rather than within reality. He also wrote *Introduction to the Traditions of Greek Theology*, which still survives. In it he surveys various mythological traditions and by means of linguistic analysis and allegorical interpretation seeks to extract what he considers to be their true meaning.

(R.S. Hays, *Lucius Annaeus Cornutus' Epidrome (Introduction to the traditions of Greek theology)*, Austin, University of Texas, 1983)

COSMAS INDICOPLEUSTES (sixth century AD)
Cosmas 'the navigator of India' came from Alexandria but, as his nickname indicates, travelled widely. He is best known for his *Christian Topography* in which he sought to produce an account of the universe that was in harmony with Christian teaching. In doing so he set himself against other Christian thinkers, in particular **John Philoponus**, who had been prepared to adopt and adapt elements of Aristotelian cosmology. Cosmas wholly rejected the idea that the universe was spherical and instead insisted that it was rectangular in plan, arguing that this was revealed by the design Moses chose for the tabernacle.

COTTA, CAIUS AURELIUS (second/first century BC)
Cotta appears as a character in *On the Nature of the Gods* by **Cicero**. There he presents the point of view of the Academy. However, he spent some time in exile and almost certainly studied Stoicism and Epicureanism as well then, including in Athens.

CRANAOUS OF POSIDONIA (fifth century BC?)
According to **Iamblichus of Chalcis**, Cranaous was a Pythagorean.

CRANTOR OF SOLI (fourth/third century BC)
Crantor was a pupil of **Xenocrates of Chalcedon, Crates of Thebes** and **Polemo of Athens**. He enticed **Arcesilaus of Pitane** away from the Lyceum to the Academy, and the two thereafter lived together. He wrote a commentary on the *Timaeus* of **Plato** [1] in which he seems to have argued that the soul can only know that which it in some way resembles. This also seems to have been the first commentary anyone wrote on a work by Plato. He was also the author of an essay on grief that was much admired by **Cicero**.
[John Dillon, *The Heirs of Plato: a study of the Old Academy (347-274 BC)*, Oxford, Clarendon Press, 2003]

CRANUS (fifth century AD)
Cranus was said to have been one of a group of philosophers who accompanied **Eudocia** on her journey from Athens to Constantinople. The story is doubted, and there is no other evidence of his existence.

CRASSICIUS PASICLES (first century BC/first century AD)
Crassicius came from Tarentum. He moved to Rome where he worked as a teacher before joining the school of Quintus **Sextius**.

CRASSUS, LUCIUS LUCINIUS (second/first century BC)
Crassus was an orator and a politician. He took a keen interest in philosophy

and at different times studied with **Metrodorus of Scepsis, Charmadas, Clitomachus of Carthage** and **Mnesarchus of Athens**.

CRATES [1] (fifth century BC)
Diogenes Laertius tells of a Crates who was the first to bring *On Nature* by **Heraclitus of Ephesus** into mainland Greece. It was the opinion of Crates that the book was very difficult.

CRATES [2] (fourth/third century BC)
Crates was a Platonist, a pupil of **Xenocrates of Chalcedon**.

CRATES [3]
According to **Diogenes Laertius**, there was a Peripatetic philosopher called Crates.

CRATES OF ATHENS (third century BC)
Crates was a Platonist and a pupil of **Crates of Thria**.

CRATES OF MALLUS or OF PERGAMUM (second century BC)
Crates studied philosophy in Tarsus and Athens before moving to Pergamum where he established his own school and became head of the library there. His main interests were language and literature, but he is also thought to have been a Stoic and **Panaetius of Rhodes** was one of his pupils. He was a promoter of the allegorical interpretation of texts, seen as a major contribution of Stoicism to literary theory.

CRATES OF TARSUS (second century BC)
Crates was a Platonist and the successor of **Carneades the Younger**. He led the Academy for forty years and was succeeded by **Clitomachus of Carthage**.

CRATES OF THEBES (fourth/third century BC)
Crates was a Cynic, a follower of **Diogenes of Sinope** and the brother of **Pasicles of Thebes**. He married **Hipparchia of Maronea** and it is said that they scandalised people by doing in public what was normally done only in private. They had a son, **Pasicles**, who was brought up as a Cynic. Crates had many pupils, including **Zeno of Citium, Cleanthes of Assus** and **Menippus of Gadara**. He is said to have written a great deal but only fragments survive. He was called 'the door opener' because of his habit of wandering uninvited into people's houses in order to harangue them.
[Luis E. Navia, *Classical Cynicism*, Westport, Greenwood Press, 1996]

CRATES OF THRIA or OF ATHENS (fourth/third century BC)
Crates was a Platonist and succeeded **Polemo of Athens** as head of the Academy. The two were close friends. They lived together and when he died, Crates was buried in Polemo's tomb. Among his pupils were **Bion of Borysthenes** and **Arcesilaus of Pitane**. He wrote a great deal but only fragments survive. When he died he was succeeded by **Socratides**.

CRATESICLEIA OF SPARTA (fifth century BC?)
According to **Iamblichus of Chalcis**, Cratesicleia was one of the most famous Pythagorean women and was married to **Cleanor of Sparta**.

CRATIPPUS OF PERGAMUM or OF MITYLENE (first century BC)
Marcus Tullius Cratippus initially studied under **Aristus of Ascalon**, but later became a Peripatetic. He taught in Mitylene for many years, and **Cicero** visited him there. Later he taught in Athens where **Horace** and **Brutus** were amongst his pupils.

CRATYLUS (fifth/fourth century BC)
Cratylus probably came from Athens. He was a follower of **Heraclitus of Ephesus**, and may also have been a teacher of the young **Plato** [1], who later named one of his dialogues after him. In that dialogue he argues that the correct names of things are natural rather than conventional. **Aristotle** [2] associates him with the belief that everything is constantly changing.

CRESCENS (second century AD)
Crescens was a Cynic in Rome. He was strongly anti-Christian and agitated for the death of **Justin Martyr** in AD 165. **Tatian** regarded him as a greedy immoral hypocrite.

CRINIS (second/first century BC)
Crinis was a Stoic who wrote on logic. He defined an argument as two or more premisses and a conclusion. He was probably the pupil of **Archedemus**.

CRISPINUS, PLOTIUS (first century BC/first century AD)
Crispinus was a Stoic and a poet. He wrote a poem setting out the tenets of Stoicism.

CRISPUS (third century AD)
Crispus is said to have been a pagan philosopher from Nicomedia, although there are doubts as to his existence.

CRITIAS (fifth century BC)
Critias was for a time a follower of Socrates but later fell out with him. He briefly headed an oligarchical government in Athens and was killed in a battle with those who sought to restore democracy. He appears in the *Protagoras* and *Charmides* of **Plato** [1] while his grandfather, who had the same name, appears in *Timaeus* and *Critias*.

CRITO OF ALOPECE (fifth century BC)
Crito was a close friend of **Socrates** and appears in some of the dialogues of **Plato** [1], including the one named after him. According to **Diogenes Laertius**, he wrote seventeen philosophical dialogues of his own, but there is no other evidence of them.

CRITO OF ARGOS
According to **Iamblichus of Chalcis**, Crito was a Pythagorean. A book on

practical wisdom in which freedom of will is emphasised was attributed to him.
(David Fideler (ed.), *The Pythagorean Sourcebook*, Grand Rapids, Phanes, 1987)

CRITOBOLUS OF ALOPECE (fifth/fourth century BC)
Critobolus was the son of **Crito of Alopece** and, like him, a follower of **Socrates**.

CRITOLAUS OF AMISUS (second century BC)
Critolaus was a Platonist and a pupil of **Carneades of Cyrene**.

CRITOLAUS OF PHASELIS (second century BC)
Critolaus succeeded **Ariston of Chios** as head of the Lyceum, and was in turn succeeded by **Diodorus of Tyre**. He was one of the philosophers sent as a deputation from Athens to Rome in 155 BC. He emphasised the relative unimportance of material comforts for the good life.

CRONIUS (second century AD)
Cronius was familiar with both Platonism and Pythagoreanism. He wrote commentaries on the works of **Plato** [1] and was a friend of **Numenius of Apamea**. He believed that evil originated from matter and that souls therefore suffered through becoming attached to bodies.

CRONIUS OF LAMPSACUS (fourth/third century BC)
Cronius studied under **Eudoxus of Cnidus** before becoming an Epicurean and a correspondent of **Epicurus**.

CTESIBIUS OF CHALCIS (fourth/third century BC)
Ctesibius was a friend of **Antigonus Gonatas** and perhaps a pupil of **Menedemus of Eretria**. He was said to be a popular dinner guest and claimed that, thanks to philosophy, for him at least there was such a thing as a free lunch. **Plutarch of Chaeronea** mentions a Ctesibius who wrote a work entitled *On Philosophy*, but it is not clear whether he is referring to Ctesibius of Chalcis or another of the same name.

CTESIPHON (second/third century AD)
Ctesiphon was a philosopher from Thasos.

CTESIPPUS (fourth/third century BC)
Ctesippus was an acquaintance of **Epicurus** and perhaps a follower.

CTESIPPUS OF PAEANIA (fifth/fourth century BC)
Ctesippus was a follower of **Socrates** and present at his death. He appears in some of the dialogues of **Plato** [1]. **Diogenes Laertius** says he was a son of **Crito of Alopece**, but he is probably mistaken.

CURBUS (fifth century AD)
Curbus was said to have been one of a group of philosophers who accompanied **Eudocia** on her journey from Athens to Constantinople. The story is doubted, as is his existence.

CYLON OF CROTON (sixth/fifth century BC)
According to **Iamblichus of Chalcis,** Cylon sought to join the circle of **Pythagoras** but was rejected because Pythagoras saw in him a tendency to violence and tyranny. In response, he led the people of Croton in a campaign against the Pythagoreans as a result of which Pythagoras had to decamp to Metapontum. But at least he left with his judgment vindicated.

CYNULCUS (second/third century AD)
Cynulcus was the nickname of a Cynic philosopher called Theodorus who appears in *Scholars at Dinner* by **Athenaeus of Naucratis.**

CYPRIAN OF CARTHAGE (third century AD)
Cyprian was originally a pagan but converted to Christianity and shortly afterwards became bishop of Carthage. This proved to be the beginning of ten turbulent years that ended with his martyrdom in AD 258. He wrote a number of works and in those dealing with ethics frequently supported his own position by citing the Stoics.
(Ante-Nicene Fathers, vol. V)

CYRIL OF ALEXANDRIA (fourth/fifth century AD)
Cyril became Patriarch of Alexandria in AD 412 and it was his supporters who killed **Hypatia of Alexandria** in AD 415. Uncompromising in both politics and theology, he was an active opponent of Neoplatonism.

CYRSAS OF CHIOS (fifth/fourth century BC)
According to **Suda,** Cyrsas travelled to Athens, slept by the tomb of **Socrates,** and talked to the philosopher in a dream.

CYRUS (fifth century AD)
Cyrus came from Alexandria where he was a doctor and a philosopher before becoming a monk.

❖ **D** ❖

DAIMACHUS (fourth century BC?)
Diogenes Laertius refers to a Daimachus who was a Platonist. He was probably an historian from Plataea.

DAMARMENUS OF METAPONTUM (fifth century BC?)
According to **Iamblichus of Chalcis,** Damarmenus was a Pythagorean.

DAMAS (fourth century BC?)
Damas wrote a life of **Eudemus of Rhodes.**

DAMASCIUS (fifth/sixth century AD)
Damascius took his name from his home city of Damascus. He studied in Alexandria under **Ammonius** and **Heliodorus of Alexandria** [2] before going on to become a pupil of **Zenodotus** [2] in Athens. A Neoplatonist, he eventually became head of the Academy, and **Simplicius** was one of his students. After Justinian wound up the schools in AD 529, Damascius led a group of philosophers to Persia, being disenchanted with life in a Christian Roman empire. The group included **Isidore of Gaza, Eulamius, Priscianus of Lydia, Hermias of Phoenicia, Diogenes** [2] and **Simplicius**. However, they did not find Persia to their taste either and returned from exile in AD 532 disappointed but protected by a treaty guaranteeing their safety. Damascius appears to have written a great deal, but only two works, a commentary on the *Parmenides* of **Plato** [1] and a treatise *On First Principles*, survive intact.
[*Routledge Encyclopaedia of Philosophy*, vol. 2]

DAMASIPPUS (first century BC)
Horace tells of a Damasippus who was converted to Stoicism by **Stertinius** at a time of personal crisis.

DAMIANES OF APHRODISIAS (fifth century AD)
Damianes was the wife of **Asclepiodotus of Alexandria** and may have been a philosopher in her own right.

DAMIANUS (fifth or sixth century AD?)
Damianus was a Platonist who wrote a work on optics in which he summarised existing theories.

DAMIPPUS (third century BC?)
The name of Damippus is attached to surviving fragments of a work on ethics. It is regarded as Pythagorean and dated to the third century BC. It is not clear whether Damippus was the actual author, or whether he lived earlier but had his name borrowed by a later writer.

DAMIS [1] (first century AD)
Damis is said to have been from Nineveh and a follower of **Apollonius of Tyana** whose written recollections of his time spent with Apollonius formed a major source for the account of his life produced by Flavius **Philostratus**. However, many have doubted whether Damis ever existed, suspecting that Philostratus invented him.

DAMIS [2] (second century AD)
Damis is an Epicurean mentioned by **Lucian of Samosata**. Opinions are divided as to whether he is to be regarded as an historical figure or not.

DAMO (sixth/fifth century BC?)
According to **Iamblichus of Chalcis**, Damo was the daughter of **Pythagoras** and mother of **Bitale**. However, her historicity is widely doubted.

DAMOCLES OF CROTON (fifth century BC?)
According to **Iamblichus of Chalcis**, Damocles was a Pythagorean.

DAMOCLES OF MESSENE (second/first century BC)
Damocles was a Stoic and a pupil of **Panaetius of Rhodes**.

DAMON OF CYRENE (second century BC)
Damon was a Platonist and pupil of **Lacydes of Cyrene**. He wrote a history of philosophy used as a source by **Diogenes Laertius**.

DAMON OF OE or OF ATHENS (fifth century BC)
Damon was a pupil of **Prodicus of Ceos**. His main interest appears to have been in music, but he evidently enjoyed a wide reputation for wisdom as well. He appears as a character in some of the dialogues of **Plato** [1], and there was a tradition that he was a teacher of **Socrates**.

DAMON OF SYRACUSE (fourth century BC)
Damon was a Pythagorean. According to **Iamblichus of Chalcis**, when Dionysius I of Syracuse condemned Damon's friend **Phintias of Syracuse** to death, Phintias asked for time to arrange his affairs, saying Damon would stand hostage for him while he was away. Dionysius was amazed when Damon agreed to the arrangement, and even more amazed when Phintias duly returned at the end of the day to accept his punishment. Dionysius was impressed and asked to join their group, but they turned him down.

DAMOPHANES (second century BC?)
Damophanes was probably an Epicurean. His name appears in fragments of a text in which an Epicurean position on religion is articulated.

DAMOPHILUS OF BITHYNIA (second century AD)
Damophilus was a sophist, historian and philosopher who wrote many works. His name sometimes appears as Demophilus and he is thought by some to have been the editor of *The Golden Verses of Pythagoras*.

DAMOSTRATUS or DEMOSTRATUS (first century BC/first century AD)
Damostratus was a Roman senator who was an historian as well as an authority on fish and fishing. He was said to have been particularly interested in paradoxes and was regarded by some as a philosopher.

DAMOTAGES OF METAPONTUM (fifth century BC?)
According to **Iamblichus of Chalcis**, Damotages was a Pythagorean.

DANDAMIS see MANDANIS

DARDANUS OF ATHENS (second/first century BC)
Dardanus was a Stoic, a pupil of **Antipater of Tarsus** and **Diogenes of Babylon**. He became the head of the school in Athens after the death of **Panaetius of Rhodes**, perhaps jointly with **Mnesarchus of Athens**.

DAVID (sixth century AD)
David, known as 'the Invincible', came from Armenia and is said to have
invented the Armenian alphabet. His name is often associated with that of
Elias, and David may have studied with him under **Olympiodorus** [1] and
succeeded him as head of the Neoplatonist school in Alexandria. A
commentary on the *Isagoge* ('Introduction') of **Porphyry** and another on the
Categories of **Aristotle** [1] may be by him, although their authorship is disputed.
As with Elias, some have questioned the likelihood of a Christian heading the
Neoplatonist school at that time.
(B. Kendall and R.W. Thompson, *Definitions and Divisions of Philosophy by David
the Invincible Philosopher*, Leuven, Peeters, 1983)
[Avedis Sanjian (ed.), *David Anhaght: the 'Invincible' Philosopher*, Atlanta,
Scholars Press, 1986]

DECIANUS (first century BC/first century AD)
Decianus was a friend of the poet Martial and probably a Stoic.

DEINARCHUS OF CORINTH (fourth/third century BC)
Deinarchus was a pupil of **Theophrastus of Eresus** at the same time as
Demetrius of Phalerum. He went on to be an orator and politician.

DEINARCHUS OF PAROS (sixth/fifth century BC?)
Deinarchus was a follower of **Pythagoras.** He seems to have been one of those
who fled Croton when the local people became hostile towards the
Pythagoreans. **Iamblichus of Chalcis** talks about the followers of Deinarchus
being killed in a battle years later, suggesting that he may have established
some kind of school of his own.

DEINIAS (third century BC)
Deinias, in collaboration with **Aristotle the Dialectician,** assassinated the
tyrant Abantidas of Sicyon. Deinias was a philosopher, and Abantidas took an
interest in philosophical issues.

DEINO (sixth/fifth century BC)
According to **Iamblichus of Chalcis,** Deino was the wife of **Brontinus,**
although some think that 'Deino' may be simply a misspelling of **Theano.**

DEINOCRATES OF TARENTUM (fifth century BC?)
According to **Iamblichus of Chalcis,** Deinocrates was a Pythagorean.

DEINOMACHUS [1] (fourth/third century BC?)
Deinomachus was the supposed recipient of a letter falsely attributed to **Crates
of Thebes.** In it, Crates enjoins Deinomachus, who is also a Cynic, to beg only
from the wise.

DEINOMACHUS [2] (third century BC?)
Deinomachus is always found in the company of **Calliphon** and appears to
have shared his views.

DELIUS OF EPHESUS see DIAS OF EPHESUS

DEMARATUS (fourth/third century BC)
Demaratus was a pupil of **Theophrastus of Eresus** and one of those to whom he bequeathed the Lyceum in his will.

DEMETRIA (fourth/third century BC)
Demetria was a member of the community of **Epicurus** and the female companion of **Hermarchus of Mitylene**.

DEMETRIUS [1] (first century BC)
Demetrius was a Platonist who belonged to the circle of Ptolemy XII of Egypt.

DEMETRIUS [2] (first century BC)
Demetrius was a Peripatetic. He was a friend of **Cato the Younger** and was with him in his final days.

DEMETRIUS [3] (first century AD)
Demetrius was a Cynic and a friend of **Seneca, Thrasea Paetus** and **Apollonius of Tyana**. Originally from Corinth, he moved to Rome, but was subsequently banished from there at least once. In AD 70 he defended one Stoic, Publius Egnatius **Celer**, against another one, **Musonius Rufus**.
[Donald R. Dudley, *A History of Cynicism from Diogenes to the Sixth Century AD*, 2nd edn, London, Bristol Classical Press, 1998]

DEMETRIUS [4] (first/second century AD?)
Marcus Aurelius mentions a Demetrius who was a Platonist.

DEMETRIUS, AURELIUS (third century AD)
Demetrius was a philosopher from Nicomedia who donated a statue of Zeus to the city.

DEMETRIUS CYTHRAS (third/fourth century AD)
Demetrius was an elderly philosopher living in Alexandria when in AD 359 he was taken to Scythopolis and tortured. The reason for his detention was that he was a devotee of the god Bes, who was often associated with divination, and at that time divination was often associated (at least by the authorities) with political conspiracy. However, he maintained that his devotion to the god was an innocent one, and was eventually released and sent back to Alexandria.

DEMETRIUS LACON (second /first century BC)
Demetrius was a notable Epicurean. He wrote a number of books on various aspects of the school's teachings. Fragments of his writings found at Herculaneum reveal a concern that some teachers were oversimplifying Epicurean philosophy in order to make it easier for their students to understand.

DEMETRIUS TULLIANUS (third century AD)
Demetrius was a philosopher from Cilicia.

DEMETRIUS OF ALEXANDRIA [1] (second century BC)
Demetrius was a Platonist and a pupil of **Carneades of Cyrene**.

DEMETRIUS OF ALEXANDRIA [2] (third/fourth century AD)
Demetrius was a Cynic and a follower of **Theombrotus** [1].

DEMETRIUS OF AMPHIPOLIS (fourth century BC)
According to **Diogenes Laertius**, Demetrius was a pupil of **Plato** [1]. He may have been the same Demetrius who was an executor of Plato's will.

DEMETRIUS OF BITHYNIA (second/first century BC)
According to **Diogenes Laertius**, Demetrius was the son of **Diphilus** [2] and a pupil of **Panaetius of Rhodes**.

DEMETRIUS OF BYZANTIUM (first century BC)
According to **Diogenes Laertius**, Demetrius was a Peripatetic philosopher.

DEMETRIUS OF MAGNESIA (first century BC)
Demetrius was the author of a work entitled *Men with the Same Name*, a collection of biographies of a variety of people, including philosophers, frequently referred to by **Diogenes Laertius**.

DEMETRIUS OF PHALERUM (fourth century BC)
Demetrius was a pupil of **Theophrastus of Eresus** and a leading figure in Athenian politics for many years. When the political tide turned against him, he went into exile in Egypt, where he died. He wrote many books on both philosophical and other topics.

DEMETRIUS OF PHOCAEA (third/second century BC)
Demetrius was a Platonist and a pupil of **Lacydes of Cyrene**.

DEMETRIUS OF SUNIUM (first/second century AD)
According to **Lucian of Samosata**, Demetrius was a Cynic and may have been a follower of **Agathobolus of Alexandria**. He is said to have travelled to India.

DEMETRIUS OF TARSUS (first/second century AD)
Demetrius was a friend of **Plutarch of Chaeronea**. He was primarily a grammarian but also took an interest in philosophy and may have been a Stoic.

DEMETRIUS OF THYATIRA (second century BC)
Demetrius was a Platonist and a pupil of **Carneades of Cyrene**.

DEMETRIUS OF TROEZEN
Demetrius wrote a work *Against the Sophists* used as a source by **Diogenes Laertius**.

DEMOCEDES OF CROTON (sixth/fifth century BC)
Democedes left Croton for Aegina where he became a famous physician. According to Herodotus, he was later captured by the Persians and helped to cure an ankle injury that was plaguing Darius I. He eventually escaped and

returned to Croton. **Iamblichus of Chalcis** says he was a Pythagorean, one of those who fled Croton during an uprising against the Pythagorean community. If this is true, it presumably happened after his return from Persia.

DEMOCLES (fourth century BC)
Democles was a pupil of **Theophrastus of Eresus**.

DEMOCRATES
Democrates is the supposed author of a collection of short ethical sayings bearing his name. Nothing is known about him, and some of the sayings are probably from **Democritus of Abdera**. As a consequence, many think that 'Democrates' is a corruption of 'Democritus'.

DEMOCRITUS (third century AD)
Democritus was a Platonist who wrote commentaries on some of the works of **Plato** [1].

DEMOCRITUS OF ABDERA (fifth/fourth century BC)
Little is known for sure about Democritus. There was even some dispute as to whether he came from Abdera or Miletus, although his name is usually associated with the former. It was said that he travelled widely, perhaps as far as India. His name often appears with that of **Leucippus** and he is assumed to have studied with him. He is also said to have been an admirer of **Pythagoras** and may have studied with **Philolaus of Croton**. **Diogenes Laertius** says he lived to be over a hundred and lists many works attributed to him, most of which deal with ethics, physics or mathematics. They were edited by **Thrasyllus** but only fragments of them survive. His pupils included **Diotimus of Tyre**, **Metrodorus of Chios**, **Protagoras of Abdera** and **Theognostus**.

From Leucippus he took the philosophy of atomism which was later taken up by **Epicurus**. He argued that atoms had to exist because if matter were infinitely divisible, in the end one would be left with nothing. Atoms were infinite in number, always in motion and made up every physical object. However, he seems to have assumed that beyond the ability to occupy space and move, atoms possessed few if any properties of their own. He also seems to have assumed that a composite object cannot possess a property that is not found in its constituent parts. Consequently he thought that many or most of the properties we ascribe to objects, such as colour, cannot belong to the objects themselves since they are not properties of atoms. They therefore arise in the way we perceive them. The extent to which he developed something resembling a sceptical approach to the problem of knowledge on the basis of this is disputed. He also developed an unusual view of the gods, regarding them as living images of a special kind, both intelligent and able to act.

In his moral philosophy he emphasised the importance of happiness or contentment as the aim of life and conscience as a guide to life. Unhappiness he saw as substantially due to the workings of the passions. However, there is some disagreement concerning how many of the surviving observations on ethics attributed to Democritus are actually his.

(Jonathan Barnes, *Early Greek Philosophy*, Harmondsworth, Penguin, 1987) [*Routledge Encyclopaedia of Philosophy*, vol. 2; Sylvia Berryman, 'Democritus', *The Stanford Encyclopedia of Philosophy* (Fall 2004 Edition), Edward N. Zalta (ed.), plato.stanford.edu/archives/fall2004/entries/democritus/]

DEMOCRITUS OF NICOMEDIA (second/third century AD)
Democritus is one of the philosophers in *Scholars at Dinner* by **Athenaeus of Naucratis**.

DEMON OF SICYON
According to **Iamblichus of Chalcis**, Demon was a Pythagorean.

DEMONAX OF CYPRUS (first/second century AD)
Demonax was a Cynic. **Lucian of Samosata** studied under him and wrote about his life. He spent most of his life in Athens and studied under a variety of philosophers including **Agathobulus of Alexandria, Epictetus, Timocrates of Heraclea** and **Demetrius of Corinth**. His own philosophy appears to have been a relatively eclectic form of Cynicism. He starved himself to death in AD 170 when he was about a hundred. He received a state funeral as a measure of the esteem in which he was held in his adopted city.

DEMOPHANES (third century BC)
Demophanes came from Megalopolis. He was a Platonist and a pupil of **Arcesilaus of Pitane**. His name sometimes appears as Megalophanes and he is usually found in the company of **Ecdelus**. They studied together, taught together and were involved in politics together. **Philopoemen** was one of their pupils. They were eventually invited to Cyrene to reform the government of the city.

DEMOPHILUS see DAMOPHILUS OF BITHYNIA

DEMOSTHENES OF MEGALOPOLIS (third century BC)
Demosthenes was a Platonist and a pupil of **Arcesilaus of Pitane**.

DEMOSTHENES OF RHEGIUM (fifth century BC?)
According to **Iamblichus of Chalcis**, Demosthenes was a Pythagorean.

DEMOSTRATUS (first or second century AD?)
According to **Porphyry**, Demostratus seems to have been a gnostic. His works were in circulation in the third century AD.

DEMOTIMUS (fourth/third century BC)
Demotimus was a Peripatetic and pupil of **Theophrastus of Eresus**, one of those to whom Theophrastus bequeathed the Lyceum when he died.

DERCYLLIDES (second/first century BC?)
Dercyllides wrote commentaries on the works of **Plato** [1]. He believed Plato's

dialogues should be divided into groups of four, an idea later taken up by **Thrasyllus**.

DEXIPPUS (fourth century AD)
Dexippus was a philosopher who is sometimes confused with an historian of the same name. He was probably a pupil of **Iamblichus of Chalcis**, who dedicated a book to him. **Seleucus** was one of his pupils. He wrote a commentary on the *Categories* of **Aristotle** [2].
(Dexippus, *On Aristotle Categories*, trans. John Dillon, London, Duckworth, 1990)

DEXITHEUS OF PAROS (fifth century BC?)
According to **Iamblichus of Chalcis**, Dexitheus was a Pythagorean.

DIADUMENUS (second/first century BC?)
Diadumenus features in a work by **Plutarch of Chaeronea** where he criticises the views of the Stoics from the point of view of Platonism.

DIAGORAS OF MELOS (fifth century BC)
Diagoras was said to have been rescued from slavery by **Democritus of Abdera** and become his pupil. He acquired a reputation as an atheist, and this led to him being condemned to death in Athens. He escaped and finally died in Corinth.

DIAPHENES OF TEMNOS (third century BC)
Diaphenes was a Stoic and a pupil of **Chrysippus of Soli**.

DIAS OF EPHESUS (fourth century BC)
Dias was a Platonist, perhaps a pupil of **Plato** [1] himself. According to Flavius **Philostratus** he was regarded as a sophist. He is probably the person also known as Delius of Ephesus.

DICAEARCHUS OF MESSENE (fourth century BC)
Dicaearchus was a pupil of **Aristotle** [1]. He was the author of several books, some on philosophy, some on other subjects. One was a life of **Pythagoras**. It has not survived but later writers make reference to it. He appears to have been dismissive of ideas of immortality and reincarnation, but emphasised the social and moral side of Pythagoreanism. He had a theory of the soul that presented it as a kind of balanced mixture of the four elements within the body, which some have interpreted as denying any independent existence to the soul at all. According to **Suda**, he also wrote a book entitled *Measurements of the Mountains in the Peloponnese*, which suggests an interest in applied geometry.

DICAEARCHUS OF TARENTUM (fifth century BC?)
According to **Iamblichus of Chalcis**, Dicaearchus was a Pythagorean.

DICAEOCLES OF CNIDUS see DIOCLES OF CNIDUS

DICAEUS OF TARSUS (second/first century BC)
Dicaeus was a Stoic and a pupil of either **Panaetius of Rhodes** or **Paramonus of Tarsus**.

DICAS OF TARENTUM (fourth century BC?)
According to **Iamblichus of Chalcis**, Dicas was a Pythagorean. He may also have been a physician.

DICINEUS (first century BC)
Dicineus was a philosopher who came from, or studied in Egypt. He travelled to Scythia where he made a favourable impression on the local people who, on his advice, tore up all their vines in order to tackle the problem of drunkenness. It is said that he wrote a book of laws for them before his death. He is also said to have become an adviser to the king of the Goths, which may be another version of the same story.

DICON OF CAULANIA (fifth century BC?)
According to **Iamblichus of Chalcis**, Dicon was a Pythagorean.

DIDYMUS [1] (first century AD?)
Clement of Alexandria mentions a Didymus who wrote a work on Pythagoreanism. A reference made by **Porphyry** may be to the same person. Some identify him with a grammarian of the first century AD.

DIDYMUS [2] (first/second century AD)
Didymus was a Cynic. He appears as a character in the dialogue by **Plutarch of Chaeronea** on the decline of oracles. He had the nickname 'Planetiades', suggesting that he was something of a wanderer.

DIDYMUS, ARIUS see ARIUS DIDYMUS

DIDYMUS, ATTIUS
Didymus was a Platonist who wrote a number of philosophical works.

DIDYMUS THE BLIND (fourth century AD)
Didymus was a Christian philosopher from Alexandria. His pupils included Tyrannius **Rufinus** and **Gregory of Nazianzus**.

DIDYMUS THE GRAMMARIAN (first century BC)
Didymus taught in Alexandria and produced an enormous volume of work. Little has survived and little bore on philosophy. He did, however, edit a large collection of proverbs, many of which derived from Peripatetic writers, and produce a book on difficult expressions in the works of **Plato** [1].

DIITREPHES
Diitrephes is portrayed as a Cynic in a work by **Parmeniscus** [2], but there are doubts concerning his historicity.

DINO… see DEINO…

DIO see DION

DIOCLEIDES (fourth century BC)
Diocleides probably belonged to the school of Megara and may have taught **Pasicles of Thebes**.

DIOCLES [1]
Diocles was a Cynic who left inscriptions on the walls of the tomb of Ramesses VI in the Valley of the Kings.

DIOCLES [2] (fourth/third century BC)
Diocles was a Peripatetic and one of the executors of the will of **Strato of Lampsacus**. Some have suggested he should be identified with Diocles of Carystus, an important physician of the period.

DIOCLES [3] (third century BC)
Chrysippus of Soli dedicated two books about language to Diocles, suggesting he was probably a Stoic himself.

DIOCLES [4] (second century AD)
According to **Lucian of Samosata**, Diocles was considered as a possible successor to the Peripatetic chair of philosophy in Athens in AD 178 when he was already an old man. Many doubt the story's reliability.

DIOCLES OF CNIDUS (third/second century BC?)
According to **Numenius of Apamea**, Diocles accused **Arcesilaus of Pitane** of only pretending to embrace Scepticism in order to avoid having to defend the views he actually believed in. The same view is sometimes found attributed to Dicaeocles of Cnidus, and it is widely supposed that the two are the same person.

DIOCLES OF MAGNESIA (first century BC?)
Diocles was the author of a number of philosophical works, all now lost, but often referred to by **Diogenes Laertius**. One was a collection of philosophical biographies, another a summary of the teachings of the major schools.

DIOCLES OF PHLIUS (fifth/fourth century BC)
According to **Iamblichus of Chalcis**, Diocles was a Pythagorean, one of those who left Italy when the Pythagorean communities there came under attack. According to **Diogenes Laertius**, he was a pupil of **Philolaus of Croton** and **Eurytus of Tarentum**.

DIOCLES OF SYBARIS (fifth century BC?)
According to **Iamblichus of Chalcis**, Diocles was a Pythagorean.

DIODORUS [1] (fifth century BC)
According to **Xenophon of Erchia**, Diodorus was a friend of **Socrates**.

DIODORUS [2] (fourth century BC?)
Diodorus wrote a work called *Memorabilia*, used as a source by **Diogenes**

Laertius in his discussion of **Speusippus**. It may be that Diodorus had been his pupil.

DIODORUS [3] (third century BC)
Diodorus was an Epicurean.

DIODORUS [4] (third century BC)
Diodorus was a Stoic and a pupil of **Chrysippus of Soli** who dedicated some of his books to him.

DIODORUS [5] (first century AD)
Diodorus was an Epicurean who committed suicide in a state of contentment and with a clear conscience, according to **Seneca**.

DIODORUS CALLIMEDES (second/third century AD)
Diodorus was a philosopher in Aphrodisias.

DIODORUS CRONUS (fourth/third century BC)
Diodorus came from Iasus and went to Megara to study with **Apollonius Cronus**, whose nickname he subsequently inherited. He was keenly interested in the practice and logic of argument and was supposed to have been the person who discovered the puzzle known as 'the horned one'. According to this, you have whatever you have not lost. So if you have not lost horns, you must have them. However, according to **Diogenes Laertius** he was outmanoeuvred in argument by **Stilpo** and as a result died a disappointed man. His pupils included **Zeno of Sidon** [1], **Zeno of Citium** and his own daughters.
[R. Gaskin, *The Sea Battle and the Master Argument*, New York, de Gruyter, 1995; *Routledge Encyclopaedia of Philosophy*, vol. 3]

DIODORUS SICULUS (first century BC)
Diodorus of Sicily wrote a history of the world that still largely survives. *The Library of History* is a valuable source of information about the thought of antiquity.
(Diodorus Siculus, *Library of History* (12 vols), trans. C.H. Oldfather et al., Loeb, 1933-67)

DIODORUS OF ADRAMYTTIUM (second/first century BC)
Diodorus was a Platonist and a pupil of **Charmadas**.

DIODORUS OF ALEXANDRIA [1] (second century BC)
Diodorus was a Platonist and a pupil of **Telecles of Phocaea**.

DIODORUS OF ALEXANDRIA [2] (first century BC)
Diodorus was a Stoic, a pupil of **Posidonius of Apamea**. His main interests were in mathematics and astronomy.

DIODORUS OF ASPENDUS (fourth century BC)
According to **Iamblichus of Chalcis**, Diodorus became a pupil of **Aresas** and

subsequently took Pythagorean teachings back to Greece. He was said to dress like a beggar and is seen by some as the precursor of the Cynics in this regard.

DIODORUS OF EPHESUS
Diodorus was the author of a life of **Anaximander** referred to by **Diogenes Laertius**.

DIODORUS OF ERETRIA
According to **Hippolytus**, Diodorus was a Pythagorean.

DIODORUS OF TARSUS (fourth century AD)
Diodorus came from Antioch, studied in Athens and became bishop of Tarsus. According to **Suda** he wrote many philosophical works addressing such topics as the soul and fate, as well as critical works on **Plato** [1], **Aristotle** [1] and **Porphyry**. He was also a friend and correspondent of **Euphronius** [2].

DIODORUS OF TYRE (second century BC)
Diodorus succeeded **Critolaus of Phaselis** as head of the Lyceum. He argued that the good life consisted of tranquillity and virtuous behaviour.

DIODORUS VALERIUS (first/second century AD)
According to **Suda**, Diodorus was a philosopher and the son of **Polio Valerius**. He appears to have written on rhetoric.

DIODOTUS [1]
According to **Diogenes Laertius**, Diodotus was a grammarian who wrote a commentary on the philosophy of **Heraclitus of Ephesus**.

DIODOTUS [2] (second/first century BC)
Diodotus was a Stoic and the young **Cicero** was one of his pupils. When he became old he lived in Cicero's house. He died there in 59 BC, and left Cicero all his property.

DIODOTUS OF SIDON (first century BC)
Diodotus was a philosopher, the brother of **Boethus of Sidon**, and like him a Peripatetic. **Strabo of Amaseia** was one of his pupils.

DIOGENES [1]
A number of fragments of Epicurean writings are ascribed to an unknown Diogenes of an unknown time and place.

DIOGENES [2] (sixth century AD)
Diogenes originally came from Phoenicia, and was a member of the group of philosophers who accompanied **Damascius** on his journey to Persia.

DIOGENES, ANTONIUS
Diogenes wrote a work drawn on by **Porphyry** for his life of **Pythagoras**.

DIOGENES LAERTIUS (third/fourth century AD?)
Little is known about Diogenes, including when he lived. However, his *Lives of*

Eminent Philosophers is a major and indispensable source of information about ancient philosophy, covering its history from its earliest days until the third century AD. He refers to a number of other works he has consulted, none of which survive. He is often criticised for being uncritical in his use of sources and not always understanding the ideas he is trying to explain.

(Diogenes Laertius, *Lives of Eminent Philosophers* (2 vols), trans. R.D. Hicks, Loeb, 1931, 1972; classicpersuasion.org/pw/diogenes/ This is a substantial but not a complete translation.)

DIOGENES OF APOLLONIA (fifth century BC)

Little is known about Diogenes other than a work of his entitled *On Nature* that is mentioned by later authors. He maintained that air was the basic principle of existence, although he seems to have been thinking primarily of living beings. He also believed that air was identical with both intelligence and the divine. Because air could be hotter or colder and drier or damper, it was possible to have a variety of living forms. **Theophrastus of Eresus** produced a compendium of his writings. It is not known which Apollonia he came from.

(Jonathan Barnes, *Early Greek Philosophy*, Harmondsworth, Penguin, 1987)

DIOGENES OF ARGOS (fourth century AD)

Little is known of Diogenes. He appears to have led a simple and quiet life in his home town of Argos while achieving a reputation as a philosopher. He may have been the brother of **Hierius** [2].

DIOGENES OF BABYLON (third/second century BC)

Diogenes was the head of the Stoa after **Zeno of Tarsus**. He was also known as Diogenes of Seleucia. **Panaetius of Rhodes** was one of his pupils. He helped to consolidate the school's teachings and make them more coherent and systematic. He had a special interest in music and wrote a work on musical theory. In 155 BC, when he was already an old man, he was one of a deputation of philosophers, the others being **Carneades of Cyrene** and **Critolaus of Phaselis**, sent to Rome to represent Athens before the Senate. Thanks to the lectures he gave during his stay there, many Romans became interested in Stoicism for the first time. When he died in 152 BC he was succeeded as head of the school by **Antipater of Tarsus**.

DIOGENES OF OENOANDA (first century BC/first century AD?)

Diogenes was an Epicurean and is known for the texts he arranged to be engraved on the walls of a colonnade (or stoa) in his home town. The texts included some written by **Epicurus** himself, some written by Diogenes and others taken from a variety of authors. In his old age Diogenes apparently wanted to share with his fellow-citizens the benefits and teachings of the philosophy he had followed.

(M.F. Smith (ed.), *Diogenes of Oinoanda: the Epicurean inscription*, Naples, Bibliopolis, 1993)

DIOGENES OF NICOMEDIA (second century BC)
Diogenes was a Platonist and a pupil of **Carneades of Cyrene**.

DIOGENES OF PTOLEMAIS
Diogenes was a Stoic. According to **Diogenes Laertius**, when he taught, he began with ethics.

DIOGENES OF SELEUCIA (second century BC)
Diogenes was an Epicurean attached to the court of Alexander Balas in Syria. During the reign of Alexander's son, he spoke out of turn and had his throat cut. He should not be confused with the Stoic **Diogenes of Babylon** who was also sometimes known as Diogenes of Seleucia.

DIOGENES OF SINOPE (fourth century BC)
Opinions are divided over whether **Antisthenes of Athens** or Diogenes was the first Cynic, but none dispute the importance of Diogenes in the history of Cynicism. However, so many stories grew up about this colourful character that it is difficult to separate fact from fiction. He is said to have been the pupil of Antisthenes and the slave of **Xeniades**. He apparently also admired **Ichthyas**, but it is difficult to identify any obvious philosophical influence coming from him. Many doubt that he ever actually met Antisthenes but at least some connection with Xeniades is entirely plausible, and certainly he spent several years in and around Corinth. He is also said to have lived in a barrel or large wine jar, which might have made writing the various works attributed to him difficult, although there is also a tradition that he wrote nothing. Surviving letters attributed to him are the product of a later age and probably date to no earlier than the first century BC.

According to Cynic tradition, Diogenes left his home town of Sinope when either he or his father, who ran the local mint, was found to have adulterated, counterfeited or defaced the currency. How literally this is intended to be taken is unclear. The Cynics opposed all they held to be artificial and found value only in what they regarded as natural. Because money is artificial, this action could be seen as a gesture designed to draw attention to the fact that its value was supported only by convention. It could also be taken as a metaphor for the Cynic philosophy which had as one of its aims the subversion of all conventions, and Diogenes adopted 'defacing the currency' as a kind of personal motto. The nickname of Cynic, meaning 'dog', may have been attached to Diogenes as an insult in the first place because people thought he behaved like an animal. However, it became a badge of pride both for him and those who were inspired by him to practise his own particular brand of self-sufficiency.

Despite his often anti-social behaviour, Diogenes attracted a significant following, his most celebrated pupil being **Crates of Thebes**. Others included **Onesicritus of Aegina** and his sons. He was also admired by many more, and after he died in Corinth a memorial was erected over his grave, consisting of a pillar fittingly topped by a statue of a dog.

The story most often told about Diogenes, that Alexander the Great visited him, is generally taken to be a fabrication, as is the tradition that the two died on the same day.
[Luis E. Navia, *Classical Cynicism*, Westport, Greenwood Press, 1996; Donald R. Dudley, *A History of Cynicism from Diogenes to the Sixth Century AD*, 2nd edn, London, Bristol Classical Press, 1998]

DIOGENES OF SMYRNA (fourth century BC)
Diogenes is said to have been a pupil of **Metrodorus of Chios** and the teacher of **Anaxarchus of Abdera**.

DIOGENES OF TARSUS (second century BC?)
Diogenes was an Epicurean. According to **Strabo of Amaseia** he travelled around teaching in various cities. He produced a book of the sayings of **Epicurus**, and another that summarised Epicurean ethics. He was also an accomplished poet.

DIOGENES THE SOPHIST (first century AD)
Although generally known as 'the Sophist', Diogenes seems to have been a Cynic. He achieved his finest hour when, in AD 75, he harangued Titus (soon to be emperor) and his mistress Berenice (never to be empress) before a crowd in the theatre at Rome. As a result, he was flogged.

DIOGENIANUS (second century AD)
Diogenianus argued against the determinism of the Stoics, suggesting that when predictions came true it was a matter of luck or coincidence rather than fate. He is thought to have been an Epicurean, though some have taken him to be a Peripatetic.
(Eusebius, *Preparation for the Gospel* (2 vols), trans. E.H. Gifford, Eugene, Wipf and Stock, 2002)

DIOGENIANUS OF PERGAMUM (second century AD)
Diogenianus was probably a pupil of **Plutarch of Chaeronea**. His father, also called Diogenianus, was a friend of Plutarch.

DIOGNETUS (second century AD)
Diognetus was a painter. As a teacher of **Marcus Aurelius**, he seems to have been the person who first fired the future emperor with enthusiasm for philosophy. Marcus Aurelius said that he learnt from him not to be distracted by trivia, to take a sceptical attitude towards those who claim to be able to work magic, and to avoid cock-fighting.

DIOMEDES (fifth century AD)
Diomedes was a student of philosophy whose efforts were undermined by the bad company he kept. He may have been a friend of **Eupeithius**.

DIOMEDON OF TARSUS (second century BC)
Diomedon was a Platonist and a pupil of **Carneades of Cyrene**.

DION [1] (third century BC)
Chrysippus of Soli dedicated two of his works on logic to Dion, suggesting he was a colleague or pupil.

DION [2] (first century BC)
Dion appears to have been an Epicurean with whom **Cicero** was acquainted but for whom he had little time or respect.

DION COCCEIANUS or OF PRUSA (first/second century AD)
Dion is often referred to by his nickname Chrysostom, meaning 'golden-mouthed' and accorded him on account of his eloquence. He had a colourful career, beginning as a sophist and teacher of rhetoric in Rome before becoming a convert to philosophy thanks to the influence of **Musonius Rufus**. According to Flavius **Philostratus**, he was also acquainted with **Apollonius of Tyana** and **Euphrates**. One of his pupils was **Favorinus**. When he was banished by Domitian from both Italy and his native Bithynia in AD 82, Dion took up the life of a wandering ascetic and teacher. Even when he was permitted to return, he continued to travel a great deal. He is generally regarded as a Cynic and many of his speeches survive.
(Dio Cocceianus, Chrysostom, *Discourses* (5 vols), trans. J.W. Cohoon and H.L. Crosby, Loeb, 1932-51)
[Donald R. Dudley, *A History of Cynicism from Diogenes to the Sixth Century AD*, 2nd edn, London, Bristol Classical Press, 1998]

DION OF ALEXANDRIA (first century BC)
Dion was a Platonist who studied under **Antiochus of Ascalon**. According to **Plutarch of Chaeronea**, he advocated noting what was said at drinking parties, and drinking may have been one of his interests. He had a brother called Topsius who was a wrestler.

DION OF EPHESUS (fourth/third century BC)
Dion was a philosopher who seems to have taught in Rome. He was honoured by a statue there.

DION OF GAZA (second century BC)
Dion was a Platonist and a pupil of **Carneades of Cyrene**.

DION OF HERACLEA (second century AD)
Dion was a Stoic who appeared in a work by **Lucian of Samosata**. He may be fictitious.

DION OF SYRACUSE (fourth century BC)
Dion was a friend of **Plato** [1] for many years. He had an erratic political career, sometimes seeking or managing to rule Syracuse either directly or through others, sometimes in exile. During one of his periods in exile he stayed at the Academy. He was eventually assassinated in 354 BC.

DION OF THRACE (second/first century BC?)
Dion was a Platonist who studied under **Theris** and was later teacher of **Dionysodorus of Smyrna**.

DIONYSIUS [1]
According to **Diogenes Laertius**, Dionysius wrote commentaries on the work of **Heraclitus of Ephesus**.

DIONYSIUS [2] (fifth/fourth century BC)
According to **Plutarch of Chaeronea**, there was a Dionysius who was a follower of **Socrates** and who came from a poor background. According to **Diogenes Laertius, Plato** [1] had a slave called Dionysius. It is just about possible that the two are one and the same, but Dionysius was a common name.

DIONYSIUS [3] (third century BC)
Dionysius succeeded **Polystratus** as head of the Epicurean school and was in turn succeeded by **Basilides of Syria**.

DIONYSIUS [4] (third century BC)
Chrysippus of Soli dedicated a number of his works on logic to a Dionysius, who was presumably a colleague or pupil.

DIONYSIUS [5] (second century BC)
Dionysius was probably a Platonist and a pupil of **Boethus of Marathon**.

DIONYSIUS [6] (second/first century BC)
Dionysius taught philosophy at Athens, but does not appear to have been attached to any of the major schools.

DIONYSIUS [7] (first century BC)
Cicero mentions a Dionysius who was a Stoic and liked to quote poetry when he was teaching.

DIONYSIUS, MARCUS POMPONIUS (first century BC)
Dionysius was the Thracian slave of Titus Pomponius **Atticus**, before being set free. Atticus and **Cicero** often referred to him in their correspondence. He was evidently a man of learning who had studied philosophy.

DIONYSIUS EXIGUUS (sixth century AD)
Dionysius was a monk and scholar. His main philosophical contribution lay in translating some works from Greek into Latin.

DIONYSIUS OF ALEXANDRIA [1] (first century AD)
According to **Suda**, Dionysius was a pupil of **Chaeremon of Alexandria** and in some way his successor.

DIONYSIUS OF ALEXANDRIA [2] (third century AD)
Dionysius was a pupil of **Origen** and became bishop of Alexandria. He wrote a work *On Nature* in which he attacked atomism, and in particular the

Epicurean version of it, arguing instead for a view of the cosmos as an ordered and unified whole guided by providence.
(Eusebius, *Preparation for the Gospel* (2 vols), trans. E.H. Gifford, Eugene, Wipf and Stock, 2002)

DIONYSIUS OF CHALCEDON (fourth century BC)
Dionysius suggested that followers of the school of Megara should be called dialecticians because of the way they structured their arguments in terms of question and answer. He is sometimes known as Dionysius the Dialectician and may have either led the school or a branch of it. **Theodorus the Atheist** was one of his pupils. He is probably the same Dionysius referred to by **Aristotle** [1] as having advanced an inadequate definition of life.

DIONYSIUS OF COLOPHON (second century BC)
Dionysius was a Platonist and a pupil of **Arcesilaus of Pitane**. According to **Diogenes Laertius**, he, in collaboration with **Zopyrus of Colophon**, may have written works attributed to **Menippus of Gadara**.

DIONYSIUS OF CYRENE (second century BC)
Dionysius was a Stoic who studied under **Diogenes of Babylon** and **Antipater of Tarsus**. He appears to have taken a leading role in exchanges between Stoics and Epicureans in his time.

DIONYSIUS OF MILETUS (first/second century AD)
Best known as a sophist and teacher of rhetoric, Dionysius taught **Alexander of Seleucia** and **Antiochus of Aegae**. According to Flavius **Philostratus**, some said Dionysius had perfected and taught an art of memory, although Philostratus himself strenuously denied even the possibility.

DIONYSIUS OF RHODES (first century AD?)
Dionysius was an Epicurean and a friend of **Diogenes of Oenoanda**.

DIONYSIUS II OF SYRACUSE (fourth century BC)
Dionysius was the ruler of Syracuse, the nephew of **Dion of Syracuse**. Interested in philosophy, he invited **Plato** [1] to his court, but Plato's attempts to put his political ideas into practice were thwarted. Dionysius was eventually deposed and went into exile in Corinth where he became a teacher.

DIONYSIUS THE AREOPAGITE (fifth/sixth century AD)
Dionysius the Areopagite was a pseudonym adopted by a writer thought to have come from Syria, the name being that of an Athenian converted to Christianity by St Paul. He is sometimes referred to as Pseudo-Dionysius. The works attributed to him first appeared in the early sixth century and constitute an attempt to reconcile Neoplatonism and Christianity. They have had a significant influence on Christian mysticism ever since, in part because of the long-standing belief that they really were written by the original Dionysius. At the heart of them is a belief in, and indication of how to achieve, a mystical union between the soul and God. It is held that humanity can be deified

through purification, illumination and contemplation. Although not its originator, Dionysius is an important figure in the history of negative theology, which maintains that God is beyond description and so beyond conceptual knowledge. According to **Suda**, he had a pupil called **Athenodorus** [5], but this is presumably a reference to the original Dionysius and not the later pseudonymous one since the two were not distinguished at the time Suda was written.

(Colm Luibhead (ed.), *Pseudo-Dionysius*, London, SPCK, 1987)

DIONYSIUS THE MUSICIAN (second century AD)
Dionysius may have been a descendant of the literary critic and historian Dionysius of Halicarnassus. He was primarily noted, as his nickname indicates, for his knowledge of music, but he evidently explored the philosophical dimensions of the subject and is said to have written a work on the subject of music in the *Republic* of **Plato** [1].

DIONYSIUS THE RENEGADE (fourth/third century BC)
Dionysius came from Heraclea in Pontus. He studied with **Heraclides of Pontus, Alexinus of Elis, Menedemus of Eretria** and **Zeno of Citium**. However, he eventually abandoned Stoicism and joined the Cyrenaics. He apparently suffered from a serious eye complaint and found that he could not practise the indifference to the pain it caused that Stoicism called for. Adopting instead the view that pleasure was the most important thing in life, he duly acquired a reputation for seeking pleasure wherever he could find it. He died by starving himself to death. He acquired his nickname because of his desertion of Stoicism, although it does not appear to have been his first switch of allegiance.

DIONYSIUS THE STOIC
Diogenes Laertius refers to Dionysius the Stoic as the source of an anecdote about **Diogenes of Sinope**.

DIONYSIUS THE THRACIAN (second century BC)
Dionysius was a grammarian whose work drew on and consolidated Aristotelian and Stoic insights into the nature of language.

DIONYSODORUS, FLAVIUS MAECIUS SEVERUS (second/third century AD)
Dionysodorus was a Platonist. He appears to have spent some time in Egypt, including Alexandria, and was honoured by a statue in Antinoopolis. Some identify him with **Severus** [2].

DIONYSODORUS OF SMYRNA (second/first century BC)
Dionysodorus was a Platonist and a pupil of **Dion of Thrace**.

DIOPEITHES OF TROY (second century BC)
Diopeithes was a Platonist and a pupil of **Carneades of Cyrene**.

DIOPHANES (third century AD)
Diophanes was a teacher of rhetoric and an acquaintance of **Plotinus**. He

taught that pupils should submit completely to their teachers, including sexually. Plotinus was shocked by this and asked **Porphyry** to come up with arguments that could be used against Diophanes on this matter.

DIOPHANTUS (fourth century AD)
Diophantus came from Egypt and was a priest as well as a philosopher. He is not to be confused with the more famous Diophantus, also from Egypt, who wrote important works on mathematics.

DIOPHANTUS OF SYRACUSE see ECPHANTUS

DIOS (seventh century BC?)
The name of Dios is attached to some Pythagorean writings on aesthetics of unknown date. It is possible that the author is supposed to have been the father of the poet Hesiod, although the texts almost certainly come from a much later period.

DIOSCURIDES [1] (third century BC)
Chrysippus of Soli dedicated some works on logic to Dioscurides, suggesting he was a pupil or a colleague.

DIOSCURIDES [2] (first century AD)
According to Flavius **Philostratus**, **Apollonius of Tyana** had at least one follower by the name of Dioscurides.

DIOSCURIDES OF CYPRUS (third century BC)
Dioscurides was a Sceptic, a pupil of **Timon of Phlius**. According to **Diogenes Laertius**, Dioscurides only had one eye, a characteristic he apparently shared with Timon.

DIOSCURUS or DIOSCORUS (fourth/fifth century AD)
Dioscurus studied philosophy in both Rome and Carthage. During his stay in Africa, he wrote a letter to **Augustine**, seeking to discuss a number of philosophical issues. Augustine replied at length, arguing that the issues were of no real importance.

DIOTIMA OF MANTINEA (fifth century BC)
Diotima appears in the *Symposium* of **Plato** [1] as the woman who taught **Socrates** about love.

DIOTIMUS (second/first century BC)
Diotimus was a Stoic celebrated for levelling various scandalous charges against the reputation of **Epicurus**. It is said that **Zeno of Sidon** [2] took legal action against Diotimus and that he was executed.

DIOTIMUS OF SEMACHIDES (third century BC)
Diotimus was an Epicurean in Athens and perhaps the pupil of **Polystratus**.

DIOTIMUS OF TYANA (first century AD)
Diotimus was a follower of **Apollonius of Tyana**.

DIOTIMUS OF TYRE (fourth century BC)
Diotimus was a follower of **Democritus of Abdera**.

DIOTOGENES (third century BC?)
The name of Diotogenes is attached to fragments of Pythagorean writings, although he may have lived before the time in which they were written. (David Fideler (ed.), *The Pythagorean Sourcebook*, Grand Rapids, Phanes, 1987)

DIPHILUS [1] (third century BC)
Diphilus was a follower of **Ariston of Chios**.

DIPHILUS [2] (second century BC)
Diphilus was a Stoic and the father of **Demetrius of Bithynia**.

DIPHILUS OF BOSPHORUS (fourth/third century BC)
According to **Diogenes Laertius**, Diphilus was a pupil of **Stilpo**. Seeking Stilpo out in order to argue against him, he instead became converted to his philosophy.

DOGMATIUS
Dogmatius was a philosopher, known only from a surviving bust.

DOLABELLA, PUBLIUS CORNELIUS (first century BC)
Dolabella was an Epicurean and for a time the son-in-law of **Cicero**. Politically active, he achieved the dubious distinction of being pronounced a public enemy by the Roman Senate. In 43 BC, utterly defeated, he ordered one of his soldiers to kill him.

DOMNINUS (fifth century AD)
Domninus was said to come from either Laodicea or Larisa and his family had Syrian origins. He studied at Athens under **Syrianus** [1] and **Proclus** [1] before going on to teach there. He was criticised by Proclus for corrupting the teachings of **Plato** [2] by introducing his own novel ideas into what he taught. His main interest was in mathematics. Very different opinions survive as to his character, suggesting he was a complex and perhaps divisive individual.

DOMNULUS (fifth century AD)
Domnulus was a friend of **Sidonius Apollinaris** and they probably studied philosophy together under **Eusebius** [2].

DOROTHEUS (second/third century AD?)
Dorotheus compiled a guide to new and foreign words in the works of **Plato** [1]. He may be the same person as the grammarian Dorotheus of Ascalon.

DOROTHEUS OF AMISUS (third century BC)
Dorotheus was a Platonist and pupil of **Arcesilaus of Pitane**.

DOROTHEUS OF TELPHOUSA (third century BC)
Dorotheus was a Platonist and a pupil of **Arcesilaus of Pitane**.

DORUS (fifth/sixth century AD)
Dorus originally came from Arabia. He first became an Aristotelian and then, due to the influence of **Isidore of Alexandria**, a Neoplatonist. He was credited with having a very sharp mind, perhaps as a result of his training in the Aristotelian logic that Isidore dismissed as pedantry.

DOSITHEUS (fourth/third century BC)
Dositheus was probably an Epicurean. A letter written to him by **Epicurus** on the death of his son **Hegesianax** [2] was copied by **Diogenes of Oenoanda**. His name sometimes appears as Sositheus.

DOSSENNUS
Dossennus appears to have been a philosopher, perhaps an Epicurean. **Seneca** mentions a monument to him with an inscription testifying to his wisdom.

DOURIS OF SAMOS (fourth/third century BC)
Douris was an historian and pupil of **Theophrastus of Eresus**. His brother was **Lyncaeus of Samos**.

DOUSARIUS OF PETRA
Dousarius took the view that there were natural connections between words and things. He believed that curses and prayers were both evidence that meanings were not merely conventional because they were understood by the gods even though the gods had nothing to do with human conventions.

DRACONTIUS (fifth century AD)
Dracontius came from North Africa and was a public official and poet. Some of his poems were written while he was a prisoner of the Vandals. Although a Christian, in one of them he sets out a vision of the world that draws heavily on Stoicism.

DRYMON OF CAULANIA (fifth century BC?)
According to **Iamblichus of Chalcis**, Drymon was a Pythagorean.

DYMAS OF CROTON (fifth century BC?)
According to **Iamblichus of Chalcis**, Dymas was a Pythagorean.

DYSCOLIUS (third/fourth century AD)
Dyscolius was probably a pupil of **Iamblichus of Chalcis**, who dedicated a book to him. He may have been the same person as the Dyscolius who was governor of Syria for a time.

❖ E ❖

ECCELO OF LUCANIA (fifth century BC?)
According to **Iamblichus of Chalcis**, Eccelo was one of the most famous Pythagorean women and **Occelo of Lucania** was her sister. However, it is thought that 'Eccelo' may be a mistake for 'Eccelus' and that Eccelo may never have existed.

ECCELUS OF LUCANIA (fifth century BC?)
According to **Iamblichus of Chalcis**, Eccelus was a Pythagorean. It is thought that fragments of a text attributed to **Polus of Lucania** may have been written by Eccelus.

ECDELUS (third century BC)
Ecdelus came from Megalopolis and was a pupil of **Arcesilaus of Pitane**. His name sometimes appears as Ecdemus, and he is usually found in the company of **Demophanes**. They studied together, taught together and were involved in politics together. **Philopoemen** was one of their pupils. They were eventually invited to Cyrene to reform the city.

ECHECLES OF EPHESUS (fourth/third century BC)
Echecles was a Cynic who studied under **Cleomenes** [1] and **Theombrotus** [1]. **Menedemus of Lampsacus** was one of his pupils.

ECHECRATEIA OF PHLIUS (fifth/fourth century BC?)
According to **Iamblichus of Chalcis**, Echecrateia was one of the most famous Pythagorean women.

ECHECRATES OF PHLIUS (fifth/fourth century BC)
Echecrates was a Pythagorean who studied with **Philolaus of Croton** and **Eurytus of Tarentum**. He appears as a character in the *Phaedo* of **Plato** [1] where he presses **Phaedo of Elis** for information about the death of **Socrates**.

ECHECRATES OF TARENTUM (fifth century BC?)
According to **Iamblichus of Chalcis**, Echecrates was a Pythagorean.

ECHECRATIDES OF METHYMNA (fourth century BC)
Echecratides was a Peripatetic, related to **Aristotle** [1] and probably one of his pupils.

ECPHANTUS OF CROTON (fifth/fourth century BC?)
According to **Iamblichus of Chalcis**, Ecphantus was a Pythagorean. He appears to be the same person referred to by **Hippolytus** as Ecphantus of Syracuse. According to Hippolytus, Ecphantus believed it was impossible to

have an accurate knowledge of things, but also believed that everything in the world was formed of size, shape and capacity. He claimed the world was a sphere, the most perfect of geometrical shapes, reflecting the fact that it was a product of the divine mind, which was also the source of all movement. A work on kings attributed to him is thought to be by a later author.

(David Fideler (ed.), *The Pythagorean Sourcebook*, Grand Rapids, Phanes, 1987)

EGNATIUS (first century BC)

Egnatius was an Epicurean who wrote a poem *On the Nature of Things*. It bears some resemblances to the work of the same name by **Lucretius** and is generally thought to have been written after it.

EIRENAEUS OF MILETUS (second/first century BC)

Demetrius Lacon dedicated one of his works to Eirenaeus, who was his pupil for some time.

EIRISCUS OF METAPONTUM (fifth century BC?)

According to **Iamblichus of Chalcis**, Eiriscus was a Pythagorean.

ELCHASAI (first/second century AD?)

According to **Hippolytus**, Elchasai was a gnostic influenced by Pythagoreanism. One of his followers, called Alcibiades, brought a book to Rome claiming that its contents had been revealed to Elchasai by an angel. The cult he founded believed in reincarnation and that Pythagorean science provided a means of predicting the future. There was also a magical healing side to the cult, and it claimed to be able to cure rabies.

ELEUCADIUS (first/second century AD)

Eleucadius was a philosopher before converting to Christianity. He later became bishop of Ravenna.

ELIAS (sixth century AD)

The name of Elias has become attached to three surviving works, two commentaries on **Aristotle** [1], and one on the *Isagoge* ('Introduction') of **Porphyry**, although their actual authorship is disputed. It is possible that they derive from the lectures of **Olympiodorus** [2]. Tradition has it that Elias succeeded Olympiodorus as head of the Neoplatonist school in Alexandria and was in turn succeeded by **David** who, like him, was a Christian. However, some have questioned whether there was a Christian Neoplatonist philosopher of that name at that time.

(L.G. Westerink, *Pseudo-Elias (Pseudo-David's) Lectures on Porphyry's Isagoge*, Amsterdam, North Holland Publishing Co., 1967)

[Christian Wildberg, 'Elias' in *The Stanford Encyclopedia of Philosophy* (Spring 2003 Edition), Edward N. Zalta (ed.), plato.stanford.edu/archives/spr2003/entries/elias/]

ELLOPION OF PEPARETHUS (fourth century BC)
According to **Plutarch of Chaeronea**, Ellopion travelled with **Plato** [1] to Egypt where they discussed philosophical matters with **Chonuphis**.

ELPIDIUS (fourth century AD)
Elpidius was a philosopher with whom the emperor **Julian** may have been in correspondence.

EMPEDOCLES (first/second century AD)
Empedocles was a friend of **Plutarch of Chaeronea**. Although he was familiar with the teachings of Pythagoreanism, it is not clear that he actually belonged to any particular school.

EMPEDOCLES OF ACRAGAS (fifth century BC)
Empedocles is one of the most interesting characters in ancient philosophy and is said to have died by casting himself into the crater of Mount Etna, although another account of his death says that he drowned at sea. Stories told about him claimed he possessed magical powers. More mundanely, he was long a leading citizen of his native city although for reasons that are unclear he was eventually sent into exile. **Diogenes Laertius** recounts a tradition according to which he was a Pythagorean who betrayed the school's code of secrecy, but this has long been a matter of dispute. Many different influences have been identified in the surviving fragments of his works, and **Parmenides of Elea, Xenophanes of Colophon** and **Anaxagoras of Clazomenae** are said to have been his teachers.

The fragments themselves are generally thought to belong to two poems, one called *Purifications* and the other *On Nature*. In *Purifications* he tells how the human race brought about its own downfall when it began to sacrifice animals and eat meat. This is the source of the impurity suggested by the poem's title. The required purification takes place through a series of reincarnations, at the end of which lies the promise of immortality and becoming godlike if not gods. In *On Nature* Empedocles claims that everything in the world is composed out of the four basic elements of earth, fire, air and water, while driving everything are two fundamental forces he calls love, a uniting power, and strife, a dividing power. They may perhaps be understood as attraction and repulsion. Precisely how the doctrines expounded in the two poems fit together is unclear and disputed.

Although there are clear similarities to Pythagoreanism in the works of Empedocles, there are also important differences. He is probably better seen as a kindred spirit than as a card-carrying member. His philosophy perhaps represents a new and bold synthesis of existing ideas, including Pythagorean ones, given an added boost by his own creative contributions. He appears not to have founded his own school (although **Gorgias of Leontini** is said to have studied with him) but Empedocles seems too original and charismatic a figure to have comfortably fitted into someone else's school.

(M.R. Wright, *Empedocles: the extant fragments*, New Haven, Yale University Press, 1981; Jonathan Barnes, *Early Greek Philosophy*, Harmondsworth, Penguin, 1987)

[Peter Kingsley, *Ancient Philosophy, Mystery and Magic,* Oxford, Clarendon Press, 1995; *Routledge Encyclopaedia of Philosophy,* vol. 3; Richard Parry, 'Empedocles', *The Stanford Encyclopedia of Philosophy* (Spring 2005 Edition), Edward N. Zalta (ed.), plato.stanford.edu/archives/spr2005/entries/empedocles/]

EMPEDOCLES OF CHALCEDON (second century BC)
Empedocles was best known for his medical work, but before taking up medicine he had studied Aristotelianism.

EMPEDOTIMUS OF SYRACUSE
According to **Heraclides of Pontus,** Empedotimus had a vision that revealed the structure of the universe. However, most now think that Empedotimus never existed and was in fact an invention of Heraclides himself.

EMPEDUS
Empedus was the author of a book of philosophical memoirs. He may have been a Stoic.

EMPEDUS OF SYBARIS (fifth century BC?)
According to **Iamblichus of Chalcis,** Empedus was a Pythagorean.

ENDIUS OF SYBARIS (fifth century BC?)
According to **Iamblichus of Chalcis,** Endius was a Pythagorean.

ENNIUS, QUINTUS (third/second century BC)
Ennius was a famous early Roman poet. In his poems he demonstrated a familiarity with various ideas from Greek philosophy, and helped to introduce these to the Roman world.

EPAMINONDAS (fifth/fourth century BC)
Epaminondas was a successful Theban general with democratic preferences. **Lysis of Tarentum** was his teacher for a while, and he seems to have taken to Pythagoreanism.

EPANDRIDES
According to **Stobaeus,** Epandrides wrote about the nature of practical wisdom.

EPICHARIDES OF TARENTUM (fourth century BC?)
Epicharides is said to have been a Pythagorean who solved the problem of not being allowed to eat living things by killing them first!

EPICHARMUS (sixth/fifth century BC)
Epicharmus came from Sicily and wrote comedies. He achieved a reputation as a philosopher although it is thought that several works attributed to him were written by others. He may have been a Pythagorean and according to **Hippobotus** he was one of the Seven Sages of ancient Greece.

EPICRATES [1] (third century BC)
Epicrates was a Peripatetic and one of the executors of the will of **Strato of Lampsacus**. He may be the same person as **Epicrates of Heraclea**.

EPICRATES [2] (third century BC)
Chrysippus of Soli dedicated some of his works on logic to Epicrates, suggesting he was a colleague or pupil.

EPICRATES OF HERACLEA (third century BC)
Epicrates was a Peripatetic who taught philosophy on Samos.

EPICTETUS (first/second century AD)
Epictetus was born at Hierapolis and spent the years of his early life as a slave. He was eventually freed, and this seems to have happened after he moved to Rome. He probably studied there under **Musonius Rufus**. He left Rome when Domitian expelled philosophers from the city in AD 89 and moved to Nicopolis where he founded his own school. He seems to have stayed there until his death in around AD 135. He wrote nothing, but one of his pupils was **Arrian**, who took copious notes and produced the work now known as *The Discourses*. Arrian also produced *The Handbook*, a brief summary of the teachings of *The Discourses* that sheds some light on the volumes of the larger work that are now lost.

Although certainly a Stoic, Epictetus was not always an orthodox one. In particular, he was inclined to take a more limited view of determinism than did some of his predecessors, allowing greater room for human freedom. In part this may reflect the fact that *The Discourses* appear to derive from relatively informal teachings, sometimes in the form of question and answer sessions, where the emphasis is frequently on what people should do. The strict moral outlook evident in his words would be undermined, rather than supported, by too strong an emphasis on the power of providence.

Although they never met, **Marcus Aurelius** was an admirer of the works of Epictetus, as also were **Clement of Alexandria** and **Origen**. Some centuries later **Simplicius** wrote an extensive commentary on *The Handbook*.
(Epictetus, *The Discourses, The Handbook, Fragments* (ed. C. Gill), London, Dent, 1995)
[A.A. Long, *Epictetus: a Stoic and Socratic guide to life*, Oxford, Clarendon Press, 2002; Keith Seddon, 'Epictetus', *Internet Encyclopaedia of Philosophy*, www.iep.utm.edu/e/epictetu.htm]

EPICURIUS (first/second century AD?)
Epicurius was an Epicurean who appears in a work by **Plutarch of Chaeronea**.

EPICURUS (fourth/third century BC)
Epicurus came from an Athenian family but was probably born on Samos in around 340 BC. Little is known about his early years. He appears to have travelled and taught in a variety of places and acquired an extensive knowledge of philosophy, especially that of **Democritus of Abdera**, but it is

unclear whether he ever formally studied under anyone. He settled in Athens in around 306 BC, bought some land there and set up the institution known as The Garden. There he lived and taught for the rest of his days. He died in around 270 BC after a prolonged period of poor health.

The essence of his teaching was that life was full of anxieties, but that these could be overcome and tranquillity achieved. Tranquillity came from the absence of pain, and the absence of pain was the same thing as pleasure. The source of anxiety was ignorance and therefore the way to overcome anxiety lay through knowledge. An understanding of pain itself was an important element of his philosophy. Physical pain could often be avoided by the exercise of common sense and a modicum of forethought. Where it could not be avoided, it could be managed, in part by the knowledge that it never lasted for long. In the view of Epicurus, it was important to separate the physical dimension of pain from the anxiety that generally attended it. The latter could always be removed even if the former could not.

Two principal sources of anxiety he identified were death and the gods. It is in his treatment of death that his debt to the atomism of Democritus is most apparent. Human beings were collections of atoms. When they died, the atoms were scattered. Because the individual dissolved at death, there was no possibility of any posthumous suffering as there was no individual left to suffer it. With regard to the gods, he took the view that they were so far removed from us in every sense that it was irrational to suppose that they took any interest in, let alone interfered in, human affairs. Phenomena sometimes associated with the gods such as lightning could, he believed, be explained purely in scientific terms, and in one of his surviving letters, that to **Pythocles**, he explains a wide variety of meteorological occurrences in this way.

The Garden was a kind of philosophical commune, and Epicurus laid great emphasis on friendship and a supportive environment. The school's tendency towards self-sufficiency and isolation, coupled with its often misunderstood interest in pleasure, led to it being the subject of considerable gossip of a salacious kind, and Epicureans, including Epicurus himself, were often accused of a variety of vices. However, the school's approach to pleasure was calculating rather than profligate and Epicurus appears to have lived relatively modestly. His views on pain bear the mark of first-hand experience.

Epicurus wrote a great deal, but only a few letters and fragments survive. When he died his pupil **Hermarchus of Mitylene** succeeded him as head of The Garden and inherited his personal library.

(Brad Inwood and L.P. Gerson (eds), *The Epicurus Reader*, Indianapolis, Hackett, 1994)

[David Konstan, 'Epicurus', *The Stanford Encyclopedia of Philosophy* (Spring 2005 Edition), Edward N. Zalta (ed.), plato.stanford.edu/archives/spr2005/entries/epicurus/; John M. Rist, *Epicurus: an introduction*, Cambridge, Cambridge University Press, 1972]

EPICURUS OF PERGAMUM (second century AD)
Epicurus was a physician, an empiricist, and a teacher of **Galen**.

EPIGANUS or EPIGONUS (fourth century AD)
Epiganus came from Cilicia and was tried for treason in AD 354. As a result of torture he confessed to being involved in a non-existent plot and was executed. In the circumstances, the comment of the historian Ammianus Marcellinus that the only similarity between Epiganus and a philosopher was the way he dressed seems somewhat harsh.

EPIGENES (fifth/fourth century BC)
According to **Clement of Alexandria**, Epigenes wrote a book on Orphic poetry in which he argued that at least some of it had been written by Pythagoreans.

EPIGENES OF CEPHISIA (fifth/fourth century BC)
Epigenes was one of the circle of **Socrates**, present both at his trial and at his death.

EPIGONUS OF SPARTA (fourth century AD)
Eunapius describes Epigonus and **Beronicianus of Sardis** as the successors of **Chrysanthius of Sardis**.

EPIMENIDES [1] (sixth century BC?)
According to **Maeandrius**, Epimenides was one of the Seven Sages of ancient Greece. From Crete, he was both a poet and a prophet. According to various traditions, he could separate his soul from his body and once slept in a cave for over fifty years.

EPIMENIDES [2] (fourth century BC?)
Epimenides is unknown except as the supposed recipient of a letter falsely attributed to **Diogenes of Sinope**. He is criticised for promising much but achieving little.

EPIPHANES (second century AD)
Epiphanes was a gnostic and the son of **Carpocrates**. According to **Clement of Alexandria**, he died young and a temple was built in his honour on his mother's native Cephallenia. He is said to have studied Platonism and believed that wives should be shared.

EPIPHANIUS (fourth century AD)
Epiphanius was a Christian from Palestine who became bishop of Salamis on Cyprus. He is best known for his *Panorion*, a work in which he attempted to refute every heresy known to him.

EPIPHRON OF METAPONTUM (fifth century BC?)
According to **Iamblichus of Chalcis**, Epiphron was a Pythagorean.

EPISYLUS OF CROTON (fifth century BC?)
According to **Iamblichus of Chalcis**, Episylus was a Pythagorean.

EPITIMIDES OF CYRENE (fourth/third century BC)
According to **Diogenes Laertius,** Epitimides was a pupil of **Antipater of Cyrene** and the teacher of **Paraebates.**

ERASISTRATUS OF CEOS (fourth/third century BC)
Erasistratus was a physician who specialised in empirical research, including vivisection. He wrote a major work of medical theory that emphasised the mechanical nature of the human body. He was generally sceptical about the ability of external factors to cause disease, holding that a cause should always produce its effect and that few if any external causes, such as cold or damp, always produced disease.

ERASTUS OF SCEPSIS (fourth century BC)
Erastus was the brother of **Coriscus of Scepsis** and studied under **Plato** [1]. He and his brother set up their own school in Assus.

ERATOSTHENES (second century AD?)
Eratosthenes was a Platonist who believed that souls always inhabited a physical body, but could move from one body to another.

ERATOSTHENES OF CYRENE (third century BC)
Eratosthenes studied in Athens under **Ariston of Chios** and **Arcesilaus of Pitane** before being invited to Egypt to teach the son of Ptolemy III. He stayed there and became head of the library in Alexandria. He wrote many works on a variety of subjects including mathematics and geography. His philosophical writings, of which only fragments remain, suggest that he was an eclectic. In the view of **Strabo of Amaseia,** despite his great learning, Eratosthenes was only a dilettante as far as philosophy was concerned.

ERATUS OF CROTON (fifth century BC?)
According to **Iamblichus of Chalcis,** Eratus was a Pythagorean.

ERENNIUS see HERENNIUS

EROTION (fourth/third century BC)
Erotion was a member of the circle of **Epicurus.** She may have been a prostitute, although the sources suggesting this are strongly anti-Epicurean.

ERYMNEUS (third century BC)
Erymneus was a Peripatetic philosopher who taught in Athens. He may have been the head of the Lyceum after **Diodorus of Tyre,** although some modern scholars think he may have had his own school.

EUBIUS OF ASCALON
Eubius was a Stoic.

EUBULIDES [1]
Eubulides was a Pythagorean who wrote about Pythagoras and claimed that 216 years separated two of his incarnations.

EUBULIDES [2] (fourth century BC?)
Eubulides wrote a book about **Diogenes of Sinope**. It is possible he is to be identified with **Eubulides of Miletus**.

EUBULIDES OF MILETUS (fourth century BC)
According to **Diogenes Laertius**, Eubulides was the teacher of **Alexinus of Elis** and **Euphantes of Olynthus**. He had his own school, although this appears to have been a continuation of the school of **Euclides of Megara**. The precise relationship between Euclides and Eubulides is unclear, but it seems likely that they were master and pupil. Diogenes Laertius says that the school's followers were first known as Megarians and then as Eristics (literally 'wranglers'). This change seems to have taken place under Eubulides, whose interests lay primarily in the direction of logic and argumentation. The extent of his originality is difficult to estimate, but he may have invented the problem of the liar. (If I say, 'I always lie' and it is true, then I do not always lie because on this occasion I am telling the truth. But if I say 'I always lie' and it is a lie, then it is not true that I always lie.) Eubulides seems to have produced a stream of writings aimed at **Aristotle** [1], presumably disputing with him on issues of logic.

EUBULUS [1]
Eubulus wrote a book called *The Sale of Diogenes*, drawn on by **Diogenes Laertius** in his account of **Diogenes of Sinope**.

EUBULUS [2] (second century BC)
Eubulus was a Platonist and a pupil of **Lacydes of Cyrene**.

EUBULUS [3] (third century AD)
Eubulus was a Platonist and head of the school in Athens. **Plotinus** was a contemporary with whom he shared a correspondence. He wrote commentaries on some of the dialogues of **Plato** [1], including *Gorgias* and *Philebus*, which suggests he may have had a particular interest in ethics.

EUBULUS OF ALEXANDRIA (second century BC)
According to **Diogenes Laertius**, Eubulus was a Sceptic, the pupil of **Euphranor of Seleucia** and the teacher of **Ptolemy of Cyrene**.

EUBULUS OF EPHESUS (second century BC)
Eubulus was a Platonist, a pupil of **Lacydes of Cyrene** and **Telecles of Phocaea**.

EUBULUS OF ERYTHRAE (second century BC)
Eubulus was a Platonist, a pupil of **Lacydes of Cyrene** and **Telecles of Phocaea**.

EUBULUS OF MESSENE
According to **Iamblichus of Chalcis**, Eubulus was a Pythagorean. He was captured by Etruscan pirates but another Etruscan called **Nausithous** recognised him as a fellow Pythagorean and secured his release.

EUCAIRIUS (fourth century BC)
Eucairius was a pupil of **Aristotle** [1].

EUCLID (third century BC)
The author of the celebrated *Elements* of geometry was said by **Proclus** [1] to be a Platonist, although the evidence for this is at best inconclusive.

EUCLIDES (fourth century AD)
Euclides was a friend of the emperor **Julian**. He may have been the author of a Neoplatonist commentary on the *Republic* of **Plato** [1].

EUCLIDES OF MEGARA (fifth/fourth century BC)
Euclides was a friend of **Theaetetus of Sunium, Plato** [1] and **Socrates**. After the execution of Socrates, Plato and others decided to stay with him for a while, finding Athens a hostile environment. His friendship for Socrates is said to have been such that, when Megarans were temporarily forbidden from entering Athens, he went to visit him disguised as a woman. His philosophy drew on elements from the teachings of not only Socrates but also **Parmenides of Elea**. From Parmenides he took the idea that everything is ultimately and really one, while from Socrates he took the primacy of ethics. Combining the two he arrived at the conclusion that if there is such a thing as virtue or the good it can only be a form or name of the ultimate unity, and the same he held to be true of god, the mind and wisdom. He is said to have written six dialogues, but nothing has survived of any of them.

Diogenes Laertius says that Euclides founded the Megaran school, although the extent to which he was responsible for establishing an actual institution is unclear. However, he may at least be credited with putting Megara on the philosophical map. **Ichthyas** and **Eubulides of Megara** are both mentioned as successors, and both were probably his own pupils.

EUCLIDES OF NICOMEDIA (first century BC)
Euclides was a Platonist and a pupil of **Carneades of Cyrene**.

EUCRATIDAS OF RHODES (second/first century BC?)
Eucratidas was an Epicurean, known only from the inscription on his gravestone, which was unearthed in Brindisi.

EUDAIMON OF HADRIANI (first/second century AD)
Eudaimon was the father of Publius Aelius **Aristides**, and a philosopher and priest in Hadriani. He may be the same Eudaimon as the one whose passing was regretted by **Marcus Aurelius**.

EUDAMUS [1] (fifth/fourth century BC)
Eudamus was said to be a philosopher, but spent much of his time selling magical charms in Athens.

EUDAMUS [2] (third century BC)
Eudamus was a Platonist and a pupil of **Arcesilaus of Pitane**.

EUDEMUS (fourth century BC)
Eudemus was an Epicurean, mentioned in a letter written by **Epicurus**.

EUDEMUS OF CYPRUS (fourth century BC)
Eudemus was a friend of **Aristotle** [1] and perhaps also a pupil of **Plato** [1].

EUDEMUS OF PERGAMUM (second century AD)
Eudemus was a Peripatetic philosopher and a friend of **Galen**. He spent many years in Rome.

EUDEMUS OF RHODES (fourth century BC)
Eudemus was a pupil of **Aristotle** [1] and friend of **Theophrastus of Eresus**. He wrote many works on a variety of subjects, including a history of mathematics. With Theophrastus, he contributed to making Aristotelian logic tidier and more formal.

EUDICUS OF LOCRI (fifth century BC?)
According to **Iamblichus of Chalcis**, Eudicus was a Pythagorean.

EUDOCIA (fourth/fifth century AD)
Originally from Athens, Eudocia went to Constantinople after her father died and became the empress of Theodosius II. She is said to have been accompanied on her journey by seven philosophers, **Apelles**, **Carus**, **Curbus**, **Cranus**, **Nervas**, **Pelops** and **Silvanus**. They are all otherwise unknown.

EUDORUS OF ALEXANDRIA (first century BC)
Eudorus probably wrote a number of works, but none have survived. Although regarded as a Platonist, his philosophy incorporated substantial elements of Pythagoreanism. Most importantly, he claimed that both **Plato** [1] and **Pythagoras** had believed that the aim of life was to become as godlike as possible. This subsequently became a central tenet of Platonism. He produced a critical commentary on the *Categories* of **Aristotle** [1] that was highly influential in Platonist and Stoic circles. According to **Strabo of Amaseia**, he also speculated on the reasons for the Nile's annual flood.
[John Dillon, *The Middle Platonists 80 BC to AD 220*, London, Duckworth, 1996]

EUDOXIUS [1] (third century AD)
Eudoxius was a friend and perhaps pupil of **Porphyry**, who dedicated a book to him.

EUDOXIUS [2] (fourth century AD)
Eudoxius was a Platonist who may have taught at Apamea. **Patricius** [1] was his pupil.

EUDOXUS OF CNIDUS (fifth/fourth century BC)
Eudoxus was a man of many talents, making contributions to a variety of disciplines. He studied with **Archytas of Tarentum** and perhaps also with **Plato** [1]. He travelled widely, spending time as a priest in Egypt and teaching in Cyzicus and elsewhere before returning to Athens. At some point he found time to draft a code of laws for his native city. His most important work was in mathematics, and he was responsible for a number of advances in geometry.

He was the originator of the theory that the universe consisted of a series of concentric spheres, later taken up by **Aristotle** [1]. According to Aristotle, he believed that pleasure is the ultimate good in life because it is universally desired and because we judge other things in terms of it.
[*Routledge Encyclopaedia of Philosophy*, vol. 3]

EUDROMUS (third/second century BC?)
According to **Diogenes Laertius**, Eudromus was a Stoic who wrote a treatise on ethics.

EUGAMUS (third century BC)
According to **Diogenes Laertius**, Eugamus was a Platonist and a pupil of **Arcesilaus of Pitane**. However, it is thought that the name should probably read 'Eudamus' and that 'Eugamus' is identical with **Eudamus** [2].

EUGATHES (third century BC?)
Eugathes was a barber from Thessaly who abandoned cutting hair in order to become an Epicurean.

EUGENES, GAIUS VALERIUS (second/third century AD)
Eugenes was commemorated by an inscription in his native Selge identifying him as a philosopher.

EUGENIUS (third/fourth century AD)
Originally from Paphlagonia, Eugenius moved to Constantinople where he gained a high reputation as a philosopher. While there he wrote a number of commentaries on the works of **Aristotle** [1]. His son was **Themistius** [2] who wrote an oration about his father's life when he died. He may have been the same Eugenius as the one, also a philosopher, who exchanged correspondence with the emperor **Julian**.

EUGNESIUS (fourth century BC?)
Eugnesius is unknown except as the supposed recipient of a letter falsely attributed to **Diogenes of Sinope**. He is assumed to have been a Cynic.

EUGNOSTUS (second century AD?)
The name of Eugnostus the Blessed is attached to a short gnostic text taking the form of a letter written by Eugnostus to his followers. In it a dualistic account of the universe is put forward, incorporating a divine realm beyond the reach of human speculation. Although scarcely orthodox Platonism, Platonist influences are apparent.
(James M. Robinson (ed.), *The Nag Hammadi Library*, Leiden, Brill, 1977)

EUHEMERUS (fourth/third century BC)
Euhemerus was a novelist. In his novel *The Sacred Record* he told of how, in a place far away, he discovered that the gods had originally been great rulers and only later deified. This idea became known as euhemerism. Much later, **Lactantius** adopted it as an explanation of the origin of pagan gods.

EULAMIUS (fifth/sixth century AD)
Eulamius came from Phrygia and was one of the group of philosophers who accompanied **Damascius** to Persia. He seems to be the same person as Eulalius who, according to **Suda**, was a teacher of Damascius, but this does not seem probable, and it is more likely that he was his pupil.

EULOGIUS (fifth century AD)
Little is known about Eulogius except that he was a philosopher and that the emperor Leo I arranged for him to be supported at public expense.

EUMARES OF PHLIUS (fifth century BC)
According to **Suda**, Eumares was a follower of **Socrates**.

EUMELUS
In his account of the life of **Aristotle [1]**, **Diogenes Laertius** refers to a work by Eumelus. He may have been a Peripatetic himself.

EUMELUS, MARCUS JULIUS (second century AD?)
The children of Eumelus erected a monument to him in Alaca identifying him as a philosopher.

EUMENES, LUCIUS VIBIUS (second century AD?)
Eumenes was a philosopher and leading citizen of Phocaea.

EUMENES OF ASPENDUS (fourth/third century BC)
Eumenes was a Platonist, probably a pupil of **Crantor of Soli**.

EUMENIUS (fourth century AD)
Eumenius studied philosophy alongside **Pharianus** and the emperor **Julian**.

EUMOIRUS OF PAROS
According to **Iamblichus of Chalcis**, Eumoirus was a Pythagorean.

EUMOLPUS (fourth century BC?)
Eumolpus was the supposed recipient of a letter falsely attributed to **Crates of Thebes** and is assumed to have been a Cynic.

EUNAPIUS (fourth/fifth century AD)
Eunapius came from Sardis and spent most of his life there. He studied with a number of sophists and became a teacher himself. His *Lives of the Philosophers and Sophists*, which survives, is a valuable source.
(Philostratus, *Lives of the Sophists* and Eunapius, *Lives of Philosophers*, trans. W.C. Wright, Loeb, 1921)

EUNOMIUS (fourth century AD)
Eunomius was a Cappadocian. He studied under **Aetius** in Alexandria and later became bishop of Cyzicus. However, he was forced to resign because of his unorthodox views, which seem to have been substantially influenced by Neoplatonism. He believed God was absolutely transcendent and unchanging, but at the same time accessible to the human intellect. He held that a correct

understanding of doctrine was much more important than any sacraments or asceticism.

EUPEITHES OF PAPHOS (second century BC)
Eupeithes was a Platonist and a pupil of **Carneades of Cyrene**.

EUPEITHIUS (fifth/sixth century AD)
Eupeithius was the son of **Hegias** and brother of **Archiadas** [2]. He is said to have had an aptitude for philosophy, but to have led a life that was unbecoming for a philosopher.

EUPHANTUS OF OLYNTHUS (fourth/third century BC)
According to **Diogenes Laertius**, Euphantus was a pupil of **Eubulides of Miletus**. He was an accomplished author who wrote a history of his period as well as poems and a number of tragedies. One of his pupils was **Antigonus Gonatas**, king of Macedonia, to whom he dedicated a work on the subject of kingship.

EUPHEMUS OF METAPONTUM (fifth century BC?)
According to **Iamblichus of Chalcis**, Euphemus was a Pythagorean.

EUPHORBUS
Euphorbus was a Trojan killed by Menelaus. According to **Heraclides of Pontus**, **Pythagoras** claimed to have been Euphorbus in an earlier life.

EUPHORION (third century BC)
Euphorion was a poet who studied under both **Lacydes of Cyrene** and **Prytanis**. According to **Diogenes Laertius**, he claimed that **Plato** [1] had rewritten the beginning of *Republic* many times.

EUPHRAEUS OF HISTIAEA or OF OREUS (fourth century BC)
Euphraeus was a student of **Plato** [1]. He became an advisor to Perdiccas III of Macedonia, and sought to ensure that the young king was surrounded by educated people. He seems to have helped to advance the career of Philip, the younger brother of Perdiccas. Philip went on to become king himself, and was the father of Alexander the Great. When Philip later tried to take control of Histiaea, Euphraeus opposed the move and was thrown into prison. He remained there until he died by committing suicide.

EUPHRANOR (third century AD?)
Euphranor was a Pythagorean who wrote a book about flutes.

EUPHRANOR OF SELEUCIA (third century BC)
According to **Diogenes Laertius**, Euphranor was a pupil of **Timon of Phlius** and the teacher of **Eubulus of Alexandria**.

EUPHRASIUS (third/fourth century AD)
According to **Eunapius**, Euphrasius was one of the most distinguished pupils of **Iamblichus of Chalcis**.

EUPHRATES (first/second century AD)
Euphrates is generally thought to have been a Stoic and a pupil of **Musonius Rufus**. It is also widely believed that Euphrates of Tyre, of Syria and of Egypt are all the same person. However, very different accounts survive of his character. Pliny the Younger, who knew him personally, describes him as a person of the highest virtue and integrity and goes so far as to compare him with **Plato** [1]. He was said to be of imposing appearance, tall and dignified with a long white beard. **Epictetus**, another contemporary and also a pupil of **Musonius Rufus**, testifies to his modesty and his emphasis on the inner philosophical life as opposed to outward posturings. However, Flavius **Philostratus**, who lived well after Euphrates had died, portrays him as a devious and jealous rival of **Apollonius of Tyana**, always seeking to ingratiate himself with those in power. A philosophical rivalry between a Stoic and a Neopythagorean would scarcely be surprising, but otherwise the different accounts are hard to reconcile. While his admirers may have been blind to some of his faults, it is difficult not to give greater weight to the testimony of Pliny and Epictetus than to that of Philostratus.

EUPHRONIUS [1]
Euphronius was said to have been an Epicurean and an atheist. He became extremely ill and only recovered his health after visiting a temple of Asclepius. He subsequently burnt the writings of **Epicurus** on the orders of the god.

EUPHRONIUS [2] (fourth century AD)
Euphronius was a philosopher whose views were criticised by **Diodorus of Tarsus**.

EUPHROSYNE
Euphrosyne is known only through an epitaph that pays tribute to her as a philosopher of great virtue and learning who died in Rome at the age of twenty.

EUREMON (fourth century BC?)
In the letter supposedly written by **Diogenes of Sinope** to **Charmides** [1], Euremon is criticised for his rather shallow grasp of philosophy and his love of money.

EURIPIDES (fifth century BC)
A number of stories link the dramatist Euripides with philosophy. **Diogenes Laertius** says he was a pupil of **Anaxagoras of Clazomenae** and that he travelled to Egypt with **Plato** [1]. That he was acquainted with philosophers of his time seems guaranteed, but beyond that much is speculative.

EURYCRATES OF SPARTA
According to **Iamblichus of Chalcis**, Eurycrates was a Pythagorean.

EURYLOCHUS (fourth/third century BC)
According to **Diogenes Laertius**, Eurylochus was a pupil of **Pyrrho of Elis**. He is said to have been prone to fits of temper, and to have had pupils of his own.

He may be the same Eurylochus to whom **Epicurus** wrote a letter insisting that he was entirely self-taught.

EURYMEDON OF TARENTUM (fifth century BC?)
According to **Iamblichus of Chalcis**, Eurymedon was a Pythagorean.

EURYPHAMUS OF SYRACUSE (sixth/fifth century BC)
According to **Iamblichus of Chalcis**, Euryphamus was a disciple of **Pythagoras**. As an indication of how seriously Pythagoreans took any agreement, Iamblichus relates how Euryphamus once asked **Lysis of Tarentum** to wait for him outside the temple of Hera. Lysis agreed. Euryphamus forgot all about him, and returned next day to find Lysis still waiting there. Some fragments of a work on life supposedly by him have survived.
(David Fideler (ed.), *The Pythagorean Sourcebook*, Grand Rapids, Phanes, 1987)

EURYPHEMUS OF METAPONTUM (sixth/fifth century BC?)
According to **Iamblichus of Chalcis**, Euryphemus was a Pythagorean, but there may be a confusion here with **Euryphamus of Syracuse**.

EURYPYLUS OF COS (third century BC)
Eurypylus was a Platonist and a pupil of **Crantor of Soli**.

EURYSTRATUS
According to **Stobaeus**, Eurystatus was a philosopher.

EURYTUS OF TARENTUM (fifth/fourth century BC?)
The information concerning Eurytus is extremely confused. **Iamblichus of Chalcis** described him as a pupil of both **Pythagoras** and **Philolaus of Croton**, while he is variously described as coming from Tarentum, Metapontum and Croton. According to **Diogenes Laertius**, **Plato** [1] visited Philolaus and Eurytus in Italy. The connections with Pythagoreanism and Italy are constants, but unless Eurytus lived an inordinately long time, it seems safer to assume either that two people by the same name have been confused with each other or that some of the information is simply wrong. The association with Philolaus is widely attested and seems unlikely to be wholly mistaken.

EUSEBIUS [1]
The name of Eusebius appears as the author of a number of fragments preserved by **Stobaeus**. It is unclear when he lived or to which philosophical school he belonged.

EUSEBIUS [2] (fourth/fifth century AD)
Eusebius was the teacher of **Sidonius Apollinaris** and **Probus**. He probably had his own school at Arelate (Arles).

EUSEBIUS OF ALEXANDRIA
Eusebius wrote a commentary on the *Categories* of **Aristotle**.

EUSEBIUS OF CAESAREA (third/fourth century AD)

Eusebius studied under **Pamphilus of Caesarea** and became bishop of Caesarea in around AD 315. He also became the friend and biographer of Constantine the Great. His most important philosophical work was *Preparation for the Gospel* which was designed as a response to *Against the Christians* by **Porphyry**. Part of its value lies in its extensive use of quotations from a variety of sources, thus preserving many philosophical fragments that would otherwise have been lost. His use of quotations is often designed to make the point that philosophers cannot agree. He also argues that the good ideas of **Plato** [1] bear an uncanny resemblance to the teachings of Moses while the bad ideas of Plato are simply wrong. The most famous work by Eusebius is his *Ecclesiastical History*, an account of the first three hundred years of Christianity. (*Nicene and Post-Nicene Fathers* series II, vol. I; Eusebius, *The History of the Church*, trans. Williamson, Harmondsworth, Penguin, 1965; Eusebius, *Preparation for the Gospel* (2 vols), trans. E.H. Gifford, Eugene, Wipf and Stock, 2002; www.tertullian.org/fathers/eusebius_pe_00_eintro.htm)
[D.S. Wallace-Hadrill, *Eusebius of Caesarea*, London, Mowbray, 1960]

EUSEBIUS OF EMESA (fourth century AD)

Eusebius taught philosophy in Antioch. **John Chrysostom** was one of his pupils.

EUSEBIUS OF MYNDUS (fourth century AD)

Eusebius studied under **Aedesius** along with **Chrysanthius of Sardis** and **Maximus of Ephesus**. Unlike them, he was suspicious of all forms of magic and believed that the truth could only be reached by rational intellectual effort. He became a friend and teacher of the emperor **Julian**.

EUSTATHIUS [1] (fourth century AD)

Eustathius was a Greek philosopher who taught in Rome. He appears in the *Saturnalia* of **Macrobius**.

EUSTATHIUS [2] (fourth century AD)

Eustathius originally came from Cappadocia and studied under **Iamblichus of Chalcis**. He spent some time in Antioch, and was sent as an envoy to Persia in AD 358 where he made such a favourable impression on Sapor II that the Persian king supposedly came close to giving up his throne in order to become a philosopher, although he was dissuaded from doing so by his advisors. Whether or not Sapor was actually so tempted, the story is consistent with the fact that Eustathius was evidently widely admired and regarded as a person of great integrity. Sometime after his return from Persia he married **Sosipatra** and they had three sons, one of whom was **Antoninus** [2]. Little is known about the philosophy of Eustathius, but he was probably a Neoplatonist and may have written a commentary on the *Categories* of **Aristotle** [1].

EUSTATHIUS OF ANTIOCH (third/fourth century BC)

Eustathius was bishop of Antioch, but was deposed and banished in AD 330.

Amongst his writings was a treatise on the soul that sought to argue the superiority of the Christian position over that of the philosophers.

EUSTOCHIUS OF ALEXANDRIA (third century AD)
Eustaochius was a physician who became a pupil of **Plotinus** and looked after him in his last years. He also produced an edition of the works of Plotinus.

EUSTROTUS OF ATHENS (first/second century AD)
Eustrotus was a pupil of Marcus Annius **Ammonius** at the same time as **Plutarch of Chaeronea**. He espoused a form of Platonism that incorporated substantial elements of Pythagoreanism, including a belief in the importance of numbers.

EUTHOSION OF RHEGIUM (fifth century BC?)
According to **Iamblichus of Chalcis**, Euthosion was a Pythagorean.

EUTHYCLES OF RHEGIUM (fifth century BC?)
According to **Iamblichus of Chalcis**, Euthycles was a Pythagorean.

EUTHYDEMUS (fifth century BC)
Euthydemus was a follower of Socrates.

EUTHYDEMUS OF CHIOS (fifth century BC)
Euthydemus appears in the dialogue by **Plato** [1] named after him. Both he and his brother Dionysodorus were specialists in martial arts. Euthydemus is generally reckoned as a sophist, but it would appear that he took a serious interest in logic.
[R.S.W. Hawtrey, *Commentary on Plato's Euthydemus*, Philadelphia, American Philosophical Society, 1981]

EUTHYNOUS OF LOCRI (fifth century BC?)
According to **Iamblichus of Chalcis**, Euthynous was a Pythagorean.

EUTHYNUS OF TARENTUM (fifth century BC?)
According to **Iamblichus of Chalcis**, Euthynus was a Pythagorean.

EUTOCIUS OF ASCALON (fifth/sixth century AD)
Eutocius was a Platonist and the teacher of **Olympiodorus** [2] and **David**. He wrote a number of works on mathematics as well as a commentary on the *Isagoge* ('Introduction') of **Porphyry**.

EUTROPIUS (fifth century AD)
Eutropius was a friend of **Sidonius Apollonaris**. He was dedicated to the philosophy of **Plotinus**, but was also chastised by Sidonius for manifesting an indifference to public service that smacked of Epicureanism.

EUXENUS (first century BC/first century AD)
According to Flavius **Philostratus**, Euxenus came from Heraclea but taught philosophy in Aegae. One of his pupils there was **Apollonius of Tyana**. He taught Pythagoreanism, but does not appear to have practised it or even understood it very well, teaching only what he had learnt by heart.

EUXITHEUS (fourth/third century BC)
Euxitheus was a pupil of **Aristotle** [1] and made a career as an orator.

EVAEON OF LAMPSACUS (fifth/fourth century BC)
According to **Diogenes Laertius**, Evaeon was a pupil of **Plato** [1].

EVAGORAS (third/fourth century AD)
Evagoras was probably a Neoplatonist and he seems to have founded his own school in Athens where **Aquila** was one of his students.

EVAGRIUS (third/fourth century AD)
Evagrius was an aristocratic philosopher based in Rome.

EVAGRIUS OF PONTUS (fourth century AD)
Evagrius spent the later years of his life as a monk and wrote a number of works that helped to make the ideas of **Origen** known to later authors such as **Dionysius the Areopagite**.

EVANDER OF ATHENS (second century BC)
Evander was a Platonist and a pupil of **Lacydes of Cyrene**.

EVANDER OF CROTON (fifth century BC?)
According to **Iamblichus of Chalcis**, Evander was a Pythagorean.

EVANDER OF METAPONTUM (fifth century BC?)
According to **Iamblichus of Chalcis**, Evander was a Pythagorean.

EVANDER OF PHOCAEA (third/second century BC)
Evander was a Platonist, a pupil of **Lacydes of Cyrene**. Lacydes chose Evander and **Telecles of Phocaea** to succeed him as head of the Academy. Evander was in turn succeeded by **Hegesinus of Pergamum**.

EVANOR OF SYBARIS (fifth century BC?)
According to **Iamblichus of Chalcis**, Evanor was a Pythagorean.

EVATHLUS (fifth century BC)
According to **Diogenes Laertius**, Evathlus was a pupil of **Protagoras of Abdera**.

EVARESTUS OF CRETE (second century AD)
Evarestus was a philosophical acquaintance of **Aelius Aristides**. They met both in Egypt and at Pergamum.

EVARETUS, QUINTUS AELIUS EGRILIUS (second century AD)
Evaretus was a philosopher in Rome, a friend of the lawyer and legal scholar Publius Salvius Julianus.

EVELTHON OF ARGOS
According to **Iamblichus of Chalcis**, Evelthon was a Pythagorean.

EVETERIUS (fourth century AD)
Eveterius was a philosopher who was arrested and tortured into betraying

several other people. The details surrounding this are uncertain, but it may have happened in connection with events in Antioch in AD 471 when a number of philosophers shared a similar fate.

EVETES OF LOCRI (fifth century BC?)
According to **Iamblichus of Chalcis**, Evetes was a Pythagorean.

EXUPERANTIA (third/fourth century AD)
Exuperantia was a philosopher in Hadrumetum. Like her husband, **Heraclamon Leonides**, she was probably an Epicurean.

❖ F ❖

FABIANUS, PAPIRIUS (first century BC/first century AD)
Fabianus made his career in public speaking but became interested in philosophy after meeting Quintus **Sextius**. He wrote a number of books and was greatly admired by **Seneca** who mentions him in his own writings on a number of occasions. Seneca describes him as someone who lived a philosophical life without being distracted by details of doctrine.

FABIUS (fifth/sixth century AD)
Fabius was a philosopher and friend of **Boethius**.

FABIUS MAXIMUS (first century BC)
Fabius Maximus was a Stoic who wrote a number of books on philosophy.

FADIUS or FABIUS GALLUS, MARCUS (first century BC)
Fadius Gallus was an Epicurean and a friend of **Cicero**.

FANNIA (first century AD)
Fannia was the daughter of **Thrasea Paetus** and **Arria Paetus the Younger** and the wife of **Helvidius Priscus**. Like them, she was part of the Stoic opposition to Nero and Vespasian.

FANNIUS, GAIUS (second century BC)
Fannius was a politician and pupil of **Panaetius of Rhodes**.

FAUSTUS OF RIEZ (fifth century AD)
Faustus probably originated from either Britain or Brittany and became bishop of Riez in around AD 459. He was a believer in free will as opposed to predestination, and held that since the soul was created it was also material, prompting **Claudianus Mamertus** to write a treatise defending its immateriality. Many of his views were condemned at the Council of Orange in AD 529 several years after his death.

FAVONIUS (first century BC)
Favonius was a Cynic. He attached himself to **Cato the Younger**, whom he sought to imitate. He was also a friend of Marcus **Brutus**, but they fell out and Brutus told him that while he only *pretended* to be a Cynic, he really *was* a dog!

FAVONIUS EULOGIUS (fourth/fifth century BC)
Favonius came from Carthage and was a pupil of **Augustine**. He wrote an analysis of *The Dream of Scipio* by **Cicero**.

FAVORINUS (first/second century AD)
Favorinus was a colourful character, said by Flavius **Philostratus** to have been an hermaphrodite. He came from Arelate (Arles) and studied with **Dion Cocceianus**. He achieved fame as a sophist, but also wrote many books on philosophy, including works on **Plato** [1], **Epictetus** and **Pyrrho of Elis**. He appears to have been a Platonist, but of a sceptical kind. He favoured a method of teaching that helped students see the arguments for and against a particular position. He studied and taught in several major cities, and spent some time in exile on Chios after falling out with the emperor Hadrian.
[J. Glucker, *Antiochus and the Late Academy*, Gottingen, Vandenhoeck and Ruprecht, 1978]

FIGULUS, PUBLIUS NIGIDIUS (first century BC)
Figulus was a friend of **Cicero** who enjoyed a great reputation for learning. However, he was on the wrong side of the civil war between **Pompey** and Julius **Caesar**, and Caesar sent him into exile. He was particularly interested in Pythagoreanism and was a leading figure in its revival in Rome. He specialised in the mystical side of Pythagoreanism and was credited with occult powers.

FIRMIANUS
Firmianus was a Roman priest and philosopher.

FIRMICUS MATERNUS, JULIUS (fourth century AD)
Firmicus was a scholar and statesman who wrote an attack on pagan religion that borrowed heavily from **Cicero**. Before his conversion to Christianity, he had been a Stoic and written a book on astrology.
(Julius Firmicus Maternus, *The Error of the Pagan Religions*, trans. C.A. Forbes, New York, Newman Press, 1970)

FIRMUS CASTRICIUS (third century AD)
Firmus was a friend of **Porphyry** and a pupil of both **Plotinus** and **Amelius Gentilianus**. He is best known because of the book *On Abstinence* that Porphyry dedicated to him, in which the arguments for vegetarianism are set out. Firmus had evidently resumed his carnivorous ways at the time the book was written.

FLAVIUS ALEXANDER, TITUS (first/second century AD)
Flavius Alexander was a sophist but is perhaps the same person as the Alexander who was an Epicurean and friend of **Plutarch of Chaeronea**.

FORTUNATIANUS (fourth century AD)
According to **Libanius** [1], Fortunatianus was a philosopher and poet who achieved high political office.

FRONTO (first century AD)
Fronto was a Stoic, mentioned by Martial in one of his epigrams.

FRONTO, DOMITIUS
Fronto was a Stoic philosopher famous enough in his time to have a statue erected in his honour in the city of Hippo, but now even when he lived is forgotten.

FRONTO, MARCUS CORNELIUS (second century AD)
Fronto was a statesman and a tutor to **Marcus Aurelius**. He seems to have had no particular philosophical allegiance, and indeed entertained something of a distrust of philosophy in general. He made a speech attacking Christians that was borrowed by **Minucius Felix** for a work of his own.
(Fronto, *The Correspondence of Marcus Cornelius Fronto* (2 vols), trans. C.R. Haines, Loeb, 1919)

FUNDANUS, GAIUS MINICIUS (first/second century AD)
Fundanus was a friend of **Plutarch of Chaeronea** and Pliny the Younger. The latter describes him as a philosopher who dedicated himself to study from an early age. It seems likely that he was a Stoic.

FURIUS PHILUS, LUCIUS (second century BC)
Furius was a scholar and statesman. He was probably a Stoic.

FUSCUS, ARISTIUS (first century BC)
Fuscus was a friend of **Horace** and probably a Stoic.

❖ **G** ❖

GAIUS (first/second century AD)
Gaius was a Platonist. Although he appears to have enjoyed a significant reputation, next to nothing is known about him. **Porphyry** mentions commentaries on **Plato** [1] by Gaius that may have been edited by his pupil **Albinus**.
[John Dillon, *The Middle Platonists 80 BC to AD 220*, London, Duckworth, 1996]

GALEN (second century AD)
After **Hippocrates of Cos**, Galen was probably the most celebrated physician in antiquity. He studied philosophy before going on to study medicine in Pergamum, Smyrna, Corinth and Alexandria. He was summoned to Rome by

Marcus Aurelius in AD 169 on account of his reputation and was greatly admired by the emperor. Much of his originality lay in his ability to bring ideas from different schools of medicine and philosophy together into a new synthesis that was also supported by his own empirical research. His principal philosophical influence was Platonism, although his father had ensured that his early education also took in Stoicism, Epicureanism and Aristotelianism. In due course he wrote many books on all of them, although most of his works on philosophy are lost. History has been kinder to his medical writings, largely because of the authority that was accorded them for centuries. He emphasised the important of logical thinking and critical argument in medicine and used these in order to expose those he thought to be impostors or simply wrong. He rejected the attack on causation led by the Sceptics and defended an account of it based on **Aristotle** [1] and the Stoics.

(Galen, *Selected Works* (ed. P.N. Singer) Oxford, Oxford University Press, 1997; Galen, *Three Treatises on the Nature of Science*, trans. R. Walzer and M. Frede, Indianapolis, Hackett, 1985; Galen, *On the Passions and Errors of the Soul*, trans. P.W. Harkins, Columbus, Ohio University Press, 1963)

[George Sarton, *Galen of Pergamum*, Lawrence, University of Kansas Press, 1954; O. Temkin, *Galenism*, Ithaca, Cornell University Press, 1973; Michael Boylan, 'Galen', *Internet Encyclopaedia of Philosophy*, www.iep.utm.edu/g/galen.htm]

GALLIO, LUCIUS JUNIUS (first century BC/first century AD)
Gallio was an orator with a reputation for his knowledge of philosophy. He adopted Lucius Annaeus **Novatus**, the elder brother of **Seneca**.

GANYMEDES (fourth/third century BC?)
Ganymedes was the supposed recipient of a letter falsely attributed to **Crates of Thebes**. In it Crates tries to persuade Ganymedes to make a whole-hearted commitment to the Cynic philosophy.

GARTYDAS OF CROTON (fifth/fourth century BC)
According to **Iamblichus of Chalcis**, Gartydas succeeded **Boulagoras** as head of the Pythagorean school. He had spent some time away from Croton and returned to a city that had been badly damaged as a result of a feud between the Pythagoreans and their opponents. He was so upset by what he found that he is said to have died of a broken heart.

GAUDENTIUS (fourth century AD?)
Gaudentius was a philosopher who wrote an important work on the theory of music that survives in parts.

GAUDENTIUS OF BRESCIA (fourth/fifth century AD)
Gaudentius was a bishop who wrote a number of sermons that still survive. Their principal philosophical interest lies in his discussion of natural law, for which he borrows from the Stoics. He argued that through the use of reason, anyone could come to a knowledge of their moral obligations.

GAURUS (third/fourth century AD)
Gaurus appears to have been a student of **Porphyry**, who may have dedicated one of his books to him.

GEDALIUS (third/fourth century BC)
Gedalius was probably a pupil of **Porphyry**, who dedicated his commentary on the *Categories* of **Aristotle** [1] to him.

GELLIUS, AULUS see AULUS GELLIUS

GELLIUS, LUCIUS (first/second century AD)
Arrian dedicated the *Discourses* of **Epictetus** to Gellius, who presumably took at least an interest in Stoicism.

GEMINA (third century AD)
Gemina was the name of a mother and daughter, both of whom were followers of **Plotinus**. During his time in Rome, Plotinus lived in the house of the elder Gemina.

GEMINUS (first century BC/first century AD?)
Geminus probably came from Rhodes and was the author of a work on astronomy. He is thought to have been a Stoic.

GENNADIUS OF MASSILIA [Marseille] (fifth century AD)
Gennasius was a Christian priest who argued that God is the only incorporeal being and that souls and angels are both material.

GEORGE OF SCYTHOPOLIS (fifth/sixth century AD)
George was the brother of **John of Scythopolis**. Like him he was a Christian and a Platonist and wrote a commentary on the works of **Dionysius the Areopagite**.

GESSIUS OF PETRA (fifth/sixth century AD)
Gessius achieved great fame as a practitioner and theorist of medicine and became a rich man as a result. However, he was also interested in philosophy and studied under **Ammonius** in Alexandria for a time. He was a friend of **Heraiscus**, sheltering him in his home and nursing him until he died.

GLAUCIAS (third/second century BC)
Glaucias was a physician of the Empiricist school. He wrote an important work, now lost, that seems to have aimed at setting medicine on a firm methodological footing.

GLAUCON (first/second century AD)
Glaucon was a physician, a Platonist, and a pupil of **Galen**.

GLAUCON OF COLLYTUS (fifth/fourth century BC)
Glaucon was a brother of **Plato** [1] and said to have been the author of a number of philosophical dialogues, none of which have survived.

GLAUCUS, TITUS FLAVIUS (second/third century AD)
Glaucus was a poet and philosopher. The nephew of Titus Flavius **Callaeschrus**, he was probably a Platonist like his uncle.

GLAUCUS OF RHEGIUM (fifth/fourth century BC)
Glaucus was an historian, used as a source by **Diogenes Laertius** who attributes to him the claim that **Democritus of Abdera** was taught by a Pythagorean.

GLYCINUS OF METAPONTUM (fifth century BC?)
According to **Iamblichus of Chalcis**, Glycinus was a Pythagorean.

GLYCO see LYCO [1]

GORGIADES (fifth/fourth century BC?)
Gorgiades is said to have been a Pythagorean, although some question his historicity and some identify him with **Gartydas of Croton**.

GORGIAS
There appears to have been a Cynic of this name, but nothing is known of him.

GORGIAS OF LEONTINI (fifty/fourth century BC)
Gorgias came from Sicily and may have studied there with **Empedocles of Acragas**. He arrived in Athens on a diplomatic mission in 427 BC and subsequently became rich through teaching rhetoric. The nature and value of rhetoric is discussed by **Plato** [1] in the dialogue named after him. Gorgias himself seems only to have written one serious work of philosophy. In it he argued that nothing existed, or if anything did exist there could be no knowledge of it, or if there could be knowledge of it, that knowledge could not be passed on from one person to another. He lived to be over a hundred and attributed his longevity to never doing anything for anyone else.
(Rosemary Kent Sprague (ed.), *The Older Sophists*, Indianapolis, Hackett, 2001) [E.R. Dodds, *Plato. Gorgias*, Oxford, Clarendon Press, 1959]

GORGIPPIDES (third century BC)
According to **Diogenes Laertius**, **Chrysippus of Soli** dedicated a number of books on logic to Gorgippides. He was presumably a Stoic and perhaps a pupil.

GORGUS OF SPARTA (second century BC)
Gorgus was a Stoic and a pupil of **Panaetius of Rhodes**.

GORGYLUS (third century BC)
Gorgyus was a Peripatetic and one of the executors of the will of **Strato of Lampsacus**.

GRACCHUS, TIBERIUS SEMPRONIUS (second century BC)
Gracchus was a Roman statesman and reformer, a friend of **Blossius of Cumae**. He may have been a Stoic himself. He was killed by a mob in 133 BC.

GRAECINUS, JULIUS (first century AD)
Graecinus was an amateur philosopher. **Seneca** described him as a man of distinction, but with little serious philosophical ability or interest.

GREGORY (fifth century AD)
Gregory was from Alexandria and the brother of **Hermias** [2]. He and his brother went to Athens with **Proclus** [1] to study with **Syrianus** [1]. Although he was a talented scholar, he seems to have been psychologically unstable. After his return to Alexandria he suffered and died from what was probably some kind of wasting disease.

GREGORY OF NAZIANZUS (fourth century AD)
Gregory came from Cappadocia and studied in Athens. Later he became an enthusiastic monk and then a reluctant bishop. He and **Basil of Caesarea** edited a collection of the writings of **Origen**.
(*Nicene and Post-Nicene Fathers* series II, vol. VII)

GREGORY OF NYSA (fourth century AD)
Gregory was the brother of **Basil of Caesarea**. He became a monk and then bishop of Nysa after an earlier career teaching rhetoric. His theological writings were influenced by Platonism and he was an admirer of the works of **Origen**.
(*Nicene and Post-Nicene Fathers*, vol. V)

GREGORY THAUMATURGUS (third century AD)
Gregory came from Neocaesarea in Pontus. After studying law and politics he became a pupil of **Origen** and later wrote about his teaching methods. He also wrote some theological works. His nickname, meaning 'wonder worker' derives from his reputation for being able to perform miracles.
(*Ante-Nicene Fathers*, vol. VI)

GYTHIUS or GYTTIUS OF LOCRI (fifth century BC?)
According to **Iamblichus of Chalcis**, Gythius was a Pythagorean.

❖ H ❖

HABROTELEIA (fifth century BC?)
According to **Iamblichus of Chalcis**, Habroteleia was the daughter of **Habroteles of Tarentum** and one of the most famous Pythagorean women.

HABROTELES OF TARENTUM (fifth century BC?)
According to **Iamblichus of Chalcis**, Habroteles was a Pythagorean and the father of **Habroteleia**.

HAGIAS (first/second century AD)
Hagias was a pupil of **Plutarch of Chaeronea**.

HAGNON OF TARSUS (second century BC)
Hagnon was a Platonist and a pupil of **Carneades of Cyrene**.

HAIMON OF CROTON (fifth century BC?)
According to **Iamblichus of Chalcis**, Haimon was a Pythagorean.

HANIOCHUS OF METAPONTUM (fith century BC?)
According to **Iamblichus of Chalcis**, Haniochus was a Pythagorean.

HARPOCRATION (fourth century AD?)
The name of Harpocration is associated with an hermetic text entitled *Cyranides* that sets out various correspondences between items in the different realms of nature. He probably came from Alexandria. Some have identified the author with a correspondent of **Libanius** [1].

HARPOCRATION OF ARGOS (second/third century AD)
Harpocration was a Platonist and a pupil of **Atticus** [1]. He wrote a commentary on **Plato** [1] and compiled a lexicon to accompany Plato's works. He appears to have held that all souls, and not just rational (which is to say, human) ones, were immortal. He also held that the material world had a beginning in time and was the source of evil.
[John Dillon, *The Middle Platonists 80 BC to AD 220*, London, Duckworth, 1996]

HAURANUS, CAIUS STALLIUS (first century BC/first century AD?)
Hauranus was a member of the Epicurean community of Neapolis (Naples).

HECATAEUS OF ABDERA (fourth/third century BC)
According to **Diogenes Laertius**, Hecataeus was a pupil of **Pyrrho of Elis**. However, the works associated with him are concerned with history and literature rather than philosophy. He is sometimes confused with **Hecataeus of Miletus**.

HECATAEUS OF MILETUS (sixth/fifth century BC)
According to **Suda**, Hecataeus was a pupil of **Protagoras of Abdera**, although he was significantly older than Protagoras. He was notable mainly as an historian and geographer.

HECATON OF RHODES (second/first century BC)
Hecaton was a Stoic and a pupil of **Panaetius of Rhodes**. He wrote a number of works drawn upon by **Diogenes Laertius**.

HECEBOLIUS (fourth century AD)
Hecebolius was primarily a sophist and taught rhetoric to the emperor **Julian**. He appears to have had flexible religious convictions (or none) and could be a pagan or Christian as the political climate demanded.

HEDEIA (fourth/third century BC)
Hedeia was a member of the circle of **Epicurus**. She may have been a prostitute, although the sources suggesting this are strongly anti-Epicurean.

HEDYLUS (third century BC?)
According to **Diogenes Laertius**, **Chrysippus of Soli** wrote some books about a kind of argument associated with Hedylus.

HEGESIANAX [1]
Nothing is known of Hegesianax except a single reference to him as a Cynic.

HEGESIANAX [2] (third century BC)
Hegesianax was probably an Epicurean. The son of **Dositheus** and brother of **Pyrson**, he died young and **Epicurus** sent a letter of consolation to his family.

HEGESIAS OF CYRENE (fourth/third century BC)
Hegesias was the pupil of **Parabaetes**. He left the Cyrenaic school to form his own, the Hegesiacs. Like the Cyrenaics he subscribed to the importance of pleasure and pain, but he also took the pessimistic view that happiness was impossible. He believed that the human body could not avoid suffering and that the human soul not only shared in this suffering but was also the source of mental torments of its own. Because of this, there was little to choose between life and death. Even the wisest of people could only hope to suffer less than others. According to **Cicero**, Hegesias argued for this position so persuasively that many who heard him committed suicide. As a result, Ptolemy I banned him from teaching in Alexandria.

HEGESIAS OF SINOPE (fourth century BC)
Hegesias was a follower of **Diogenes of Sinope** and rejoiced in the nickname of 'dog collar'. He was rebuked by Diogenes for wanting to study Cynic writings when he had a living example of Cynic teaching, Diogenes himself, in front of him.

HEGESINUS OF PERGAMUM (third/second century BC)
Hegesinus succeeded **Evander of Phocaea** as head of the Academy, and was succeeded in turn by **Carneades of Cyrene**. He is probably the person referred to by **Clement of Alexandria** as Hegesilaus.

HEGIAS (fifth/sixth century AD)
Hegias came from Athens and was a friend of **Damascius** and **Proclus**. He was said to have had a considerable natural aptitude for philosophy, but not to have fulfilled it because of his inability to detach himself from a variety of material interests. Despite that, he may have become the head of the Neoplatonist school at Athens after the death of **Isidore of Alexandria**. It appears he had a generous nature, but because of this he attracted many undesirable hangers-on.

HELANDRUS OF TARENTUM (fifth century BC?)
According to **Iamblichus of Chalcis**, Helandrus was a Pythagorean.

HELICAON OF RHEGIUM (fifth century BC)
According to **Iamblichus of Chalcis,** Helicaon was a Pythagorean. He was renowned as a legislator and helped to revise the constitution of Rhegium.

HELICON OF CYZICUS (fourth/third century BC)
Helicon studied under **Eudoxus of Cnidus** and **Polyxenus.** He was best known as an astronomer.

HELIODORUS [1] (first century AD)
Heliodorus was a Stoic philosopher in the time of Nero. He appears to have also been an informer with regard to at least one of the many plots of the period.

HELIODORUS [2] (first/second century AD)
Heliodorus was an Epicurean and close friend of the emperor Hadrian. He succeeded Popillius **Theotimus** as head of the school in Athens.

HELIODORUS OF ALEXANDRIA [1] (third century AD)
Heliodorus was a Peripatetic and contemporary of **Plotinus.** He wrote a number of books, but nothing is known about them.

HELIODORUS OF ALEXANDRIA [2] (fifth/sixth century AD)
Heliodorus was the son of **Hermias** [2] and **Aedesia,** and the brother of **Ammonius.** Born in Alexandria, Aedesia took him and his brother to Athens after their father died. There they studied under **Proclus** [1]. Although regarded as less talented than Ammonius, Heliodorus taught philosophy when he returned to Alexandria, **Damascius** being one of his pupils. He also took an interest in astronomy.

HELIODORUS OF ANTIOCH (third/second century BC)
Heliodorus was an Epicurean who held a senior position at the court of Seleucus IV. He fell out with the king over a political matter and assassinated him.

HELIODORUS OF EMESA (fourth century AD)
Heliodorus wrote the novel *Ethiopica.* It contains a handful of historical philosophical references and many have sought to impose on it a philosophical interpretation.

HELIODORUS OF LARISA (fifth/sixth century AD?)
Heliodorus appears to have been a scientist and philosopher who wrote a book on optics. He may have been a Platonist.

HELIODORUS OF MALLUS (first century BC)
Heliodorus was a Platonist and a pupil of **Charmadas.**

HELLESPONTIUS (fourth century AD)
Hellespontius came from Galatia and travelled widely to satisfy his thirst for knowledge. In old age he went to Sardis and met **Chrysanthius of Sardis.** This encounter led him to conclude that the knowledge he had sought for so many

years was of little real value. Unfortunately, his conversion to philosophy had come very late in the day and he soon left for Apamea where he died.

HELORIPPUS OF SAMOS
According to **Iamblichus of Chalcis**, Helorippus was a Pythagorean.

HELORIS OF SAMOS
According to **Iamblichus of Chalcis**, Heloris was a Pythagorean.

HELPIDIUS [1] (fourth century AD)
Helpidius was a philosopher and the recipient of a letter attributed to the emperor **Julian**.

HELPIDIUS [2] (fourth century AD)
Helpidius studied gnosticism and became the teacher of **Priscillian**. A Christian, his views were condemned as heretical at a synod in AD 380.

HELVIDIUS PRISCUS (first century AD)
Helvidius was the husband of **Fannia** and the son-in-law of **Thrasea Paetus**. A Stoic involved in politics, he spent periods in exile but was admired as a man of principle.

HEMINA, LUCIUS CASSIUS (second century BC)
Hemina was an historian who may also have been a Pythagorean.

HERACLAMON LEONIDES (third/fourth century AD)
Heraclamon was an Epicurean from Hadrumetum. His wife was **Exuperantia**.

HERACLAS (third century AD)
Heraclas was a pupil of **Origen** and became his teaching assistant. When Origen left Alexandria, Heraclas took over his school, and not long after became bishop of Alexandria as well.

HERACLEODORUS [1] (fourth century BC)
Heracleodorus was said to have been a pupil of **Plato [1]**.

HERACLEODORUS [2] (first century BC)
Heracleodorus was one of those criticised by **Philodemus of Gadara** in his book on poetic theory. He may also have been the target of the work by **Aristocritus [1]** entitled *Positions against Heracleodorus* referred to by **Clement of Alexandria**. Exactly what Heracleodorus stood for is unclear.

HERACLEON (second century AD)
According to **Hippolytus**, Heracleon was a follower of **Valentinus** and a Platonist and Pythagorean rather than a Christian.

HERACLEON OF MEGARA (first/second century AD)
Heracleon was probably a pupil of **Plutarch of Chaeronea**.

HERACLEUS (third century BC)
Heracleus was one of those to whom **Lyco** [1] bequeathed the Lyceum on his death. He had presumably been a pupil there for some time.

HERACLIAN (fourth/fifth century AD)
Heraclian was a bishop of Chalcedon who wrote a long work attacking the philosophy of **Mani**. He was evidently a gifted philosopher and a noted scholar.

HERACLIDES [1] (third century BC)
Heraclides was a Stoic, a pupil of **Chrysippus of Soli** who dedicated a book to him.

HERACLIDES [2] (second/first century BC)
According to **Diogenes Laertius**, Heraclides was a Sceptic, the pupil of **Ptolemy of Cyrene** and teacher of **Aenesidemus of Cnossus**.

HERACLIDES [3] (first/second century AD)
Heraclides is mentioned by **Plutarch of Chaeronea** as someone who objected to his attack on Epicureans and Epicureanism. It may be that he was an Epicurean himself.

HERACLIDES [4] (second century AD)
Heraclides was a Platonist who received a letter from someone called **Theon** [2] in which a number of Stoic texts were discussed.

HERACLIDES, AURELIUS (second century AD)
Heraclides was a leading Stoic in Athens.

HERACLIDES LEMBUS (second century BC)
Although **Suda** says Heraclides came from Oxyrhynchus, according to **Diogenes Laertius** he may have come from Callatis or Alexandria. The sources are agreed that he had the nickname of Lembus, meaning 'small boat', although it is not at all clear why. He wrote works on the history of philosophy.

HERACLIDES OF AENUS (fourth century BC)
According to **Diogenes Laertius**, Heraclides was a pupil of **Plato** [1]. In around 360 BC, he and his brother **Python** assassinated Cotys, the ruler of Thrace. **Aristotle** [1] believed their motives for doing so were personal rather than philosophical.

HERACLIDES OF BARGYLIA
According to **Diogenes Laertius**, Heraclides was the author of a work attacking the philosophy of **Epicurus**.

HERACLIDES OF PONTUS (fourth century BC)
Heraclides studied at the Academy under **Plato** [1] and **Speusippus**. When Speusippus died, Heraclides hoped to succeed him but was thwarted in this ambition by **Xenocrates of Chalcedon**. This prompted him to return to his

native Heraclea where he gained a reputation as a writer. According to **Diogenes Laertius** his output was considerable, but he was sometimes criticised for being too interested in myths and exotica at the expense of more serious material.

[H.B. Gottschalk, *Heraclides of Pontus*, Oxford, Clarendon Press, 1980]

HERACLIDES OF TARENTUM (second/first century BC)
Heraclides wrote a large work expounding the Empiricist philosophy of medicine which attracted the admiration of **Galen**.

HERACLIDES OF TARSUS (second century BC)
Heraclides was a Stoic, a pupil of **Antipater of Tarsus**. He argued that there are degrees of moral imperfection.

HERACLITUS [1] (first century AD)
Heraclitus compiled a commentary on Homer. His extensive use of allegorical interpretation is generally attributed to his being a Stoic.

HERACLITUS [2] (first/second century AD)
Heraclitus was a friend of **Epictetus** and may also have been a Stoic. According to Epictetus, he valued justice over property and reputation.

HERACLITUS OF EPHESUS (sixth/fifth century BC)
Little is known of the life of Heraclitus. He came from a noble family and probably spent his whole life in his home town of Ephesus. He appears to have cared little for his fellow citizens, and the lack of affection seems to have been mutual. **Timon of Phlius** described him as a man of riddles, and later generations gave him the nickname 'the Obscure'. The obscurity appears to have been intentional, although its purpose remains conjectural. His best known observation, that it is impossible to step into the same river twice, reflects the importance he attached to the idea of change in his understanding of the world. However, constant change was only one part of the picture. Underlying it was a single primal essence that Heraclitus called 'fire'. The significance of this choice seems to be that unlike other traditional elements such as air and water, fire is more like a process than a thing and so is better suited to being at the heart of a world of constant change. Fire is an instrument of transformation employed by a principle of reason, the *logos*, which is identified with both universal law and the divine. It is a principle of cosmic order and human reason is a microcosmic manifestation of it. The *logos* can also be understood as analogous to the modern principle of the conservation of energy. Just as that principle says that energy is neither created nor destroyed, so in a universe regulated by the *logos* what fire takes with one hand it gives with the other.

The cosmology of Heraclitus therefore acknowledges the changing nature of things while containing this change within a unifying structure. Change is not the same thing as chaos. Unlike his contemporary **Parmenides of Elea**, Heraclitus accepted the reality of change that is urged upon us by the evidence

of our senses, but denied that it made knowledge or philosophy problematic. Many elements of his cosmology were later taken up by the Stoics, but he seems to have founded no school himself.
(Jonathan Barnes, *Early Greek Philosophy*, Harmondsworth, Penguin, 1987)
[Charles H. Kahn, *The Art and Thought of Heraclitus*, Cambridge, Cambridge University Press, 1979; Daniel Graham, 'Heraclitus', *Internet Encyclopaedia of Philosophy*, www.iep.utm.edu/h/heraclit.htm]

HERACLITUS OF RHODIAPOLIS (first century AD)
Heraclitus was a physician, poet and Epicurean.

HERACLITUS OF TYRE (second/first century BC)
Heraclitus was a Platonist, a pupil of **Clitomachus of Carthage** and **Philo of Larisa**. He later taught in Alexandria.

HERACLIUS (fourth century AD)
Heraclius was a Cynic. He invited the emperor **Julian** to one of his lectures in Constantinople, hoping to make an impression. He did, but it was an unfavourable one and Julian duly produced a written piece critical of him.

HERAISCUS (fifth century AD)
Heraiscus may have had the distinction of being the last person to be mummified in Egypt. He was the brother of **Asclepiades of Alexandria** and uncle of **Horapollon** (who later became his son-in-law as well). He spent many years away from Egypt, including a period in Constantinople. He was said to have been a gifted philosopher, but apparently had other gifts as well, including psychic ones. His brother even came to believe (as the result of a vision) that he was an incarnation of the god Bacchus. After his return to Alexandria, he was arrested along with Horapollon and they were both tortured, but Heraiscus revealed nothing. Later he hid in the house of **Gessius of Petra**, where he was looked after until he died. After his death, Asclepiades arranged to have him mummified.

HERAS (first century AD)
Heras was a Cynic who emulated the antics of **Diogenes the Sophist** by publicly criticising Titus and his mistress in a packed Roman theatre. Unfortunately for Heras, while Diogenes had only been flogged, he was beheaded.

HERAS, CAIUS CINATUS (first/second century AD)
Heras was a citizen of Oxyrhynchus. His personal seal bore the figure of a philosopher, suggesting he was probably one himself.

HERCULIANUS (fourth/fifth century AD)
Herculianus came from Egypt, where he studied under **Hypatia of Alexandria**. One of his fellow students was **Synesius of Ptolemais**. They became lifelong friends, and often corresponded.

HEREAS (third century BC)
Hereas was a pupil of **Chrysippus of Soli**.

HERENNIUS or ERENNIUS (third century AD)
According to **Porphyry**, Herennius was a student of **Ammonius Saccas**. He, **Origen** and **Plotinus** all undertook not to reveal what Ammonius had taught them, but Herennius broke his word. Unfortunately, what he revealed is not known.

HERILLUS OF CARTHAGE (third century BC)
Herillus was an early Stoic, having studied under **Zeno of Citium** himself in Athens. However, he later broke with Zeno and set up his own school, although it does not seem to have long survived him. He took an intellectual approach to the good life, arguing that knowledge was the most important thing, and the worst was a life lived in ignorance. However, his understanding of knowledge itself held that it was, or at least involved, a kind of mental tranquillity. Whereas Zeno advocated life in accordance with nature, it might be said that Herillus advocated life in accordance with the *knowledge* of nature.

HERMAGORAS (third century BC)
Hermagoras was from Amphipolis and a pupil of **Persaeus of Citium**. A Stoic, he wrote a number of lost works, including a dialogue entitled 'Dog Hater' (presumably an attack on Cynicism?), a book about divination with eggs, and another accusing the followers of **Plato** [1] of being sophists.

HERMAISCUS (fourth/third century BC?)
Hermaiscus was the supposed recipient of a letter falsely attributed to **Crates of Thebes** and is assumed to have been a Cynic.

HERMARCHUS OF MITYLENE (fourth/third century BC)
Hermarchus was an Epicurean who succeeded **Epicurus** as head of the school. He had been a student of rhetoric before being converted to philosophy by Epicurus. He is said to have written works on **Empedocles of Acragas**, **Plato** [1] and **Aristotle** [1]. When he died he was succeeded by **Polystratus**.

HERMIAS [1] (second/third century AD?)
Hermias was a Christian who wrote a work mocking pagan philosophers for their views on the soul and the nature of the universe and for the extent to which they disagreed with each other on them.

HERMIAS [2] (fifth century AD)
Hermias came from Alexandria. He was the husband of **Aedesia** and the father of **Ammonius** and **Heliodorus of Alexandria** [2]. He studied in Athens with his brother **Gregory** and **Proclus** [1] under **Syrianus** [1]. After returning to Alexandria he became a teacher of philosophy. He was known and respected for his integrity and generosity. A Neoplatonist, he wrote a surviving commentary on the *Phaedrus* of **Plato** [1].

HERMIAS OF ATARNEUS (fourth century BC)

Hermias ruled Atarneus and Assus in Mysia as a vassal of the Persian king. There are various stories about him, including one that he had been a slave and became a eunuch, but their reliability is disputed. He may have heard **Plato** [1] lecture at the Academy, but this again is uncertain. However, it is generally agreed that he became a close friend of **Aristotle** [1], probably when Aristotle left Athens for Assus after the death of Plato, and Aristotle may have married his daughter or niece. When Hermias was executed, probably in 341 BC, as a result of political miscalculations, Aristotle erected a cenotaph at Delphi to his memory. It is said that he wrote a book on the soul, claiming it to be immortal.

HERMIAS OF PHOENICIA (fifth/sixth century AD)

Hermias came from Phoenicia and was one of the group of philosophers who accompanied **Damascius** on his journey to Persia.

HERMINUS [1] (second century AD)

Herminus was a Peripatetic who wrote a number of commentaries on the works of **Aristotle** [1]. He may have come from Pergamum.

HERMINUS [2] (second/third century AD)

Herminus was a Stoic, apparently a contemporary of **Plotinus**. He confined his activities mainly to teaching and wrote little or nothing.

HERMIPPUS OF SMYRNA (third century BC)

Hermippus was a Peripatetic who wrote a number of philosophical biographies, including works on **Pythagoras**, **Aristotle** [1] and **Theophrastus of Eresus**. None of these survive, but **Diogenes Laertius** acknowledged Hermippus as one of his sources.

HERMOCRATES, FLAVIUS (second century AD)

Hermocrates was a philosopher honoured in his native Phocaea.

HERMODAMUS OF SAMOS (seventh/sixth century BC)

Hermodamus appears in the story of **Pythagoras**. According to **Iamblichus of Chalcis**, Hermodamus and Pythagoras fled Samos together to go and study under **Pherecydes of Syros** and others. However, according to **Diogenes Laertius**, Pythagoras returned to Samos after Pherecydes died in order to study with Hermodamus. The connection between the two seems strong if unclear.

HERMODORUS (fourth century BC)

Hermodorus came from Syracuse and became a student and biographer of **Plato** [1], presumably when Plato visited Sicily. He also wrote a history of mathematics. According to **Suda**, he took Plato's books and sold them. It is not clear what is meant by this, or why it is apparently meant as a criticism of Hermodorus.

[John Dillon, *The Heirs of Plato: a study of the Old Academy (347-274 BC)*, Oxford, Clarendon Press, 2003]

HERMODOTUS (first century AD)
If he existed, Hermodotus was a Cynic, but some doubt his historicity.

HERMOGENES (second/third century AD)
Hermogenes seems to have been at once a Christian, a Platonist and a gnostic. He is known principally because of the attacks on him found in the writings of **Tertullian** and **Hippolytus**. He argued that even God could not create something out of nothing, and so the world must have been shaped from existing matter.

HERMOGENES OF ALOPECE (fifth century BC)
Hermogenes was a follower of **Socrates** and one of those present at his death. He appears as a principal character in the *Cratylus* of **Plato** [1].

HERMOGENES OF PONTUS (fourth century AD)
Hermogenes studied philosophy when young before pursuing a successful political career. On the occasions when he was out of favour, he returned to his studies. He and **Libanius** [1] were regular correspondents.

HERMOTIMUS OF CLAZOMENAE (eighth/seventh century BC?)
The historicity of Hermotimus is questionable, but the erection of a temple to him at Clazomenae suggests some basis in fact. The legends surrounding him point to some kind of wonderworker, reputed to be able to leave his body for long periods. (It is said he died when his body was cremated while he was outside it.) He also became recognised as one of the 'pre-incarnations' of **Pythagoras**.

HERMOTIMUS OF COLOPHON (fourth century BC)
Hermotimus was a mathematician who may have spent time studying at the Academy.

HERODES ATTICUS (first century AD)
Herodes became one of the richest and best-connected people in the Roman empire. More of a sophist and a friend of philosophers than a philosopher himself, he condemned the Stoics for their lack of feeling.

HERODICUS (second century BC)
Herodicus was a pupil of **Crates of Mallus**. He was more interested in language and literature than in philosophy. However, because **Plato** [1] had said in *Republic* that he would ban the works of Homer from his ideal city, Herodicus, a great admirer of Homer, became an anti-Platonist, extending his criticisms to **Socrates** as well.

HERODOTUS (fourth/third century BC)
Herodotus was a follower of **Epicurus** and is best known because a letter Epicurus wrote to him has survived. In it, Epicurus sets out his views about the nature of the world. **Diogenes Laertius** suggests, although not very clearly, that Herodotus may have turned against Epicurus at some point.

HERODOTUS OF NICOMEDIA (first century BC)
Herodotus was a Platonist and a pupil of **Carneades of Cyrene**.

HERODOTUS OF TARSUS (first/second century AD)
Herodotus was a Sceptic. According to **Diogenes Laertius,** he was taught by **Menodotus of Nicomedia** and was the teacher of **Sextus Empiricus**. He seems to be the person called Herodotus of Philadelphia in **Suda** and perhaps also the Herodotus who studied under Claudius **Agathinus**.

HEROPHILUS (first/second century AD?)
Herophilus was the author of an introduction to Stoicism referred to by **Origen**.

HEROPHILUS OF CHALCEDON (third century BC)
Herophilus was a physician and medical researcher who wrote a major work on anatomy. He appears to have been influenced in his work by both Aristotelianism and Scepticism.

HESTIAEUS OF MILETUS (third century BC?)
Hestiaeus was a Platonist, commemorated as such in an inscription on his tomb in Miletus.

HESTIAEUS OF PERINTHUS (fourth century BC)
Hestiaeus was a pupil of **Plato** [1]. He was interested in physics and developed a theory of vision that treated objects as the source of the light by which they were seen.

HESTIAEUS OF TARENTUM (fifth/fourth century BC?)
According to **Iamblichus of Chalcis,** Hestiaeus was a Pythagorean. **Suda** suggests he may have been the father of **Archytas of Tarentum**.

HESYCHIUS OF MILETUS (sixth century AD)
Hesychius was an historian whose works were drawn on by **Suda,** particularly on biographical matters.

HICETAS (fifth/fourth century BC?)
Hicetas was a Pythagorean from Syracuse. He appears to have been interested in astronomy and speculated on the movement of the Earth relative to the rest of the universe.

HIERAX [1] (second/third century AD?)
Hierax wrote a work *On Justice*. It is thought that he was a Platonist, perhaps from Egypt.

HIERAX [2] (fourth century AD)
Hierax was a priest from Alexandria Troas who may also have been a philosopher.

HIERAX [3] (fifth century AD)
Hierax came from Alexandria. He went to Athens at the same time as

Ammonius and **Heliodorus of Alexandria** [2], presumably to study under **Proclus** [1] with them.

HIERAX, SILVANUS DOROTHEUS (fourth century AD)
Hierax was the proud possessor of a certificate confirming that he was a philosopher.

HIERIUS [1] (third/fourth century AD)
Hierius was a Neoplatonist, a pupil of **Iamblichus of Chalcis** and the teacher of **Maximus of Ephesus**.

HIERIUS [2] (fourth century AD)
Hierius was probably a Neoplatonist and may have been the brother of **Diogenes of Argos**.

HIERIUS OF ATHENS (fifth century AD)
Hierius was a pupil of **Proclus** [1] and the son of **Plutarch of Athens**. He may have taught **Pamprepius**.

HIEROCLES (second century AD)
Hierocles was a Stoic who probably taught in Athens. A number of his sayings are preserved by **Stobaeus** and seem to come from lectures on ethics. The name of Hierocles is also attached to an introductory work on ethics and the author is generally assumed to be the same person. It deals with self-awareness and regard for others.
[*Routledge Encyclopaedia of Philosophy*, vol. 4]

HIEROCLES, SOSSIANUS (third/fourth century AD)
Hierocles was a governor of Bithynia whose name is associated with a work entitled *The Lover of Truth* in which Christianity was attacked and in which Jesus was compared with **Apollonius of Tyana**. The extent to which he actually wrote the work is disputed and he may have borrowed much of it from elsewhere, perhaps from **Porphyry**. **Macarius of Magnesia** appears to have responded to it.

HIEROCLES OF ALEXANDRIA (fourth/fifth century AD)
Hierocles was a pupil of **Plutarch of Athens**. He wrote a great deal, including a commentary on *The Golden Verses of Pythagoras* that still survives, as well as a treatise on fate and some other shorter works. He was a Platonist, although **Damascius** was critical of the level of his accomplishments in this regard. His version of Platonism certainly seems to have owed much to Pythagoreanism, although the two had long been intertwined. He taught philosophy in Alexandria where **Aeneas of Gaza** and **Theosebius** were two of his pupils. On a visit to Constantinople he found himself arrested, flogged and sent into exile, although eventually he managed to return to Alexandria. Some of his writings have survived.
(David Fideler (ed.), *The Pythagorean Sourcebook*, Grand Rapids, Phanes, 1987)

HIEROCLES OF HYLLARIMA (second century AD?)
Hierocles was a famous athlete before he took up philosophy. He may have been a Stoic.

HIERONYMUS OF RHODES (third century BC)
Hieronymus was a Peripatetic who wrote a number of works both philosophical and literary. According to **Diogenes Laertius**, he was a prominent critic of **Arcesilaus of Pitane**. According to **Clement of Alexandria**, he taught that the good life was one of tranquillity by which, according to **Cicero**, he meant freedom from pain.

HIEROTHEUS (sixth century AD)
Hierotheus was a philosopher and astrologer said to have encouraged the emperor Justinian to pave the floor of Hagia Sophia with silver. The story is doubted, and so is his existence.

HILAPIUS (fifth century AD)
Hilapius was a philosopher from Antioch much admired by **Asclepiodotus of Alexandria**. Some identify him with **Hilarius of Antioch**.

HILARIUS (fourth century AD)
Hilarius was a philosopher from Achaea. Apart from a visit he paid to Antioch in AD 388, when he made the acquaintance of **Libanius** [1], little is known about him.

HILARIUS OF ANTIOCH (fifth century AD)
Hilarius was a man of great learning, but became seriously interested in philosophy only late in life when he had already enjoyed a career in politics. On discovering that his protégé was having an affair with his wife, he gave up his wife, his house and his property and left Antioch. After a period spent travelling, he arrived in Athens. There he tried to become a pupil of **Proclus** [1], but Proclus turned him away on the basis that he led too luxurious a life for a philosopher. He left Athens, and that is the last that is heard of him. Some identify him with **Hilapius**.

HILARIUS OF BITHYNIA (fourth century AD)
Hilarius was a painter and philosopher from Bithynia. He spent his later years in Athens and was a friend of **Eunapius**. He met an unfortunate end in AD 395 when the Goths captured him near Corinth and beheaded him along with his servants.

HIMERIUS (fourth century AD)
Himerius came from Bithynia and was probably the son-in-law of **Nicagoras**. He was primarily known as a sophist but he had a strong interest in Platonism. A number of his known works deal with philosophical themes. He became a close friend of the emperor **Julian**.

HIPPARCHIA OF MARONEA (fourth/third centuries BC)
Hipparchia was a Cynic, the sister of **Metrocles of Maronea**. She became the

wife of **Crates of Thebes** although her parents were opposed to the match, but no one, not even Crates, could dissuade her. She was evidently possessed of a sharp mind and **Suda** says she wrote a book critical of **Theodorus the Atheist**. **Diogenes Laertius** says merely that she put Theodorus down at a banquet.

HIPPARCHIDES OF RHEGIUM (fifth century BC?)
According to **Iamblichus of Chalcis**, Hipparchides was a Pythagorean.

HIPPARCHUS [1] (fifth century BC?)
Hipparchus was the supposed recipient of a letter attributed to **Lysis of Tarentum** in which he was reproached with revealing Pythagorean teachings to people who had not been properly prepared to receive them. It is doubted whether the letter ever had anything to do with Lysis, and many think that Hipparchus is to be identified with **Archippus of Tarentum**, **Hippasus of Metapontum**, or an amalgam of both. His probable non-existence did not prevent a work on tranquillity being attributed to him.
(David Fideler (ed.), *The Pythagorean Sourcebook*, Grand Rapids, Phanes, 1987)

HIPPARCHUS [2] (fourth/third century BC)
Hipparchus was a pupil of **Theophrastus of Eresus**, and one of those to whom Theophrastus bequeathed the Lyceum when he died.

HIPPARCHUS OF NICAEA (second century BC)
Although **Suda** describes Hipparchus as a philosopher, he is best known for his work on astronomy and wrote commentaries on the works of **Aratus of Soli** and **Eratosthenes of Cyrene**.

HIPPARCHUS OF SOLI (first century BC)
Hipparchus was a Platonist and pupil of **Carneades of Cyrene**.

HIPPARCHUS OF STAGIRA (fourth century BC)
Hipparchus was a friend and pupil of **Aristotle** [1]. According to **Suda**, he wrote about the problem of gender in gods, and also on marriage.

HIPPARCHUS OF TROY (first century BC)
Hipparchus was a Platonist and pupil of **Carneades of Cyrene**.

HIPPASUS OF METAPONTUM (sixth/fifth century BC)
Hippasus was one of the early followers of **Pythagoras**. He seems to have been particularly interested in mathematics and musical theory. His name is usually connected with the division of the Pythagoreans into two schools, the *akousmatikoi*, or Hearers, and the *mathematikoi*, or Learners. The precise difference between the two groups is unclear and disputed, but both claimed to stay true to the teachings of Pythagoras. However, one interpretation of the groups' names is that the Hearers kept strictly to what Pythagoras had actually said whereas the Learners sought to take his ideas further. Another is that the Hearers were content with the practical side of Pythagoreanism while the Learners were more inclined to theorise. In any event, it seems Hippasus was

a member of, and perhaps the first leader of, the Learners. It is said he died at sea as a result of daring to reveal secrets of Pythagorean geometry.
(Jonathan Barnes, *Early Greek Philosophy*, Harmondsworth, Penguin, 1987)

HIPPASUS OF SYBARIS (sixth/fifth century BC?)
According to **Iamblichus of Chalcis**, Hippasus was a Pythagorean. He is probably the same person as **Hippasus of Metapontum**.

HIPPIAS OF ELIS (fifth century BC)
Hippias was a sophist who appears as a principal participant in three dialogues of **Plato** [1], including two named after him (although many regard the *Greater Hippias* as the work of someone else). He appears to have had a range of accomplishments. He was probably an authority on mathematics, and according to **Xenophon of Erchia** he had developed an art of memory.
(Rosemary Kent Sprague (ed.), *The Older Sophists*, Indianapolis, Hackett, 2001)
[*Routledge Encyclopaedia of Philosophy*, vol. 4]

HIPPIAS OF PTOLEMAIS (fourth century AD?)
Hippias was a Platonist who went to Egyptian Thebes and wrote his name in the Valley of the Kings.

HIPPO see HIPPON

HIPPOBOTUS (second or first century BC?)
Hippobotus was an historian of philosophy whose works were drawn on by **Diogenes Laertius**. He appears to have written at least two works, one of which traced various philosophical genealogies and another that divided philosophy up into nine schools, those of Megara, Eretria, Cyrene, **Epicurus**, **Anniceris of Cyrene**, **Theodorus the Atheist**, the Stoa, the Old Academy, and the Peripatetic. He refused to identify the Sceptics as a school on the basis that they had no positive doctrines.

HIPPOCLIDES (fourth/third century BC)
Hippoclides was an Epicurean. According to **Valerius Maximus**, he was born on the same day as **Polystratus**, was close to him all his life, and died on the same day as he did.

HIPPOCRATES (third century BC)
Hippocrates was a Peripatetic and one of the executors of the will of **Strato of Lampsacus**.

HIPPOCRATES OF CHIOS (fifth century BC)
Hippocrates was a mathematician and astronomer. He is thought by some to have been a Pythagorean or at least influenced by Pythagorean ideas.

HIPPOCRATES OF COS (fifth/fourth century BC)
Hippocrates was the first great name in Greek medicine. Little is known about him and most if not all of the writings attributed to him were the work of others. He is credited with putting medicine on a new footing based on observation

and reason, in line with the philosophical and scientific thought of his time. The 'Hippocratic Oath' still has a role to play in medicine.
(G.E.R. Lloyd, (ed.), *Hippocratic Writings*, Harmondsworth, Penguin, 1978)
[Michael Boylan, 'Hippocrates', *Internet Encyclopaedia of Philosophy*, www.iep.utm.edu/h/hippocra.htm]

HIPPODAMUS OF MILETUS (fifth century BC)
Hippodamus achieved fame as a town planner, regarded by the Greeks as the originator of the grid layout. One of the cities he designed was Thurium, and he is sometimes referred to as 'the Thurian'. Although it is doubted whether he ever had any connections with Pythagoreanism, fragments of Pythagorean writings on happiness and politics were later attributed to him.
(David Fideler (ed.), *The Pythagorean Sourcebook*, Grand Rapids, Phanes, 1987)

HIPPOLYTUS (second/third century AD)
Hippolytus was a leading theologian in Rome. His book, *The Refutation of all Heresies*, is a valuable source of information on ancient philosophy. He begins by setting out many philosophical theories before accusing heretics of being led astray by them.
(*Ante-Nicene Fathers*, vol. V)

HIPPOMEDON OF ARGOS (fifth century BC?)
According to **Iamblichus of Chalcis**, Hippomedon was a Pythagorean, but he was probably the same person as **Hippomedon of Asine**.

HIPPOMEDON OF ASINE (fifth century BC?)
According to **Iamblichus of Chalcis**, Hippomedon was a Pythagorean. He said that when teaching, **Pythagoras** had presented the basic principles of his philosophy to his students, and then gone on to explain and justify them. However, over time the explanations and arguments had been forgotten, with the result that the basic principles had come to be interpreted differently by different groups of Pythagoreans. He was probably the same person as **Hippomedon of Argos**.

HIPPON (fourth/third century BC?)
Hippon was the supposed recipient of a letter falsely attributed to **Diogenes of Sinope** and appears in it as a Cynic. The letter purports to be a response to a question about death.

HIPPON OF SAMOS (fifth century BC)
Although Hippon is said by **Iamblichus of Chalcis** to have come from Samos, other sources attach him to Rhegium, Croton or Metapontum. However, these are all places with strong connections to Pythagoreanism, so at least his philosophical affiliation seems clear. There are also conflicting testimonies as to what he believed. It seems clear that he put forward a metaphysical theory arguing that moisture (though not necessarily water as such) was a fundamental principle, but some say that he regarded heat as

equally fundamental, and that the action of the one on the other created the world.
(Jonathan Barnes, *Early Greek Philosophy*, Harmondsworth, Penguin, 1987)

HIPPOSTHENES OF CROTON (fifth century BC?)
According to **Iamblichus of Chalcis**, Hipposthenes was a Pythagorean.

HIPPOSTHENES OF CYZICUS
According to **Iamblichus of Chalcis**, Hipposthenes was a Pythagorean.

HIPPOSTRATUS OF CROTON (fifth century BC?)
According to **Iamblichus of Chalcis**, Hippostratus was a Pythagorean.

HIPPOTHALES OF ATHENS (fourth/third century BC)
According to **Diogenes Laertius**, Hippothales was a pupil of **Plato** [1]. He may have been the same Hippothales as the one mentioned in Plato's *Lysis*.

HIPPYS OF RHEGIUM (fifth century BC?)
Hippys was an historian, thought by some to have been a Pythagorean.

HIRTIUS, AULUS (first century BC)
Hirtius was an Epicurean and a correspondent of **Cicero**, although none of their letters survive.

HODIUS OF CARTHAGE
According to **Iamblichus of Chalcis**, Hodius was a Pythagorean.

HONORATUS (second century AD)
Honoratus was a Cynic who took to the habit of wearing a bearskin.

HORACE [QUINTUS HORATIUS FLACCUS] (65-8 BC)
Best known as a poet, as a young man Horace was sent by his father to Athens where he studied philosophy. His time there was cut short when civil war broke out after the assassination of Julius **Caesar**. His works frequently advocate the simple country life, and a number of the letters he published in the last decade of his life indicate a continuing, perhaps renewed, interest in philosophy. Although he had Epicurean friends and was clearly familiar with Epicurean philosophy, it is not clear that he ever belonged to any particular school.
(Horace, *Complete Works*, London, Dent, 1911)

HORAPOLLON (fifth century AD)
Horapollon was the son of **Asclepiades of Alexandria**. He was taught by his father, but showed only a limited aptitude for philosophy. He and his uncle **Heraiscus** were arrested and tortured by the authorities when they were searching for **Isidore of Alexandria**, but they refused to talk. It is possible that he was the same Horapollon as the one who wrote a surviving book on hieroglyphics, but opinions are divided.
(G. Boas (ed.), *The Hieroglyphics of Horapollo*, Princeton, Princeton University Press, 1993)

HORTENSINUS (second century AD?)
Hortensinus was a physician from Rome who also took an interest in, and perhaps taught, philosophy.

HORUS (fourth century AD)
Horus was a Cynic from Egypt who appears in the *Saturnalia* of **Macrobius**. He achieved distinction as a boxer, carrying off a prize at games held in Antioch in AD 364, before turning to philosophy.

HOSTILIANUS (first century AD)
Hostilianus was one of the philosophers the emperor Vespasian banished from Rome in AD 74. He was probably a Stoic.

HOSTILIANUS HESYCHIUS (third century AD)
Hostilianus came from Apamea. He was adopted by **Amelius Gentilianus**, who wrote up notes of the lectures of **Plotinus** for his benefit. He was presumably a Neoplatonist.

HYLLUS OF SOLI (third century AD)
Hyllus was a Stoic who studied under both **Sphaerus of Borysthenes** and **Chrysippus of Soli**.

HYPATIA OF ALEXANDRIA (fourth/fifth century AD)
Hypatia was the daughter of **Theon of Alexandria** and one of the most educated women of her time, being accomplished in mathematics, philosophy and astronomy. A Platonist, amongst her pupils were **Herculianus, Olympius** [2] and **Synesius of Ptolemais**. Much admired by many for her beauty as well as her intelligence, she also attracted enemies and was killed by a Christian mob in AD 415.
[M. Dzielska, *Hypatia the Alexandrian*, Cambridge, Harvard University Press, 1995]

HYPERIDES (fourth century BC?)
Lucian of Samosata wrote about a Cynic called Hyperides who walked around with a club. He may be Lucian's own invention.

HYPERIDES OF ATHENS (fourth century BC)
Acording to **Diogenes Laertius**, Hyperides was an Athenian orator who studied with **Plato** [1]. He joined the revolt against the Macedonians after the death of Alexander the Great, which led to his execution. Accounts differ as to whether his tongue was cut out by the Macedonians, tired of listening to his invectives against them, or by himself in order to make it impossible for him to reveal any secrets.

HYPSAEUS
Stobaeus mentions a philosopher called Hypsaeus, but nothing more is known about him.

❖ **I** ❖

IAMBLICHUS (fourth century AD)
Iamblichus is said to have been a philosopher who dabbled in divination. Some suspect he may never have existed, some identify him with **Iamblichus of Apamea**.

IAMBLICHUS OF APAMEA (fourth century AD)
Iamblichus was the grandson of **Sopater of Apamea**. He was also related to **Libanius** [1], under whom he studied and who acknowledged him as a philosopher with a knowledge of **Pythagoras, Plato** [1] and **Aristotle** [1].

IAMBLICHUS OF CHALCIS (third/fourth century AD)
Iamblichus came from Syria. He studied under **Anatolius** and **Porphyry** and taught philosophy at Apamea for several years where his pupils included **Aedesius, Euphrasius** and **Eustathius** [2]. His son **Ariston** [2] married **Amphicleia**, a follower of **Plotinus**. According to **Eunapius**, Iamblichus believed himself to have magical powers. Whether this is true or not, he is generally credited with taking Neoplatonism in a more occult direction and took a keen interest in ritual as well as reason. Also according to Eunapius, he wrote in a dense and difficult style, and what survives of his writings bears that out. His best known and best preserved works are a life of **Pythagoras** and *Exhortation to Philosophy*. While the historical reliability of *On the Pythagorean Life* is often questionable, its aim, like that of most ancient biographies, was to set an example others might admire and follow. Iamblichus regarded Pythagoras as not only divinely inspired, but also as someone who had drawn on the most ancient teachings of Egypt and Mesopotamia in shaping his philosophy. Those who responded positively to his portrayal of Pythagoras could then read *Exhortation to Philosophy* to find out more about the teachings of his school, as well as those of **Aristotle** [1] and **Plato** [1].

The teachings of Iamblichus himself embraced both the theoretical and the practical. From Porphyry he took the metaphysics of Plotinus but made it more complex. Alongside it he developed a programme for the mystical life that drew heavily on the power of symbols. In the work usually referred to as *On the Mysteries of the Egyptians*, written under the pseudonym of **Abammon**, Iamblichus defends this dimension of Neoplatonism against the sceptical approach taken towards it by Porphyry in his *Letter to Anebo*. Where Porphyry, following Plotinus, emphasised the importance of individual effort in the process of spiritual development, Iamblichus emphasised the importance of seeking and securing the assistance of the divine. As such, he presents himself as both priest and philosopher.

(Iamblichus, *On the Pythagorean Life*, trans. G. Clark, Liverpool, Liverpool University Press, 1989; Iamblichus, *The Exhortation to Philosophy; including the Letters of Iamblichus and Proclus' Commentary on the Chaldean Oracles*, trans. T. Johnson, Grand Rapids, Phanes, 1988; *On the Mysteries*, trans. T. Taylor, Hastings, Chthonios Books, 1989; John Dillon and Lloyd P. Gerson, *Neoplatonic Philosophy: introductory readings*, Indianapolis, Hackett, 2004)
[*Routledge Encyclopaedia of Philosophy*, vol. 4]

IAMBULUS (third century BC?)
Iambulus wrote a utopian novel mentioned by **Diodorus Siculus**. Various attempts have been made to read Cynic and/or Stoic ideas into it.

IARCHAS (first century AD)
According to Flavius **Philostratus**, Iarchas was a philosopher whom **Apollonius of Tyana** met in India. The name is suspiciously similar to *acharya*, an Indian title meaning 'teacher'.

ICCIUS (first century BC)
Iccius was a friend of **Horace**. He appears to have studied Stoicism, as in one of his odes Horace depicts him constantly looking out for works by **Panaetius of Rhodes**. However, the poet also berates his friend for neglecting his studies in favour of more trivial pursuits.

ICCUS OF TARENTUM (sixth/fifth century BC)
Iccus was a celebrated sportsman, a victor in the pentathlon at the Olympic Games. He was admired by **Plato** [1] in *Laws* for his self-discipline, and according to **Iamblichus of Chalcis** he was also a Pythagorean.

ICHTHYAS (fifth/fourth century BC)
According to **Diogenes Laertius**, Ichthyas was a follower of **Euclides of Megara** and perhaps his successor as head of the school. He was admired by **Diogenes of Sinope** and was probably the teacher of **Thrasymachus of Corinth**.

ICOCAESIUS (fifth century AD)
Icocaesius came from Aegae in Cilicia and achieved a reputation as a philosopher, although he was principally known as a sophist. He spent most of his life in Antioch and became a Christian there.

IDAEUS OF HIMERUS (fifth century BC)
According to **Sextus Empiricus**, Idaeus believed that everything in the world was derived from a single element, and that was air.

IDOMENEUS OF LAMPSACUS (fourth/third century BC)
Idomeneus was a pupil of **Epicurus** and married **Batis**. Epicurus wrote his last letter to him, fondly recalling their conversations over the years and commending his attitude towards philosophy. **Diogenes Laertius** refers to a book he wrote about **Socrates** and his circle.

IOBATES
Iobates was a king of Libya who collected Pythagorean texts. He is not to be confused with the Iobates of legend who was a king of Lycia.

IOLAUS OF BITHYNIA (second century BC)
Iolaus was a physician and perhaps an Epicurean.

IOLLAS OF SARDIS (first century BC)
Iollas was a Platonist.

ION OF CHIOS (fifth century BC)
Ion was famous as a poet, but also wrote about philosophy. **Suda** connects him with the name 'Xuthus', leading some to believe that the Pythagorean philosopher **Xuthus** and Ion were one and the same. Some of the few surviving fragments attributed to Ion concern **Pythagoras**, and Ion may have been a Pythagorean whether he was the same person as Xuthus or not.
(Jonathan Barnes, *Early Greek Philosophy*, Harmondsworth, Penguin, 1987)

IONICUS OF SARDIS (fourth century AD)
According to **Eunapius**, Ionicus was trained as a sophist. He also practised medicine and carried out a great deal of experimental research. He studied the different schools of philosophy and was adept at divination.

IPHICLES (fourth century AD)
Iphicles was a philosopher unwillingly sent from Epirus as an envoy to the emperor Valentinian I in AD 375. He may have been the same Iphicles who had taught in Antioch and been a friend of the emperor **Julian**, who described him as a Cynic.

IRENAEUS OF LYONS (second century AD)
Irenaeus was a theologian and bishop of Lyons. His *Against Heresies* is a valuable source of information on gnosticism and other Christian heterodoxies of his time.
(*Ante-Nicene Fathers*, vol. I)

IRENAEUS OF MILETUS (second/first century BC)
Irenaeus was an Epicurean and a pupil of **Demetrius Lacon**.

ISAEUS (first/second century AD)
Isaeus came from Assyria. He had a reputation as a sophist who had led a dissipated youth. However, according to Flavius **Philostratus** in later life he became a model of asceticism and more akin to a philosopher.

ISAGORAS OF THESSALY (first/second century AD)
According to Flavius **Philostratus**, Isagoras was a pupil of **Apollonius of Tyana**.

ISIDORE [1] (first century AD)
Isidore was a Cynic at the time of Nero. On one occasion he publicly harangued the emperor in the street and was banished as a result.

ISIDORE [2] (second century AD)
Isidore was the son and follower of the gnostic teacher **Basilides**. According to **Clement of Alexandria**, he wrote a book *About the Soul*.

ISIDORE [3] (fourth/fifth century AD)
Suda refers to a philosopher called Isidore who was married to **Hypatia of Alexandria**. Although such a marriage is generally thought never to have happened it is not clear whether Isidore himself is also an invention.

ISIDORE OF ALEXANDRIA (fifth/sixth century AD)
Isidore studied philosophy under **Asclepiades of Alexandria** and **Heraiscus**, probably in Alexandria. He also studied under **Proclus** [1] and **Marinus of Neapolis** in Athens. His main interest was in the philosophy of **Plato** [1]. Proclus admired him and encouraged him to pursue the philosophical life, although for some reason he was disturbed by the fact that Isidore had a habit of imitating bird calls. Isidore returned to Egypt with **Sallustius of Syria** and began to teach philosophy. However, he was found guilty of practising magic and decided to go back to Athens. He was there when Proclus died in AD 485 and Marinus became the head of the school. When Marinus died, Isidore succeeded him. **Damascius**, one of his pupils, wrote a biography of him. His main philosophical interests were in metaphysics.

ISIDORE OF GAZA (sixth century AD)
Isidore was one of the group of philosophers who accompanied **Damascius** on his journey to Persia.

ISIDORE OF PELUSIUM (fourth/fifth century AD)
Isidore was a Christian philosopher who became a monk. He became involved in doctrinal disputes in Egypt, and wrote hundreds of letters, many of which have survived.

ISIDORE OF SEVILLE (sixth/seventh century AD)
Isidore was bishop of Seville and an encyclopaedist whose works are a significant source of information about ancient philosophy.

ISIDORE OF THMOUIS (second/third century AD)
Isidore was a Platonist honoured at Delphi.

ISOCRATES (fourth century BC)
Acording to **Suda**, Isocrates was the son of **Amyclus of Heraclea**, and a pupil of **Plato** [1]. He also studied under **Isocrates of Erchia** and continued his work after he died.

ISOCRATES OF ERCHIA (fifth/fourth century BC)
Isocrates studied under **Prodicus of Ceos**, **Theramenes of Stiria** and **Gorgias of Leontini**, but he went on to become critical both of the sophists and of the more abstract thinkers such as **Plato** [1]. He taught oratory to some of the leading figures of his time and became immensely rich. However, because he

distrusted the political ambitions of Philip II of Macedonia, he died, at the age of 98, a disappointed man, perhaps by starving himself to death. (Isocrates (3 vols), trans. G. Norlin, Loeb, 1928-45)

ISSUS (fourth century BC)
Issus is said to have been a pupil of **Aristotle** [1].

ITALICUS, SILIUS (first century AD)
Italicus had a career in politics before retiring to his villa near Neapolis (Naples) where he pursued his interests of philosophy and poetry. He was a Stoic, an acquaintance of **Epictetus** and admired by Pliny the Younger. He starved himself to death because of terminal health problems.

ITANAEUS OF CROTON (fifth century BC?)
According to **Iamblichus of Chalcis**, Itanaeus was a Pythagorean.

IUNCUS (second century AD?)
Iuncus was the author of a philosophical dialogue about old age. Some think he was the son-in-law of Titus Varius **Cailianus**.

❖ J ❖

JACOB (fifth century AD)
Jacob was a physician in Alexandria. He was regarded as a philosopher by some and may have had Pythagorean leanings.

JASON OF ATHENS (second/first century BC)
Jason was a Platonist, a disciple of **Carneades of Cyrene**.

JASON OF NYSA (first century BC)
Jason was the grandson of **Posidonius of Apamea**, succeeding him as head of school when he died. He wrote a history of philosophy, amongst other works.

JASON OF PAROS (second century BC)
Jason was a Platonist, a disciple of **Carneades of Cyrene**.

JOHN (seventh century AD)
John was a philosopher who may have been a correspondent of **Maximus Confessor**.

JOHN CHRYSOSTOM (fourth/fifth century AD)
John studied under **Libanius** [1] and **Diodorus of Tarsus**. He took up the monastic life, then became a preacher, and was eventually made patriarch of Constantinople. A lack of tact on his part coupled with political scheming on that of others led to his deposition, exile and eventual death. Large numbers of

his *Homilies* have survived, mainly dedicated to the literal interpretation of the scriptures.
(*Nicene and Post-Nicene Fathers* series I, vols IX-XIV)

JOHN PHILOPONUS (sixth century AD)
John was a Christian Neoplatonist and a pupil of **Ammonius**. He taught grammar at Alexandria but wrote on many subjects, including philosophy. Some of his writings, including commentaries on the works of **Aristotle** [1], survive, although they are at least in part based on the lectures of Ammonius. John also wrote a book on **Proclus** [1], criticising him, amongst other things, for believing that the world was eternal. His most important work generally was in the field of metaphysics, where he sought to achieve a degree of simplification by dismissing or ignoring whatever could not be proven to exist or lacked explanatory power. He was also a theologian, but his views were rejected as heretical by the Church. His substantial output earned him the nickname of Philoponus, meaning 'industrious'.
(Philoponus, *Corollaries on Place and Void*; *On Aristotle On the Soul*; *On Aristotle On Coming-to-Be and Perishing*; *On Aristotle Physics*; etc: London, Duckworth, 1987-)
[Richard Sorabji (ed.), *Philoponus and the Rejection of Aristotelian Science*, London, Duckworth, 1987]

JOHN OF LYDIA (fifth/sixth century AD)
John came from Philadelphia. In Constantinople he studied the philosophy of **Plato** [1] and **Aristotle** [2] with **Agapius**. However, he was attracted to public life and made his career there. Only when he retired in around AD 552 did he return to his studies and begin to write. He is often referred to as John Lydus.

JOHN OF SCYTHOPOLIS (fifth/sixth century AD)
Some have suggested that John was the author of the works that appeared under the name of **Dionysius the Areopagite**, but this view has little support. Nevertheless there is a connection between the two as John wrote a commentary on them. He argued that they were orthodox from both a Christian and a Platonist point of view. His brother was **George of Scythopolis**.

JOVIAN
Jovian may have written one or more commentaries on the logical works of **Aristotle** [1].

JOVIUS (fourth/fifth century AD)
Jovius was the son of **Paulinus of Nola**. From a letter written to him by his father, it appears he was a keen student of philosophy.

JULIA DOMNA (second/third century AD)
Julia Domna was the wife of emperor Septimius **Severus** and the mother of Caracalla. She had a wide range of interests and helped to make the imperial court a significant centre of culture. It was due to her encouragement that

Flavius **Philostratus** wrote his book about the life of **Apollonius of Tyana**. **Galen** was another who benefited from her support. Her nickname, 'the Philosopher', was a testimony to her intellectual pursuits. She committed suicide in AD 217 after Caracalla had been murdered.

JULIAN (fourth century AD)
Julian was a Platonist who visited Egypt and left an inscription in the tomb of Ramesses VI.

JULIAN, EMPEROR (AD 331-363)
Julian, sometimes known as 'the Apostate', was Roman emperor from AD 361 to 363 before dying at the early age of 32. A naturally gifted scholar, he studied under **Maximus of Ephesus** and had many philosophical friends and acquaintances including Saturninus Secundus **Salutius**, **Priscus** and **Himerius**. Although his philosophical outlook was generally eclectic, he had a special fondness for Platonism and a particular hostility to the Cynics of his day. Although keen to restore paganism to its prior pre-eminence, he nevertheless left Christians in peace, but removed some of their privileges. A number of letters and speeches by Julian, some on philosophical issues but not all thought to be genuine, survive.
(Julian, *The Works of Emperor Julian* (3 vols), trans. W.C. Wright, Loeb, 1913-23)
[Polymnia Athanassiadi, *Julian: an intellectual biography*, London, Routledge, 1992]

JULIAN POMERIUS (fifth/sixth century AD)
Julian came from North Africa but ended his days as a priest in Gaul. He wrote a work on the soul, and another, *The Contemplative Life*, that contains an attack on the Stoic theory of the passions.
(Julianus Pomerius, *The Contemplative Life*, trans. M.J. Suelzer, Westminster, Newman, 1947)
[Marcia L. Colish, *The Stoic Tradition from Antiquity to the Early Middle Ages: 2. Stoicism in Christian Latin thought through the sixth century*, Leiden, Brill, 1990]

JULIAN OF ECLANUM (fourth/fifth century AD)
Julian was a follower of **Pelagius**. As a result he was deposed from his position as bishop of Eclanum in AD 417 and appears to have led an unsettled life thereafter. His works survive in the use made of them by **Augustine** in *Against Julian the Defender of the Pelagian Heresy* and the so-called *Incomplete work against Julian*, left unfinished by Augustine at his death. Julian opposed Augustine's doctrine of original sin and entertained a more positive conception of human nature.
(*Nicene and Post-Nicene Fathers*, vol. V)

JULIAN OF TRALLES (first/second century AD?)
Julian argued that the world's soul dictated the movements of the heavens. It is thought he may have been a Platonist or an Aristotelian.

JULIAN THE CHALDAEAN (first/second century AD) and JULIAN THE THEURGIST (second century AD)
Julian the Chaldaean and Julian the Theurgist were father and son. Little is known about their lives, but they are both associated with a celebrated book known as the *Chaldaean Oracles*. It was claimed to contain divine revelations, many of them attributed to Apollo, although it is generally supposed that they were the work of father or son or both. The revelations contained many instructions of a moral nature, commanding this or prohibiting that. The work seems to have had little impact when it first appeared and might have been forgotten altogether had **Porphyry** not come across it many years later and become convinced that it was genuinely a work of divine wisdom. Between the time of Porphyry and that of **Proclus** [1], the *Chaldaean Oracles* was a favourite book of Neoplatonists, and a number of commentaries on it were produced developing the more magical and cosmological elements of the work.
[Hans Lewy, *Chaldaean Oracles and Theurgy*, Cairo: L'Institut Français d'Archéologie Orientale, 1956]

JULIUS AFRICANUS, SEXTUS (third century AD)
Julius was a Christian author and encyclopaedist. He probably came from Libya, but spent most of his life in Palestine where some say he was born. One of his surviving letters is to **Origen**. **Suda** identifies him as a philosopher.
(*Ante-Nicene Fathers*, vol. VI)

JULIUS CASSIANUS (second century AD)
Julius came from Alexandria and was a follower of **Valentinus**. According to **Clement of Alexandria**, he wrote a work entitled *Concerning Continence and Celibacy* in which he argued for abstinence from sex because it is association with physical bodies that leads souls to corruption.

JULIUS ISIDORUS (first century AD?)
Julius was a philosopher in Egypt.

JULIUS JULIANUS (third century AD?)
Julius was a philosopher from Rome who was killed during an attack on the city.

JUNIOR (fourth century AD)
Junior was a philosopher who wrote, or edited, a short work on geography in about AD 350.

JUNIUS MAURICIUS (first century AD)
Junius was a Stoic and one of the senators who opposed Nero.

JUSTIN (second century AD?)
Justin is cited by **Hippolytus** as the originator of what he regards as a pagan form of gnosticism in which a wide variety of disparate elements are brought together.

JUSTIN MARTYR (second century AD)
Justin came from Neapolis (Nablus). He studied various schools of philosophy before converting to Christianity. He wrote a defence of his religion addressed to the emperor Antoninus Pius, known as the *First Apology*, and a second shorter work in the same vein. His *Dialogue with Trypho* is an argument for the superiority of Christianity over Judaism. His martyrdom in AD 165 is said to have been engineered by **Crescens**.
(*Ante-Nicene Fathers*, vol. I)

JUVENAL [DECIMUS JUNIUS JUVENALIS] (first/second century AD)
Juvenal was renowned for writing poetic satires in which it is possible to identify a variety of philosophical interests if not influences.
(Juvenal, *The Satires of Juvenal*, trans. H. Creekmore, New York, Mentor, 1963)

❖ K ❖

KANUS JULIUS (first century AD)
It is not clear whether Kanus was this person's first or second name, and some refer to him as Canus or Canius. He was a Stoic and one of those who opposed Caligula. When the emperor ordered him to be executed, Kanus is said to have thanked him and to have gone to meet his death calmly and without apparent concern. He was admired for his exemplary demeanour by **Seneca** and **Boethius**.

❖ L ❖

LACHARES OF ATHENS (fifth century AD)
Lachares studied under **Syrianus** [1] with **Proclus** [1], but went on to a career as a sophist. However, according to **Suda** he deserved to be regarded as a philosopher because he led a virtuous life.

LACON OF SAMOS
According to **Iamblichus of Chalcis**, Lacon was a Pythagorean.

LACRATES OF METAPONTUM (fifth century BC?)
According to **Iamblichus of Chalcis**, Lacrates was a Pythagorean.

LACRITUS OF METAPONTUM (fifth century BC?)
According to **Iamblichus of Chalcis**, Lacritus was a Pythagorean.

LACTANTIUS (third/fourth century AD)
Lactantius was a pupil of **Arnobius of Sicca**. He wrote a number of works arguing that Christianity was superior to the philosophy of the schools and that philosophy was of only limited use in the search for truth. However, in his attacks on Epicureanism and Stoicism in particular, he is a useful source of information on the thinking of the schools. He died in AD 326.
(*Ante-Nicene Fathers*, vol. VII)
[Marcia L. Colish, *The Stoic Tradition from Antiquity to the Early Middle Ages: 2. Stoicism in Christian Latin thought through the sixth century*, Leiden, Brill, 1990]

LACYDAS OF METAPONTUM (fifth century BC?)
According to **Iamblichus of Chalcis**, Lacydas was a Pythagorean.

LACYDES (fourth century BC?)
Lacydes was the supposed recipient of two letters falsely attributed to **Diogenes of Sinope** and is assumed to have been a Cynic. According to the letters, he was a Macedonian.

LACYDES OF CYRENE (third century BC)
Lacydes succeeded **Arcesilaus of Pitane** as head of the Academy in around 241 BC. The ancient sources are divided over whether he simply continued the work of his former teacher, or whether he took the Academy in a significantly different direction. He was an acquaintance of **Timon of Phlius** and taught **Chrysippus of Soli** for a while. He became the first head of the Academy to resign his post when he stood down in favour of his chosen successors **Evander of Phocaea** and **Telecles of Phocaea**. He seems to have died soon afterwards from the effects of drinking too much.

LAELIUS, GAIUS (second century BC)
Laelius was a statesman and orator who took a keen interest in philosophy, becoming an acquaintance of the Stoics **Diogenes of Seleucia** and **Panaetius of Rhodes**. He was given the nickname of *sapiens*, 'the sage'. According to **Cicero**, this was because of his self-control. Cicero greatly admired him and featured him in a number of his philosophical works.

LAETUS, OFELLIUS (first century AD)
Laetus was a Platonist from Ephesus.

LAMISCUS OF TARENTUM (fourth century BC)
Lamiscus was a Pythagorean and friend of **Archytas of Tarentum**. When **Plato** [1] ran into trouble in Syracuse in 360 BC, Archytas sent Lamiscus to rescue him.

LAMPRIAS [1] (first/second century AD)
Lamprias was the brother of **Plutarch of Chaeronea**. He appears in some of Plutarch's works and compiled a catalogue of them.

LAMPRIAS [2] (fourth century AD)
Lamprias came from Argos. Along with another philosopher, **Diogenes of Argos**, he was sometimes called upon to act as an envoy for his city.

LAMPRIAS OF ERETRIA (fourth century BC)
Lamprias was a teacher of **Aristoxenus of Tarentum**, although he seems to have taught him music rather than philosophy.

LAODAMAS (third century BC)
Chrysippus of Soli dedicated some works on logic to Laodamas, suggesting he was a pupil or colleague.

LAPHAON OF METAPONTUM (fifth century BC?)
According to **Iamblichus of Chalcis**, Laphaon was a Pythagorean.

LASTHENIA OF MANTINEA or OF ARCADIA (fourth century BC)
Lasthenia is one of two women said to have been students of both **Plato** [1] and **Speusippus**. The other was **Axiothea of Phlius**.

LASUS (sixth century BC)
Lasus was a poet from Hermione. He appears in some lists of the Seven Sages of ancient Greece.

LEANAX OF SYBARIS (fifth century BC?)
According to **Iamblichus of Chalcis**, Leanax was a Pythagorean.

LEANDER OF MILETUS see MAEANDRIUS

LEO see LEON

LEOCRITUS OF CARTHAGE
According to **Iamblichus of Chalcis**, Leocritus was a Pythagorean.

LEOCYDES OF METAPONTUM (fifth century BC?)
According to **Iamblichus of Chalcis**, Leocydes was a Pythagorean.

LEODAMAS or LAODAMAS OF THASOS (fourth century BC)
Leodamas was a mathematician who studied under **Plato** [1].

LEON OF BYZANTIUM (fourth century BC)
Leon was a pupil of either **Plato** [1] or **Aristotle** [1]. He made a career as a sophist, and is sometimes credited with dissuading Philip of Macedonia from attacking his home city, although according to one version of the story his attempts backfired, and the people of Byzantium turned on him, prompting him to commit suicide. He is said to have been extremely fat.

LEON OF METAPONTUM (sixth/fifth century BC)
According to **Iamblichus of Chalcis**, Leon was a Pythagorean. He is probably the Leon to whom **Alcmaeon of Croton** dedicated a book.

LEON OF PELLA (fourth century BC)
Leon wrote a work, purporting to be a letter from Alexander the Great, in which he argued that the Egyptian gods had originally been kings.

LEON OF PHLIUS (sixth century BC)
Leon was the ruler of Phlius and is said to have had many discussions with **Pythagoras** on matters of philosophy.

LEONIDES (fourth century BC)
According to **Suda**, Leonides was a student of **Plato** [1] and assassin of **Clearchus of Heraclea**.

LEONIDES OF RHODES (second century BC)
According to **Strabo of Amaseia**, Leonides was a Stoic.

LEONTION (fourth/third century BC)
Leontion was an Epicurean. She is described by **Diogenes Laertius** as an Athenian prostitute who lived with **Metrodorus of Lampsacus** [2].

LEONTIUS or LEONTICHUS OF CYRENE (third century BC)
Leontius was a member of the Academy when **Lacydes of Cyrene** was its head.

LEONTIUS OF LAMPSACUS (fourth/third century BC)
According to **Diogenes Laertius**, Leontius was a pupil of **Epicurus**, as was his wife **Themista of Lampsacus**. They named their son Epicurus in his honour.

LEONTIUS OF TARENTUM (fifth century BC?)
According to **Iamblichus of Chalcis**, Leontius was a Pythagorean.

LEONTIUS THE HERMIT (fifth/sixth century AD)
Leontius was a Christian philosopher who taught in Constantinople. He is generally regarded as a Platonist, but he was clearly also familiar with the works of **Aristotle** [1]. He believed that the only way to truth was through faith, and that evil had its origin in the soul.

LEOPHANTUS (sixth century BC?)
Leophantus appears in some lists of the Seven Sages of ancient Greece. He probably came from either Ephesus or Lebedus.

LEOPHRON OF CROTON (fifth century BC?)
According to **Iamblichus of Chalcis**, Leophron was a Pythagorean.

LEPIDUS OF AMASTRIS (second century AD)
Lepidus was an Epicurean who studied under **Timocrates of Heraclea**. Amastris appears to have been a substantial centre of Epicureanism in his time.

LEPTINES (third century BC)
Chrysippus of Soli dedicated a book on the use of reason to Leptines, suggesting he was probably a pupil.

LEPTINES OF SYRACUSE (fifth century BC?)
According to **Iamblichus of Chalcis**, Leptines was a Pythagorean.

LESBONAX (first century BC/first century AD)
Lesbonax was a sophist from Mitylene. According to **Suda** he wrote many philosophical works, but this may be a confused reference to an earlier philosopher of the same name who is otherwise unknown. He had a son called Potamo who was a teacher of rhetoric.

LEUCIMUS
According to **Clement of Alexandria**, Leucimus was a Peripatetic who believed that true happiness lay in celebration of what was good. Some believe the name should read 'Lyciscus', but both names are otherwise unknown.

LEUCIPPUS (fifth century BC)
Although he may have been the originator of atomism, little is known about Leucippus. According to **Diogenes Laertius**, some said he had been born in Elea, some in Abdera and yet others in Miletus. The associations with the first two could be explained by the fact that he was said to have been a pupil of **Zeno of Elea** and the teacher of **Democritus of Abdera**. He believed that the universe was infinite in size and contained an infinite number of atoms of different shapes and sizes. Things are formed when atoms join together. The one sentence of his own writing that survives indicates that Leuicippus believed that everything happens because of necessity.
(Jonathan Barnes, *Early Greek Philosophy*, Harmondsworth, Penguin, 1987)
[John Burnet, *Early Greek Philosophy*, London, Macmillan, 1930; *Routledge Encyclopaedia of Philosophy*, vol. 5; Sylvia Berryman, 'Leucippus', *The Stanford Encyclopedia of Philosophy* (Fall 2004 Edition), Edward N. Zalta (ed.), plato.stanford.edu/archives/fall2004/entries/leucippus/]

LIBANIUS [1] (fourth century AD)
Libanius came from Antioch and spent most of his life there apart from a period studying rhetoric in Athens and time spent teaching it in Constantinople and Nicomedia. He was a friend of the emperor **Julian** and supported his attempts to revive paganism, but he was also a friend and teacher of many Christians. His importance lives mainly in his friends, as many of his letters to them survive in which he discusses many issues and ideas of the day.
(Libanius, *Selected Works* (2 vols), trans. A.F. Norman, Loeb, 1969, 1977; Libanius, *Autobiography and Selected Letters* (2 vols), trans. A.F. Norman, Loeb, 1992)

LIBANIUS [2] (fourth century AD)
Libanius was a Pythagorean mentioned by **Libanius** [1].

LIBERALIS, AEBUTIUS (first century AD)
Liberalis was a friend of **Seneca** and lived in Lugdunum (Lyons) at a time when it was destroyed by fire. He was presumably a Stoic and Seneca points out that

although Liberalis was accustomed to dealing with everyday difficulties, he had found an unexpected catastrophe on this scale difficult to handle.

LICENTIUS (fourth century AD)
Licentius was a pupil of **Augustine** from Tagaste. He achieved a modest reputation as a poet before dying young.

LINUS (seventh century BC?)
Linus was a semi-mythical figure, and the stories surrounding him are confused. His name became associated with that of Hermes and with texts of a philosophical and mystical nature. Some reckon him amongst the Seven Sages of ancient Greece. According to **Diogenes Laertius**, he came from Thebes and wrote a poem on the nature of the universe. His name appears on the list of Seven Sages drawn up by **Hippobotus**.

LIVY [TITUS LIVIUS] (first century BC/first century AD)
Although famous as one of the great Roman historians, as a young man Livy studied philosophy, probably in his home town of Patavium (Padua) and even wrote some philosophical dialogues, though they have not survived.

LOBON OF ARGOS (fourth/third century BC)
Lobon produced a book *On Poets* used as a source by **Diogenes Laertius**. It brought together materials from various poets, mainly of the sixth century BC, who had composed pithy wise sayings.

LONGINUS, CASSIUS (third century AD)
Longinus originally came from Syria. As a young man he travelled widely and spent some time in Alexandria as a pupil of **Ammonius Saccas** and others. He then moved to Athens where he became close friends with **Porphyry** and probably his teacher. Longinus was an admirer of the philosophy of **Plotinus**, but also very critical of it. They seem to have had very different views on how to understand **Plato** [1], in particular his Theory of Forms. When Plotinus read the works of Longinus, he expressed admiration for his scholarship but questioned whether he was really a philosopher. He was long thought to be the author of a work on poetry and its production entitled *On the Sublime*, but most now think it was by someone else. Longinus moved to Palmyra to become an adviser to **Zenobia**. It proved to be an unfortunate decision. Zenobia was defeated by the Romans, but whereas she was taken off to Rome, Longinus was executed.
(Aristotle/Horace/Longinus, *Classical Literary Criticism*, trans. T.S. Dorsch, Harmondsworth, Penguin, 1965)

LONGINUS, GAIUS CASSIUS (first century AD)
Longinus was a legal scholar and theorist.

LUCAN [MARCUS ANNAEUS LUCANUS] (first century AD)
Lucan was the nephew of **Seneca** who achieved fame with a poem about the

civil war between Julius **Caesar** and Pompey. Born in Cordoba, he moved to Rome where he studied Stoicism under Lucius Annaeus **Cornutus**.
(Lucan, *Pharsalia*, trans. R. Graves, Harmondsworth, Penguin, 1956)

LUCCEIUS, LUCIUS (first century BC)
Lucceius was an historian and a friend of **Cicero**. Some of Cicero's letters to Lucceius suggest that he may have been an Epicurean.

LUCIAN (second century AD)
Lucian was a gnostic, probably a follower of **Cerdo**.

LUCIAN OF SAMOSATA (second century AD)
Lucian trained as a lawyer in Antioch before studying philosophy in Rome. He claims his teacher there was **Nigrinus**, but some suspect this is his invention and that he in fact studied under **Albinus** [1], a Platonist. He was also influenced by **Demonax**, whose philosophical outlook was more eclectic, although he is generally regarded as a Cynic. Lucian is famous for his essays and dialogues, mostly satirical, many of which have survived. A number of philosophers appear in them, although not all may have existed. As a satirist he is more interested in mocking pomposity and exposing hypocrisy than in advocating any positive doctrine.
(Lucian (8 vols), trans. A.M. Harmon et al., Loeb, 1913-67)
[*Routledge Encyclopaedia of Philosophy*, vol. 5]

LUCILIUS, GAIUS (second century BC)
Lucilius was a poet who wrote many satirical works. Although philosophy was one of his subjects, many of his writings were concerned with social morals and standards of public life. Only fragments survive. **Clitomachus of Carthage** dedicated a work on the suspension of judgment to him.
(*Remains of Old Latin*, vol. 3, trans. E.H. Warmington, Loeb, 1940)

LUCILIUS THE YOUNGER, GAIUS (first century BC)
Lucilius was both a poet and philosopher. He is best known as the friend of **Seneca** to whom 124 letters were written discussing a wide range of issues from a primarily Stoic point of view.

LUCIUS [1] (first century AD)
Lucius was a pupil of **Musonius Rufus**. He was responsible for publishing some of his master's teachings.

LUCIUS [2] (first/second century AD)
Lucius was a Pythagorean who appears as a character in some of the writings of **Plutarch of Chaeronea**. He was a pupil of **Moderatus of Gades**.

LUCIUS [3] (first/second century AD)
Lucius was a Cynic and an opponent of **Favorinus**.

LUCIUS [4] (second century AD)
Lucius was a friend of **Herodes Atticus**. A pupil of **Musonius of Tyre**, he was renowned for his learning and wit.

LUCRETIUS [TITUS LUCRETIUS CARUS] (first century BC)
Lucretius is known only for his long poem *On the Nature of Things* in which he sets out the doctrines of Epicureanism. As the only substantial systematic work of Epicureanism to survive from antiquity, it is a work of considerable significance. Unfortunately, it is difficult to judge how accurate an account it is of the school's teachings as there is little with which to compare it. However, the Epicureans tended towards conservatism in doctrinal matters and so it is unlikely Lucretius strayed far from orthodoxy. The first two books of the poem are mainly concerned with expounding atomism, the middle two are concerned with human nature and knowledge, and the last two analyse a number of natural phenomena.
(Lucretius, *On the Nature of Things*, trans. M.F. Smith, Indianapolis, Hackett, 2001; classics.mit.edu/Browse/browse-Carus.html)
[*Routledge Encyclopaedia of Philosophy*, vol. 5; David Simpson, 'Lucretius', *Internet Encyclopaedia of Philosophy*, www.iep.utm.edu/l/lucretiu.htm]

LUCULLUS, LUCIUS LICINIUS (second/first century BC)
Lucullus was a rich Roman who made a career in public and military life. He was a friend and pupil of **Antiochus of Ascalon**, although his philosophical tastes appear to have been quite eclectic. He spend his last years quietly going insane.

LYCANDER OF NICAEA (second century BC?)
Lycander was a Stoic, commemorated by an inscription in his home town.

LYCISCUS see LEUCIMUS

LYCO [1] (third century BC)
Lyco came from Troy and succeeded **Strato of Lampsacus** as head of the Lyceum. Because of the sweetness of his voice, some called him Glyco, meaning 'sweet'. He led the Lyceum for 44 years but seems to have achieved relatively little during this time. According to **Diogenes Laertius**, he was an accomplished wrestler. When he died he was probably succeeded by **Ariston of Ceos**.

LYCO [2] (third century BC)
Lyco was a nephew of Lyco [1]. Mentioned in his uncle's will, it seems he studied at the Lyceum.

LYCO OF IASUS (fourth century BC?)
Lyco was a Pythagorean who dressed like a beggar. He wrote an account of the life of **Pythagoras**.

LYCO OF NICAEA (second century BC)
Lyco was a Stoic and a disciple of **Panaetius of Rhodes**.

171

LYCO OF TARENTUM (fifth century BC?)
According to **Iamblichus of Chalcis**, Lyco was a Pythagorean.

LYCOMEDES (third century BC)
Lycomedes was one of those to whom **Lyco** [1] bequeathed the Lyceum on his death. He had presumably been a pupil there for some time.

LYCON see LYCO

LYCOPHRON [1] (fifth/fourth century BC)
Lycophron was a pupil of **Gorgias of Leontini**. Primarily a sophist, he nevertheless appears to have taken positions on philosophical matters. For example, he declared that being from a noble family was worthless in itself as its value depended solely on the esteem in which the family was held.
(Rosemary Kent Sprague (ed.), *The Older Sophists*, Indianapolis, Hackett, 2001)

LYCOPHRON [2] (fourth/third century BC)
According to **Plutarch of Chaeronea**, Lycophron was an Epicurean. **Leontius of Lampsacus** corresponded with him.

LYCURGUS OF ATHENS (fourth century BC)
Lycurgus was a statesman who was a pupil of **Plato** [1] for a while.

LYDUS (second century AD?)
Porphyry mentions a Lydus who appears to have been the author of gnostic treatises in circulation in his time.

LYNCAEUS OF SAMOS (fourth/third century BC)
Best known as a grammarian, Lyncaeus was a pupil of **Theophrastus of Eresus**. His brother was **Douris of Samos**.

LYRAMNUS OF PONTUS
According to **Iamblichus of Chalcis**, Lyramnus was a Pythagorean.

LYSIADES OF CATANA (fifth century BC?)
According to **Iamblichus of Chalcis**, Lysiades was a Pythagorean.

LYSIBIUS OF TARENTUM (fifth century BC?)
According to **Iamblichus of Chalcis**, Lysibius was a Pythagorean.

LYSIMACHUS [1] (fourth/third century BC)
Lysimachus was a pupil of **Theophrastus of Eresus**.

LYSIMACHUS [2] (first century BC)
Lysimachus was a follower of **Antiochus of Ascalon**.

LYSIMACHUS [3] (second/third century AD)
Lysimachus was a Stoic who taught **Amelius Gentilianus**. As Amelius came from Etruria, that may have been the home of Lysimachus as well.

LYSIMACHUS [4] (fourth century AD?)
Lysimachus was a Platonist known to have visited, or come from, Egypt. He wrote his name inside the tomb of Ramesses VI in the Valley of the Kings.

LYSIMACHUS OF COS (second/first century BC)
Lysimachus was a physician who wrote a book criticising the work of **Demetrius Lacon.**

LYSIS (fourth/third century BC?)
Lysis was the supposed recipient of a letter falsely attributed to **Crates of Thebes**. Lysis is addressed as a fellow Cynic and reprimanded for drinking too much.

LYSIS OF TARENTUM (fifth/fourth century BC)
Lysis was a Pythagorean. When the Pythagoreans were being persecuted in Italy, he escaped and made his way to Thebes. There he taught **Epaminondas,** the city's military leader. A letter to **Hipparchus** [1] long attributed to Lysis is almost certainly not by him.

❖ M ❖

MACARIUS OF MAGNESIA (third/fourth century AD?)
Macarius wrote a work entitled *Apocriticus* in which he sought to defend Christianity against the objections of Neoplatonists.

MACEDO (second century AD)
Macedo was a philosopher and a friend of **Aulus Gellius.**

MACEDO, CALPURNIUS COLLEGA (fourth century AD)
Macedo came from Antioch in Pisidia. An inscription commemorates him as a philosopher in the tradition of **Plato** [1] and **Socrates.**

MACEDONIUS (fourth century AD)
Macedonius had a book dedicated to him by **Iamblichus of Chalcis** and was probably one of his followers.

MACEDONIUS OF CYRRHUS (fourth century AD)
Macedonius was once a pupil of **Libanius** [1], who says he was a philosopher. He appears to have been in demand as an envoy representing his home town of Cyrrhus on a number of occasions.

MACROBIUS, AMBROSIUS THEODOSIUS (fourth/fifth century AD)
Macrobius is best known as the author of *Saturnalia*, a semi-philosophical dialogue that covers a wide range of topics, although its principal one is the poetry of **Virgil**. However, there are also some reflections on religion and

matters of psychology. More interesting philosophically is a commentary he wrote for his son on the 'Dream of Scipio' by **Cicero** (an extract from his *Republic*). In it he explores the nature of the soul, mainly from a Neoplatonist point of view. The soul's immortality and divine nature are discussed in the light not only of philosophy but also in that of the science of his day.

(P.V. Davies, *Macrobius: The Saturnalia*, New York, University Presses of California, Columbia and Princeton, 1984)

MAEANDRIUS (fourth/third century BC)
Maeandrius was a source used by **Diogenes Laertius** in his account of **Thales of Miletus**. He may be the same person as Leander of Miletus who wrote a history of his home town.

MAGNILLA (first or second century AD)
Magnilla was a philosopher in her own right as well as being either the wife or daughter of another. She came from Apollonia in Mysia where she was commemorated in an inscription.

MAGNUS OF NISIBIS (fourth century AD)
According to **Eunapius**, Magnus drew on the work of **Aristotle** [1] in his profession as a healer, apparently by emphasising the role of the will in causing and curing sickness. He was also a sophist and taught at Alexandria, where he enjoyed a considerable reputation. **Libanius** [1] wrote to him on more than one occasion.

MALCHION (third century AD)
Malchion was a Christian scholar from Antioch, a man of great learning skilled in logic and rhetoric.

MALION OF DARDANIA
According to **Iamblichus of Chalcis**, Malion was a Pythagorean.

MAMMARION (fourth/third century BC)
Mammarion was a follower of **Epicurus**. It is said she was a prostitute but this was not an unusual accusation to be made against Epicurean women.

MANDANIS (fourth century BC)
Mandanis was one of the Indian philosophers Alexander the Great met in Taxila. He was said to be familiar with the thought of **Pythagoras, Socrates** and **Diogenes of Sinope**. He is sometimes known as Dandamis.

MANDROLYTUS OF PRIENE (sixth century BC)
Mandrolytus was a pupil of **Thales of Miletus**.

MANI or MANES or MANICHAEUS (third century AD)
Mani was a philosopher and prophet. His thought was shaped by various influences, including those to which he was exposed in Persia and India. The central idea guiding the movement he founded was a cosmic ethical dualism in which the world was seen as a stage on which the struggle between good

and evil was played out. Evil is associated, more or less closely, with both darkness and matter. All else follows from this. Mani taught a form of asceticism that included vegetarianism and the avoidance of procreation. Even the building of houses was frowned upon as this had clear connotations of making oneself at home in the physical world. However, these requirements only applied in full to those who devoted themselves wholly to the movement. There was a less demanding regime for lay members, one of whom, for nine years, was **Augustine**. Mani sought to integrate elements from Christianity, Buddhism and Zoroastrianism into a single philosophy of life with himself as its prophet. What Buddhists felt about this is not known, but Christianity rejected him as a gnostic heretic and Zoroastrians appear to have instigated his execution in AD 277.

[Hans Jonas, *The Gnostic Religion*, Boston, Beacon, 1963]

MANILIUS, MARCUS (first century AD)
Manilius was a Stoic, astronomer and poet. He wrote a long poem on astronomical matters, part of which survives. He took an extreme position on the subject of fate, believing that not even thoughts were exempt from its influence.
(Manilius, *Astronomica*, trans. G.P. Goold, Loeb, 1977)

MARAS (fifth century AD)
Maras came from Beroea in Syria. He was widely respected for his generosity and the kind of life he led, as a result of which he was given the nickname 'the Just'.

MARCELLA (third century AD)
Marcella was the wife of **Porphyry**. When he married her she was a widow with five children. He dedicated a book to her, but the extent of her interest in philosophy is unclear.

MARCELLINUS (fifth century AD)
Marcellinus was a friend of **Anthemius** [2]. He was probably a Neoplatonist and may have been a pupil of **Sallustius of Syria**.

MARCELLUS, MARCUS CLAUDIUS [1] (first century BC)
Marcellus was a pupil of **Cratippus of Pergamum**. He had a career in public life and was one of those opposed to Julius **Caesar**. Caesar pardoned him but he was murdered in Piraeus when on his way back to Rome in 45 BC. He was buried in the grounds of the Academy.

MARCELLUS, MARCUS CLAUDIUS [2] (first century BC)
Marcellus was the nephew of the emperor Augustus and, until his death, his chosen heir. He spent some time as a pupil of **Nestor of Tarsus**.

MARCELLUS, TULLIUS
Marcellus came from Carthage. He wrote about logic, including a book on syllogisms.

MARCIANUS (second century AD)
Marcianus was a philosophy teacher to **Marcus Aurelius**.

MARCION (second century AD)
Marcion came from Pontus and was probably a pupil of **Cerdo**. According to **Hippolytus**, he was also influenced by the philosophy of **Empedocles of Acragas**. He distinguished between the wrathful God of Judaism and the loving God of Christianity, leading him to put together a canon of texts from which what is now known as the Old Testament was excluded altogether. The church's response to this led to the first recognisable Bible. He espoused a form of ethical dualism and advocated an ascetic existence.
(Arland J. Hultgren and Steven A. Haggmark (eds), *The Earliest Christian Heretics*, Minneapolis, Fortress Press, 1996)

MARCUS [1] (second/third century AD)
According to **Hippolytus**, Marcus was a gnostic and a follower of **Valentinus**. Hippolytus took the view that the philosophical system of Marcus was based on Pythagoreanism because of the importance it attached to the significance of numbers. Hippolytus also accused Marcus of being both a sorcerer and a fraud.

MARCUS [2] (third century AD)
There is a tradition, seeming to date from a significantly later period, that Marcus was a philosopher who ruled the Roman empire between the death of Gordian III in AD 244 and the accession of Philip the Arab, usually thought to have taken place that same year. There may have been a philosopher by that name in Rome at that time, but there is no evidence that such a person ever ruled anything.

MARCUS AURELIUS (AD 121-180)
Marcus Aurelius was the adopted son of Antoninus Pius. Antoninus had also adopted Lucius **Verus**, and after he died in AD 161 Marcus and Verus jointly ruled the empire. When Verus died, Marcus continued to rule alone. His own death marks the end of a period regarded as a golden age in Roman imperial history when a series of childless emperors adopted their chosen successors. Marcus had the misfortune of having a natural son, Commodus, who succeeded him but proved inadequate to the task.

According to his own testimony, it was **Diognetus** who first interested Marcus in philosophy and encouraged him to attend the lectures of **Bacchius of Paphos**, **Tandasis** and **Marcianus**. He also studied with **Herodes Atticus**, Marcus Cornelius **Fronto**, **Apollonius of Chalcedon** and **Sextus of Chaeronea**. However, perhaps the strongest influence on him was Quintus Junius **Rusticus** for whom Marcus had particular respect and affection. All these people and more receive a mention in the book usually known as *Meditations*, although its title is more correctly translated as *To Himself*.

The book, written while the emperor was on a military campaign, is a series of reflections both on his own life and on life in general. Through them Marcus constantly reminds himself of the ideals of conduct and thought to which he aspires. Although these ideals have their strongest roots in Stoicism, he is prepared to take his inspiration from wherever he can find it. For this reason his brand of Stoicism is sometimes seen as a rather eclectic one. This is mirrored in the fact that in AD 176 he established professorial chairs in Platonism, Aristotelianism and Epicureanism as well as Stoicism in Athens. Curiously, given his interest in philosophy, he delegated the task of deciding who should be appointed to these chairs to **Herodes Atticus**.

(Marcus Aurelius, *Meditations*, trans. M. Staniforth, Harmondsworth, Penguin, 1964, and many other editions; classics.mit.edu/Browse/browse-Antoninus.html)

[Anthony R. Birley, *Marcus Aurelius: a biography*, London, Routledge, 2000; R.B. Rutherford, *The Meditations of Marcus Aurelius: a study*, Oxford, Clarendon Press, 1989; Pierre Hadot, *The Inner Citadel: the Meditations of Marcus Aurelius*, trans. M. Chase, Cambridge, Harvard University Press, 1998; John Sellars, 'Marcus Aurelius', *Internet Encyclopaedia of Philosophy*, www.iep.utm.edu/m/marcus.htm]

MARCUS OF SAMNIUM (second century BC)
Marcus was a Stoic and a pupil of **Panaetius of Rhodes**.

MARIA OF EGYPT (second century AD?)
Maria was primarily an alchemist and appears to have been responsible for technical developments in her field. She was also interested in philosophy, especially Hermeticism.

MARINUS OF NEAPOLIS [Nablus] (fifth century AD)
Marinus was originally a Samaritan but later became a pagan. He studied under **Proclus** [1] and succeeded him as head of the Platonist school in Athens when he died. He is known to have produced a commentary on the *Parmenides* of **Plato** [1], and a biography of Proclus, but otherwise he seems to have written little. Before his death he appointed **Isidore of Alexandria** as his successor.

MARIUS VICTORINUS AFER (third/fourth century AD)
Marius was a teacher of rhetoric before he converted to Christianity in later life. As a pagan he wrote commentaries on **Cicero**, **Porphyry** and **Aristotle** [1], and translated **Plotinus** into Latin. He does not appear to have affiliated himself to any school in particular, but was familiar with all of the leading ones. As a Christian he made use of his wide knowledge of philosophy in constructing arguments against those whom he considered heretics, as well as in the development of orthodox Christian theology.

[A.H. Armstrong (ed.), *The Cambridge History of Later Greek and Early Medieval Philosophy*, Cambridge, Cambridge University Press, 1970]

MARSANES (second/third century AD?)
Marsanes was a gnostic, perhaps from Syria. A work by him has survived in

badly damaged form that indicates the influence of Platonism. It is significantly less radically dualistic than many other gnostic texts.
(James M. Robinson (ed.), *The Nag Hammadi Library*, Leiden, Brill, 1977)

MARTIANUS CAPELLA (fifth century AD)
Martianus was the author of an encyclopaedic work covering all of the seven traditional liberal arts (grammar, dialectic, rhetoric, geometry, arithmetic, astronomy and music). The sections dealing with these are preceded by others articulating a myth concerning the marriage of Philology and Mercury, hence the book's title, the *Philologia*. Although Martianus seems to have been an eclectic pagan, there are strong elements of Neoplatonism running through the myth and later centuries came to regard it as an important Platonist text.
(W.H. Stahl and R.W. Johnson, *Martianus Capella and the Seven Liberal Arts* (2 vols), New York, Columbia University Press, 1971, 1977)

MARTIN OF BRAGA (sixth century AD)
Martin was a Christian who believed that Christianity and Stoicism were in harmony with each other, at least as far as ethics was concerned. He wrote a treatise on the cardinal virtues, borrowing heavily from **Seneca** and emphasising the importance of practical wisdom above all other virtues.
(Martin of Braga, *Formula vitae honestae*, trans. Barlow, Washington, Catholic University of America Press, 1969)
[Marcia L. Colish, *The Stoic Tradition from Antiquity to the Early Middle Ages: 2. Stoicism in Christian Latin thought through the sixth century*, Leiden, Brill, 1990]

MATIUS, GAIUS (first century BC)
Matius was a friend of both **Cicero** and Julius **Caesar**. He may also be identical with the Matius who wrote on food and trees. He took an interest in philosophy and some think he was an Epicurean. However, in a letter to Cicero he expressed a desire to retire to Rhodes, a place more associated with Stoicism at that time.

MATRIS (fourth century BC)
Matris was a pupil of **Plato** [1], as was his son **Chion**.

MAXIMIANIUS (sixth century AD)
Maximianus is said to have been a philosopher and astrologer who encouraged the emperor Justinian to pave the floor of Hagia Sophia with silver. It probably never happened and he may never have existed.

MAXIMUS [1] (first/second century AD)
Maximus was an Epicurean and a friend of Pliny the Younger. He was sent by Rome to reform the constitutions of Greek cities. He was an acquaintance of **Epictetus** and a supposed discussion between them is preserved in *Discourses* III.7.
(Epictetus, *The Discourses, The Handbook, Fragments* (ed. C. Gill), London, Dent, 1995)

MAXIMUS [2] (third century AD)
Maximus came from a poor background but went on to study philosophy, which he appears to have been determined to put to practical uses. He helped to defend Marcianopolis (presumably his home town) from an attack by the Goths in AD 248.

MAXIMUS [3] (fourth century AD)
Maximus came from Lycia and taught philosophy in Athens where **Severus** [2] was one of his pupils.

MAXIMUS [4] (fourth century AD)
Maximus was a philosopher from Constantinople who may have been the father of **Euclides**. It is also possible that he was a Christian.

MAXIMUS [5] (fourth century AD)
Maximus studied philosophy under **Hierius** [1].

MAXIMUS [6] (fourth century AD)
Maximus was a philosopher praised by **Symmachus** for his knowledge of the arts and the way he lived.

MAXIMUS [7] (fourth/fifth century AD)
Maximus was a pagan philosopher to whom **Isidore of Pelusium** wrote one of his many letters.

MAXIMUS HERO OF ALEXANDRIA (fourth century AD)
Maximus claimed to be both a Cynic and a Christian. After a dubious early career in Alexandria, he moved to Constantinople where he managed to get himself appointed bishop in AD 380. However, his supporters soon abandoned him and he was deposed. **Gregory of Nazianzus** composed an oration praising his philosophical accomplishments before turning against him.

MAXIMUS OF AEGAE (first century AD)
Maximus was a source used by Flavius **Philostratus** for his life of **Apollonius of Tyana**. Apollonius spent some time in Aegae as a young man, and it was on this period of his life that Maximus was able to shed light. Maximus himself is said to have been responsible for the emperor's Greek correspondence, the emperor in question probably being **Tiberius**.

MAXIMUS OF BYZANTIUM
Suda mentions a Maximus of Byzantium or Epirus, but the description given seems to fit **Maximus of Ephesus** so closely that they are probably one and the same person.

MAXIMUS OF EPHESUS (fourth century AD)
Maximus was a Neoplatonist and a teacher of **Julian** before he became emperor. When he did, he invited Maximus to join him in Constantinople. He was present at Julian's death-bed in AD 363, where they discussed the

immortality of the soul. He decided to stay in Constantinople but subsequently fell foul of the emperor Valens and was sent back to Ephesus to be beheaded in AD 371. He was recognised as a man of considerable learning. Philosophically he favoured the more mystical Neoplatonism of **Iamblichus of Chalcis** passed on to him by **Hierius** [1]. He wrote a number of works, perhaps including commentaries on **Aristotle** [1], but nothing survives. His brothers were **Claudianus of Smyrna** and **Nymphidianus of Smyrna**.

MAXIMUS OF MADAURA (fourth century AD)
Maximus was a teacher of grammar. He exchanged letters with **Augustine** in which they discussed monotheism, with Maximus articulating a pagan version of it.

MAXIMUS OF NICAEA (third/fourth century AD)
Maximus was a Neoplatonist who wrote a commentary on the *Republic* of **Plato** [1].

MAXIMUS OF TYRE (second century AD)
Little is known of Maximus except for the lectures he gave in Rome between AD 180 and AD 185, some of which have survived. They cover a range of philosophical and in particular ethical topics. They are not particularly sophisticated in philosophical terms, although this may reflect the abilities of the audience for which they were intended as much as those of Maximus himself. Opinions are divided as to which school, if any, he belonged to and the influences of Platonism, Stoicism and Cynicism have all been detected.
[John Dillon, *The Middle Platonists 80 BC to AD 220*, London, Duckworth, 1996]

MAXIMUS THE CONFESSOR (sixth/seventh century AD)
Maximus held high office in the Byzantine empire before becoming a monk. He became deeply involved in the theological disputes of the day, as a result of which he was at various times exiled and tortured. Philosophically, his most interesting work involved an interpretation of history that saw its purpose as making humanity divine.
[A.H. Armstrong (ed.), *The Cambridge History of Later Greek and Early Medieval Philosophy*, Cambridge, Cambridge University Press, 1970]

MEDIUS [1] (fourth century BC)
Medius was a pupil of **Chrysippus of Cnidus** and the teacher of **Erasistratus of Ceos**. His name sometimes appears as Metrodorus. He married **Pythias**, the daughter of **Aristotle** [1], but his interests were primarily medical rather than philosophical.

MEDIUS [2] (third century AD)
Medius was a Stoic and a contemporary of **Plotinus**. He wrote a number of books, but nothing is known of them.

MEGALOPHANES see DEMOPHANES

MEGASTHENES (fourth/third century BC)
Megasthenes was an historian who wrote about Asia, and especially India. According to **Clement of Alexandria**, he believed that both Indian and Jewish philosophers held the same views about nature as did their Greek counterparts.

MEGILLUS (fifth/fourth century BC?)
Megillus was a Pythagorean who wrote a book about numbers. He may be the same person as the Megillus of Sparta who appears in the *Laws* of **Plato** [1].

MEGISTIAS OF METAPONTUM (fifth century BC?)
According to **Iamblichus of Chalcis**, Megistias was a Pythagorean.

MELAMPUS (third century BC?)
Melampus was perhaps a philosopher and certainly had a special interest in divination. Some short works by him have survived dealing with divination by moles (the blemishes, not the animals) and twitches. The name may be a pseudonym adopted from a celebrated legendary seer. (www.isidore-of-seville.com/astdiv/melampus.html)

MELANIPPIDES OF TARENTUM (fourth century BC)
Melanippides was the author of a number of tragedies. He appears to have practised a relatively ascetic version of Pythagoreanism.

MELANIPPUS OF CYRENE
According to **Iamblichus of Chalcis**, Melanippus was a Pythagorean.

MELANTAS
Melantas had a book on **Plato** [1] dedicated to him by **Boethus** [1]. He was presumably a Platonist.

MELANTES (fourth/third century BC)
Melantes, along with his brother **Pancreon**, was a follower of **Theophrastus of Eresus** and a major beneficiary in his will.

MELANTHIUS OF RHODES (second century BC)
Melanthius was a Platonist, a contemporary, and perhaps pupil, of **Carneades of Cyrene**. **Aeschines of Neapolis** was one of his pupils.

MELEAGER (third century BC)
Chrysippus of Soli dedicated two books on logic to Meleager, suggesting he was either a colleague or a pupil.

MELEAGER OF GADARA (second/first century BC)
Meleager was a Cynic and a poet, the author of a number of philosophical satires. He also wrote and collected epigrams.

MELESIAS OF METAPONTUM (fifth century BC?)
According to **Iamblichus of Chalcis**, Melesias was a Pythagorean.

MELISIPPE (fourth century BC?)
Melisippe was the supposed recipient of a letter falsely attributed to **Diogenes of Sinope** and is assumed to have been a Cynic.

MELISIPPUS (fourth century BC?)
Melisippus was the supposed recipient of two letters falsely attributed to **Diogenes of Sinope** and is assumed to have been a Cynic. In one of the letters, Diogenes recounts the beating he received from drunk Athenian youths.

MELISSA OF SAMOS
The name of Melissa is attached to some surviving fragments of Pythagorean writings.

MELISSUS OF SAMOS (fifth century BC)
In 441 BC Melissus made his mark on history by leading the people of Samos to victory in a sea battle against the Athenians. According to **Diogenes Laertius**, he was a pupil of **Parmenides of Elea**. Although some question the literal truth of this, the strongest philosophical influence on him was certainly Parmenides, but he may also have been acquainted with **Heraclitus of Ephesus** and Pythagoreanism. Beginning from the proposition that it was impossible for something to emerge from nothing, he developed a theory of the cosmos that held it to be a changeless unity, homogeneous, eternal and infinite. He also argued that it could not be physical, but it is not clear quite what kind of non-physical thing he conceived it to be. All change, including any kind of motion, he regarded as illusory, and our belief in the reality of any such change he attributed to the unreliability of the senses.
(Jonathan Barnes, *Early Greek Philosophy*, Harmondsworth, Penguin, 1987)
[John Burnet, *Early Greek Philosophy*, London, Macmillan, 1930]

MELITIUS OF PONTUS (third/fourth century AD)
According to **Eusebius of Caesarea**, Melitius was a man of exceptional learning and scholarship, accomplished in all areas of learning, which can hardly have excluded philosophy.

MELITO (second century AD)
Melito was bishop of Sardis and wrote a defence of Christianity addressed to **Marcus Aurelius**. He may have been a eunuch.

MEMMIUS, GAIUS (first century BC)
Memmius is an enigmatic character. **Lucretius** dedicated his great Epicurean poem to him and he acquired the ruins of the house in Athens that had once been the home of **Epicurus**. However, it is not at all clear that he was ever an Epicurean himself and he fell out with **Patro** because he would not donate the house to the school.

MENAECHMUS (fourth century BC)
Menaechmus probably came from Alopeconnessus and was a pupil of **Eudoxus of Cnidus**. He was a Platonist and wrote a number of philosophical works,

including a commentary on the *Republic* of **Plato** [1]. He was also noted for his work in geometry.

MENANDER [1] (fourth/third century BC)
Known as a writer of comic dramas, Menander also had a serious side. He probably studied under **Theophrastus of Eresus** and is known to have been a friend of both **Demetrius of Phalerum** and **Epicurus**. He died while swimming.

MENANDER [2] (first/second century AD)
Menander was a philosopher to whom Marcianus **Aristides** is thought to have written.

MENANDER DRYMUS
Menander was a pupil of **Diogenes of Sinope**. He was apparently also a great admirer of Homer. The meaning of his nickname Drymus, meaning 'oak wood', is wholly obscure.

MENECLES (first century BC)
Menecles was a Sceptic, probably from Cyme. An inscription found in the area claimed that he had attained the Sceptic's goal of tranquillity.

MENECRATES [1] (third century BC)
Chrysippus of Soli dedicated a book on logic to Menecrates, suggesting he was either a colleague or a pupil.

MENECRATES [2] (second/first century BC)
Menecrates was a pupil of **Antiochus of Ascalon**.

MENECRATES OF ELEA (fourth century BC)
Menecrates was a pupil of **Xenocrates of Chalcedon**.

MENEDEMUS OF ERETRIA (fourth/third century BC)
Menedemus first encountered philosophy when he visited the Academy in Athens during a period of military service in neighbouring Megara. This was enough to convince him of where his future lay. His friend **Asclepiades of Phlius** persuaded him to study first under **Stilpo**, and then at the school of Elis at a time when **Anchipylus** and **Moschus** may have been its heads. Subsequently Asclepiades and Menedemus took over the school and moved it to Eretria, from which it thereafter took its name. According to **Diogenes Laertius**, Menedemus was a rather chaotic teacher although he had a sharp mind. Exactly what he taught is unclear, and some apparently regarded him as a Cynic. The only positive doctrine explicitly attributed to him is that there is only one virtue, although it may be called by different names. The school also acquired a reputation for skill in argument and **Arcesilaus of Pitane** is said to have been influenced by its work in this direction. Menedemus enjoyed parties and became popular in Eretria to the point where he was asked to govern it. For reasons that are unclear, he seems to have died at the court of **Antigonus Gonatas**.

MENEDEMUS OF LAMPSACUS (third century BC)
Menedemus was a Cynic, a pupil first of **Colotes of Lampsacus** and then of **Echecles of Ephesus**. According to **Diogenes Laertius**, he claimed to have come from Hades to observe and report back on human immorality.

MENEDEMUS OF PYRRHA (fourth century BC)
Menedemus was a pupil of **Plato** [1]. He sought to become head of the Academy in 339 BC when **Speusippus** died, but **Xenocrates of Chalcedon** was chosen instead.

MENEDEMUS OF RHODES (fourth century BC?)
Menedemus is said to have been an Aristotelian and perhaps head of the Peripatetic school for a time. However, it is possible that he is to be identified with **Eudemus of Rhodes**.

MENELAUS (fourth century BC?)
Menelaus belonged to the school of Megara and may have been a pupil of **Eubulides of Miletus**.

MENEPHYLUS (first/second century AD)
Menephylus was a Peripatetic and friend of **Plutarch of Chaeronea**.

MENESTOR OF SYBARIS (fifth century BC?)
According to **Iamblichus of Chalcis**, Menestor was a Pythagorean.

MENESTRATUS (fourth/third century BC)
Menestratus was an Epicurean, a pupil of **Metrodorus of Lampsacus** [2].

MENEXENE (fourth/third century BC)
According to **Clement of Alexandria**, Menexene was the daughter of **Diodorus Cronus** and an accomplished philosopher in her own right.

MENEXENUS (fifth/fourth century BC)
Menexenus was a follower of **Socrates**, and one of those present at his death. **Plato** [1] named a dialogue after him.

MENIPPUS OF GADARA (third century BC)
Menippus was born in Gadara, spent many years in Pontus, and ended up as a citizen of Thebes. He was a Cynic, a pupil of **Crates of Thebes** and perhaps also of **Metrocles of Maronea**. He was a slave, but secured his freedom. He then went on to make a large fortune but committed suicide by hanging himself when he was swindled out of it. A number of books were attributed to him, although there were rumours that other people had written them. The works, as listed by **Diogenes Laertius**, indicate a baffling array of subjects including necromancy, wills, and the birth of **Epicurus**. He was renowned for his humour, but his wit had a bite to it. Long after his death, he appeared as a character in the satires of **Lucian of Samosata**.
[R. Bracht Branham and Marie-Odile Goulet-Cazé (eds), *The Cynics: the Cynic movement in antiquity and its legacy*, Berkeley, University of California Press, 1996]

MENIPPUS OF LYCIA (first century AD)
Menippus was a noted Cynic of his time. According to Flavius **Philostratus,** he attached himself to **Apollonius of Tyana** for a time. Philostratus also relates that Menippus became infatuated with a woman, not realising she was a vampire until Apollonius unmasked her.

MENIPPUS OF PONTUS see MENIPPUS OF GADARA

MENIPPUS OF SINOPE see MENIPPUS OF GADARA

MENNEAS (first century AD?)
Menneas was an Epicurean and a friend of **Diogenes of Oenoanda.**

MENODORUS (fourth century BC?)
In a letter supposedly written by **Diogenes of Sinope** to **Apolexis,** reference is made to 'Menodorus the Philosopher'. He may have come from Megara.

MENODOTUS OF NICOMEDIA (first/second century AD)
Menodotus was a Sceptic, the pupil of **Antiochus of Laodicea** and teacher of **Herodotus of Tarsus.** He was also a physician of the Empiricist school. He may be the same Menodotus who wrote a history of Scepticism drawn on by **Diogenes Laertius.**

MENOECEUS (fourth century BC)
Menoeceus is remembered not for anything he did but because **Epicurus** wrote a letter to him that survives. In it Epicurus sets out the basic principles of his philosophy, that there is nothing to fear and that pain can be avoided.

MENON (fourth century BC)
Menon was a pupil of **Aristotle** [1] and wrote an encyclopaedic work on Greek medicine.

MENON OF CROTON (sixth/fifth century BC)
According to **Iamblichus of Chalcis,** Menon was a Pythagorean, and perhaps the son-in-law of **Pythagoras** himself.

MENTOR OF BITHYNIA (second century BC)
Mentor was a pupil of **Carneades of Cyrene.** However, they fell out over a woman and Mentor was banished from the Academy.

MEROPIUS (third/fourth century AD)
Meropius originally came from Tyre. Early church historians describe him as a philosopher who travelled to India and was killed on his return journey.

MESSALLA CORVINUS, MARCUS VALERIUS (first century BC)
Messalla was an Epicurean and a friend of **Horace.** As young men, they studied together in Athens. He opposed Julius **Caesar** but eventually made his peace with Augustus. As an author he wrote a number of works, including philosophical treatises, but none survive.

METELLUS NUMIDICUS, QUINTUS CAECILIUS (second/first century BC)

Metellus was a Roman general and politician who studied philosophy in Rhodes and in Athens under **Carneades of Cyrene**.

METHODIUS OF OLYMPUS (third/fourth century AD)

Methodius was a bishop who was probably martyred during the reign of Diocletian. He wrote a great deal, although only some of his works have survived. He was an opponent of both **Origen** and **Porphyry** and a defender of free will.

(*Ante-Nicene Fathers*, vol. VI)

METON OF PAROS (sixth/fifth century BC)

According to **Iamblichus of Chalcis**, Meton was a Pythagorean.

METOPUS (fifth century BC?)

According to **Iamblichus of Chalcis**, Metopus was a Pythagorean from Sybaris, but **Stobaeus** says he came from Metapontum. Fragments of a work on virtue attributed to him survive.

(David Fideler (ed.), *The Pythagorean Sourcebook*, Grand Rapids, Phanes, 1987)

METROCLES OF MARONEA (fourth/third century BC)

Metrocles was a Cynic and the brother of **Hipparchia of Maronea**. He became a pupil of **Theophrastus of Eresus** but was highly self-critical. Matters came to a head when he was forced to urinate at a very inopportune moment, as a result of which he decided to kill himself. **Crates of Thebes** became aware of this and persuaded him that the calls of nature demanded to be answered, illustrating his case by both word and deed. In gratitude, Metrocles left Theophrastus for Crates. Little is known of his thought, but he appears to have attached importance to the distinction between what could be bought and what could not. Eventually, as an old man, he did commit suicide by holding his breath.

METRODORUS [1] (fifth century BC)

According to **Iamblichus of Chalcis**, Metrodorus was a Pythagorean and the son of **Epicharmus**. He appears to have practised as a physician.

METRODORUS [2] (third century BC)

Chrysippus of Soli dedicated many of his books to Metrodorus who must have been a Stoic and perhaps a pupil.

METRODORUS [3] (second century BC)

Metrodorus was a philosopher and a painter.

METRODORUS [4] (third/fourth century AD)

Metrodorus originally came from Persia, but seems to have moved to Constantinople, perhaps in order to study philosophy there. He later travelled to India, where he was well received despite the fact that at some point he seems to have stolen some valuable jewels. He returned with gifts for the emperor Constantine, but claimed to have been robbed of some of them while he was travelling across Persia. Whether this story was true or not, it was apparently sufficient to prompt Constantine to cancel a treaty he had with the Persians.

METRODORUS see also MEDIUS

METRODORUS OF APAMEA (second century BC)
Metrodorus was a pupil of **Carneades of Cyrene**.

METRODORUS OF CHIOS (fourth century BC)
Metrodorus was a pupil of **Democritus of Abdera** or **Nessus of Chios** and a teacher of **Diogenes of Smyrna**. **Diogenes Laertius** recounts a tradition that Metrodorus denied all knowledge of anything, including the knowledge that he knew nothing, suggesting that he was familiar with the teachings of the Sceptics. However, he is generally reckoned to have been an atomist and the author of a work on nature based on atomist principles.

METRODORUS OF CYZICUS (second/first century BC)
Metrodorus was a pupil of **Charmadas**.

METRODORUS OF LAMPSACUS [1] (fifth century BC)
Metrodorus was a pupil of **Anaxagoras of Clazomenae**.

METRODORUS OF LAMPSACUS [2] (fourth/third century BC)
Metrodorus was a close friend of **Epicurus** and probably became his pupil in Lampsacus. Thereafter the two were rarely apart until Metrodorus died only a few years before Epicurus himself. His position in the school was inferior only to that of its founder. He wrote a number of works, none of which survive, that were accorded canonical status by later Epicureans. He was the brother of **Batis** and the lover of **Leontion**, with whom he seems to have had children, a boy called Epicurus and a girl whose name is unknown.

METRODORUS OF PITANE (second/first century BC)
Metrodorus was a Platonist and pupil of **Metrodorus of Stratonicea**.

METRODORUS OF SCEPSIS (second/first century BC)
Metrodorus was a pupil of **Charmadas** who later abandoned Platonism for rhetoric. He was credited with having an exceptional memory.

METRODORUS OF STRATONICEA (second/first century BC)
Metrodorus was a pupil of **Carneades of Cyrene**. Unlike **Clitomachus of Carthage**, Metrodorus developed and put forward an interpretation of Carneades that attributed specific positive doctrines to him rather than complete Scepticism. This interpretation later helped to shape the thought of **Philo of Larisa**. According to **Diogenes Laertius**, Metrodorus was a pupil of **Epicurus** before transferring his allegiance to Carneades. However, Epicurus died more than fifty years before Carneades was born. It is possible that Metrodorus was an Epicurean before joining the Academy or that some other Metrodorus of Stratonicea studied with Epicurus.

METRODORUS THE THEORIST (fourth/third century BC)
Metrodorus studied under **Theophrastus of Eresus** before becoming a pupil of **Stilpo**.

METRON (fourth/third century BC)
Metron was a pupil of **Theophrastus of Eresus**.

METRONAX (first century AD)
Metronax was a popular teacher of philosophy in Neapolis (Naples), where **Seneca** attended some of his lectures. He was probably a Stoic.

METROPHANES OF EUCARPIA (third/fourth century AD?)
Metrophanes was a Platonist, although his main interest appears to have been rhetoric. He also wrote a book about his native Phrygia.

MICCYLUS (fourth/third century BC)
Miccylus was an acquaintance of **Crates of Thebes** and perhaps a Cynic himself.

MILON
Milon was a philosopher unknown except for fragments of a work he wrote on nature that were preserved by **Stobaeus**.

MILON OF CROTON (sixth/fifth century BC)
According to **Iamblichus of Chalcis**, Milon was a Pythagorean, one of those who studied with **Pythagoras** himself. He died when an anti-Pythagorean mob burnt his house down when he was inside it. He is not to be confused with another Milon of Croton, a close contemporary, who was a wrestler.

MILTAS OF THESSALY (fourth century BC)
Miltas was a soothsayer and may also have been a pupil of **Plato** [1].

MILTIADES [1] (third century BC)
Miltiades was a pupil of **Ariston of Chios**.

MILTIADES [2] (second century AD)
Miltiades was a Christian who wrote a defence of Christianity and an attack on Greek philosophy.

MILTIADES OF CARTHAGE
According to **Iamblichus of Chalcis**, Miltiades was a Pythagorean.

MIMNOMACHUS OF TARENTUM (fifth century BC?)
According to **Iamblichus of Chalcis**, Mimnomachus was a Pythagorean.

MINUCIUS FELIX, MARCUS (second/third century AD)
Minucius was a Christian, best known for having written a surviving dialogue, *Octavius*, between a Christian and a pagan. The pagan attacks Christians for their immorality, dogmatism and lack of respect for tradition. His attack draws heavily on an anti-Christian speech made by Marcus Cornelius **Fronto**. The

Christian defends Christian virtue and argues that pagan philosophers, and in particular the Stoics, have produced a number of arguments for the existence of God. He also draws on **Tertullian**. The dialogue ends with the pagan completely convinced by his opponent.
(*Ante-Nicene Fathers*, vol. IV)

MITHRES or MITHRAS (fourth/third century BC)
Mithres came from Syria. He was a friend of **Epicurus**, who dedicated a book about diseases and death to him. It is unclear whether he studied with Epicurus or **Metrodorus of Lampsacus** [2] or both.

MNASAGORAS (second century BC)
Mnasagoras was a Stoic, probably from Alexandria Troas. He was a pupil of **Antipater of Tarsus** or **Diogenes of Babylon** or both.

MNASEAS (third century BC?)
Mnaseas was a Sceptic.

MNASEAS OF TYRE (second/first century BC)
Mnaseas was a Platonist and a pupil of **Antiochus of Ascalon**.

MNASILAS or MNASILEAS
Mnasilas is unknown apart from a reference to him as a philosopher in a papyrus found at Herculaneum.

MNASO (fourth/third century BC?)
Mnaso was the supposed recipient of a letter falsely attributed to **Crates of Thebes**, and is assumed to have been a Cynic.

MNASO OF PHOCIS (fourth century BC)
Mnaso was a pupil of **Aristotle** [1].

MNESARCHUS or MNEMARCHUS (sixth/fifth century BC)
Mnesarchus was the son of **Pythagoras**. He led the Pythagorean school after the death of **Aristaeus of Croton**.

MNESARCHUS OF ATHENS (second/first century BC)
Mnesarchus was a Stoic who studied with **Panaetius of Rhodes** and **Diogenes of Babylon**. He taught in Athens at the same time as **Dardanus of Athens**, and there is some indication that they may have jointly headed the school there after the death of Panaetius. His name sometimes appears as Mnesarchides.

MNESIBULUS OF RHEGIUM (fifth century BC?)
According to **Iamblichus of Chalcis**, Mnesibulus was a Pythagorean.

MNESIGENES (third century BC)
Mnesigenes was a Peripatetic and one of the executors of the will of **Strato of Lampsacus**.

MNESISTRATUS OF THASOS (fourth century BC)
Mnesistratus was probably a pupil of **Plato** [1].

MOCHUS or OCHUS
According to both **Suda** and **Diogenes Laertius,** despite the different versions they give of the name, Mochus or Ochus was a very early Phoenician philosopher.

MODERATUS OF GADES (first century AD)
Moderatus was a Neopythagorean and friend of **Plutarch of Chaeronea.** He was convinced that both **Plato** [1] and **Aristotle** [1] had taken ideas from Pythagoreanism without acknowledging their debt. However, his evidence for this belief probably consisted of spurious Pythagorean writings he had edited that were actually written well after the time of both Plato and Aristotle. He believed that the interest **Pythagoras** took in numbers was due to the fact they could express important and fundamental truths that words could not. He believed that matter was the source of all evil in the universe, although he stops short of a cosmic dualism. In fact, he adheres to a kind of monism that may owe at least as much to Plato and **Parmenides of Elea** as it does to Pythagoras.
[Charles H. Kahn, *Pythagoras and the Pythagoreans: a brief history*, Indianapolis, Hackett, 2001]

MOIRAGENES (second century AD?)
Moiragenes wrote a work on the life of **Apollonius of Tyana.** Flavius **Philostratus** consulted it in composing his own biography but generally rejected its material because of its hostile approach to its subject.

MONIMUS OF SYRACUSE (fourth century BC)
Monimus was a slave who became a follower of **Diogenes of Sinope.** In order to free himself from his owner, who was a banker, he pretended to be mad and started throwing around all the money he could find in the banker's house. This was enough to ensure his dismissal. When he became a Cynic, his former owner was *convinced* he was mad. As well as Diogenes, Monimus was also an admirer of **Crates of Thebes,** and in due course became highly regarded himself. **Menander** [1] paid tribute to his wisdom in one of his plays. Monimus himself wrote relatively little, producing only two books and a number of shorter pieces.

MOSCHION OF MALLUS (third century BC)
Moschion was a Platonist and pupil of **Lacydes of Cyrene.**

MOSCHUS (fourth century BC)
Moschus belonged to the Elian school during the period between the death of **Phaedo of Elis** and the arrival of **Menedemus of Eretria.** He was probably a pupil of Phaedo himself and may have headed the school for a time, perhaps with **Anchipylus.** He may be the same Moschus who is said to have lived in Elis on a diet of water and figs.

MUMMIUS, SPURIUS (second century BC)
Mummius was a Stoic and a distinguished orator who wrote a number of letters on ethical issues.

MUSONIUS (second/third century AD)
Porphyry mentions a Musonius who appears to have been a Stoic teaching in Athens. **Suda** also mentions a philosopher called Musonius who was taught by the sophist Hermogenes of Tarsus (who was born in around AD 160). Both references may be to the same person.

MUSONIUS OF TYRE (second century AD)
According to Flavius **Philostratus**, Musonius was a philosopher and the teacher of **Lucius** [4]. He appears to have emphasised the value of self-control and moderation.

MUSONIUS RUFUS, GAIUS (first century AD)
Musonius was a Stoic, but with some leanings towards Cynicism. **Epictetus** and **Athenodotus** were among his pupils. Based in Rome, he was exiled from there at least three times as the political tide ebbed and flowed. He appears to have written nothing himself, but others, including Epictetus, have preserved some of his teachings. Despite his admiration for the Cynics, he advocated a surprisingly conventional life, recommending marriage and large families. However, because he believed in the equality of women, he saw marriage as a true partnership. It is thought that the character of Musonius of Babylon in the life of **Apollonus of Tyana** written by Flavius **Philostratus** is fictional but based on the real Musonius Rufus.
[*Routledge Encyclopaedia of Philosophy*, vol. 6]

MYES OF POSIDONIA
According to **Iamblichus of Chalcis**, Myes was a Pythagorean. Someone called Myes abridged an historical work by **Hippys of Rhegium**, but it is not clear whether it was the same person.

MYIA OF CROTON (sixth/fifth century BC)
Myia was probably the daughter of **Pythagoras** and **Theano**, and the wife of **Milon of Croton**. She was regarded as one of the most famous Pythagorean women.

MYLLIAS OF CROTON (fifth century BC?)
According to **Iamblichus of Chalcis**, Myllias was a Pythagorean. He is said to have been one of a group of Pythagoreans who were ambushed, but found their escape route blocked by a field of beans. Being prohibited by Pythagorean precepts from touching beans, they preferred death to betraying their principles.

MYONIDES (third century AD)
Myonides was a Pythagorean.

MYRMEX (fourth/third century BC)
Myrmex was a pupil of **Stilpo**. He originally sought out Stilpo in order to argue against him, but in the event became won over to his teachings.

MYRONIANUS OF AMASTRIS
Myronianus wrote a book entitled *Historical Parallels* that contained biographies of philosophers later drawn upon by **Diogenes Laertius**.

MYRTILUS OF THESSALY (second/third century AD)
Myrtilus is one of the philosophers in *Scholars at Dinner* by **Athenaeus of Naucratis**. He was a Cynic and the son of a shoemaker.

MYS (fourth/third century BC)
Mys was a slave of **Epicurus** and a follower of his master's philosophy. Epicurus gave him his freedom in his will.

MYSON (seventh/sixth century BC)
Myson is generally reckoned to have been one of the Seven Sages of ancient Greece and to have been recognised as the wisest man of his day by the oracle of Apollo at Delphi. The little that is known of him suggests a reasonable measure of common sense but nothing more profound.

❖ **N** ❖

NASTAS OF CAULONIA (fifth century BC?)
According to **Iamblichus of Chalcis**, Nastas was a Pythagorean.

NAUCRATES THE SAGE
Naucrates is mentioned by **Stobaeus** but it is not clear who is meant. The name does not appear on any of the usual lists of the Seven Sages, although there was more than one noted poet by that name, as well as an important mathematician.

NAUCYDES (fourth century BC)
Naucydes is said to have been a teacher of **Epicurus**.

NAUSICYDES OF CHOLARGES (fifth century BC)
Nausicydes was one of a philosophical circle that also included **Andron of Gargettus, Callicles** and **Tisander**. They agreed that while the study of philosophy was valuable, it should not be taken too far.

NAUSIPHANES OF TEOS (fourth century BC)
According to **Diogenes Laertius**, Nausiphanes was a pupil of **Pyrrho of Elis** and a teacher of **Epicurus**, although Epicurus sometimes denied having any teachers. However, Nausiphanes was probably responsible for introducing Epicurus to the theory of atomism developed by **Democritus of Abdera**.

NAUSITHOUS
According to **Iamblichus of Chalcis,** Nausithous was an Etruscan Pythagorean who rescued another Pythagorean, **Eubulus of Messene,** from pirates.

NEANTHES OF CYZICUS (third century BC)
Neanthes was a pupil of **Philiscus of Melos.** He appears to have been an authority on the history of Syria, and according to **Clement of Alexandria** claimed that **Pythagoras** was a Syrian. **Diogenes Laertius** draws on unnamed works by Neanthes in his accounts of **Heraclitus of Ephesus** and **Plato** [1] amongst others.

NEARCHUS OF TARENTUM (third/second century BC)
Nearchus was a Pythagorean. He played host to Cato the Elder when Cato recaptured Tarentum from the Carthaginians in around 208 BC.

NEBRIDIUS (fourth century AD)
Nebridius was a wealthy Carthaginian who became a pupil of **Augustine.** Under his influence he became both a Platonist and a Christian. A number of letters exchanged by the two have survived in which they discuss, amongst other things, whether thoughts are always accompanied by images.
(*Nicene and Post-Nicene Fathers,* vol. I)

NECHEPSO
The name of Nechepso is often found linked with that of **Petosiris** in the context of Egyptian astrology. He was said to have been a king of Egypt, but none by that name is known.

NELEUS OF SCEPSIS (fourth/third century BC)
Neleus was the son of **Coriscus of Scepsis** and studied under **Theophrastus of Eresus.** He was one of the group of philosophers who inherited the Lyceum when Theophrastus died and he personally inherited his teacher's library.

NEMESIUS OF EMESA (fourth/fifth century AD)
Nemesius wrote a work *On Human Nature* in which he sought to give an account of the soul acceptable to both Platonists and Christians. In doing so, he helpfully mentions the views of a number of other philosophers on the subject. He became bishop of Emesa, but otherwise nothing is known about his life.
(*Library of Christian Classics,* vol. 4, Philadelphia, Westminster Press, 1955)
[John Dillon, *The Middle Platonists 80 BC to AD 220,* London, Duckworth, 1996]

NEOCLES (fourth/third century BC)
Neocles was a brother of **Epicurus** (their father was also called Neocles). Thanks to the influence and urging of Epicurus, he took up the study of philosophy himself.

NEOCRITUS OF ATHENS
According to **Iamblichus of Chalcis,** Neocritus was a Pythagorean.

NEPOS, CORNELIUS (second/first century BC)
Nepos was a biographer who wrote on the lives of hundreds of people, including philosophers.

NERINTHUS (fourth century BC?)
Aristotle [1] wrote a dialogue named after Nerinthus in which he is portrayed as a farmer from Corinth who reads the *Gorgias* of **Plato** [1] and leaves his land to search out its author. The extent to which this was based on historical fact is unclear.

NERO (second/first century BC)
Demetrius Lacon dedicated a book to Nero, making it likely he was an Epicurean himself.

NERVAS (fifth century AD)
Nervas was said to have been one of a group of philosophers who accompanied **Eudocia** on her journey from Athens to Constantinople. The story is doubted, and his existence is questionable.

NESSUS OF CHIOS (fifth/fourth century BC)
Nessus was a teacher of **Metrodorus of Chios**.

NESTOR OF TARSUS [1] (second century BC)
Nestor was a Stoic in Athens.

NESTOR OF TARSUS [2] (first century BC)
Nestor was a Platonist and a tutor to Marcus Claudius **Marcellus** [2], the nephew of Augustus. He took over the running of his home city from another philosopher, **Athenodorus of Tarsus**.

NESTORIUS (fourth century AD)
Nestorius was the father of **Plutarch of Athens** and may have been a philosopher in his own right.

NICAGORAS (third/fourth century AD)
Nicagoras was a Platonist based in Athens and may have been the father-in-law of **Himerius**. He held an official position at Eleusis and is known to have visited Egypt. He appears to have helped to push Platonism in a more mystical direction.

NICAGORAS OF CYPRUS
The name of Nicagoras is linked with a theory concerning the flooding of the Nile and another, similar to that of **Euhemerus**, concerning the origins of the gods. It is not clear whether both references are to the same person.

NICANDER (fourth/fifth century AD)
Nicander was a philosopher and a friend of **Synesius of Ptolemais** when he was in Constantinople.

NICANDER OF ALEXANDRIA
According to **Suda**, Nicander wrote a book about the students of **Aristotle** [1].

NICANDER OF BITHYNIA (second century BC)
Nicander was a Stoic and a pupil of **Panaetius of Rhodes**.

NICANOR (fourth/third century BC)
Nicanor was a follower of **Epicurus**. Epicurus made provision for him in his will.

NICARETE (fourth/third century BC)
Nicarete was the mistress of **Stilpo** and perhaps also one of his pupils.

NICASICRATES (third/second century BC?)
The name of Nicasicrates is usually found together with that of **Timasagoras**, but there is no consensus as to which school they belonged to. They had a theory about anger which was attacked by the Epicureans **Thespis** and **Basilides of Syria**. It is unclear whether this was a dispute amongst Epicureans or between Epicureans and representatives of another school.

NICIAS [1] (third century BC)
Chrysippus of Soli dedicated a book on language to Nicias, suggesting he was either a colleague or a pupil.

NICIAS [2] (fourth century AD)
Nicias was a philosopher and friend of **Symmachus**.

NICIAS OF NICAEA (first century AD?)
Nicias wrote a history of philosophy in which he traced a number of philosophical lineages.

NICION (first century AD?)
Nicion appears in the *Banquet of the Cynics* by **Parmeniscus** [2]. She is portrayed as a prostitute with the unflattering nickname of 'Dog Fly', presumably because she kept the company of Cynics.

NICIPPUS (fourth/third century BC)
Nicippus was a pupil of **Theophrastus of Eresus**. He was one of those to whom Theophrastus bequeathed the Lyceum on his death.

NICOLAUS (first century BC?)
According to **Diogenes Laertius**, Nicolaus was an opponent of Epicureanism. Some identify him with **Nicolaus of Damascus**.

NICOLAUS OF DAMASCUS (first century BC)
Nicolaus was a highly educated man. He studied grammar, literature, rhetoric, music, mathematics and the sciences before turning to philosophy. He described education as a kind of journey, but philosophy as home. His philosophical home became Aristotelianism, athough he may have had some familiarity with Platonism as well. Amongst his pupils were the children of Mark Antony and Cleopatra. He wrote a great deal, including a lengthy history of the world, biographies, tragedies and comedies. He also wrote an account of

the early years of Augustus, and the two became friends. Another friend was Herod the Great. Nicolaus spent some time with him as his personal philosophy teacher and Herod named a species of date after him. Some identify him with **Nicolaus**.

(H.J. Drossart Lulofs, *Nicolaus of Damascus on the Philosophy of Aristotle*, Leiden, Brill, 1965)

NICOLOCHUS OF RHODES (fourth/third century BC)
According to **Diogenes Laertius**, Nicolochus was a Sceptic and pupil of **Timon of Phlius**.

NICOMACHUS (fourth century BC)
Nicomachus was the son of **Aristotle** [1] and, if ancient gossip is to be believed, the lover of **Theophrastus of Eresus**. In any event he seems to have studied under Theophrastus, and perhaps Aristotle too. He was once thought to have been the author of Aristotle's *Nicomachaean Ethics*, but his connection with the work, if any, does not go beyond editorship.

NICOMACHUS OF GERASA (first/second century AD)
Nicomachus was a Neopythagorean who was particularly interested in mathematics and music. His *Introduction to Arithmetic* was a standard textbook for centuries while his *Handbook of Harmonics* was an important statement of Pythagorean musical theory. Both books survive, and the aim of both was to articulate an understanding of the basic nature of the universe in terms that are ultimately numerical. He also wrote an account of the life of **Pythagoras**, but that has long since disappeared. Centuries after his death, **Proclus** [1] believed himself to be Nicomachus' reincarnation.

(Nicomachus of Gerasa, *Introduction to Arithmetic*, trans. M.L. D'Ooge, Ann Arbor, University of Michigan Press, 1938; A. Barker, *Greek Musical Writings*, vol. II: *Harmonic and Acoustic Theory*, Cambridge, Cambridge University Press, 1989)

[John Dillon, *The Middle Platonists 80 BC to AD 220*, London, Duckworth, 1996; Charles H. Kahn, *Pythagoras and the Pythagoreans: a brief history*, Indianapolis, Hackett, 2001]

NICOMEDES
According to **Diogenes Laertius**, Nicomedes wrote a commentary on the works of **Heraclitus of Ephesus**.

NICOSTRATUS OF ALEXANDRIA (second century BC)
Nicostratus was a pupil of **Carneades of Cyrene**.

NICOSTRATUS OF ATHENS (second century AD)
Claudius Nicostratus was a Platonist. He is mentioned by **Simplicius** in his commentary on the *Categories* of **Aristotle** [1]. He was honoured at Delphi at the same time as **Bacchius of Paphos, Zosimus of Athens** and **Cornelianus of Mallus**.

NICOTELES OF CYRENE (fourth/third century BC)
Nicoteles was a philosopher and the brother of **Anniceris of Cyrene**. According to **Suda**, one of his pupils was called Posidonius, perhaps a reference to **Posidonius of Olbiopolis**.

NIGRINUS (second century AD)
Nigrinus is said to have been a Platonist and the teacher of **Lucian of Samosata**, who wrote a dialogue about him. However, some doubt his historicity, and think Lucian may have been making a joke changing the 'white' **Albinus** [1] into the 'black' Nigrinus.

NILUS [1] (first century AD)
According to Flavius **Philostratus**, Nilus was one of the group of naked philosophers encountered in Egypt by **Apollonius of Tyana**. They appear to have lived in a community about a day's walk from Thebes. He is said to have become a follower of Apollonius and accompanied him on a journey up the Nile.

NILUS [2] (fourth century AD)
Nilus was attacked in a letter sent by the emperor **Julian** for turning down an office he had been offered. Julian appears to have regarded Nilus as someone whose philosophical outlook led him to be uninterested in public duty. Although he is not specifically described as a Cynic, he may have been one.

NILUS THE MONK or THE ASCETIC (fourth/fifth century AD)
Nilus probably came from Ancyra, and studied in Constantinople under **John Chrysostom**. He then went, or returned, to Ancyra (Ankara) and founded a monastery near it. He wrote a great deal on moral and ascetic matters, with special emphasis on the demands of monastic life. He also produced a large number of letters to a wide variety of people, many of which survive. He believed that the spiritual life was the practice of Christian philosophy.

NINON OF CROTON (fifth century BC)
Ninon was one of the leaders of the anti-Pythagorean movement in Croton. He claimed that the Pythagoreans were elitist and anti-democratic. He also claimed to have a knowledge of their secret teachings and published it in a book. However, according to **Iamblichus of Chalcis**, Ninon knew nothing of what the school taught and the book was a work of pure invention.

NOETUS [1] (third century BC)
Noetus was a pupil of **Chrysippus of Soli**.

NOETUS [2] (first/second century AD)
Noetus came from Smyrna and taught the utter unity and indivisibility of God. As a result he fell out with his fellow Christians because he argued that if Jesus was identical with God and Jesus died, then God died too.

NOMUS (fifth century AD)
Nomus was an amateur philosopher who was much admired by **Damascius**.

He was noted for his honesty and modesty and was knowledgeable about both philosophy and literature.

NOVATUS, LUCIUS ANNAEUS (first century BC/first century AD)

Novatus was the elder brother of **Seneca**, and was adopted by Lucius Junius **Gallio**, subsequently taking his name. Seneca dedicated two of his philosophical dialogues to him. Seneca's exhortations suggest that if Novatus was not actually a Stoic himself, he was at the very least a sympathiser.

NUMA POMPILIUS (eighth/seventh century BC)

According to tradition, Numa was the second king of Rome, the successor of Romulus. He was said to favour the simple life and be a reluctant ruler. **Clement of Alexandria** believed that he was a Pythagorean, but **Livy** seems right to argue that Numa must have died long before **Pythagoras** was born.

NUMENIUS OF APAMEA (second century AD)

Numenius defies easy categorisation. Although he is usually referred to as a Pythagorean or Neopythagorean, the fact that **Tryphon** could accuse **Plotinus** of plagiarising Numenius indicates the narrowness of the gap between what counted as Pythagoreanism and what counted as Platonism at that time. Furthermore, even in a period that favoured eclecticism, he went further than most, famously suggesting that **Plato** [1] was no more than Moses speaking Greek and that the religions of India, Persia and Egypt were all in harmony both with each other and with Platonism. Only the Sceptics, who claimed to believe nothing, seem to have attracted his genuine enmity. Numenius envisaged a kind of original or primeval wisdom to which every worthwhile philosophy or religion was related in some way, however distant or decadent a descendant it might be. His complex reconstruction of this wisdom in metaphysical terms incorporates a divine trinity (although one of the three gods is supreme) combined with a peculiar form of dualism in which evil souls are produced from matter. The cosmic opposition between spirit and matter is reflected in the internal opposition in each individual between a good and an evil soul. Despite the protestations of **Amelius Gentilianus** to the contrary, many later thinkers have taken the view that even if Plotinus did not technically plagiarise Numenius, he was nevertheless greatly influenced by him. As a result, Numenius is sometimes seen as the last of the Pythagoreans because after his time Pythagoreanism and Platonism became difficult to disentangle.

(Eusebius, *Preparation for the Gospel* (2 vols), trans. E.H. Gifford, Eugene, Wipf and Stock, 2002)

[John Dillon, *The Middle Platonists 80 BC to AD 220*, London, Duckworth, 1996; Charles H. Kahn, *Pythagoras and the Pythagoreans: a brief history*, Indianapolis, Hackett, 2001]

NYMPHIDIANUS OF SMYRNA (fourth century AD)

Nymphidianus was the brother of **Claudianus of Smyrna** and **Maximus of**

Ephesus. Like them he took an interest in philosophy, but he seems not to have had the same talent or success in this field. The emperor **Julian** entrusted him with his Greek correspondence and he helped to draft official documents.

NYMPHIS (third century BC)
Nymphis was a pupil of **Chrysippus of Soli**.

NYSIUS OF SAMNIUM (second century BC)
Nysius was a pupil of **Panaetius of Rhodes**.

❖ O ❖

OCCELO OF LUCANIA (fourth century BC?)
According to **Iamblichus of Chalcis**, Occelo was one of the most famous Pythagorean women and **Eccelo of Lucania** was her sister. However, some think that Iamblichus was mistaken and that Occelo is in fact **Occelus of Lucania** and therefore not a woman at all.

OCCELUS OF LUCANIA (fourth century BC?)
According to **Iamblichus of Chalcis**, Occelus was a Pythagorean and brother of **Occilus of Lucania**. He appears to have held that the number three was the key to understanding the world. However, according to **Hippolytus**, he also believed that in addition to the four elements (earth, fire, air and water) there was a fifth principle which was circular motion. **Philo of Alexandria** says he believed it was possible to prove that the world was indestructible.
(David Fideler (ed.), *The Pythagorean Sourcebook*, Grand Rapids, Phanes, 1987)

OCCILUS OF LUCANIA (fourth century BC?)
According to **Iamblichus of Chalcis**, Occilus was a Pythagorean and brother of **Occelus of Lucania**.

OCHUS see MOCHUS

ODAENATHUS (fifth century AD)
Odaenathus was originally from Syria and became a pupil of **Plutarch of Athens**. He thought that it was impossible to attain to knowledge of the divine through speculation and generally saw little point in philosophical discussion.

OENOMAUS OF GADARA (second century AD?)
Oenomaus was a Cynic. He appears to have written a great deal, including some tragedies. Substantial extracts from a work entitled *The Detection of Impostors*, which drew the ire of the emperor **Julian**, survive. In it he denounces oracles as fraudulent and derides the Stoics for believing in them. He argues that because the future is not predestined, there can be no foreknowledge of it.

And if the future were predestined, it could not be changed so foreknowledge of it would be useless. People should therefore concentrate on taking control over their own lives in the present rather than seeking to know what the future will bring.

(Eusebius, *Preparation for the Gospel* (2 vols), trans. E.H. Gifford, Eugene, Wipf and Stock, 2002)

[Donald R. Dudley, *A History of Cynicism from Diogenes to the Sixth Century AD*, 2nd edn, London, Bristol Classical Press, 1998]

OENOPIDES OF CHIOS (fifth century BC)
Oenopides was renowned as an expert on geometry, although his interest appears to have been at least in part motivated by practical problems in astronomy. He also had a theory about why the Nile flooded. He is generally thought to have been a Pythagorean.

OLYMPIADES (fourth century BC)
Olympiades was a pupil of **Xenocrates of Chalcedon**.

OLYMPICHUS (third century BC)
Olympichus was a Peripatetic and one of the executors of the will of **Strato of Lampsacus**.

OLYMPICUS OF GAZA (second century BC)
Olympicus was a pupil of **Carneades of Cyrene**.

OLYMPIODORUS [1] (fourth/fifth century AD)
Olympiodorus was from Alexandria and taught philosophy there. One of those who studied under him was **Proclus** [1] whom he wished, but failed, to acquire as a son-in-law. Another pupil was **Ulpian of Gaza**. Olympiodorus had a reputation for speaking so quickly when he taught that his students found him hard to follow.

OLYMPIODORUS [2] (fifth/sixth century AD)
Olympiodorus was from Alexandria and studied there under **Ammonius**. Commentaries on the works of **Plato** [1] and **Aristotle** [1] by him survive, although they are mainly compiled from his students' lecture notes. He probably taught **Elias**. He may be the same Olympiodorus who took an interest in alchemy and wrote a commentary on the work of **Zosimus**, which also survives. He may also be the same Olympiodorus as the one who taught **Stephanus of Alexandria**.

OLYMPIUS [1] (fourth century AD)
Olympius was a friend of **Iamblichus of Chalcis** and the recipient of letters from him on philosophical matters. He was probably a Platonist.

OLYMPIUS [2] (fourth/fifth century AD)
Olympius came from a wealthy Syrian family. He studied under **Hypatia of Alexandria** and became a friend and correspondent of **Synesius of Ptolemais**.

OLYMPIUS [3] (fourth/fifth century AD)
Olympius came from Cilicia and studied philosophy in Alexandria. When the
city became an uncomfortable place for pagans, he moved to Italy.

OLYMPIUS OF ALEXANDRIA (third century AD)
Olympius studied under **Ammonius Saccas** and became a rival of **Plotinus**.
According to **Porphyry**, the rivalry grew so bitter that Olympius even resorted
to magic in his attempts to do Plotinus harm, but in the end had to concede
defeat.

ONASANDER (first century AD)
Onasander was a Platonist. He wrote commentaries on the *Republic* of **Plato** [1]
as well as two books on military matters.
(Aeneias Tacticus, Asclepiodotus, Onasander, trans. Illinois Greek Club, Loeb,
1923)

ONATAS or ONATUS OF CROTON or OF TARENTUM (fifth century BC?)
Onatas was a Pythagorean. Opinions differ as to whether some surviving
fragments of text are to be ascribed to him or not.

ONESICRITUS OF AEGINA (fourth century BC)
Onesicritus was a follower of **Diogenes of Sinope**. He sent his sons
Androsthenes of Aegina and **Philiscus of Aegina** to Athens where they both
attached themselves to Diogenes. In due course he joined them. He is
sometimes confused with **Onesicritus of Astypalaea**.

ONESICRITUS OF ASTYPALAEA (fourth century BC)
Onesicritus was a Cynic who joined the army of Alexander the Great and wrote
an account of his leader's education. When the army was in Taxila he met the
Indian philosophers **Mandanis** and **Calanus**. He is sometimes confused with
Onesicritus of Aegina.
[T.S. Brown, *Onesicritus*, Berkeley, University of California Press, 1949]

ONETOR (third century BC)
Chrysippus of Soli dedicated a book on logic to Onetor, suggesting that he was
either a colleague or a pupil.

ONOMACRITUS (sixth century BC?)
According to **Aristotle** [1], there was a tradition that **Onomacritus** came from
Locri and studied the art of legislation in Crete. He was also adept at divination.
His name was sometimes associated with that of **Zaleucus of Locri**, perhaps
pointing to a link between Onomacritus and Pythagoreanism.

OPILLUS, AURELIUS (second century BC)
Opillus was originally the slave of an Epicurean and may have been one
himself. In any event, when he was freed he became a teacher of philosophy,
although he later switched to rhetoric and grammar. When Publius Rutilius
Rufus was sent into exile, Opillus went with him.

OPSIMUS OF RHEGIUM (fifth century BC?)
According to **Iamblichus of Chalcis**, Opsimus was a Pythagorean.

ORESTADAS OF METAPONTUM (sixth century BC)
According to **Iamblichus of Chalcis**, Orestadas was a Pythagorean. He is probably to be identified with the Orestades, also a Pythagorean, who is said by **Diogenes Laertius** to have freed **Xenophanes of Colophon** from slavery.

ORIBASIUS (fourth century AD)
Oribasius was primarily known for his work in medicine, but according to **Eunapius** no philosopher could fail to benefit from his acquaintance. He became the personal physician of the emperor **Julian**, whose enthusiasm for a pagan revival he shared. After Julian's death he was sent into exile, living and working amongst the Goths, before subsequently being recalled. All his surviving works are on medicine.

ORIGEN (second/third century AD)
Debates have long raged over whether there was a Christian Origen and a Platonist Origen, or whether the two were one and the same person. The Platonist Origen is known through **Porphyry**, who claims that **Herennius**, **Plotinus** and Origen were all pupils of **Ammonius Saccas**. Only two works, both lost, are attributed to him. Most of what is known about the Christian Origen's life derives from **Eusebius of Caesarea**, but many of his own works also survive. He studied under **Clement of Alexandria** and went on to found his own school in Caesarea. He wrote a great deal, but his writings were later condemned and most of them were destroyed. His unwelcome views included the belief that in the end all souls would be saved and so there was no such thing as eternal damnation. As a young man he is said to have castrated himself in an act of zeal, and in later life he was imprisoned and tortured. The principal argument for insisting that the Platonist Origen must be distinguished from the Christian one is that the works attributed to the former are said to date to after the latter's death.
(*Ante-Nicene Fathers*, vols IV and X)
[Jean Daniélou, *Origen*, trans. Mitchell, London, Sheed and Ward, 1955; Edward Moore, 'Origen of Alexandria', *Internet Encyclopaedia of Philosophy*, www.iep.utm.edu/o/origen.htm]

ORION [1] (fourth/third century BC?)
Orion was the supposed recipient of a letter falsely attributed to **Crates of Thebes**. In it Crates enjoins Orion to send his sons to study philosophy, which they had both studied, perhaps together, as young men.

ORION [2] (fourth/third century BC?)
According to **Diogenes Laertius**, Orion was an Epicurean, possibly a pupil of **Epicurus** himself.

ORION [3] (fourth/fifth century AD)
Orion came from Thebes in Egypt and produced a book of wise sayings that he sent to **Eudocia**.

ORRONTIUS, MARCELLUS (third century AD)
According to **Porphyry**, Orrontius was a senator and a follower of **Plotinus**.

OURANIUS (sixth century AD)
Ouranius is said to have been a physician and philosopher from Palestine. He claimed to be a Peripatetic, but the extent of his understanding of the school's teachings are unclear. He spent time in Constantinople before travelling to Persia where he met and impressed **Chosroes I**.

OURANIUS CYNICUS
The name, meaning 'Heavenly Dog' was written on the wall of a tomb in the Valley of the Kings. It was presumably the chosen pseudonym of a Cynic.

❖ **P** ❖

PACCIUS (first/second century AD)
Paccius was an orator and friend of **Plutarch of Chaeronea**. He may have been a Platonist and certainly took an interest in philosophical issues.

PACTIUM OF TARENTUM (fifth century BC?)
According to **Iamblichus of Chalcis**, Pactium was a Pythagorean.

PAEONIUS (fourth/third century BC)
According to **Diogenes Laertius**, Paeonius was a pupil of **Stilpo**, having previously studied under **Aristides** [1].

PALAEPHATUS [1] (fifth or fourth century BC?)
According to **Suda**, Palaephatus came from either Paros or Priene. He wrote a lengthy work on *Incredible Things* in which he sought to establish rational explanations for them. The name may have been a pseudonym.

PALAEPHATUS [2] (fourth century BC)
According to **Suda**, Palaephatus was an historian from Abydos who studied under **Aristotle** [1]. Gossip said the two were lovers.

PALAMEDES
Palamedes was supposedly the grandson of Poseidon and cousin of Agamemnon. He embodied wisdom in the way that his rival Odysseus embodied cunning. He was said to have been a poet and an inventor, the originator of all or part of the Greek alphabet. The extent to which he is to be regarded as a genuine historical figure is problematic, but there is no obvious

reason why he should not be accorded the same degree of historicity as his famous cousin.

PALLADIUS (fifth century AD)
Palladius is known to have been a philosopher from references to that effect in some letters of **Theodoret**.

PAMPHILA OF EPIDAURUS (first century BC/first century AD)
Pamphila was the author of at least two books, *Memorabilia* and *Commentaries*, both of which were sources for **Diogenes Laertius**.

PAMPHILUS [1] (sixth century BC?)
According to **Dicaearchus of Messene**, Pamphilus was one of the Seven Sages of ancient Greece.

PAMPHILUS [2] (fourth century BC)
According to **Diogenes Laertius**, Pamphilus was a Platonist and a teacher of **Epicurus** at his school on Samos. A Pamphilus is also said to have taught **Aristotle** [1], but it is not clear whether it is the same person.

PAMPHILUS [3] (sixth century AD)
Little is known about Pamphilus other than that he was a philosopher who died by drowning at sea.

PAMPHILUS PHILOPRAGMATUS (fourth century BC?)
A confusing entry in **Suda** refers to a philosopher of this name from Neapolis or Sicyon or Amphipolis. Part of the confusion may arise from the fact that he wrote on art, amongst other things, and a famous painter by the name of Pamphilus came from Amphipolis and taught in Sicyon. It is therefore possible that the painter was confused with a philosopher from Neapolis. Philopragmatus is a rather unflattering nickname meaning 'busybody'.

PAMPHILUS OF CAESAREA (third/fourth century AD)
Pamphilus came from Berytus (Beirut) and studied in Alexandria. He became influenced by the ideas of **Origen** and later wrote a defence of them. As bishop of Caesarea, he encountered **Eusebius of Caesarea** who became his pupil. He was martyred in AD 309, but his library in Caesarea survived for hundreds of years.

PAMPHILUS OF MAGNESIA (second century BC)
Pamphilus was a pupil of **Carneades of Cyrene**.

PAMPREPIUS (fifth century AD)
Pamprepius was a poet and polymath from Panopolis. He was a pupil of **Proclus** [1] and perhaps also of **Hierius of Athens**.

PANACEUS
Panaceus is said to have been a Pythagorean who wrote about music.

PANAETIUS
According to **Suda**, Panaetius was from Rhodes and wrote many philosophical

works. However, none have survived, and there is some doubt as to whether there was ever more than one philosopher of note from Rhodes called Panaetius.

PANAETIUS OF RHODES (second century BC)
Panaetius studied under **Crates of Mallus** at Pergamum and then at Athens with **Diogenes of Babylon** and **Antipater of Tarsus**, eventually succeeding Antipater as head of the school in 129 BC. He is one of the major figures of the period known as the Middle Stoa, although his teachers are generally credited with having initiated it. His principal contributions came in the area of ethics where he helped to make Stoicism's demands less idealistic and more realistic. The early Stoics had maintained an uncompromising absolutism where virtue was the only good and perfection the only worthwhile attainment. The Middle Stoa found a place for relative goods, such as health and material comforts (even though they were no part of virtue as such), and degrees of imperfection, so that progress was open to everyone. Exactly what contribution Panaetius made to these developments is unclear as none of his own works survives, although the *On Moral Duties* of **Cicero** was based on one of them. He is credited with denying the possibility of divination, suggesting he challenged traditional Stoic views on determinism, and he seems to have taken the view that while excessive emotions were certainly to be reined in, not all emotion had to be extinguished. This helped to make Stoicism appear more human. Like his teachers, but unlike the early Stoa, Panaetius was also prepared to incorporate ideas from Platonism and Aristotelianism into his thinking.

The fate of the school in Athens after the death of Panaetius in 110 BC is unclear. Even while head of the school there he appears to have spent substantial periods of time in Rome, as well as maintaining close links with his native Rhodes. His natural successor, **Posidonius of Apamea**, established himself in Rhodes and there is no evidence of a rival in Athens. The influence of Panaetius lived on in Rome thanks to the impression he had made on people such as **Scipio** and **Scaevola**.
[*Routledge Encyclopaedia of Philosophy*, vol. 7]

PANARETUS (third century BC)
Panaretus was a pupil of **Arcesilaus of Pitane**.

PANCRATES (second century AD)
According to Flavius **Philostratus**, Pancrates was a Cynic who taught philosophy near Corinth. He once saved the sophist Lollianus from being stoned to death by an angry Athenian mob.

PANCREON (fourth/third century BC)
Pancreon was a follower of **Theophrastus of Eresus**, and one of the beneficiaries of his will. Jointly with his brother **Melantes** he inherited all the property of Theophrastus in Eresus, and a share of the Lyceum in Athens as long as he wished to continue studying philosophy there.

PANSA, CAIUS VIBIUS (first century BC)
Pansa was an Epicurean, achieving high political rank as a consul.

PANNYCHUS (first century AD)
An epigram by Martial addresses Pannychus as someone versed in the doctrines of the various philosophical schools.

PANTACLEA (fourth/third century BC)
According to **Clement of Alexandria**, Pantaclea was a daughter of **Diodorus Cronus** and an accomplished philosopher.

PANTAENUS (second century AD)
Pantaenus appears to have been educated as a Stoic, but later became a Christian. His origins are unclear, but he is generally associated with Alexandria where he became the first known head of the Catechetical School there, perhaps being succeeded by his pupil **Clement of Alexandria**. He was one of the first to see the potential of philosophy as a valuable adjunct to Christian theology. He is said to have travelled to India as a missionary at some stage in his career.

PANTHOIDES (fourth/third century BC)
According to **Diogenes Laertius**, Panthoides was a logician who taught **Lyco** [1].

PANYASSIS OF HALICARNASSUS
Two celebrated people by the name of Panyassis seem to have come from Halicarnassus. The elder was a famous poet, but a younger one was a philosopher who wrote a book on dreams.

PAPIRIUS PAETUS (first century BC)
Papirius was an Epicurean and a friend of **Cicero**. Cicero wrote him a letter in which he rebuked Papirius for his use of obscenities.

PAPPUS OF ALEXANDRIA (fourth century AD)
Pappus wrote on a wide variety of topics, although he was principally interested in mathematics. He also produced commentaries on the work of **Ptolemy** [1] and a study of dreams.

PAPUS (third/fourth century AD)
Papus was a follower of **Mani** who taught in Egypt.

PARAEBATES (fourth/third century BC)
According to **Diogenes Laertius**, Paraebates was a member of the Cyrenaic school, the pupil of **Epitimides of Cyrene** and teacher of **Hegesias of Cyrene** and **Anniceris of Cyrene**.

PARAMONUS OF TARSUS (second century BC?)
Paramonus was a Stoic and a pupil of **Panaetius of Rhodes**.

PARMENIDES OF ELEA (fifth century BC)
Little is known about the life of Parmenides. He came from Elea, probably

spent most of his life there, and may have written the city's constitution. It is said that he was converted to philosophy by **Ameinias** [1], a Pythagorean. The extent to which his own philosophy was influenced by Pythagoreanism is a matter of dispute and interpretation.

Unlike most philosophers before and after his time, he chose to write in verse and substantial sections survive of a poem he wrote that was apparently intended to sum up his philosophy. It begins with a prologue that tells of a journey in a chariot in which he is carried into the heavens to visit a goddess. While this is usually understood in allegorical terms, it is possible it reflects a genuine vision. The goddess then teaches him about the nature of the world, and the rest of the poem is divided into two sections. The first, entitled 'The Way of Truth', sets out the theory Parmenides is putting forward, and substantial portions of this have been preserved. The purpose of the second section, of which fewer lines survive, is less clear.

According to 'The Way of Truth', what exists is one, eternal, indivisible, immobile and unchanging. At the heart of it is the belief that what exists and what does not exist are so fundamentally different that it is incomprehensible how one could ever become the other or how they could possibly co-exist. Consequently what does not exist is banished from reality altogether. But if what exists cannot cease to exist, then the world is unchanging in its composition. However, Parmenides goes further than this, presumably on the basis that if something changes in any way, then it becomes something it was not before, and this could be interpreted as something that did not previously exist coming into existence, which is not allowed. Therefore change of any kind, including movement, is incompatible with existence. But if that is the case, it is clear, if nothing else is, that how the world really is, is very different from how we experience it to be. In this way Parmenides went significantly beyond **Thales of Miletus** and **Anaximenes of Miletus**. While they argued that *ultimately* the world could be understood in terms of a single element, they did not dispute that the world really did contain multiple manifestations of that element. Furthermore, in order for that element to be able to appear in those manifestations, it had to have the capacity for change. Thales and Anaximenes sought to explain the world of everyday experience but did not dispute its existence. Parmenides was far more radical and his explanation of the nature of the world challenged every aspect of everyday experience and common sense.

Although **Zeno of Elea** seems to have been his only direct and immediate follower, the influence of Parmenides was substantial. In putting forward such a drastic and radical account of the true nature of the world, he helped to set the agenda for metaphysics for decades, if not centuries, to come.

(D. Gallop, *Parmenides of Elea*, Toronto, Toronto University Press, 1984; Jonathan Barnes, *Early Greek Philosophy*, Harmondsworth, Penguin, 1987) [S. Austin, *Parmenides: being, bounds and logic*, New Haven, Yale University Press, 1986]

PARMENISCUS [1] (sixth/fifth century BC)
According to **Favorinus**, there was a tradition that **Xenophanes of Colophon** had been sold into slavery and rescued from that fate by Parmeniscus, a Pythagorean.

PARMENISCUS [2] (first century AD?)
Parmeniscus was the author of a work entitled *Banquet of the Cynics* and it is thought he was a Cynic himself. The work is quoted at length by **Cynulcus** in *Scholars at Dinner* by **Athenaeus of Naucratis**. The historicity of the characters he portrays is disputed.

PARMENISCUS OF ALEXANDRIA
Parmeniscus was a scholar with a wide range of interests. He wrote on history, grammar, astrology and astronomy. He produced an important commentary on the work of **Aratus of Soli**.

PARMISCUS OF METAPONTUM (sixth/fifth century BC?)
According to **Iamblichus of Chalcis**, Parmiscus was a Pythagorean. It is possible that he is to be identified with **Parmeniscus [1]**.

PASEAS OF CYRENE (third century BC)
Paseas was a pupil of **Lacydes of Cyrene**.

PASICLES (fourth/third century BC)
Pasicles was the son of **Crates of Thebes** and **Hipparchia of Maronea**. He was raised as a Cynic.

PASICLES OF RHODES (fourth century BC)
Pasicles is thought to have been a student of **Aristotle [1]**.

PASICLES OF THEBES (fourth/third century BC)
Pasicles was the brother, and perhaps the student, of **Crates of Thebes**. However, there is also a strong tradition that he was a Megarian rather than a Cynic, perhaps having studied with **Diocleides**. He may have been a teacher of **Stilpo**. The son of Crates was also called **Pasicles**.

PASIPHILIUS (fourth century AD)
Pasiphilius was a philosopher in Antioch who was tortured after helping someone falsely accused of treason to escape. He refused to give his torturers what they wanted, and was beheaded.

PASIPHON (fourth century BC?)
Pasiphon belonged to the school of Eretria. He was said by some to have been the real author of dialogues attributed to **Aeschines of Sphettus**.

PASYLUS (third century BC)
According to **Diogenes Laertius**, **Chrysippus of Soli** dedicated some of his works on logic to Pasylus. He was presumably a Stoic, and perhaps a pupil.

PATAECUS (sixth century BC?)
In his account of the life of **Solon**, **Plutarch of Chaeronea** mentions Pataecus,

who claimed to have inherited the soul of Aesop. This suggests he may have been a Pythagorean.

PATERIUS (fourth century AD)
Paterius was a Neoplatonist who probably taught in Athens. He wrote a number of commentaries.

PATRICIUS [1] (fourth century AD)
Patricius was a philosopher who had a large villa near Heliopolis (Baalbek). He had it decorated with a series of mosaics depicting the early life of Alexander the Great and testifying to his own wisdom and piety.

PATRICIUS [2] (fifth century AD)
Patricius was a philosopher said by **Damascius** to have confused philosophy and theology.

PATRO (first century BC)
Patro was a leading Epicurean in Athens. He was a pupil of **Phaedrus** and succeeded him as head of the school. He was a close friend of Titus Pomponius **Atticus**.

PATROCLES (fourth/third century BC?)
Patrocles was the supposed recipient of a letter falsely attributed to **Crates of Thebes**. Crates advises him to model himself on **Diogenes of Sinope**.

PAUL OF ALEXANDRIA (fourth century AD)
According to **Suda**, Paul was a philosopher who was particularly interested in astrology and wrote a number of books on the subject.

PAULINUS OF NOLA (fourth/fifth century AD)
Paulinus was a wealthy man who had a career in public life before becoming a monk. He wrote many poems and letters, some of which survive. Some see the influence of Stoicism on his views concerning the monastic life. His son was **Jovius**.
(Paulinus of Nola, *Letters* (2 vols), trans. P.G. Walsh, New York, Newman Press, 1966-67; Paulinus of Nola, *The Poems*, trans. P.G. Walsh, New York, Newman Press, 1975)

PAULINUS OF SCYTHOPOLIS (third century AD)
Paulinus was a pupil of **Plotinus**, but had a reputation for not being a very good student of philosophy. He was also a doctor.

PAULUS (third century BC)
According to **Clement of Alexandria**, Paulus was a pupil of **Lacydes of Cyrene**. When tortured, he bit his tongue off and spat it out rather than betray a secret.

PAUSANIAS
Diogenes Laertius mentions an author of this name who wrote commentaries

on **Heraclitus of Ephesus**, earning for himself the nickname Heracleitistes ('imitator of Heraclitus').

PAUSANIAS OF ACRAGAS (fifth century BC)
Pausanias was a friend and follower of **Empedocles of Acragas**, the dedicatee of one of his poems, and the author of an account of his life and death.

PAUSANIAS OF PONTUS (second century BC)
Pausanias was a pupil of **Panaetius of Rhodes**.

PEISICRATES OF TARENTUM (fifth century BC?)
According to **Iamblichus of Chalcis**, Peisicrates was a Pythagorean.

PEISIRRODUS OF TARENTUM (fifth century BC?)
According to **Iamblichus of Chalcis**, Peisirrodus was a Pythagorean.

PEISIRRODE OF TARENTUM (fifth century BC?)
According to **Iamblichus of Chalcis**, Peisirrode was one of the most famous Pythagorean women.

PEISON (second century BC)
Peison was a pupil of **Panaetius of Rhodes**.

PELAGIUS (fourth/fifth century AD)
Pelagius was a British monk and teacher, famous for his defence of the doctrine of free will, which he believed to be the only sound basis for an adequate account of moral responsibility. He held that people were free to choose between good and evil, and that the good was embodied in divine law. As such, he was opposed to the doctrine of original sin insisted upon by **Augustine**. As a result of Augustine's attacks on him, Pelagius was excommunicated in AD 417, along with his follower **Celestius**, and his views were condemned as heretical. Pelagius probably died not long afterwards. Another follower, **Julian of Eclanum**, continued to support the Pelagian cause.
[John Ferguson, *Pelagius: an historical and theological study*, Cambridge, Heffer, 1957]

PELOPS (fifth century AD)
Pelops is one of a group of seven philosophers said to have accompanied **Eudocia** on her journey from Athens to Constantinople. Various sayings were attributed to them.

PEMPELUS OF THURII
The name of Pempelus is attached to some surviving fragments of Pythagorean writings on parenthood.
(David Fideler (ed.), *The Pythagorean Sourcebook*, Grand Rapids, Phanes, 1987)

PEREGRINUS PROTEUS (second century AD)
Peregrinus was an extremely colourful character, the subject of an essay by **Lucian of Samosata**. Originally from Parium, he fled from there on suspicion

of killing his father, eventually arriving in Palestine where he made the acquaintance of a number of Christians, either becoming or pretending to be one himself. Some time later he got into difficulties with the local authorities and returned to Parium. At that point he seems to have become a Cynic, or at least adopted the appearance of one. He went back to Palestine, where he fell out with the Christians and decided to move on to Egypt. While there he studied with **Agathobolus of Alexandria**. After a while he moved on again, this time to Italy. There he annoyed the authorities sufficiently for them to banish him, so he went to Greece. In Athens he had contact with **Herodes Atticus** (whom he pestered and frequently abused) and **Demonax**. He is best known for his dramatic death, jumping onto a funeral pyre at the Olympic Games in AD 165. He had advertised his intentions well in advance, and **Theagenes of Patras** was on hand to advertise his teacher's impending fate and ensure that he died before a large audience. Opinions differ as to the motives of Pereginus. His self-immolation was regarded by some as a demonstration of philosophical imperturbability in the face of death, while others dismissed it as a bizarre publicity stunt. He is said to have written some works of Christian apologetics, but if he did, none have survived. Neither has the explanation of his nickname 'Proteus', which perhaps suggests that he was regarded as something of a slippery character.

PERIANDER (seventh/sixth century BC)
Periander was a generally unpleasant character but for some reason the ancient Greeks chose to regard him as one of their Seven Sages. He ruled Corinth as a tyrant for many years and killed his wife in a fit of rage. The fact that sayings attributed to him include one praising democracy above tyranny and another warning of the dangers of impetuosity scarcely seems like adequate compensation.

PERICLES (fifth century AD)
Pericles originally came from Lydia, but moved to Athens. He was active as a philosopher there at the same time as **Proclus** [1].

PERICLES OF CHOLARGES (fifth century BC)
Famous for being one of the great statesmen of Athens, Pericles was also at one time a pupil of **Anaxagoras of Clazomenae** and for twenty years had **Aspasia** as his companion.

PERICTIONE
The name of Perictione is attached to some surviving fragments of Pythagorean writings about a woman's life. The author appears to have borrowed the name from the mother of **Plato** [1].
(David Fideler (ed.), *The Pythagorean Sourcebook*, Grand Rapids, Phanes, 1987)

PERSAEUS OF CITIUM (third century BC)
Persaeus was a close friend of **Zeno of Citium**, and they shared a house together during their time in Athens. He wrote a number of works, although

not all of them were philosophical in nature. He believed that everything that was wrong or bad was equally wrong or bad, and that even the wise were bound to base their actions on opinions sometimes. He also held the view that many 'gods' were in fact originally things that were useful to people, or human beings who had made important discoveries. Because of this he was sometimes regarded as an agnostic or even an atheist. He became an enemy of **Menedemus of Eretria** because they disagreed on matters of politics, as a result of which Menedemus called him the worst man alive

PERSIUS, FLACCUS AULUS (first century AD)
Persius is best known as a satirical poet, but in his youth he studied with Lucius Annaeus **Cornutus**, to whom he wrote a poetical tribute and to whom he left his works on his death. A strong belief in the value of Stoic ethics lies beneath much of his satire. He was a friend of **Thrasea Paetus**, and was related to him by marriage. Through this connection he became associated with the Stoic opposition to Nero, but died before the emperor took action against them.
(Juvenal and Persius, trans. S.M. Broad, Loeb, 2004)

PETOSIRIS (fourth/third century BC?)
According to **Suda**, Petosiris was a philosopher from Egypt who edited some astrological and religious texts. Certainly his name, along with that of **Nechepso,** became associated with Egyptian astrology. It is possible that this Petosiris is to be identified with the builder of a tomb discovered in ancient Hermopolis in 1919 and who was a priest of Thoth, the god of wisdom.

PETRON OF HIMERA (sixth/fifth century BC?)
Petron was an early Pythagorean from Sicily who claimed that there were 183 worlds arranged in the form of a triangle, sixty on each side and one at each angle.

PETRONIUS ARISTOCRATES (first century AD)
Petronius came from Magnesia and was a friend of **Persius**. He was an accomplished philosopher and led a scholarly and pious life.

PETRUS (sixth/seventh century AD)
Petrus came from Arabia and went to Alexandria to study philosophy. His principal claim to fame is that he helped the Persians to enter the city when they attacked it in AD 617.

PHAEDO OF ELIS (fifth/fourth century BC)
Phaedo was a young follower of **Socrates** and was present at his death, according to **Plato** [1], who named after him the dialogue that recounted the events of Socrates' last day. Some time later he returned to Elis where he founded his own school. Unfortunately, it is not at all clear what the school taught. There are doubts as to whether he ever wrote anything, but if he did, nothing has survived. **Plistanus of Elis** took over the school when he died.

PHAEDO OF POSIDONIA
According to **Iamblichus of Chalcis**, Phaedo was a Pythagorean.

PHAEDRUS (second/first century BC)
Phaedrus was an Epicurean who taught in both Rome and Athens. In Rome, the young **Cicero** was one of his pupils. In Athens he may have succeeded **Zeno of Sidon** [2] as head of the school. He died in 70 BC.

PHAENYLUS (fourth century BC?)
Phaenylus was the supposed recipient of a letter falsely attributed to **Diogenes of Sinope** and is assumed to have been a Cynic.

PHAETES OF PHOCAEA (third century BC)
Phaetes was a pupil of **Lacydes of Cyrene**.

PHANIAS (first century BC)
Phanias was a pupil of **Posidonius of Apamea**.

PHANIAS OF ERESUS (fourth century BC)
Phanias was a Peripatetic and a friend of **Theophrastus of Eresus**. According to **Diogenes Laertius**, he wrote a book on **Socrates** and his followers.

PHANOMACHUS (fourth century BC?)
Phanomachus was the recipient of a letter falsely attributed to **Diogenes of Sinope** and is assumed to have been a Cynic.

PHANTO OF PHLIUS (fifth century BC?)
Phanto was an early Pythagorean who moved to Italy and seems to have left there again when the community at Rhegium broke up.

PHARIANUS (fourth century AD)
Pharianus was a friend of the emperor **Julian**. As young men they studied philosophy together, along with **Eumenius**.

PHARNACES (first/second century AD)
Pharnaces appears as a Stoic in a dialogue by **Plutarch of Chaeronea**. Many question his historicity.

PHEMONOË
Antisthenes of Rhodes attributed the famous proverb 'Know thyself' to Phemonoë. She was said to have been a priestess of Apollo, and the first to deliver the god's oracles in verse.

PHERECYDES OF SYROS (sixth century BC)
Pherecydes was said to have been a pupil of **Pittacus** and the teacher of **Pythagoras**. He was credited with miraculous powers of foresight, and with being the first Greek to write in prose. His subject was the origins of the gods and the world. He was claimed to have had access to secret Phoenician books, but opinions differ on how great an oriental influence can be detected in his

thought. There are numerous and contradictory accounts of his death, including one that he threw himself down the mountainside at Delphi.

PHILADELPHUS OF PTOLEMAIS (second/third century AD)
Philadelphus is one of the philosophers in *Scholars at Dinner* by **Athenaeus of Naucratis**.

PHILARCHUS (third century BC)
Chrysippus of Soli dedicated a book on logic to Philarchus, suggesting he was either a colleague or a pupil.

PHILINUS OF COS (third century BC)
Philinus was one of the founders of the Empiricist school of medicine, a slightly younger contemporary of **Serapion**.

PHILIP (third century BC)
Chrysippus of Soli dedicated a book on logic to Philip, suggesting he was either a colleague or a pupil.

PHILIP OF MEGARA
Diogenes Laertius quotes Philip, who had written about the life of **Stilpo**. He is described as a philosopher, and was perhaps a member of the school of Megara himself.

PHILIP OF OPUS (fourth century BC)
Philip was a pupil of **Plato** [1] and achieved fame mainly as an astronomer. He is widely thought to have edited Plato's *Laws* and written the appendix to it known as the *Epinomis*. He is sometimes known as Philip of Mende, although his most likely birthplace was Medma, an Italian colony of Opus. The *Epinomis* is notable for its treatment of the subject of daemons.
[John Dillon, *The Heirs of Plato: a study of the Old Academy (347-274 BC)*, Oxford, Clarendon Press, 2003]

PHILIP OF PRUSA (first/second century AD)
Philip was a Stoic and historian. He was a contemporary of **Plutarch of Chaeronea** and appears as a character in some of his writings.

PHILIPONUS see JOHN PHILOPONUS

PHILIPPUS (fourth/fifth century AD)
The only thing known about Philippus is that he was a philosopher who died in AD 423.

PHILISCUS (second century AD)
Philiscus was one of two Epicureans (the other was **Alcius**) expelled from Rome sometime between AD 150 and AD 175.

PHILISCUS OF AEGINA (fourth century BC)
Philiscus was a follower of **Diogenes of Sinope** and the brother of another follower, **Androsthenes of Aegina**. He was also said to be a pupil of **Stilpo** and

a teacher to Alexander the Great, but it is extremely unlikely that he was all of these things. The tragedies sometimes attributed to Diogenes may have in fact been written by Philiscus.

PHILISCUS OF MELOS (first century AD)
Philiscus was a follower of **Apollonius of Tyana**. He fell ill and Apollonius nursed him until he died.

PHILISTION (fourth century BC)
Philistius was a Platonist and a pupil of **Xenocrates of Chalcedon**.

PHILO [1] (fourth century BC)
Philo was a pupil of **Aristotle** [1].

PHILO [2] (fourth/third century BC?)
According to **Diogenes Laertius, Chrysippus of Soli** wrote two books that were replies to works by Philo. It is not clear which Philo is meant, and neither book is actually addressed to him, suggesting he was either not alive or not a Stoic. Some think this Philo may be **Philo the Dialectician.**

PHILO OF ALEXANDRIA or PHILO JUDAEUS (first century BC/first century AD)
Philo was a Jew who lived in Egypt and wrote in Greek. He came from a wealthy family and spent his whole life in Alexandria, active in the Jewish community there. Philosophically, he is generally regarded as a Platonist, although some have regarded him as a gnostic. He was certainly only a Platonist up to a point and it may be best to regard him as an eclectic. Above all, however, he was a Jew and the bulk of his surviving writings are discussions of the Pentateuch. In them he develops an allegorical method of interpretation that had earlier emerged within Stoicism and would later be adopted by Christian commentators. He postulated a transcendent God, knowable mystically but not intellectually. God's first creation is the Logos, Philo's account of which incorporates elements from Platonism, Stoicism and gnosticism. The Logos is a key intermediary between the transcendent and the material world. Philo's philosophy is sometimes seen as a forerunner of Neoplatonism, and had an influence on the development of Christian theology. Perversely, perhaps, his impact within Judaism appears to have been relatively slight.
(*The Works of Philo*, trans. C.D. Yonge, New York, Hendrickson, 1993)
[A.H. Armstrong (ed.), *The Cambridge History of Later Greek and Early Medieval Philosophy*, Cambridge, Cambridge University Press, 1970; John Dillon, *The Middle Platonists 80 BC to AD 220*, London, Duckworth, 1996; Marian Hillar, 'Philo of Alexandria', *Internet Encyclopaedia of Philosophy*, www.iep.utm.edu/p/philo.htm]

PHILO OF ATHENS (fourth/third century BC)
Philo was a friend and follower of **Pyrrho of Elis**. He had a reputation for relishing debate.

PHILO OF LARISA (second/first century BC)

Philo was a Platonist, and first studied philosophy in his home town with **Callicles of Larisa**. He then moved to Athens to study with **Clitomachus of Carthage**, and eventually succeeded him as head of the Academy in 109 BC. In 88 BC, when Athens was caught up in the war between Mithridates and the Romans, he decided to remove himself to Rome, taking his pupil **Antiochus of Ascalon** with him. There he continued to teach, one of his students being **Cicero**. He died a few years later in 83 BC.

Philo appears to have changed his philosophical position more than once during his career. The Academy he inherited was already sceptical, but interpretations of what Scepticism actually meant differed. Philo was first of all prepared to concede that if knowledge was not possible, then something very close to it was possible, something that, for practical purposes, was tantamount to knowledge. Later, he came to believe that what was possible was not just tantamount to knowledge, but knowledge itself. However, in both cases he retained the distinction between having knowledge and knowing that one had it. One could have knowledge, but one could never be sure one had it. In this sense, he always remained a Sceptic since claims to certainty were always problematic under each position he adopted. After Philo, **Antiochus of Ascalon** led the Academy in a more eclectic direction.

[H. Tarrant, *Scepticism or Platonism? The Philosophy of the Fourth Academy*, Cambridge, Cambridge University Press, 1985]

PHILO THE DIALECTICIAN (fourth/third century BC)

According to **Diogenes Laertius**, Philo was a friend of **Zeno of Citium**. He was also probably a pupil of **Diodorus Cronus**, and was responsible for making advances in the development of logic. He is sometimes referred to as Philo of Megara.

[*Routledge Encyclopaedia of Philosophy*, vol. 7]

PHILOCHORUS (third century BC)

Philochorus was primarily known as an historian, but his writings also embraced philosophical topics. He is said to have written a book on Pythagorean women.

PHILOCRATES (third/second century BC)

Philocrates was a nephew and pupil of **Chrysippus of Soli**, and the brother of **Aristocreon**.

PHILODAMUS OF LOCRI (fifth century BC?)

According to **Iamblichus of Chalcis**, Philodamus was a Pythagorean.

PHILODEMUS OF GADARA (first century BC)

Philodemus was an Epicurean who studied in Athens before moving to Italy. He became friends with **Piso Caesoninus** who gave him a villa at Herculaneum in which to live and work. There he wrote and taught for many years, with Piso himself being one of his pupils. Philodemus composed many poems in

addition to producing a number of prose works which included a history of philosophy. After he died, his personal library remained at the villa in Herculaneum where it was subsequently buried by the eruption of Vesuvius in AD 79. Since excavations began at Herculaneum in the eighteenth century, a number of items from the library have been recovered and more may remain buried.
[*Routledge Encyclopaedia of Philosophy*, vol. 7]

PHILOLAUS OF CROTON or OF TARENTUM (fifth century BC)
According to **Iamblichus of Chalcis**, Philolaus was a pupil of **Pythagoras**, but the evidence suggests that he was born after Pythagoras died. However, he is generally credited with being the first Pythagorean to set the school's teachings down in writing. He put forward a theory of metaphysics that posited two fundamental principles, the unlimited and the limiting, which were the source of everything else. Because these two principles were opposites, they could co-exist only on the basis of some kind of harmony. For the Pythagoreans, harmony was understood in mathematical terms, consequently number seems to have played an important, although not entirely clear, role in the cosmology of Philolaus. He also wrote on astronomy and his work in this area is notable for the fact that he does not place Earth at the centre of the cosmos, but instead has it orbiting a central fire. How much of his thought was original and how much was taken directly from Pythagoras is impossible to know and has often been disputed. **Eurytus of Tarentum** was probably a pupil of Philolaus and the two names are often linked. **Simmias of Thebes** and **Cebes of Thebes** are also thought to have been his pupils, and Philolaus is said to have taught in Thebes after leaving Italy when the Pythagorean school in Croton was disbanded. There was a tradition that **Democritus of Abdera** was another student, but this is less well-founded.
(Jonathan Barnes, *Early Greek Philosophy*, Harmondsworth, Penguin, 1987)
[C.A. Huffman, *Philolaus of Croton: Pythagorean and Presocratic*, Cambridge, Cambridge University Press, 1993]

PHILOMATHES (third century BC)
According to **Diogenes Laertius, Chrysippus of Soli** dedicated a number of his books on logic to Philomathes. The title of one of them indicates that Philomathes was himself an author of works on logic. He was presumably also a Stoic.

PHILOMELUS (third century BC?)
Philomelus was a Sceptic.

PHILONICUS (fourth century BC?)
Philonicus belonged to the school of Megara.

PHILONIDES (second century BC)
Philonides was an Epicurean with a special interest in mathematics. He was a pupil of both **Basilides of Syria** and **Thespis**. He established himself in Antioch

at the court of the Seleucids and converted **Antiochus Epiphanes** to his philosophy. Many seem to have studied with him there. He collected all the works of **Epicurus** for the royal library and produced summaries of a number of them. His name is sometimes associated with Laodicea because he was sent there to govern the city.

PHILONIDES OF TARENTUM (fifth/fourth century BC)
According to **Iamblichus of Chalcis**, Philonides was a Pythagorean. Someone of the same name is mentioned in the ninth letter of **Plato** [1], and it is thought that he may be the same person.

PHILONIDES OF THEBES (fourth/third century BC)
According to **Diogenes Laertius**, Philonides was a pupil of **Zeno of Citium**. When Antigonus, the king of Macedonia, wrote to Zeno asking for a teacher, he sent Philonides to him, along with **Persaeus**.

PHILOPATOR (first/second century AD)
Philopator was a Stoic, and contributed to the debate within the school on fate and determinism. He believed it was possible for people to be genuinely responsible for their actions even if they could not have acted other than the way they did.

PHILOPOEMEN (third/second century BC)
Philopoemen came from Megalopolis and was a leader of the Greeks in their battle against Roman domination. He was a pupil of **Demophanes** and **Ecdelus**.

PHILOPONUS see JOHN PHILOPONUS

PHILOSTRATUS, FLAVIUS (second/third century AD)
The family of Philostratus came from Lemnos, although he spent most of his life in Athens. Exactly what he wrote is uncertain, but it is generally accepted that a life of **Apollonius of Tyana** (written at the request of **Julia Domna**) and a collection of *Lives of the Sophists* are by him, both of which survive. They are valuable, although not always reliable, sources of information. Some other works bearing the name of Philostratus may be by him or by members of the same family, which had something of a literary tradition.
(Philostratus, *Lives of the Sophists* and Eunapius, *Lives of the Sophists*, trans. W.C. Wright, Loeb, 1921; Philostratus, *Life of Apollonius of Tyana* (2 vols), trans. C.P. Jones, Loeb, 2005; Philostratus, *Life of Apollonius*, trans. C.P. Jones, Harmondsworth, Penguin, 1970)

PHILOSTRATUS THE EGYPTIAN (first century BC)
According to Flavius **Philostratus**, Philostratus the Egyptian studied philosophy alongside Cleopatra. The extent to which she was actually interested in the subject is unclear. There were some philosophers amongst her inner circle of friends in Alexandria, but Philostratus was probably not one of them. He claimed to be a Platonist, but was dismissed by most as a mere sophist. Certainly his reputation appears to have been limited to oratory.

PHILOXENUS [1] (fifth century BC)
According to a surviving fragment of a work attributed to **Aeschines of Sphettus**, Philoxenus was a pupil of **Anaxagoras of Clazomenae** and a generally undesirable character. Some think that **Protagoras of Abdera** is meant here rather than Anaxagoras.

PHILOXENUS [2] (fourth century BC)
Aristotle [1] dedicated one of his books to a Philoxenus, possibly a well-known poet or painter of the time.

PHILTYS OF CROTON (fifth century BC?)
According to **Iamblichus of Chalcis**, Philtys was one of the most famous Pythagorean women.

PHINTIAS OF SYRACUSE (fourth century BC)
Phintias was a Pythagorean. It was said that Dionysius I of Syracuse, at the instigation of others, condemned him to death on trumped up charges in order to test his moral strength. Phintias calmly asked for time to arrange his affairs, and said that his friend **Damon of Syracuse** would stand in for him while he was gone. Dionysius was amazed when Damon agreed to the arrangement, and even more amazed when Phintias duly returned at the end of the day to accept his punishment.

PHOCION CHRESTOS (fourth century BC)
Phocion was best known as an Athenian statesman and military leader, but he also took an interest in philosophy. He is variously said to have been a pupil of **Plato** [1], **Xenocrates of Chalcedon** and **Diogenes of Sinope**, and he may have associated with all of them at one time or another. He led a very simple life, suggesting that he may have favoured Cynicism more than Platonism. His nickname of Chrestos meaning 'the Good' or 'the Honest', indicated the public esteem in which he was held. He was renowned for his incorruptibility and integrity. However, he also always made a point of voting against the majority, in the belief that the majority was always wrong. He eventually became the victim of political machinations, and was condemned to death by the Athenian assembly in 318 BC. Like **Socrates** he was obliged to drink hemlock and like Socrates he was said to have met his death calmly.

PHOEBION (third century AD)
Phoebion was a Stoic. All his writings are lost, but he appears to have concerned himself with some of the finer details of the school's teaching.

PHOENIX OF COLOPHON (fourth/third century BC)
Phoenix was a poet who wrote a number of works that touched on ethical issues. He may have been a Cynic.

PHORMIO OF ELIS (fourth century BC)
Phormio was a pupil of **Plato** [1]. The people of Elis secured his services to reform their laws.

PHORMIO OF EPHESUS (third/second century BC)
Phormio was a Peripatetic philosopher whose name became synonymous with people who try to teach things they know nothing about. The origins of this unfortunate association was an occasion when Phormio held forth on military matters to an audience that included the Carthaginian general Hannibal, who was completely unimpressed and made no secret of the matter.

PHRAOTES (first century AD)
According to Flavius **Philostratus**, Phraotes was the king of Taxila and the pupil of **Iarchas**.

PHRASIDEMUS (fourth/third century BC)
According to **Diogenes Laertius**, Phrasidemus was a Peripatetic who became a pupil of **Stilpo**. He was particularly interested in questions about the nature of the world.

PHRONTIDAS OF TARENTUM (fifth century BC?)
According to **Iamblichus of Chalcis**, Phrontidas was a Pythagorean.

PHRYNICHUS OF LARISA (fourth century BC)
Phrynichus is said to have been a pupil of **Diogenes of Sinope**.

PHRYNICHUS OF TARENTUM (fifth century BC?)
According to **Iamblichus of Chalcis**, Phrynichus was a Pythagorean.

PHYCIADAS OF CROTON (fifth century BC?)
According to **Iamblichus of Chalcis**, Phyciadas was a Pythagorean.

PHYNTIS (fifth century BC?)
Phyntis is said to have been a Pythagorean and is probably to be identified with **Philtys**. Fragments of a book on the moderation of women are attributed to her. (David Fideler (ed.), *The Pythagorean Sourcebook*, Grand Rapids, Phanes, 1987)

PHYTIUS OF RHEGIUM (fifth century BC?)
According to **Iamblichus of Chalcis**, Phytius was a Pythagorean, and renowned as a lawmaker.

PIERIUS (third/fourth century BC)
According to **Eusebius of Caesarea**, Pierius was an elder of the church in Alexandria. He led a life of poverty while pursuing his philosophical studies.

PISISTRATUS (sixth century BC)
Pisistratus ruled Athens from 546 BC until his death in 529 BC. He was regarded as a benevolent dictator and some reckoned him amongst the Seven Sages of ancient Greece.

PISISTRATUS OF EPHESUS
Pisistratus was a source used by **Diogenes Laertius**. He denied that the writings attributed to **Aeschines of Sphettus** were actually by him.

PISITHEUS (third/fourth century AD)
Pisitheus was a Neoplatonist and a pupil of **Theodorus of Asine**. He wrote a commentary on the *Timaeus* of **Plato** [1].

PISO CAESONINUS, LUCIUS CALPURNIUS (first century BC)
Piso was the father-in-law of Julius **Caesar**, and spent many years of his active political life trying to prevent civil war. In later life he became interested in Epicureanism, studying with **Philodemus of Gadara**. For some time, Philodemus lived in Piso's villa at Herculaneum, and his library has been discovered there.

PISO FRUGI CALPURNIANUS, MARCUS PUPIUS (first century BC)
Piso was a friend of **Cicero**, although in later life they fell out. Cicero uses him in his *On Moral Ends* to articulate the philosophy of **Antiochus of Ascalon**. According to Cicero, he and Piso had attended lectures of Antiochus together. Piso had also studied with **Staseas of Neapolis**.

PITTACUS OF MYTILENE (seventh/sixth century BC)
Pittacus was often reckoned as one of the Seven Sages of ancient Greece. He was credited with having helped to free Lesbos from tyranny and then governing wisely for ten years before retiring from office. He appears to have coined the odd pithy saying, such as 'Know your opportunity!', as well as writing many songs and poems.

PLATO [1] (fifth/fourth century BC)
Although one of the most famous of all Western philosophers, surprisingly little is known with certainty about the life of Plato. The facts have become overlain with a great deal of legend and the two are often difficult to separate. He was evidently from an aristocratic family in Athens and as a young man attached himself to the circle of **Socrates**. After the death of Socrates he spent some time away from Athens before returning to found the Academy in around 385 BC. He visited Sicily both before and after this time, where he became friends with **Dion of Syracuse** as well as other members of the city's ruling family. On his last visit in around 360 BC he became a virtual prisoner there and had to be rescued with the help of **Archytas of Tarentum**. The remainder of his life seems to have passed without further incident and when he died he was buried at the Academy, which at that time was probably still little more than a meeting place.

The interpretation of Plato's philosophy has usually taken one of two main options. In the ancient world it was generally assumed that his philosophy was fully formed from the outset and that individual works could all be reconciled with each other within one grand scheme. In the modern world it is more often assumed that his philosophy developed and evolved over time. Consequently, while ancient scholars such as **Thrasyllus** sought to arrange Plato's dialogues according to the arrangement that made most sense thematically, modern scholars have been more concerned with ascertaining the order in which they were written. There have also been disputes over the authenticity of a handful of them.

The modern view is that Plato's earlier works owe most to the direct influence of Socrates, while the later ones reveal the emergence of a philosophy that is distinctively his own. Whereas earlier ones often end with no firm conclusion, later ones tend to be more dogmatic in tone. Although Socrates continues to appear as a character in the dialogues, it is thought that the views he expresses are increasingly those of Plato. In what is usually accepted to be Plato's last work, *Laws*, Socrates does not appear at all. Furthermore, the dialogue form, used to great dramatic effect in earlier works, is retained there but has little real purpose.

It is generally agreed that Plato's first work was the *Apology*. It presents the speech made by Socrates in his own defence at his trial. Although, as was the custom of the times, a few liberties are taken in the name of artistic licence, it is thought to be authentic in its essentials.

Beyond broad agreement concerning his first and last compositions, unanimity is harder to find. The *Symposium*, for example, in which the subject of beauty is discussed, is regarded by some as an early dialogue, by some as a late one, and by some as falling in a middle period between the two. The same is true of *Phaedo* which deals with the subject of immortality. There tends to be more consensus concerning the late dialogues, with few disputing the right of *Timaeus, Critias, Philebus, Sophist* and *Statesman* to count as such. On the other hand *Laches, Lysis, Crito* and *Euthyphro* are normally regarded as early. It is widely thought that *Republic* began as an early work, which then became the first part of a later and longer one.

Some of the major dialogues harder to date are *Gorgias, Theaetetus* and *Parmenides. Gorgias*, like *Republic*, is about justice, but also sets out to clearly distinguish the concerns of philosophy from those of rhetoric. *Theaetetus* is concerned with the theory of knowledge, while *Parmenides* is one of the dialogues in which Plato talks about his Theory of Forms.

The Theory of Forms, or Theory of Ideas, is one of the most distinctive elements of Plato's thought, although he never sets it out systematically and so it has to be pieced together from observations scattered over a number of dialogues. This is one of the areas where uncertainties over the consistency and dating of Plato's works create problems. Did Plato have one single Theory of Forms that never changed? If he did, then apparently conflicting statements on the subject need to be reconciled with each other. If he did not, then later expositions of the theory should presumably be viewed as more authoritative, having been made in the light of criticisms of earlier ones.

The principal aim of the Theory of Forms seems to have been to make knowledge possible in a changing world. This was thought to be problematic because knowledge was supposed to be something fixed and stable whereas the world appeared to be a place where nothing was fixed or stable. Plato's solution was to remove the foundations of knowledge from the everyday world of experience to another realm beyond it. This was the intelligible world, so called because its contents could only be apprehended by the intellect, as opposed to the everyday sensible world, the contents of which could be grasped by the physical senses. The Forms in the intelligible world were the pure and unchanging archetypes of all the contents of the sensible world. The possibility of knowledge was bought at the price of making it both other-worldly and elitist, since it was envisaged that only a small minority of people would be able to attain to it. At the same time, knowledge was unified in the sense that all the Forms were to be found in one place. There was also a tendency, more pronounced in later Platonists than in Plato himself, to assimilate Forms to each other and so to unify knowledge in that way as well. There was another dimension to Plato's theory of knowledge based on his belief in the immortality and pre-existence of the soul. In *Meno* this is used to explain apparently innate knowledge which is presented as a kind of remembering.

Other dialogues by Plato generally accepted as authentic are *Cratylus*, *Charmides*, *Protagoras*, *Euthydemus*, *Phaedrus* and the *Lesser Hippias*. Opinions are more divided regarding *Menexenus*, *Ion*, *Greater Hippias* and *Alcibiades*, although the present tendency is to accept them in the absence of conclusive grounds for rejecting them.

Although by far his most famous pupil was **Aristotle** [1], on his death in 348 or 347 BC Plato was succeeded as head of the Academy by his nephew **Speusippus**.

(Plato, *The Collected Dialogues*, Princeton, Bollingen, 1961; Plato, *Complete Works*, Indianapolis, Hackett, 1997; also many editions of individual dialogues, especially *Republic*; classics.mit.edu/Browse/browse-Plato.html)
[Paul Friedlander, *Plato* (3 vols), trans. H. Meyerhoff, London, Routledge and Kegan Paul, 1958-69; G. Grube, *Plato's Thought*, London, Athlone Press, 1980; Richard Kraut, *The Cambridge Companion to Plato*, Cambridge, Cambridge University Press, 1992; Richard Kraut, 'Plato', *The Stanford Encyclopedia of Philosophy* (Summer 2004 Edition), Edward N. Zalta (ed.), plato.stanford.edu/archives/sum2004/entries/plato/]

PLATO [2] (fourth century BC)
According to **Diogenes Laertius**, Plato was a Peripatetic philosopher who had been a pupil of **Aristotle** [1] himself.

PLATO [3] (third century BC)
According to **Diogenes Laertius**, Plato was a pupil of **Praxiphanes**.

PLATO OF RHODES (second century BC)
Plato was a Stoic and a pupil of **Panaetius of Rhodes**.

PLATO OF SARDIS (first century BC)
Plato was an Epicurean who taught in Athens.

PLISTANUS OF ELIS (fourth century BC)
Plistanus was a follower of **Phaedo of Elis**, and became head of the school at Elis when Phaedo died.

PLOTINA, POMPEIA (first/second century AD)

Plotina was the empress of Trajan. She came from Nemausus (Nimes), and Trajan's successor Hadrian, her adopted son, erected a memorial to her there when she died. She was actively involved in Epicureanism and a benefactress of the school in Athens. Thanks to her intervention, Hadrian gave his permission for the school to elect someone who was not a Roman citizen as its head.

PLOTINUS (third century AD)

Plotinus probably came from Egypt. He studied philosophy in Alexandria under **Ammonius Saccas** for several years before joining an expedition to Persia. After this ran into difficulties, he made his way to Rome where he remained for most of the rest of his life. There he began to teach and attract a circle of followers. Most of what is known about his life is due to the biography written by **Porphyry**, who became one of his pupils and edited his writings into the book known as *Enneads*. Plotinus was evidently a popular and charismatic figure who attracted many devotees such as the senator **Rogatianus** and **Eutochius of Alexandria**, a physician who took care of him. For the last few years of his life he moved to Campania and died there in around AD 270.

He is generally regarded as the founder of Neoplatonism, although the term itself is a modern one. It is a strongly mystical interpretation of Platonism, and Plotinus had some kind of profound mystical experience on four occasions during his life. He interpreted these as a form of union with the divine source of all spiritual being. His philosophy can be seen as an attempt to make sense of these experiences and produce a metaphysical structure within which they were understandable. His philosophy was also an attempt to show others how such experiences, which he regarded as providing access to the ultimate truth, could be achieved. Consequently, while his metaphysical system describes how one level of being emerged from another, the practical purpose of this is to show how one may ascend through these levels to reach what is at once the divine, truth, goodness and unity.

Plotinus was convinced that the spiritual philosophical life was worthwhile, because of the superior kind of happiness and ultimate knowledge it could bring, but he also believed it was difficult. This seems to have been one of the reasons why he was so strongly opposed to gnosticism, as he apparently took the view that the gnostics were promising an easy route to something that could in fact be achieved only with great difficulty. However, while Plotinian mysticism stood firmly against any hint of the magical, it was always strongly ethical. Spiritual progress was made through an arduous process of purification, and this involved shedding concerns about the physical body and the passions.

How much the Neoplatonism of Plotinus owes to Ammonius Saccas is impossible to know, but the debt is usually assumed to be substantial. With regard to **Plato** [1], his most significant and substantial borrowings were from *Timaeus, Symposium, Phaedo* and *Phaedrus*. However, while he always cites Plato

in good faith, it is difficult to avoid the conclusion that, in the end, Plato serves Plotinus rather than the other way round.
(Plotinus (6 vols), trans. A.H. Armstrong, Loeb, 1966-87; Plotinus, *The Enneads*, trans. S. MacKenna, Harmondsworth, Penguin 1991 (an abridged translation); classics.mit.edu/Browse/browse-Plotinus.html)
[Lloyd P. Gerson (ed.), *The Cambridge Companion to Plotinus*, Cambridge, Cambridge University Press, 1996; D.J. O'Meara, *Plotinus: an introduction to the Enneads*, Oxford, Oxford University Press, 1993; Lloyd Gerson, 'Plotinus', *The Stanford Encyclopedia of Philosophy* (Fall 2003 Edition), Edward N. Zalta (ed.), plato.stanford.edu/archives/fall2003/entries/plotinus/]

PLUMBA (sixth century AD)
Plumba is said to have been a philosopher who composed a poem honouring the empress Sophia. However, while the empress certainly existed, Plumba may not have done.

PLUTARCH OF ATHENS (fourth/fifth century AD)
Plutarch was the son of **Nestorius**. A Neoplatonist, he was head of the Academy in Athens, eventually succeeded in that position by **Syrianus** [1]. He wrote many commentaries on the works of **Plato** [1]. Although they were highly regarded, none have survived.

PLUTARCH OF CHAERONEA (first/second century AD)
Plutarch studied under Marcus Annius **Ammonius**, and became a priest of Apollo at Delphi, not far from his native Chaeronea where he spent the greater part of his life. He was a prolific writer and many of his works survive including *Moralia*, a long set of essays including a number of philosophical ones, and *Lives*, in which he compares major figures from the histories of Greece and Rome, always with an eye to making a moral point. Some of his essays recount conversations, real, imaginary or embellished, to which he was a party in one way or another, giving the impression that under his influence Chaeronea for a while became a magnet for intellectuals of all kinds. Some of his essays were more polemical than philosophical, with the Epicureans being a favourite target. Plutarch himself is generally regarded as a Platonist, although he appears to have been an unorthodox one. One of the influences on his thought was Zoroastrianism, and this led him to regard evil as a distinct force in its own right rather than simply an absence of good.
(Plutarch, *Moralia* (15 vols), trans. F.C. Babbitt et al., Loeb, 1927-76)
[John Dillon, *The Middle Platonists 80 BC to AD 220*, London, Duckworth, 1996]

PLUTIADES (first century BC?)
According to **Strabo of Amaseia**, Plutiades was a philosopher from Tarsus who led the life of an itinerant teacher.

POEMENIUS (third/fourth century AD)
Poemenius had a work by **Iamblichus of Chalcis** dedicated to him, and it is assumed that he was a Neoplatonist.

POLEMARCHUS (fourth century BC)
Polemarchus was the pupil of **Eudoxus of Cnidus** and the teacher of **Callippus of Cyzicus**.

POLEMARCHUS OF TARENTUM (fifth century BC?)
According to **Iamblichus of Chalcis**, Polemarchus was a Pythagorean.

POLEMARCHUS OF THURII (fifth century BC)
Polemarchus came from a very rich family and owned the house in Piraeus where the *Republic* of **Plato** [1] is set and in which he is featured as a participant. He had lived most of his life in Italy, but spent his last decade or so in Athens, where he became interested in philosophy. He fell foul of the rulers of the city and was condemned to death in 404 BC. The events of his last days are recounted in Plato's *Lysis*.

POLEMAIUS OF SYBARIS (fifth century BC?)
According to **Iamblichus of Chalcis**, Polemaius was a Pythagorean.

POLEMARCHUS (fourth century BC)
Polemarchus was a pupil of **Eudoxus of Cnidus** and taught **Callipus of Cyzicus**.

POLEMO OF ATHENS (fourth/third century BC)
Polemo became head of the Academy in 314 BC on the death of his teacher **Xenocrates of Chalcedon**. Before becoming interested in philosophy, he had led a dissolute life, and first met Xenocrates when, at the instigation of his friends, he wandered drunk into the Academy wearing a garland of flowers on his head. Xenocrates simply ignored him and carried on with his lecture. After this inauspicious start, Polemo went on to become the school's star pupil. As a result of his philosophical endeavours, he became a changed person, a model husband, and totally unflappable. Even the bite of a mad dog could not disturb him. Although he received public honours, he preferred the quiet of the Academy where he could work with his students, one of whom, for a while, was **Zeno of Citium**. He was succeeded as head of Academy in around 276 BC by **Crates of Thria**. Polemo appears to have reacted against the attempts of **Speusippus** and Xenocrates to make the philosophy of **Plato** [1] more systematic, and his interests were more practical than theoretical. He taught that life should be lived in accordance with nature, which Zeno made a central tenet of Stoicism.
[John Dillon, *The Heirs of Plato: a study of the Old Academy (347-274 BC)*, Oxford, Clarendon Press, 2003]

POLEMO OF TROY (second century BC)
Polemo was a Stoic, probably a pupil of **Panaetius of Rhodes**. He published a book of inscriptions and another attacking **Eratosthenes**.

POLIADES OF SIKYON
According to **Iamblichus of Chalcis**, Poliades was a Pythagorean.

POLITES (third century BC)
Polites was a pupil of **Lacydes of Cyrene.**

POLLIO, GAIUS ASINIUS (first century BC)
Pollio played a leading role in Rome's political and cultural life. He was a friend of both **Virgil** and **Horace,** and when he went into retirement wrote a history of the civil war. His philosophical views are not known, but he was evidently not a Peripatetic as one of his books was entitled *Against Aristotle.* According to **Suda,** he also wrote about the philosopher Musonius. This cannot be **Musonius Rufus,** who was born after Pollio died, but there is no obvious earlier candidate. It may be that the work in question was written by a later Pollio, perhaps **Pollio Valerius.**

POLLIO VALERIUS (first/second century AD)
Pollio came from Alexandria and had a son, **Diodorus Valerius.** He wrote a number of philosophical works, as well as a dictionary of Attic Greek.

POLLIS (third century BC)
Chrysippus of Soli dedicated two books to Pollis, one on logic and one on ethics. He was probably either a colleague or a pupil.

POLLIUS FELIX (first century AD)
Pollius was an Epicurean and a patron of the poet Statius.

POLLUX or POLYDEUCES OF NAUCRATIS (second century AD)
Julius Pollux was a grammarian and teacher of rhetoric. He became a personal friend of the emperor Commodus to whom he dedicated his *Onomasticon,* a thematically arranged dictionary containing many excerpts from other writers.

POLUS OF LUCANIA
Polus is said to have been a Pythagorean, although some think he was a spelling mistake and should be identified with **Eccelus of Lucania.** A work on justice was attributed to him.
(David Fideler (ed.), *The Pythagorean Sourcebook,* Grand Rapids, Phanes, 1987)

POLYAENUS, TITUS AVIANUS BASSIUS (second/third century AD)
Polyaenus was a Stoic from Hadriani.

POLYAENUS OF LAMPSACUS (fourth/third century BC)
Polyaenus was an early follower of **Epicurus** and had previously been an eminent mathematician. He is said to have been convinced by Epicurus that geometry was a waste of time. He became one of the senior members of the school and his son, also called Polyaenus, became one of his pupils.

POLYBUS (fourth century BC)
Polybius was probably both the son-in-law and pupil of **Hippocrates of Cos.**

POLYCTOR OF ARGOS
According to **Iamblichus of Chalcis,** Polyctor was a Pythagorean.

POLYMNASTUS OF PHLIUS (fifth/fourth century BC)
According to **Iamblichus of Chalcis**, Polymnastus was a Pythagorean. According to **Diogenes Laertius** he studied with **Philolaus of Croton** and **Eurytus of Tarentum**. **Aristoxenus of Tarentum** met him and perhaps studied with him.

POLYSTRATUS (third century BC)
Polystratus was the third head of the Epicurean school after **Epicurus** himself and **Hermarchus of Mitylene**. He was in turn succeeded by **Dionysius** [3]. One of his works, *Contempt for the Irrational*, was found in the villa of **Piso Caesoninus** at Herculaneum. He criticised the Sceptics for questioning the evidence of the senses.

POLYSTRATUS OF ATHENS (third century BC)
Polystratus was a pupil of **Theophrastus of Eresus**. According to **Athenaeus of Naucratis** he was known as 'the Etruscan' and enjoyed wearing the dress of female 'entertainers'.

POLYXENUS (fourth century BC)
Polyxenus studied under **Euclides of Megara**. He was a friend of **Bryson of Heraclea** and a teacher of **Helicon of Cyzicus**.

POLYZELUS
The name of Polyzelus is known from a text of **Alexander of Aphrodisias** in which he discusses the subject of fate. He is assumed to have been a Peripatetic, but it is not possible to say where or when.

POMPEDIUS (first century AD)
According to the historian Josephus, Pompedius was an Epicurean senator. However, some believe that 'Pompedius' should read 'Pomponius' and take this as a reference to Publius Pomponius Secundus, a statesman and author.

POMPEIUS, SEXTUS (second/first century BC)
Sextus Pompeius was an uncle of the famous Roman general **Pompey**. He was well versed in Stoicism and a man of considerable learning, especially in the area of geometry.

POMPEY [GNAIUS POMPEIUS MAGNUS] (106-48 BC)
Pompey was a statesman and general ultimately defeated in a civil war against Julius **Caesar**. When he was 20 he met **Posidonius of Apamea** in Rome. It is said that this meeting had a great effect on him, but it is not clear to what extent he became a Stoic as such.

POMPYLUS (fourth/third century BC)
Pompylus was a slave of **Theophrastus of Eresus**, and is said also to have been a philosopher.

PONTIANUS OF NICOMEDIA (second/third century AD)
Pontianus is one of the philosophers in *Scholars at Dinner* by **Athenaeus of Naucratis**.

PORPHYRY (third century AD)

Porphyry came from Tyre and was originally called Malchus. He probably studied under Cassius **Longinus** in Athens before moving to Rome where he became a pupil of **Plotinus** as well as his biographer. He later moved to Sicily for several years and dedicated himself to writing before returning to Rome to teach. **Iamblichus of Chalcis** was one of his many pupils. He edited the *Enneads* of Plotinus and wrote a number of works of his own, some of which survive in whole or in part. One of them, *On Abstinence*, he wrote for his friend **Firmus Castricius** who had abandoned vegetarianism. He wrote a commentary on the *Categories* of **Aristotle** [1] that survives and many other commentaries on works by **Plato, Theophrastus of Eresus, Ptolemy** [1] and Plotinus that are lost. His introduction (*Isagoge*) to Aristotle's *Categories* became widely used as a logic textbook. He wrote a long work attacking Christianity which drew responses from **Apollinarius of Laodicea** and **Eusebius of Caesarea**, amongst others, and which was formally burnt in AD 448. Some suspect he may have been a Christian himself in his youth but he appears to have taken a sceptical approach to all religions for most of his life. He was a loyal follower of Plotinus more than an original thinker, but his surviving works shed important light on early Neoplatonism.

(Porphyry, *On Aristotle Categories*, trans. S. Strange, London, Duckworth, 1992; Porphyry, *On Abstinence from Killing Animals*, trans. G. Clark, London, Duckworth, 2000; E. Warren, *Porphyry the Phoenician: Isagoge*, Toronto, Pontifical Institute of Medieval Studies, 1975; John Dillon and Lloyd P. Gerson, *Neoplatonic Philosophy: introductory readings*, Indianapolis, Hackett, 2004)

[A. Smith, *Porphyry's Place in the Neoplatonic Tradition*, Hague, Nijhoff, 1974; *Routledge Encyclopaedia of Philosophy*, vol. 7]

POSIDONIUS, FLAVIUS (fourth/fifth century AD)

Posidonius came from Hermopolis and was referred to as a philosopher in a document he witnessed there.

POSIDONIUS OF ALEXANDRIA (fourth century BC)

According to **Hippobotus**, Posidonius was a pupil of **Zeno of Citium**. His principal writings appear to have been in the field of history.

POSIDONIUS OF APAMEA (second/first century BC)

Posidonius studied in Athens under **Panaetius of Rhodes**. He travelled widely before founding his own school in Rhodes, where his students included **Cicero**. They had met when Posidonius visited Rome on diplomatic business in 87 BC. A polymath, he wrote on a wide variety of topics including history, astronomy, mathematics and meteorology. He argued for a connection between the tides and the phases of the moon and devised a method for measuring the earth's circumference. His philosophical writings were also extensive, but nothing survives.

Like Panaetius, Posidonius is seen as a major figure of the Middle Stoa but he took its eclectic tendencies even further. He had a particular interest in the

Timaeus of **Plato** [1] and in what he took to be the Pythagorean influences that lay behind it. However, the ideas he tried to combine from different systems did not always sit easily together, and his metaphysical outlook strains to reconcile the ultimate unity of reality with large doses of dualism. His conception of the soul strives to be Stoic, Platonist and Pythagorean at the same time. He differed with Panaetius on the question of divination and took a more traditional Stoic line on determinism. He also formulated a philosophy of history that emphasised the importance and role of wisdom in the unfolding of events in the human world.

He was an influential figure in a variety of ways, and **Pompey** claimed that meeting him changed his life. Although posterity remembers him principally as a philosopher, his contemporaries recognised the full range of his achievements. For Posidonius they were all part of an attempt to demonstrate the unity and rationality of the world. When he died his grandson **Jason of Nysa** took over his school.

(L. Edelstein and I.G. Kidd (eds), *Posidonius*, vol. 1: *The Fragments*, Cambridge, Cambridge Unversity Press, 1972)

[I.G. Kidd, *Posidonius*, vol. 2: *The Commentary*, Cambridge, Cambridge University Press, 1988]

POSIDONIUS OF OLBIOPOLIS (third/second century BC?)
According to **Suda**, Posidonius was a sophist and historian whose works were sometimes confused with those of **Posidonius of Alexandria**.

POSSIDIUS (fourth/fifth century AD)
Possidius was a pupil of **Augustine** who became bishop of Calama. He wrote the first biography of Augustine.

POTAMO OF ALEXANDRIA (first century BC)
Potamo was the founder of an eclectic school in Alexandria, borrowing and bringing together ideas from all the main philosophical movements of that time. He believed that truth was based on reason and accurate observation. He believed that everything could be defined in terms of what it was made of, how it was made, where it was made, and the properties it was given. These he regarded as four basic principles. He believed that the good life was the virtuous life, and that material benefits, such as health, were necessary for it.

PRAETEXTATUS, VETTIUS AGORIUS (fourth century AD)
Praetextatus achieved high office under the emperor **Julian**. A man of considerable learning, he was a Neoplatonist and translated some of the works of **Themistius** [2].

PRAXAGORAS (fourth century AD)
Praxagoras was a philosopher from Athens, primarily known as an historian who wrote lives of Alexander the Great and Constantine the Great, amongst others. He is not to be confused with Praxagoras of Cos, a fourth-century BC physician who believed that the arteries contained air rather than blood.

PRAXIPHANES (fourth/third century BC)

Praxiphanes, who came from either Mitylene or Rhodes, is said to have been a pupil of **Theophrastus of Eresus** and a teacher of **Epicurus, Aratus of Soli** and **Callimachus of Cyrene**. While it is not absolutely impossible that all this is true, many doubt it, believing either that two different people called Praxiphanes are involved or that there never was a teacher of Epicurus by that name.

PRAYLUS OF THE TROAD (third century BC)

Praylus may have been a pupil of **Timon of Phlius,** and so a Sceptic. He is said to have been possessed of great personal courage and to have met his undeserved execution without a word of complaint.

PREPON (second century AD)

According to **Hippolytus,** Prepon was a follower of **Marcion**. He argued that in addition to there being principles of good and evil, there was a third and intermediate one of justice.

PRISCIAN OF LYDIA (sixth century AD)

Priscian wrote books on the philosophy of **Theophrastus of Eresus**. Most of them were commentaries but the only one that survives is a paraphrase of an original work by Theophrastus (although some suspect that a commentary on **Aristotle** [1] credited to **Simplicius** is actually by Priscianus). He also wrote a book on philosophical issues addressed to **Chosroes I**, king of Persia, and he was one of those who accompanied **Damascius** on his journey to Persia and back again. He is sometimes confused with another slightly older Priscianus who was a famous grammarian.
(Priscian, *On Theophrastus On Sense Perception*, trans. P. Huby, London, Duckworth, 1997)

PRISCIANUS (fourth century AD)

Priscianus was a philosopher at Rome, and a friend of **Symmachus**.

PRISCILLIAN (fourth century AD)

Priscillian and his followers had the dubious distinction of being the first people put to death for heresy by the Christian church. He espoused a form of gnosticism, and believed that the physical world was an evil place to which souls were sent as a punishment.

PRISCUS (fourth century AD)

Priscus originally came from Epirus and studied philosophy in Pergamum under **Aedesius**. He became a personal friend of the emperor **Julian** and accompanied him on his expedition to Persia. After Julian's death he settled in Antioch, where he was accused of being a magician. However, he suffered no ill effects from the experience and left for Athens where he taught for many years. He was a Neoplatonist and a great admirer of the works of **Iamblichus of Chalcis.**

PROBUS (fourth/fifth century AD)
Probus studied under **Eusebius** [2] at the same time as **Sidonius Apollinaris** and may have assisted Eusebius in his teaching. He married the cousin of Sidonius, who may also have been the daughter of **Simplicius**.

PROCLES (fourth century BC)
According to **Plutarch of Chaeronea**, Procles was a student at the Academy at the same time as **Xenocrates of Chalcedon**.

PROCLES OF METAPONTUM (fifth century BC?)
According to **Iamblichus of Chalcis**, Procles was a Pythagorean.

PROCLINUS (third century AD)
Proclinus was a Platonist who produced some compilations and editions of the works of earlier writers.

PROCLUS [1] (fifth century AD)
Proclus was born in Constantinople, although he is sometimes referred to as 'the Lycian' after the place where he spent most of his childhood and from which his family originally came. He went to Alexandria where he studied first under a sophist called Leonas and then under **Olympiodorus** [1]. It is said that during his time with Olympiodorus he learnt by heart all the writings of **Aristotle** [1] on logic. He moved to Athens where he became a pupil of both **Plutarch of Athens** and **Syrianus** [1]. When Syrianus died, he succeeded him as head of the school. He was a popular and hard working teacher who led a simple life. He claimed he could achieve such occult acts as influencing the weather and came to regard himself as the reincarnation of the Pythagorean **Nicomachus of Gerasa**. When Proclus died in AD 485 he was succeeded by **Marinus of Neapolis**, one of his many accomplished pupils who also included **Ammonius, Asclepiodotus of Alexandria, Hierius of Athens** and **Isidore of Alexandria**.

Proclus is said to have written a large number of books, including works on **Pythagoras, Plato** [1], Hesiod and Homer, but only a few survive. The best known is his *Elements of Theology*, an attempt to present the teachings of Neoplatonism in a systematic format borrowed from the celebrated work on geometry by **Euclid** (claimed by Proclus to be a Platonist himself). In it the whole of reality is presented within a single structure which is formed of a complex set of triads. The single structure represents the ultimate unity of reality while the triads represent the multiplicity of experience. Read downwards, the hierarchy explains the process of emanation whereby things come into being, read upwards it explains the process of mystical identification with the divine. The extent to which the *Elements of Theology* is or is intended to be original is disputed, but it remains a defining text of Neoplatonism. In the Middle Ages, a paraphrase of it was in circulation, but it was mistakenly believed to be the work of **Aristotle** [1] rather than Proclus.
(Proclus, *The Elements of Theology*, trans. E.R. Dodds, Oxford, Clarendon Press,

1963, *Proclus' Commentary on Plato's Parmenides*, trans. G.R. Morrow and John Dillon, Princeton, Princeton UP, 1987; Proclus, *On the Existence of Evils*, trans. J. Opsomer and C. Steel, London, Duckworth, 2003; John Dillon and Lloyd P. Gerson, *Neoplatonic Philosophy: introductory readings*, Indianapolis, Hackett, 2004)
[A.H. Armstrong (ed.), *The Cambridge History of Later Greek and Early Medieval Philosophy*, Cambridge, Cambridge University Press, 1970]

PROCLUS [2] (fifth/sixth century AD)
Proclus probably came from Athens. Although recognised as a philosopher, he was also an inventor and helped to develop a kind of flame-thrower for use at sea.

PROCLUS [3] (fifth/sixth century AD)
Proclus was known both as a philosopher and as an interpreter of dreams. He probably lived and taught in Constantinople, and interpreted a dream for the emperor Athanasius not long before the emperor died.

PROCLUS OF MALLUS
According to **Suda**, Proclus was a Stoic who wrote a book *Against Epicurus*.

PROCOPIUS (fourth/fifth century AD)
Procopius was a friend of **Hellespontius**. On his death bed Hellespontius exhorted Procopius to become a follower of **Chrysanthius of Sardis**, which he did.

PROCOPIUS OF GAZA (fifth/sixth century AD)
Procopius was primarily known as a sophist and theologian, writing a number of works on books of the Bible. A work criticising the philosophy of **Proclus [1]** has also been attributed to him by some, although it may have been written by an earlier person of the same name.

PRODICUS OF CEOS (fifth century BC)
Procicus features in a number of the dialogues of **Plato [1]**, where he is represented as someone especially interested in the precise use of language. Originally from the island of Ceos, he made his name there before travelling further afield and making a reputation for himself as a teacher and intellectual. He wrote a number of works but only fragments survive and it is difficult to get a sense of his thought from them. However, he seems to have taken an interest in many different areas of philosophy, although he is sometimes dismissed as a sophist. One of his pupils was **Theramenes of Stiria**.
(Rosemary Kent Sprague (ed.), *The Older Sophists*, Indianapolis, Hackett, 2001)
[W.K.C. Guthrie, *The Sophists*, Cambridge, Cambridge University Press, 1971]

PRORUS OF CYRENE (fifth/fourth century BC?)
According to **Iamblichus of Chalcis**, Prorus was a Pythagorean. He tells how, when Prorus was in financial difficulties, another Pythagorean, **Clinias of Tarentum**, selflessly went to his aid. This is intended as an illustration of the

special nature of Pythagorean friendship. **Aristippus of Cyrene** dedicated a work to someone called Prorus, but it is not clear if it is the same person.

PROSENES or PROSENAS (third century AD)
Prosenes was a Peripatetic philosopher who believed that **Plato** [1] had borrowed a great deal of his philosophy from earlier thinkers (including **Protagoras of Abdera**) without acknowledging the fact. He suggested that this was not widely known because the works of Plato's predecessors were difficult to find. He seems to have taught in Athens and was a friend of both **Porphyry** and Cassius **Longinus**.

PROTAGORAS
According to **Diogenes Laertius**, there was a Stoic philosopher called Protagoras.

PROTAGORAS OF ABDERA (fifth century BC)
Protagoras was one of the leading sophists of his age, and features in the dialogue of **Plato** [1] named after him. He is said to have first studied philosophy with **Democritus of Abdera** before moving to Athens where he taught for many years and amassed a considerable sum of money by doing so. It is said that he was expelled from Athens for atheism and drowned while sailing to Sicily. However, the story is widely doubted. He did not deny the existence of the gods, but denied knowing whether they existed or not. This appears to have been in keeping with his general approach to knowledge which in some ways bordered on Scepticism, but in other ways looks more like relativism. He did not so much deny the existence or possibility of truth as deny the existence of a criterion whereby one claim to it could be judged inferior or superior to another. His famous observation that 'Man is the measure of all things' is often taken to be a statement of the principle of relativism, although how far he extended its application is unclear, and there have been many different interpretations of the observation.
(Rosemary Kent Sprague (ed.) *The Older Sophists*, Indianapolis, Hackett, 2001) [W.K.C. Guthrie, *The Sophists*, Cambridge, Cambridge University Press, 1971; Plato, *Protagoras*, trans. C.C.W. Taylor, Oxford, Clarendon Press 1991; Carol Poster, 'Protagoras', *Internet Encyclopaedia of Philosophy*, www.iep.utm.edu/p/protagor.htm]

PROTARCHUS OF BARGYLIA (second century BC)
Protarchus is said to have been an Epicurean and the teacher of **Demetrius Lacon**.

PROTERIUS OF CEPHALLENIA (fourth century AD)
Proterius is mentioned by **Eunapius** as one of those philosophers who was killed by the Goths at the end of the fourth century AD. Exactly what his philosophical interests were is not known, but he was evidently a well-respected individual.

PROTOGENES OF TARSUS (first/second century AD)
Protogenes was a friend of **Plutarch of Chaeronea** and appears in some of his dialogues. He became a teacher of grammar, but may have studied Platonism as a young man.

PROXENUS OF POSIDONIA
According to **Iamblichus of Chalcis**, Proxenus was a Pythagorean.

PROXENUS OF SYBARIS (fifth century BC?)
According to **Iamblichus of Chalcis**, Proxenus was a Pythagorean.

PRUDENTIUS, AURELIUS CLEMENS (fourth century AD)
After Prudentius retired from a career in public service he took up writing poetry. Most of his works are defences of Christianity in one form or another. His account of the origin of sin shows the influence of Stoicism and emphasises how people bring suffering on themselves by making bad choices. His *Psychomachia* depicts a struggle between pagan vice and Christian virtue. (Prudentius (2 vols), trans. H.J. Thompson, Loeb 1949, 1953)
[Marcia L. Colish, *The Stoic Tradition from Antiquity to the Early Middle Ages: 2. Stoicism in Christian Latin thought through the sixth century*, Leiden, Brill, 1990]

PRYTANIS (fourth/third century BC)
Prytanis was a Peripatetic and a teacher of **Euphorion**. He was invited by the people of Megalopolis to reform their laws.

PSENOPHIS OF HELIOPOLIS (seventh/sixth century BC)
According to **Plutarch of Chaeronea**, Psenophis was an Egyptian priest and philosopher visited by **Solon**.

PTOLEMAIS (first century AD?)
Ptolemais came from Cyrene and was mainly interested in music. She wrote a work on Pythagorean musical theory.

PTOLEMY [1] [CLAUDIUS PTOLEMAIUS] (second century AD)
Ptolemy spent most of his working life in Alexandria, becoming head of the famous Museum there. His great achievement was the *Almagest*, a work on astronomy that dominated the subject for well over a thousand years. However, he also wrote on a range of other subjects, including musical theory where he combined Pythagorean mathematics with his own observations. Philosophically, his most interesting work was *On the Faculty of Judgement* in which he tackled problems relating to the theory of knowledge and scientific method. His position is that the senses are generally trustworthy, but that critical rational reflection on the evidence of the senses is needed to eliminate error.
(H. Blumenthal, A.A. Long et al., '*On the Kriterion and Hegemonikon*: Claudius Ptolemaeus' in P. Huby and G. Neal (eds), *The Criterion of Truth: essays in honour of George Kerferd*, Liverpool, Liverpool University Press, 1989; J.L. Berggren,

Ptolemy's Geography: an annotated translation of the theoretical chapters, Princeton, Princeton University Press, 2000)
[*Routledge Encyclopaedia of Philosophy*, vol. 7]

PTOLEMY [2] (second century AD)
According to **Hippolytus**, Ptolemy was a gnostic and follower of **Valentinus**.

PTOLEMY [3] (third century AD)
Ptolemy was a Peripatetic and a highly regarded scholar.

PTOLEMY [4] (third/fourth century AD)
Ptolemy was a Neoplatonist. He wrote a commentary on the *Timaeus* of **Plato** [1] and a number of works on **Aristotle** [1].

PTOLEMY [5] (fourth century AD)
Ptolemy was a philosopher from Alexandria who was also active in political life. On one occasion he was flogged for an unknown real or imagined offence.

PTOLEMY OF CYRENE (second century BC?)
Ptolemy was a Sceptic. **Diogenes Laertius** gives two accounts of the history of Scepticism after the death of **Timon of Phlius**. The first is that he had no successors, but that the school was later revived by Ptolemy. The second is that one of his pupils, **Euphranor of Seleucia**, taught **Eubulus of Alexandria**, who in turn taught Ptolemy. Both versions make Ptolemy an important figure in the history of Scepticism between Timon and **Aenesidemus of Cnossus**.

PTOLEMY THE BLACK (third century BC?)
According to **Diogenes Laertius**, Ptolemy was a noted Epicurean from Alexandria. His nickname probably refers to the colour of his skin as a means of distinguishing him from his contemporary **Ptolemy the White**.

PTOLEMY THE WHITE (third century BC?)
According to **Diogenes Laertius**, Ptolemy was a noted Epicurean from Alexandria. His nickname probably refers to the colour of his skin as a means of distinguishing him from his contemporary **Ptolemy the Black**.

PUDENTIANUS (second century AD?)
Pudentianus was an Epicurean. **Galen** wrote a lost work about him.

PYRALLIANUS (second century AD)
Pyrallianus was a philosophical acquaintance of **Aelius Aristides** during the time they both spent in Pergamum. He had a considerable knowledge of the dialogues of **Plato** [1].

PYRRHO OF ELIS (fourth/third century BC)
There was a tradition that Pyrrho was a painter, although not a very good one, before he took up philosophy. He may have travelled to Persia and India but most of his years seem to have been spent in his home town of Elis. He was a friend of **Anaxarchus of Abdera** and perhaps through him became acquainted

with the thought of **Metrodorus of Chios**. He is also said to have admired the philosophy of **Democritus of Abdera**. **Diogenes Laertius** mentions a tradition that he studied with **Bryson of Megara**, although this seems unlikely for chronological reasons.

Pyrrho is usually regarded as the founder of Scepticism, and early Scepticism is often referred to as Pyrrhonism. However, he wrote nothing and it is not at all clear that he ever founded any kind of school. Most of what is known about his thought comes through the testimony of **Timon of Phlius**, an early and enthusiastic follower. Central to his philosophy was the idea of the suspension of judgment. The suspension of judgment involves the refusal to assent to anything that is not certain. If nothing is certain, nothing should be assented to. According to **Antigonus of Carystus**, Pyrrho doubted the evidence of his senses to the extent that friends had to follow him around to ensure that he came to no harm, because he might do something like fall over a cliff while suspending judgment as to whether it really existed or not. **Aenesidemus of Cnossus** disputed this, claiming that when it came to everyday life Pyrrho had behaved like anyone else whatever his philosophical views. This appears to be consistent with the evidence, such as it is, of Timon, and with Pyrrho's long life. Nevertheless, the anecdotes about him recounted by **Diogenes Laertius** at least point to a reputation for being a somewhat unworldly figure.

The precise reasoning behind Pyrrho's suspension of judgment is unknown. The sophists of his time made familiar the idea that an argument for a position could always be juxtaposed with another against it. If Pyrrho travelled to India he may well have encountered a form of systematic Scepticism in the form of Buddhism, while his travels themselves would have exposed him to the realities of cultural relativism. The atomism of Democritus may have suggested to him that the world our senses present to us may bear no resemblance to how things really are, and that how they really are lies beyond our knowledge. In the end, the extent to which the 'modes' of scepticism, later formulated or systematised by others such as **Agrippa**, actually derive from the thought of Pyrrho himself has to remain a matter for speculation.

[Richard Bett, *Pyrrho: his antecedents and his legacy*, Oxford, Oxford University Press, 2000; Richard Bett, 'Pyrrho', *The Stanford Encyclopedia of Philosophy* (Fall 2002 Edition), Edward N. Zalta (ed.), plato.stanford.edu/archives/fall2002/entries/pyrrho/]

PYRRHO OF METAPONTUM (fifth century BC?)
According to **Iamblichus of Chalcis**, Pyrrho was a Pythagorean.

PYRRHO OF PHLIUS (third century BC)
According to **Suda**, Pyrrho was a Sceptic and a pupil of **Timon of Phlius**.

PYRRHUS OF DELOS
According to **Heraclides of Pontus**, **Pythagoras** claimed to have been reincarnated a number of times, and could remember all his previous lives.

His last reincarnation before he became Pythagoras was as Pyrrhus, a fisherman.

PYRSON (third century BC)
Pyrson was the son of **Dositheus** and brother of **Hegesianax** [2]. He was probably an Epicurean.

PYTHAGORAS OF SAMOS (sixth century BC)
Pythagoras is a mysterious figure around whom many legends grew up. A great deal was written about him, but much of it long after his death and on the basis of dubious evidence. Apart from the fact that he was born in Samos, little is known about his life until he moved to Croton in around 530 BC, although there was a tradition that he studied with **Pherceydes of Syros**. In Croton he founded a community, but for some reason he was later forced to leave Croton and settle in nearby Metapontum, where he died. Although they suffered mixed fortunes, Pythagorean communities seem to have survived in one place or another in southern Italy until the fourth century BC. They had a reputation for being close-knit, being bound together not only by common doctrines and practices but also by vows of secrecy and a strong belief in the value of friendship.

Exactly what Pythagoras taught is difficult to ascertain. He wrote nothing himself but later authors were sometimes guilty of ascribing to him views that he probably never held. It seems certain that he believed in the transmigration of souls and in the soul's immortality. According to **Heraclides of Pontus**, Pythagoras could remember his own earlier incarnations, the last one being as **Pyrrhus of Delos**, a fisherman. He advocated a distinctive dietary regime, although this does not appear to have amounted to full vegetarianism. There was also a prohibition on eating beans that has puzzled many over the centuries and invited a good deal of speculation as to its origin and purpose. It is clear that the Pythagoreans, at least in the time of Pythagoras himself and during the period immediately after, comprised as much a cult as a philosophical school.

The celebrated theorem of geometry with which his name has become associated was almost certainly not the brainchild of Pythagoras himself and some modern scholars have questioned the extent to which he was interested in mathematics at all. On the other hand, it would seem unlikely that his followers would become so closely identified with an area in which he had little or no interest within what appears to have been a relatively short time after his death. In any event, Pythagoreans were regarded as adherents to the view that the key to understanding the universe was number, and they also seem to have made significant advances in applying mathematics to the problem of understanding musical harmonics.

Many later philosophers sought to develop genealogies that linked all the major figures of the past and writers like **Iamblichus of Chalcis** identified large numbers of people as pupils of Pythagoras himself or Pythagoreans of a later generation. How many actually were is a matter of dispute.

The wife of Pythagoras, **Theano,** was said to have been an accomplished philosopher in her own right, as was their son **Mnesarchus,** who became leader of the school when the immediate successor of Pythagoras, **Aristaeus of Croton,** died. However, by this time the school was already fragmented with one faction led by **Hippasus of Metapontum.**
[Walter Burkert, *Lore and Science in Ancient Pythagoreanism,* trans. E.L. Minar, Cambridge, Harvard University Press, 1972; Charles H. Kahn, *Pythagoras and the Pythagoreans,* Indianapolis, Hackett, 2001; Carl Huffman, 'Pythagoras', *The Stanford Encyclopedia of Philosophy* (Spring 2005 Edition), Edward N. Zalta (ed.), plato.stanford.edu/archives/spr2005/entries/pythagoras/]

PYTHEAS (fourth century BC)
Pytheas came from Massilia (Marseille) and achieved fame in a number of different fields. As well as being a philosopher he was also a mathematician, astronomer, geographer and explorer.

PYTHIAS (fourth century BC)
Pythias was the daughter of **Aristotle** [1], the mother of **Aristotle** [3] and the wife of **Medius** [1].

PYTHIODORUS TRICO (fourth century AD)
Pythiodorus came from Thebes in Egypt. He seems to have studied philosophy in Alexandria and become a priest. During the reign of the emperor **Julian,** he took a leading role in the pagan revival there.

PYTHOCLES (fourth/third century BC)
Pythocles was a follower of **Epicurus** and the recipient of one of his surviving letters. In it he sets out his views on many aspects of nature such as the sun, moon, stars, clouds, storms and earthquakes.

PYTHODORUS [1] (fifth century BC)
Pythodorus was a pupil of **Zeno of Elea.**

PYTHODORUS [2] (third century BC)
Pythodorus was a pupil of **Arcesilaus of Pitane** and produced written versions of some of his lectures.

PYTHODORUS OF CYZICUS
According to **Iamblichus of Chalcis,** Pythodorus was a Pythagorean.

PYTHON (third century BC)
Python was one of those to whom **Lyco** [1] bequeathed the Lyceum on his death. He had presumably been a pupil there for some time.

PYTHON OF AENUS (fourth century BC)
According to **Diogenes Laertius,** Python was a pupil of **Plato** [1]. Along with his brother **Heraclides of Aenus,** he assassinated Cotys, the ruler of Thrace, in *c.* 360 BC. It seems Cotys may have earlier killed their father.

PYTHONAX (third century BC)
Chrysippus of Soli dedicated two books on reason to Pythonax, suggesting that he was either a colleague or a pupil.

QUADRATUS (second century AD)
Quadratus was a teacher of **Varus of Perge**. He was apparently a gifted speaker who was well-versed in philosophy, and achieved high political office. He is not to be confused with the apologist of the same name who headed the Christian community in Athens.

QUEEN CLEOPATRA (second century AD)
The Cleopatra in question was not the ruler of Egypt but rather a celebrated alchemist, given the accolade of 'Queen' for her accomplishments. Her work was influenced by Hermeticism and traditional Egyptian cosmology.

QUINTILIUS VARUS (first century BC)
Quintilius Varus was an Epicurean. He studied under **Siro** with **Virgil**, and perhaps also under **Philodemus of Gadara**. He was the author of at least two philosophical essays, one on flattery and one on greed.

RABIRIUS (first century BC)
Rabirius was an Epicurean teacher in Italy. He was criticised by **Cicero** for oversimplifying the school's doctrines in order to reach a wider audience.

RECTUS (first century AD)
Rectus was a Stoic from Antioch. He was a pupil of **Kanus**.

RHEGINUS
Rheginus was the author of a work on friendship, fragments of which were preserved by **Stobaeus**.

RHESUS (fourth century BC?)
Rhesus was the supposed recipient of a letter falsely attributed to **Diogenes of Sinope**. According to the letter, he came from Argos, but it is unclear whether he was a Cynic himself.

RHEXIBIUS OF METAPONTUM (fifth century BC?)
According to **Iamblichus of Chalcis**, Rhexibius was a Pythagorean.

RHODIPPUS OF CROTON (fifth century BC?)
According to **Iamblichus of Chalcis**, Rhodippus was a Pythagorean.

RHOSANDER (second century AD)
Rhosander was a philosopher who became an acquaintance of **Aelius Aristides** during the time they were both staying at Pergamum.

RHYNDACUS OF LUCANIA see BINDACUS OF LUCANIA

ROGATIANUS (third century AD)
Rogatianus was a senator who gave up his privileged life to become a pupil of **Plotinus**. He thereafter lived a frugal existence, eating only every other day, to which he attributed his recovery from gout.

ROGUS, TERTILIUS (second/first century BC)
Rogus was a pupil of **Philo of Larisa** when Philo was in Rome.

RUBELLIUS PLAUTUS (first century AD)
Rubellius Plautus was a Stoic related by marriage to **Tiberius** [1]. Perceived as a threat by Nero, he was first sent to Asia and then killed there in AD 62. He was a friend of **Coeranus** and **Musonius Rufus**.

RUFINUS OF CYPRUS (second century AD)
Rufinus was a Peripatetic, but may also have studied under **Demonax**.

RUFINUS, TYRANNIUS (fourth/fifth century AD)
Rufinus came from Aquileia and spent many years in Alexandria and Jerusalem. He translated a number of theological works from Greek into Latin, including several by **Origen**, whose views he defended.

RUFUS, PUBLIUS RUTILIUS (second/first century BC)
Rufus was a Stoic who studied with **Panaetius of Rhodes**. He became involved in public life and made a number of enemies. They managed to have him found guilty of extortion in 92 BC and he went into exile in Smyrna. There he became extremely popular and wrote an important work of history.

RUFUS OF PERINTHUS (second century AD)
Rufus was a pupil of **Herodes Atticus**. Although best known for his wealth and his oratory, he appears to have led an austere life and been admired for his benevolence.

RUSTICUS, QUINTUS JUNIUS (second century AD)
Rusticus was a Stoic and friend of **Marcus Aurelius**. According to Marcus, amongst other things he learnt from him were the importance of both character development and careful study. He also introduced him to the works of **Epictetus**. He taught law and presided over the trial of **Justin Martyr**, condemning him to death.

❖ S ❖

SABELLIUS (third century AD)
Sabellius struggled with the Christian problem of the Trinity. He believed that the three dimensions of the Trinity should be understood as modes of a single being rather than as separate persons. Known as modalism, this view was condemned as heretical.

SABINILLIUS (third century AD)
Sabinillius was a senator who was also a follower of **Plotinus**.

SALLUSTIUS
Sallustius assembled a collection of materials by and about **Empedocles of Acragas**.

SALLUSTIUS OF SYRIA (fourth/fifth century AD)
Sallustius studied in Emesa, Athens and Alexandria, and became attached to the circle of the Neoplatonist **Isidore of Alexandria**. However, he appears to have converted to Cynicism, and practised a very austere life. **Simplicius** tells of someone by this name who placed a burning coal on his own thigh in order to test his ability to withstand pain, and it is probably he. He came to embrace the extreme view that philosophy was not so much difficult as impossible, and this may have been the basis of his dispute with **Proclus** [1].

SALMOXIS see ZALMOXIS

SALUTIUS, SATURNINUS SECUNDUS (fourth century AD)
Salutius was a close friend of the emperor **Julian**, and was offered the throne on the latter's death, but declined on account of his own advanced age and poor health. He led an active political life and was regarded as incorruptible. Known to have been well-versed in both Greek literature and philosophy, he was probably the author of *On the Gods and the World Order*, although there is some doubt about this, with some ascribing it to **Sallustius of Syria** or a Flavius Sallustius. The work is a Neoplatonist theology, and was dedicated to the emperor.

SALVIAN (fifth century AD)
Salvian was a Christian from Gaul who wrote a book in which he tried to understand why there was so much suffering in his country in his time. He took an approach that was at once religious, historical and philosophical. Philosophically his greatest debt was to the Stoics.
(Salvian, *On the Governance of God*, trans. E.M. Sanford, New York, Columbia University Press, 1930)

[Marcia L. Colish, *The Stoic Tradition from Antiquity to the Early Middle Ages: 2. Stoicism in Christian Latin thought through the sixth century*, Leiden, Brill, 1990]

SARAPION (fifth century AD)
Sarapion was a philosopher and mystic who led a very simple and frugal life. When he died his only belongings were a few books which he bequeathed to **Isidore of Alexandria**.

SARAPION, MARA BAR (first/second century AD)
Sarapion was a Stoic from Syria imprisoned by the Romans in around AD 73.

SARAPION OF ALEXANDRIA (second century AD)
Sarapion was a sophist who wrote a variety of works. They were mainly on rhetoric, but he also wrote on **Plato** [1].

SARAPION OF NICOMEDIA (second century BC)
Sarapion was a pupil of **Carneades of Cyrene**.

SARAPION see also SERAPION

SARPEDON [1] (second/first century BC)
According to **Diogenes Laertius**, Sarpedon was a Sceptic and a pupil of **Ptolemy of Cyrene**.

SARPEDON [2] (fourth century AD)
Sarpedon taught philosophy and was a friend of **Libanius** [1].

SATURNILUS (second century AD)
Saturnilus (who was also known as Satornilus and Saturninus) was a gnostic from Antioch. He taught that God was unknowable and that the world had been created by angelic beings.

SATURNINUS CYTHENAS (second/third century AD)
According to **Diogenes Laertius**, Saturninus was a Sceptic and a pupil of **Sextus Empiricus**.

SATYRUS OF CALLATIS (third/second century BC)
Satyrus was a source used by **Diogenes Laertius**. He wrote about the lives of many famous people, including a number of philosophers. He was probably a Peripatetic.

SAUFEIUS, LUCIUS (second/first century BC)
Saufeius came from a rich and privileged Praeneste family. He was a close friend of Titus Pomponius **Atticus** who intervened to save his property from confiscation in 43 BC. Saufeius was in Athens at the time, studying philosophy at the Epicurean school there.

SCAEVOLA, QUINTUS MUCIUS (second/first century BC)
Known as 'the Augur', Scaevola was a Stoic and an expert on law, which he taught to **Cicero**, amongst others. Cicero expressed his admiration for him by

making him a character in some of his philosophical works. He studied under **Panaetius of Rhodes**, from whom he probably borrowed his approach to theology. He distinguished between the theology of the poets, the philosophers and the politicians. That of the poets was fanciful and false, that of the philosophers was true but unsuitable for the masses, and that of the politicians was traditional and socially beneficial.

SCIPIO AEMILIANUS AFRICANUS, PUBLIUS CORNELIUS (second century BC)
Scipio was a statesman, military leader and scholar. More a patron of philosophers than a philosopher himself, he was particularly close to **Panaetius of Rhodes**. **Cicero** regarded him sufficiently highly to include him as a character in some of his philosophical works. He was much admired for his moral courage and integrity.

SCOPELIAN OF CLAZOMENAE (first/second century AD)
Scopelian was celebrated above all as an orator, but his talents were many and various. He was much in demand for his persuasive skills in his adopted city of Smyrna, and appears to have been valued as a wise counsellor there.

SCYLAX OF HALICARNASSUS (second century BC)
Scylax was an astronomer and statesman. He was a friend and perhaps student of **Panaetius of Rhodes** and denied the possibility of divining the future through the study of the stars.

SCYTHINUS OF TEOS (fourth/third century BC)
Scythinus was a satirical poet. He produced an account of the philosophy of **Heraclitus of Ephesus** in verse form.

SEBASMIUS (third/fourth century AD)
Sebasmius was a philosopher mentioned on a list of priests and philosophers belonging to the Roman aristocracy dated to around AD 320.

SECUNDUS (second century AD)
According to **Hippolytus**, Secundus was a gnostic who believed that the world was divided into light and darkness.

SECUNDUS OF ATHENS (first/second century AD)
Secundus was a teacher of **Herodes Atticus**. Although mainly interested in rhetoric, he also appears to have also addressed himself to ethical issues.

SECUNDUS THE SILENT (first/second century AD)
Secundus acquired his nickname on account of a vow of silence he took following the death of his mother. Some regarded him as a Pythagorean, but he appears to have led the life of a Cynic. Even the emperor Hadrian could not get him to break his vow, although Secundus may have provided written answers to some of the philosophical questions he posed.

SELEUCUS (fourth century AD)
Seleucus was a pupil of **Dexippus** and is mentioned in one of his philosophical works.

SELEUCUS THE GRAMMARIAN
According to **Diogenes Laertius**, Seleucus wrote a book called *On Philosophy*.

SELINUNTIUS OF RHEGIUM (fifth century BC?)
According to **Iamblichus of Chalcis**, Selinuntius was a Pythagorean.

SELLIUS, CAIUS (second/first century BC)
Sellius was a pupil of **Philo of Larisa** when Philo was in Rome.

SELLIUS, LUCIUS (second/first century BC)
Sellius was a pupil of **Philo of Larisa** when Philo was in Rome.

SENECA, LUCIUS ANNAEUS (first century BC/first century AD)
One of the most famous of Roman philosophers, Seneca was born in Cordoba at the very end of the first century BC. He is sometimes known as 'the Younger' to distinguish him from his father who bore the same name. He became a lawyer, a statesman, a tragedian and tutor to the future emperor Nero. His philosophical status owes more to the fact that many of his philosophical writings survive than to any particular achievements. One of his early teachers was **Sotion of Alexandria** [1], but he regarded himself as a Stoic for most of his life. He wrote a number of philosophical essays, but better known are his letters to **Lucilius the Younger**. In these he reflects on various issues thrown up by everyday existence, constantly exhorting his friend to lead an ever better life. His Stoicism is not of the most orthodox variety and he is prepared to acknowledge the virtues of philosophers from other schools, even, most unusually for a Stoic, **Epicurus**.

His involvement in politics led to him to a period of exile under Claudius and eventually in AD 65 a death sentence under Nero. According to Tacitus, he first tried to bleed himself to death, then took poison and a warm bath and finally suffocated in a steam room. The death of Seneca became a powerful image of Stoicism and the subject of a number of works of art.
(Seneca, *Ad Lucilium epistolae morales* (3 vols), trans. R. Gummere, Loeb, 1917-25; Seneca, *Moral Essays* (3 vols), trans. J.W. Basore, Loeb, 1928-35)
[Miriam Griffin, *Seneca: a philosopher in politics*, Oxford, Clarendon Press, 1992]

SERAPIO (first century AD)
In one of his letters, **Seneca** mentions the philosopher Serapio. According to **Lucilius the Younger**, Serapio was given to talking very quickly when he taught. He seems to have been a Stoic, originally from Asia Minor.

SERAPION (third century BC)
Along with **Philinus of Cos**, Serapion was one of the founders of the Empiricist school of medicine, generally regarded as an offshoot of Scepticism. Its

approach was based upon observation and induction, along with a measure of guesswork. Theoretical speculation was frowned upon.

SERAPION see also SARAPION

SERAPION OF ALEXANDRIA (third century AD)
Serapion was a friend of **Plotinus**. He had studied rhetoric, but then began to study philosophy as well. However, he was unable to give it very much attention because of his continuing business interests.

SERENIANUS (fourth century AD)
Serenianus was a Cynic who visited the emperor **Julian**.

SERENUS, AELIUS
According to **Stobaeus**, Serenus wrote a book of philosophical memoirs.

SERENUS, ANNAEUS (first century AD)
Serenus was a Stoic and friend of **Seneca**, who dedicated some of his works to him. In his dialogue *On the Tranquillity of Mind*, Seneca depicts them discussing the problems Serenus has with maintaining his firmness of resolve.

SEVERIANUS (fifth/sixth century AD)
Severianus came from Alexandria. His father wanted him to become a lawyer but he had a desire to study philosphy. When his father died he went to Athens and became a pupil of **Proclus** [1]. However, he later abandoned philosophy for a career in public life.

SEVERUS [1] (second century AD)
Severus was a Platonist who wrote a work *On the Soul* in which he maintained that the soul was wholly divine and wholly rational.

SEVERUS [2] (fourth century AD)
Severus came from Lycia and studied philosophy in Athens along with **Libanius** [1]. He then returned to Lycia where he became a teacher of philosophy, although he appears to have had reservations about doing so.

SEVERUS ALEXANDER (third century AD)
Severus Alexander studied philosophy with **Stilio**. He became emperor in AD 222 at the young age of fourteen when his cousin Elagabalus was assassinated. His reign, largely dominated by his mother, was not a success and they were both assassinated in AD 235.

SEVERUS, CLAUDIUS (second century AD)
Severus was a Peripatetic and a friend of **Marcus Aurelius**.

SEVERUS, MESSIUS PHOEBUS (fifth century AD)
Severus was a Neoplatonist teaching in Alexandria when he was summoned by **Anthemius** [2] to take up the position of consul in Constantinople.

SEVERUS, SEPTIMIUS (second/third century AD)
Severus ruled the Roman empire from AD 193 to 211. It is said that he was well-versed in philosophy, although his wife **Julia Domna** would appear to have taken a greater interest in it.

SEXTIUS, QUINTUS (first century BC/first century AD)
Sextius founded his own school in Rome that drew heavily on both Pythagoreanism and Stoicism. He preached an ascetic way of life, which included vegetarianism, and exhorted his followers (known as Sextians) to reflect at the end of each day on their moral failings and accomplishments. When he died, his son became head of the school, but it did not long survive him. However, one of the Sextians was **Sotion of Alexandria** [1], who taught **Seneca**, and Seneca himself was influenced by the school's teachings for some time.

SEXTUS (second century AD?)
Sextus was the compiler of a collection of sayings known as the *Sentences of Sextus*. They are mainly of an ethical nature and show signs of a variety of influences including traditional wisdom literature, Stoicism and Christianity. They proclaim that wisdom is attained through the conquest of the passions.
(Henry Chadwick, *The Sentences of Sextus*, Cambridge, Cambridge University Press, 1959)

SEXTUS EMPIRICUS (second/third century AD)
Sextus Empiricus is a key figure in the history of Scepticism, and his works constitute by far the largest body of literature on the subject surviving from antiquity. Little is known about his life, but he appears to have been a physician and 'Empiricus' is probably a nickname indicating that he belonged to the Empiricist school of medicine. His *Outlines of Pyrrhonism* is a concise treatment of the tenets of Scepticism, while his other book, usually known as *Against the Mathematicians*, is an attack on all who make unwarranted claims to knowledge. Owing to the scarcity of earlier materials, it is impossible to know how faithful Sextus was to the teachings of **Pyrrho of Elis**, although he makes no claims to originality.

His fundamental argument is that judgment should always be suspended because for every opinion it is always possible to come up with a contrary one of equal force. In the absence of any compelling reason for accepting one or the other, the only rational position is to sit on the fence. This, he believed, was not only logical but also beneficial, in that it leads to detachment and the tranquillity that goes with it. Only those who are attached to things get upset about them.
(Sextus Empiricus (4 vols), trans. R.G. Bury, Loeb, 1933-39; Julia Annas and Jonathan Barnes, *Sextus Empiricus, Outlines of Scepticism*, Cambridge, Cambridge University Press, 1994; Richard Bett, *Sextus Empiricus, Against the Ethicists*, Oxford, Clarendon Press, 1997)
[Richard Bett, *Pyrrho: his antecedents and his legacy*, Oxford, Oxford University Press, 2000; R.J. Hankinson, *The Sceptics*, London, Routledge, 1995]

SEXTUS OF CHAERONEA (second century AD)
Sextus is best known for having been a tutor to **Marcus Aurelius**. He was also probably the nephew of **Plutarch of Chaeronea**. Marcus regarded him as something of a role model and greatly admired the morality and humanity of both his life and his teachings. He was a Platonist, though **Suda** calls him a Sceptic as a result of confusing him with **Sextus Empiricus**.

SIDONIUS APOLLINARIS (fifth century AD)
Sidonius followed a political career before changing direction and becoming a bishop. He wrote a number of poems in which he made reference to philosophers and philosophical issues, and claimed that **Cleanthes of Assus** bit his nails.
(Sidonius Apollinaris, *Poems and Letters* (2 vols), trans. W.B. Anderson, Loeb, 1936, 1965)
[Marcia L. Colish, *The Stoic Tradition from Antiquity to the Early Middle Ages: 2. Stoicism in Christian Latin thought through the sixth century*, Leiden, Brill, 1990]

SILVANUS [1] (second century AD?)
The name of Silvanus was attached to a document found at Nag Hammadi. The teachings contained within it recognisably belong within the tradition of wisdom literature, but also show the influence of Platonism and Stoicism.
(James M. Robinson (ed.), *The Nag Hammadi Library*, Leiden, Brill, 1977)

SILVANUS [2] (fifth century AD)
Silvanus is one of a group of seven philosophers said to have accompanied **Eudocia** on her journey from Athens to Constantinople. However, there are doubts as to whether any of the philosophers actually existed, although various sayings were attributed to them.

SIMIAS (first/second century AD?)
Simias was a Stoic. If not the teacher of **Aephicianus**, he certainly influenced him.

SIMICHIAS OF TARENTUM (fifth century BC?)
According to **Iamblichus of Chalcis**, Simichias was a Pythagorean.

SIMMIAS (fourth/third century BC)
According to **Diogenes Laertius**, Simmias was a pupil of **Stilpo** having previously studied with **Aristotle of Cyrene**.

SIMMIAS OF THEBES (fifth/fourth century BC)
Simmias was a friend of **Socrates** and appears as a character in some of the dialogues of **Plato** [1]. He was at least influenced by Pythagoreanism, and may have been a pupil of **Philolaus of Croton**. There is some dispute as to what he may have written, partly because none of his writings have survived.

SIMON OF ATHENS (fifth/fourth century BC)
Simon is a curious character. According to **Diogenes Laertius**, he was a cobbler and friend of **Socrates**. When Socrates visited his shop and talked to people there, he tried to write down what he heard. This resulted in a number of short

dialogues by him, all of which have since been lost. **Phaedo of Elis** is said to have written a dialogue in which Simon was a character, and that is also lost.

SIMONIDES (fourth century AD)
Simonides was a young philosopher, perhaps a Neoplatonist, well-known for living a principled and disciplined life. However, he was accused of involvement in a plot against the emperor Valens in AD 371. His refusal to betray any secrets led to him being burnt alive.

SIMPLICIUS (sixth century AD)
Simplicius came from Cilicia, and studied in both Alexandria and Athens, with **Ammonius** and **Damascius** amongst his teachers. He was one of the group of philosophers who travelled to Persia with Damascius. He also spent some time in Syria, and may have died there. He is best known for his surviving commentaries, three on works of **Aristotle** [1] (*Physics, Categories* and *On the Heavens*) and one on the *Handbook* of **Epictetus**. He also wrote on **Iamblichus of Chalcis** and **Euclid**. Despite the range of his subject matter, he was himself a Neoplatonist. He was a stern critic of **John Philoponus**, although it seems the two never actually met.
(Simplicius, *On Aristotle Categories* (4 vols); *On Aristotle Physics* (8 vols); *On Aristotle On the Heavens* (5 vols); *On Epictetus Handbook* (2 vols); etc: various translators, London, Duckworth, 1992-)

SIMUS OF POSIDONIA
According to **Iamblichus of Chalcis**, Simus was a Pythagorean.

SIRO (first century BC)
Originally from Greece, Siro established an Epicurean community in Naples, of which **Virgil** was a member for a few years. **Horace** may have been another. The community enjoyed some success and Siro attracted a number of followers. At his death in 42 BC his house passed to Virgil and the subsequent fate of the community is unknown.

SISENNA, LUCIUS CORNELIUS (second/first century BC)
Sisenna achieved acclaim as an historian. **Cicero** suggests he was an Epicurean, but not a very consistent one.

SOCHARES (fourth/third century BC?)
Sochares was a Cynic.

SOCRATES (469-399 BC)
One of the most famous characters in the history of Western philosophy, Socrates is nevertheless something of an elusive figure since the solid facts known about his life turn out to be surprisingly few. He was married with three sons, spent time on military service in his late thirties and early forties, and was condemned to death by drinking hemlock. It is not at all clear when or why he first became interested in philosophy, but it seems to have occupied at least the last twenty-five years of his life. He may have studied with **Archelaus of Athens** for a while, but he seems to have found the teachings of the

Pythagoreans more congenial. He founded no formal school but attracted around himself a variety of enthusiasts and admirers, in particular **Plato** [1]. Because his style of philosophy involved challenging people to justify their claims to knowledge and going on to demonstrate their ignorance, it is not surprising that he made enemies as well as friends. Whether it was intended to be understood ironically or not, Socrates seems to have claimed that he knew nothing himself either, but that at least he knew that he knew nothing.

It is by no means easy to know what Socrates taught owing to what has become known as the Socratic problem. The main source of information is Plato, but it is accepted that the dialogues in which Socrates appears are not meant to be read as verbatim accounts of actual conversations. On the other hand, it is generally thought that at least in the earlier dialogues the authentic voice of Socrates is discernible. The Socratic problem therefore concerns how much of the historical Socrates can be found in the Socrates of Plato's dialogues. Apart from Plato the only other substantial sources are **Xenophon of Erchia**, the playwright Aristophanes and **Aristotle** [1]. Although Xenophon was a personal friend of Socrates, the reliability of his memoirs is often questioned, as is the extent of his philosophical understanding. However, the picture he paints is not inconsistent with that to be found in Plato's early dialogues and Socrates emerges as a self-controlled man of principle who is largely indifferent to material matters but always concerned about the welfare of his friends. He claimed to receive messages from the gods and enjoyed debate. In the *Clouds* of Aristophanes, on the other hand, he more resembles a sophist and is depicted as responsible for introducing new gods, one of the crimes of which he was accused, along with corrupting the youth. Aristotle indicates that the principal philosophical interests of Socrates were in ethics.

It is evident that even in and shortly after his own time there were differences of opinion concerning what the core teachings of Socrates were, and more than one school would go on to claim to be the true inheritor of his legacy. As a bare minimum it is probably safe to conclude that Socrates regarded living well or virtuously as the most important thing in life. In *Gorgias* Plato makes Socrates say that it is better to suffer wrong than to do it, and this seems likely to have been a genuine Socratic sentiment. If nothing else it helps to make sense of why he stayed and accepted his death sentence even though he knew it was unjust and even though he had the chance to escape. Outside of ethics, he may have taken a more sceptical line, although it is not clear whether he thought that rational debate, if properly pursued, could lead to truth or whether he believed it could only reveal the absence of knowledge. Although he did not go as far as some Cynics would in rejecting material comforts, he seems to have preferred the simple life.

None of this adequately explains the impact Socrates had on those around him or the extent to which he has been admired by philosophers ever since, but it is beyond doubt that his influence has been incalculable.

[John Ferguson, *Socrates: a source book*, London, Macmillan, 1970; Gregory Vlastos, *Socrates: ironist and moral philosopher*, Ithaca, Cornell University Press, 1991]

SOCRATES OF BITHYNIA
According to **Diogenes Laertius**, Socrates was a Peripatetic.

SOCRATIDES (fourth/third century BC)
Socratides was a Platonist who was elected to succeed **Crates of Thria** as head of the Academy. He seems to have been chosen on the grounds of his seniority and little else. He proved not to be up to the task and soon stood aside in favour of **Arcesilaus of Pitane**.

SOLON (seventh/sixth century BC)
Solon was a poet and legislator in Athens. He was invited to reform the laws of the city and achieved a reputation for his wisdom and fairness, although in this regard posterity judged him more favourably than did his contemporaries. He travelled a great deal and is said to have spent time studying philosophy in Egypt with **Psenophis of Heliopolis** and **Sonchis of Sais**. According to **Plutarch of Chaeronea**, he learnt from them the story of Atlantis. He is generally regarded as one of the Seven Sages and **Diogenes Laertius** attributes to him the saying 'Nothing to excess'.

SONCHIS OF SAIS (seventh/sixth century BC)
According to **Plutarch of Chaeronea**, Sonchis was an Egyptian priest and philosopher visited by **Solon**.

SOPATER OF APAMEA (fourth century AD)
Sopater was a Neoplatonist who headed the school after the death of **Iamblichus of Chalcis**. He found favour with Constantine the Great, but others schemed against him and Constantine was persuaded to order his execution.

SOPATER THE YOUNGER (fourth century AD)
Sopater the Younger was the son of **Sopater of Apamea**. Like his father, he was a philosopher and close to the imperial family.

SOPOLIS (fourth century BC?)
Sopolis was the supposed recipient of a letter falsely attributed to **Diogenes of Sinope** and is assumed to have been a Cynic.

SORANUS, BAREA (first century AD)
Part of the Stoic opposition to Nero, Soranus was betrayed by his friend Publius Egnatius **Celer,** who also betrayed Servilia, the daughter of Soranus. Both were condemned to death at the same time as **Thrasea Paetus.**

SORANUS OF EPHESUS (first/second century AD)
Soranus was a physician of the Methodist school founded by **Themison of Laodicea**. He took the movement in a more theoretical direction, allowing speculation to supplement observation. He wrote a number of works, including medical biographies and a manual of gynaecology.

SOSIBIUS

According to **Diogenes Laertius**, Sosibius was a critic of **Anaxagoras of Clazomenae**.

SOSICRATES OF RHODES (second century BC)

Sosicrates was primarily an historian, but he also wrote a book called *Successions* containing the biographies of various philosophers. It does not survive, but it was one of the sources used by **Diogenes Laertius**.

SOSIGENES [1] (third century BC)

Chrysippus of Soli wrote a book on logic addressed to Sosigenes and **Alexander** [1]. They were almost certainly Stoics and probably colleagues or pupils of Chrysippus.

SOSIGENES [2] (second century BC)

Sosigenes was a Stoic and pupil of **Antipater of Tarsus**.

SOSIGENES OF ALEXANDRIA (second century AD)

Sosigenes was a teacher of **Alexander of Aphrodisias**.

SOSIPATRA (fourth century AD)

Sosipatra was born near Ephesus. According to **Eunapius**, as a child she was taught by strange people who turned out to be spirits. As a result she came to possess a great reputation for wisdom, and was able to explain all manner of things to all kinds of people. She married the philosopher **Eustathius** [2] and they had three sons. After his death she moved to Pergamum where she had many students. In addition to her intellectual powers she appears to have possessed clairvoyant ones as well.

SOSISTRATUS OF LOCRI (fifth century BC?)

According to **Iamblichus of Chalcis**, Sosistratus was a Pythagorean.

SOSITHEUS see DOSITHEUS

SOSPIS (second century AD)

According to Flavius **Philostratus**, Sospis was a well-known philosopher who was also a priest.

SOSTHENES OF SICYON

According to **Iamblichus of Chalcis**, Sosthenes was a Pythagorean.

SOSTRATUS HERACLES (second century AD)

Sostratus came from Boeotia and lived in the wild on Mount Parnassus. Some take him to have been a Cynic, although the evidence is far from conclusive. He was probably given the nickname of Heracles because of his extensive labours in building roads and bridges in the area where he lived. The idea that his neighbours literally believed him to be Heracles has little to commend it. He also had the nickname Agathion, or 'goodfellow'.

SOSUS (second century BC)
Sosus was a Stoic from Ascalon. He studied under **Panaetius of Rhodes** and **Antiochus of Ascalon** dedicated a dialogue to him.

SOTADAS or SOTAS OF BYZANTIUM (first century BC/first century AD?)
Sotadas is referred to as a philosopher in a work by **Aristocles of Messene** and may have been his student.

SOTADES OF ATHENS
Sotades wrote a book *On the Mysteries*, but it has not survived.

SOTADES OF MARONEA (third/second century BC)
Sotades was a poet who produced satirical works reflecting the outlook of the Cynics. By this means he managed to gain enemies in high places, and it is said that Ptolemy II of Egypt had him sewn up in a sack and thrown into the sea.

SOTAS OF PAPHOS (first century BC)
Sotas was a pupil of **Panaetius**.

SOTERICHUS OF THE OASIS (third/fourth century AD)
Soterichus was a poet who produced an account of the life of **Apollonius of Tyana**.

SOTION (third/second century BC?)
Sotion wrote *The Succession of Philosophers*, a long work on the history of philosophy structured in terms of intellectual lineages whereby every philosopher is the 'successor' of another. **Diogenes Laertius** was familiar with it and often took a very similar approach. **Eunapius** also made use of it. Sotion himself was probably a Peripatetic.

SOTION OF ALEXANDRIA [1] (first century BC/first century AD)
Sotion was a teacher of **Seneca**. He was a follower of **Sextius** and practised vegetarianism. He argued that the avoidance of meat led to a healthier diet and was morally preferable since the provision of meat involved cruelty.

SOTION OF ALEXANDRIA [2] (first century AD?)
Sotion was a Peripatetic who wrote a commentary on the *Categories* of **Aristotle** [1]. He was the younger brother of **Apollonius of Alexandria**.

SPEUSIPPUS (fifth/fourth century BC)
Speusippus was the nephew of **Plato** [1] and became head of the Academy on his uncle's death. According to **Diogenes Laertius** he could be very bad tempered and on one occasion threw his favourite dog down a well. He did not enjoy good health and may eventually have committed suicide in 339 BC. The systematisation of Plato's philosophy probably began under him and was continued under his successor **Xenocrates of Chalcedon**. One of his main interests was biology, but he wrote on a wide range of other subjects as well, including mathematics and language. In ethics he advanced the view that pleasure in itself was neither good nor bad.
[John Dillon, *The Heirs of Plato: a study of the Old Academy (347-274 BC)*, Oxford,

Clarendon Press, 2003; Russell Dancy, 'Speusippus', *The Stanford Encyclopedia of Philosophy* (Summer 2003 Edition), Edward N. Zalta (ed.), plato.stanford.edu/archives/sum2003/entries/speusippus/]

SPHAERUS OF BORYSTHENES (third century BC)
Sphaerus was a Stoic who studied under both **Zeno of Citium** and **Cleanthes of Assus**. The Stoics held him in particularly high esteem for the elegance and precision of his definitions. He advanced the view that the wise man will have no opinions, which is to say that the wise man does not claim to know anything he does not know with certainty. Sphaerus is sometimes referred to as 'of the Bosphorus' rather than Borysthenes. He is probably the same person as the Sphaerus to whom **Chrysippus of Soli** dedicated one of his books.

SPHODRIAS
Sphodrias wrote a book on love and is thought to have been a Cynic.

SPINTHARUS (fifth/fourth century BC?)
Spintharus may have been the teacher of **Aristoxenus of Tarentum**, although according to some Peripatetics sources he was only his father.

STASEAS or STATEAS OF NEAPOLIS [Naples] (first century BC)
Staseas was the first Peripatetic philosopher to take up residence in Rome. He defended the Aristotelian position that virtue was not sufficient for happiness, a position some Peripatetics were prepared to compromise on in order to achieve a reconciliation with Stoic ethics.

STATILIUS (first century BC)
Statilius was an Epicurean, a friend of **Cato the Younger** and **Marcus Brutus**, and a staunch opponent of Julius **Caesar**.

STEPHANUS (sixth/seventh century AD)
Stephanus came from Athens and achieved fame practising and teaching medicine. He wrote many works on the subject, none of which have survived. He is sometimes also referred to as a philosopher, but it is not known what his philosophical interests were.

STEPHANUS OF ALEXANDRIA (sixth/seventh century AD)
Stephanus was a Neoplatonist who became a Christian. He spent some years teaching both philosophy and mathematics in Alexandria having studied in Constantinople under **Theodorus** [5]. Later, he returned to Constantinople as a professor of philosophy. He wrote commentaries on the works of **Aristotle** [1], as well as a book on astronomy. He may also have at least dabbled in alchemy, and some identify him with the Stephanus who predicted the Arab invasion of Egypt.

STEPHANUS OF LAODICEA (third/fourth century AD)
According to **Eusebius of Caesarea**, Stephanus was bishop of Laodicea during the persecutions of Diocletian. He was an accomplished philosopher, but Eusebius criticises him for failing to act like a philosopher when tested.

STERTINIUS (first century BC)
Stertinius was a Stoic based in Rome. **Damasippus** became his pupil.

STESAGORAS (third century BC)
According to **Diogenes Laertius, Chrysippus of Soli** dedicated some of his books on logic to Stesagoras. He was probably a colleague or pupil.

STHENONIDAS or STHENIDAS OF LOCRI (fifth century BC?)
According to **Iamblichus of Chalcis**, Sthenonidas was a Pythagorean. **Stobaeus** preserves a fragment of a work on kingship attributed to a Sthenidas, and this is thought to refer to the same person, although the true author was probably someone else altogether.
(David Fideler (ed.), *The Pythagorean Sourcebook*, Grand Rapids, Phanes, 1987)

STILIO (second/third century AD)
Stilio was a philosopher from Syria who taught the emperor **Severus Alexander**.

STILO, LUCIUS AELIUS (second/first century BC)
Stilo was a highly accomplished scholar who wrote books on a variety of subjects including grammar, literature, history and law. Although he became a Stoic, he is not known to have produced any specifically philosophical writings. **Cicero** and **Varro** were amongst those he taught.

STILPO (fourth/third century BC)
Stilpo succeeded **Eubulides of Miletus** as head of the Megarian school. He was a popular teacher with a ready wit and attracted a number of notable pupils, including **Zeno of Citium** and perhaps **Crates of Thebes**. At one time he may have been a pupil of **Diogenes of Sinope** or **Antisthenes of Athens**, and he is sometimes regarded as a Cynic. He led a simple life and gained a wide reputation for his indifference towards most things. According to **Diogenes Laertius**, when an attack was launched on Megara, special measures were taken by the attackers to protect his house and property. However, Stilpo was wholly unperturbed by the event, remarking that his most valued possession was his learning. He wrote a number of philosophical works, none of which have survived. His primary philosophical interests were in logic and ethics. He taught the value of self-sufficiency and indifference to pleasure and pain.

STOBAEUS, JOHN (fifth/sixth century AD)
Stobaeus was an anthologist and his works are valuable resources for the study of ancient philosophy.

STRABO OF AMASEIA (first century BC/first century AD)
Best known for his famous work on geography, Strabo was a pupil of **Xenarchus of Seleucia** and **Boethus of Sidon**. He was also influenced by the work of **Posidonius of Apamea**, and his outlook seems generally to have been that of a Stoic.

(Strabo, *The Geography of Strabo* (8 vols), trans. H.L. Jones, Loeb, 1917-32; classics.mit.edu/Browse/browse-Strabo.html)

STRATIPPUS (second century BC)
Stratippus was a pupil of **Carneades of Cyrene**.

STRATIUS OF SICYON
According to **Iamblichus of Chalcis**, Stratius was a Pythagorean.

STRATO OF LAMPSACUS (fourth/third century BC)
Strato succeeded **Theophrastus of Eresus** as head of the Lyceum. He had previously studied under him before leaving to spend some time in Alexandria, where he taught Ptolemy II Philadelphus and may have had a hand in founding the famous library there. He was sometimes nicknamed 'the Physicist' because it was in the sciences that his major interests lay. He appears to have developed a much more experimental approach to the sciences than had his predecessors, while his theorising on the nature of the universe brought him much closer to **Democritus of Abdera** than to **Aristotle** [1] on a number of points. He believed that everything was affected by gravity, and that the world could be understood in scientific terms without invoking any kind of divine forces. He thought that minds and perception went together, such that anything that perceived had to have a mind of some kind. Similarly, minds could not function without perception and, as he understood perception to be a physical process, he held that the mind could not survive the death of the body. **Diogenes Laertius** mentions another Strato, also a Peripatetic philosopher, of Alexandria, but since Strato of Lampsacus spent some time in Alexandria, it is possible that they are one and the same person.

STRATOCLES OF RHODES (second/first century BC)
Stratocles wrote a history of Stoicism. He was the pupil of **Panaetius of Rhodes** and later taught **Antipater of Tyre**.

SUDA or SUIDAS
Suda was long thought to be the name of a person who wrote a book of reference, perhaps in the tenth century AD. It is now treated as the name of the book itself. It is an extensive, although not always reliable, source of information about ancient philosophy, amongst other things.

SUETONIUS, GAIUS TRANQUILLUS (first/second century AD)
Suetonius is now best known for his account of the lives of the early Roman emperors, but his literary output amounted to much more than this, even if most of it is lost. Amongst his works was a commentary on the *Republic* of **Cicero**.
(Suetonius, *The Twelve Caesars*, trans. R. Graves, Harmondsworth, Penguin, 1957)

SURA, LUCIUS LUCINIUS (first/second century AD)
Sura was a successful politician and general as well as being a man of considerable learning. He was a friend of Pliny the Younger, who consulted him on whether or not ghosts existed.

SYLLUS OF CROTON (fifth century BC?)
According to **Iamblichus of Chalcis**, Syllus was a Pythagorean. The Pythagoreans were very reluctant to take oaths as they felt that using the names of the gods in this way shows a lack of proper reverence. As evidence of this, Syllus is said to have preferred to hand over money rather than take an oath.

SYMBULUS (fifth/sixth century AD?)
Symbulus was said to have been a philosopher and astrologer who, with **Hierotheus** and **Maximinianus**, persuaded the emperor Justinian to pave the floor of the church of Hagia Sophia with silver. The story is doubted, as is the existence of Symbulus.

SYMMACHUS, QUINTUS AURELIUS (fourth century AD)
Symmachus was a priest and man of considerable learning who achieved high office as a consul.

SYNESIUS (fifth/sixth century AD?)
Nothing is known about Synesius except a passing reference to him as a philosopher.

SYNESIUS OF PTOLEMAIS (fourth/fifth century AD)
Synesius originally came from Cyrene and went to Alexandria to study under **Hypatia of Alexandria**. In due course, he renounced Neoplatonism for Christianity and became bishop of Ptolemais in AD 410, only a few years before his death. Some of his writings survive from his pre-Christian period including a satirical attack on sophists, a discussion of dreams, and *Dion*, which defends the intellectual life while rejecting extreme forms of asceticism. After his conversion, he went on to write a number of hymns. Works on astrology and alchemy are sometimes attributed to him, but his connection with them is questionable.

SYRIANUS [1] (fourth/fifth century AD)
Syrianus was an important figure in the history of Neoplatonism. Originally from Alexandria, he moved to Athens and became the head of the Academy there after the death of **Plutarch of Athens**. One of his pupils, and his own successor when he died in AD 437, was **Proclus** [1]. His main interests were in metaphysics, and he sought to reconcile Platonism and Pythagoreanism with Orphism. He also wrote commentaries on the works of **Plato** [1] and **Aristotle** [1].

SYRIANUS [2] (fifth century AD)
Syrianus was a friend of **Isidore of Alexandria** and probably taught philosophy in Athens.

❖ **T** ❖

TANDASIS (second century AD)
Tandasis was one of the teachers of **Marcus Aurelius**. It is unclear which school he belonged to, but he evidently taught in Rome.

TATIAN (second century AD).
Tatian came from Assyria, studied Greek philosophy, and became a Christian in Rome. He wrote an *Oration to the Greeks* that poured scorn on philosophers for their dogmatism, their inability to agree with each other, their mercenary tendencies, and their arrogance (a failing of which he himself was duly accused by **Irenaeus of Lyons**). An increasingly pessimistic view of human nature led him to join (or perhaps found) an ascetic movement called the Encratites ('the self-controlled ones') whose beliefs at least verged on gnosticism. **Hippolytus** regarded them as more like Cynics than Christians.
(*Ante-Nicene Fathers*, vol. II)

TAURISCUS (second century BC)
Tauriscus was a pupil of **Crates of Mallus**.

TAURUS, LUCIUS CALVENUS (second century AD)
Taurus came from Berytus (Beirut). He was a Platonist, but may have taught at his own school. He wrote a *Commentary on the Timaeus* and took an interest in metaphysical matters, such as why the gods send souls into the world (although his followers appear to have been divided on the matter). In ethics he took a Peripatetic line, believing that complete happiness required more than just living virtuously; considerations such as health and material comforts were necessary too.
[John Dillon, *The Middle Platonists 80 BC to AD 220*, London, Duckworth, 1996]

TAURUS OF TYRE (first/second century AD)
Taurus was a Platonist, and one of the teachers of **Herodes Atticus**. Many of his works sought to clarify the differences between the philosophies of **Plato** [1] and **Aristotle** [2].

TELAUGES OF SAMOS (sixth/fifth century BC)
Telauges was the son born late in life to **Pythagoras**, who died when he was young. **Aeschines of Sphettus** wrote a dialogue in which a Telauges appears, unconventionally dressed, in a discussion with **Socrates** about asceticism. He is identified as a Pythagorean and is probably the same person, although whether such a conversation ever actually took place is another matter. He may have been a teacher of **Empedocles of Acragas**. He

seems to have represented a rather eccentric form of Pythagoreanism, something more akin to Cynicism.

TELECLES OF METAPONTUM (third century BC)
Telecles was a pupil of **Arcesilaus of Pitane**.

TELECLES OF PHOCAEA (third/second century BC)
Telecles was a Platonist. When **Lacydes of Cyrene** resigned his position as head of the Academy, he handed over his responsibilities to Telecles and **Evander of Phocaea**. As **Diogenes Laertius** mentions only Evander having a successor, it may be that Telecles was regarded as the junior partner in this arrangement, or perhaps he was the first to die.

TELEPHUS OF PERGAMUM (second century AD)
Telephus was a Stoic and a grammarian. One of his pupils was Lucius **Verus**.

TELES OF MEGARA (third century BC)
Teles was a Cynic and a teacher whose surviving fragmentary writings are useful sources of information about earlier Cynics, and in particular **Bion of Borysthenes**, whom he greatly admired. He produced a number of diatribes, the Cynics' preferred literary genre, and his are the earliest surviving examples.
[E.N. O'Neil, *Teles: the Cynic teacher*: Missoula: Scholars Press, 1977]

TERILLUS OF SYRACUSE (fifth/fourth century BC)
Terillus is mentioned in a letter from **Plato** [1] to **Dionysius II of Syracuse**, the authenticity of which is widely doubted. He is described there as someone who divides his time between Syracuse and Athens, and who is not only a philosopher, but also a man of much learning.

TERPSION OF MEGARA (fifth/fourth century BC)
Terpsion was a friend of **Theaetetus of Sunium** and **Euclides of Megara**. According to **Plato** [1], he was one of those present at the death of **Socrates**. In Plato's *Theaetetus* he displays a clear interest in Socratic philosophy.

TERTULLIAN [QUINTUS SEPTIMIUS FLORENS TERTULLIANUS]
(second/third century AD)
Tertullian was born in Carthage, and for some time pursued a career as a lawyer, probably in Rome. He studied the works of **Plato** [1] and the Stoics, and wrote a philosophical treatise on the soul. In around AD 195, he converted to Christianity and became a formidable propagandist for the cause, while at the same time infusing his understanding of it with ideas taken from Stoicism. A powerful writer, he coined the memorable phrase, 'I believe it because it is impossible.' In later life he became an adherent of Montanism, an ascetic sect, although he seems to have rejected the more extreme forms of its asceticism.
(*Ante-Nicene Fathers*, vols III, IV)
[*Routledge Encyclopaedia of Philosophy*, vol. 9]

THALES OF MILETUS (seventh/sixth century BC)
Thales is by long tradition the first Western philosopher. Amongst the Greeks he was also revered as one of the Seven Sages, and the only one amongst them readily recognisable as a philosopher today. He appears to have been a wide-ranging thinker who may have made some important discoveries in mathematics. He is also said to have predicted an eclipse of the sun in 585 BC. Unfortunately only the most fragmentary of references to his works remain, making it difficult to know what he really thought or did. The most tantalising fragment comes from **Aristotle** [1] who in his *Metaphysics* attributes to Thales the belief that ultimately everything comes from water. It is sometimes thought that the basis of this claim is the observation that in the everyday world water can exist in solid, liquid and gaseous forms and so it presents itself as something that can take on a variety of forms and modes of existence. An alternative view is that Thales may have been thinking more of water as the source of animal and vegetable life.

(Jonathan Barnes, *Early Greek Philosophy*, Harmondsworth, Penguin, 1987)
[Partricia F. O'Grady, *Thales of Miletus: the beginnings of Western science and philosophy*, Aldershot, Ashgate, 2002; Patricia O'Grady, 'Thales of Miletus', *Internet Encyclopaedia of Philosophy*, www.iep.utm.edu/t/thales.htm]

THAUMASIUS [1] (third century BC)
Thaumasius was a relative of **Arcesilaus of Pitane**. In his will, Arcesilaus refers to Thaumasius in terms suggesting he was also a pupil.

THAUMASIUS [2] (third century AD)
Thaumasius was a pupil of **Plotinus** and **Porphyry** but he found their style of teaching through questions and answers uncongenial, preferring instead formal lectures.

THEAETETUS see THEROCLES

THEAETETUS OF SUNIUM (fifth/fourth century BC)
Theaetetus was an associate of **Plato** [1], who named one of his dialogues after him. He was mainly interested in mathematics, but the extent to which the mathematical ideas in the dialogue genuinely derive from him is disputed. It was long thought that he taught mathematics in the Academy, but this view is now seriously challenged. Some think he may even have died before the Academy came into existence.

THEAGENES (sixth century BC)
Theganes came from Rhegium. He argued that myths should be interpreted allegorically and that what people regarded as acts of the gods were only natural phenomena.

THEAGENES OF PATRAS (second century AD)
Theagenes was a Cynic and a follower of **Peregrinus**, whose praises he constantly sang. He established himself as a teacher in Rome, where he gave

public lectures daily in the Forum of Trajan. He is said to have died when **Attalus** gave him the wrong treatment for a liver problem.

THEAGES (fifth century BC)
According to **Iamblichus of Chalcis**, Theages was a Pythagorean who sought to introduce more democratic institutions into Croton. **Stobaeus** preserves fragments of a book on virtue attributed to him, but in fact the work of a later author.
(David Fideler (ed.), *The Pythagorean Sourcebook*, Grand Rapids, Phanes, 1987)

THEAGES OF ANAGYRUS (fifth/fourth century BC)
Theages makes a brief appearance in the *Republic* of **Plato** [1]. **Socrates** characterises him as someone who is a student of philosophy even though he would rather not be. He has political ambitions, but poor health prevents him from pursuing them.

THEANO (sixth/fifth century BC).
Theano is generally thought to have been the wife of **Pythagoras** and the mother of his children. She is said to have been an accomplished thinker in her own right, in particular in the area of mathematics, as well as a poet. After her husband's death, she married his successor, **Aristaeus of Croton**. She may have been the daughter of **Brontinus**, although there is some confusion over this. According to one tradition she was the wife of Brontinus and only the pupil of Pythagoras. It is not impossible that there were two women of this name, perhaps mother and daughter.

THEANOR OF CROTON (fifth/fourth century BC?)
Theanor was a Pythagorean who appears as a character in some of the works of **Plutarch of Chaeronea**. He is believed by some to be fictitious.

THEARIDAS
According to **Clement of Alexandria**, Thearidas wrote a book entitled *On Nature*, arguing that everything came from one single first principle. He came from Metapontum and may have been a Pythagorean.

THEARUS (third century BC)
Chrysippus of Soli dedicated one of his books on logic to Thearus, who was probably a colleague or a pupil.

THEDOUSAor THEADOUSA OF SPARTA
According to **Iamblichus of Chalcis**, Thedousa was one of the most famous Pythagorean women.

THEIODAS OF LAODICEA (first century AD?)
According to **Diogenes Laertius**, Theiodas was a Sceptic, a pupil of **Antiochus of Laodicea**. He may be the same person as **Theodas of Laodicea**.

THEMISON OF LAODICEA (first century BC/first century AD)
Themison was probably the founder of the Methodist school of medicine, and

the teacher of **Thessalus**. The Methodists followed an approach to health heavily influenced by Scepticism. They believed that all that was required was observation of the ways in which a patient's body was 'out of balance', and the application of remedies to restore the balance.

THEMISTA OF LAMPSACUS (fourth/third century BC)
Themista and her husband **Leontius of Lampsacus** were early converts to the philosophy of **Epicurus**, who wrote a number of letters to her.

THEMISTIUS [1] (third century BC)
Themistius was a pupil of **Arcesilaus of Pitane**.

THEMISTIUS [2] (fourth century AD)
Themistius was the son of **Eugenius**. For many years he taught philosophy in Constantinople while at the same time pursuing a lucrative career in public life. Like many Platonists of his time he had strong eclectic tendencies, not only believing that **Plato** [1] and **Aristotle** [2] had been in substantial agreement with each other, but also arguing that Christianity and the religion of the Greeks were in essence the same. Perhaps this helps to explain why he earned the respect of a succession of Christian emperors despite the fact that he remained a pagan. His philosophical writings mainly concentrated on Aristotle, and he produced a number of commentaries on his works as well as summaries of them.
(Themistius, *On Aristotle On the Soul*, trans. R.B. Todd, London, Duckworth, 1996; Themistius, *On Aristotle Physics 4*, trans. R.B. Todd, London, Duckworth, 2003)

THEMISTOCLES [1] (third century AD)
Themistocles was a Stoic and author of some lost books on unknown topics.

THEMISTOCLES [2] (fourth century AD)
Themistocles was a philosopher in Constantinople. It seems unlikely he was the same person as the trouble-making young Athenian of that name mentioned by **Eunapius**, unless he matured with age.

THEO, CAIUS JULIUS (first century BC/first century AD)
Theo was a Stoic philosopher from Alexandria. He was a friend of **Arius Didymus**.

THEO see THEON

THEOCLES (fifth century BC)
According to **Iamblichus of Chalcis**, Theocles was a Pythagorean who helped to produce a new code of law for Rhegium. However, Iamblichus also mentions a Theaetetus in exactly the same context, suggesting that they are probably the same person.

THEODAS OF LAODICEA (first century AD?)
Theodas was a physician of the Empiricist school. He may be the same person as **Theiodas of Laodicea**.

THEODECTES OF PHASELIS (fourth century BC)
Theodectes achieved fame as a dramatist, producing fifty plays before dying at the age of 41. However, as a young man he had studied with both **Plato** [1] and **Aristotle** [2].

THEODORA (fifth/sixth century BC)
Damascius dedicated his life of **Isidore of Alexandria** to Theodora. She had studied philosophy with them both, as had her sisters.

THEODORET (fourth/fifth century AD)
Theodoret was born in Antioch. He reluctantly became bishop of Cyrrhus in AD 423 and spent most of the rest of his life there. He was convinced that Christianity was superior to paganism both philosophically and morally, and wrote a treatise comparing the views of the Church and the philosophers on a variety of issues such as human nature and the end of the world.
(*Nicene and Post-Nicene Fathers*, series II, vol. III)

THEODORIDAS OF LINDUS (first century AD?)
Theodoridas was a philosophical acquaintance of **Diogenes of Oenoanda**. He was probably an Epicurean.

THEODORUS [1]
According to **Diogenes Laertius**, Theodorus wrote a book attacking **Epicurus**. It is possible the author is to be identified with either **Theodorus of Chios** or **Theodorus of Miletus**.

THEODORUS [2]
Theodorus produced an edited version of the works of **Teles of Megara**.

THEODORUS [3] (fourth century AD)
Theodorus was a Platonist who became a priest. He had been a pupil of **Maximus of Ephesus** and was a friend of the emperor **Julian**.

THEODORUS [4] (fifth century AD)
Theodorus was a friend of **Proclus** [1]. He wrote a book on fate, and Proclus wrote one in return. However, his main interest was engineering rather than philosophy.

THEODORUS [5] (sixth century AD)
Theodorus taught philosophy at Constantinople where one of his pupils was **Stephanus of Alexandria**.

THEODORUS, FLAVIUS MANLIUS (fourth/fifth century AD)
Theodorus was a statesman and author who wrote on a wide range of subjects. He is best known for a technical work on poetry but also produced translations of Greek philosophical works.

THEODORUS OF ASINE (third/fourth century AD)
Theodorus was a Neoplatonist who studied with both **Porphyry** and

Iamblichus of Chalcis. He wrote commentaries on the *Timaeus* and *Phaedo* of **Plato** [1]. A group opposed to the innovations of Iamblichus, known as the Theodorites, may have been founded by him. He is described by **Eunapius** as a particularly virtuous individual.

THEODORUS OF BYZANTIUM (fifth century BC)
Theodorus was renowned for his eloquence and wrote a number of works on rhetoric. In *Phaedrus*, **Plato** [1] called him *Logodaedalus*, a 'Daedalus of words'.

THEODORUS OF CHIOS
Theodorus is mentioned by **Diogenes Laertius** as a Stoic philosopher.

THEODORUS OF CYRENE (fifth/fourth century BC)
Theodorus features in three dialogues of **Plato** [1]. He is portrayed as an accomplished mathematician, and also a friend of **Protagoras of Abdera**. Plato may have gone to Cyrene to study with him, although in the dialogues he is said to be teaching in Athens. He should not be confused with **Theodorus the Atheist** who is also sometimes referred to as Theodorus of Cyrene.

THEODORUS OF GADARA (first century BC/first century AD)
Theodorus had a wide range of interests and wrote many books but was best known as a theoretician of rhetoric. He had a school on Rhodes where the future emperor **Tiberius** attended his lectures.

THEODORUS OF MILETUS
Theodorus is mentioned by **Diogenes Laertius** as a Stoic philosopher.

THEODORUS OF SOLI (fourth and/or third century BC)
Theodorus had a theory that there were five elements and that they corresponded to five geometrical solids, ranging from the pyramid to the dodecahedron. He seems to have developed this from ideas put forward by **Plato** [1] in his *Timaeus*.

THEODORUS OF TARENTUM (fifth century BC?)
According to **Iamblichus of Chalcis**, Theodorus was a Pythagorean.

THEODORUS THE ATHEIST (fourth/third century BC).
Theodorus acquired his nickname because of his professed opposition to the religious beliefs of his time. According to **Diogenes Laertius**, he studied under **Aristippus Metrodidactus**, **Anniceris of Cyrene** and **Dionysius of Chalcedon**, subsequently attracting his own group of followers who became known as the Theodoreans. He took the view that pleasure and pain were the only important things in life, and that conventional morality should be treated with a degree of flexibility. He regarded himself as a citizen of the world, and lived in a number of different places. This was not always a matter of choice as on more than one occasion he was asked to move on. His flexible approach to morality may have been a contributory factor. He ended his days in Cyrene, even though it had earlier thrown him out. His views on religion may have influenced **Epicurus**.

THEODORUS THE MONK (sixth/seventh century AD)

Two people called Theodorus who were monks as well as philosophers are said to have been teachers in Alexandria around the end of the sixth century AD. One taught both philosophy and theology and wrote works attacking heresy, the other was renowned for his simple life. It is possible that they were one and the same person.

THEODOSIUS OF TRIPOLIS (second/third century AD?)

The name of Theodosius is associated with two works, one entitled *Sceptical Chapters* and the other a commentary on a text of **Theudas**. The author of at least one of them seems to have been Theodosius of Tripolis, who has often been confused with Theodosius of Bithynia, a mathematician of the second century BC.

THEODOTUS [1]

According to **Clement of Alexandria**, Theodotus was a Pythagorean.

THEODOTUS [2] (third century AD)

Theodotus was a Platonist and at one time headed the school in Athens.

THEODOTUS [3] (fifth/sixth century AD?)

All that is known of Theodotus is that a book on his life written by **Tribonianus** described him as a philosopher.

THEODOTUS OF BYZANTIUM (second/third century AD)

Theodotus was a shoemaker or tanner and a Christian who founded the movement known as adoptionism. For this he was excommunicated. Fearing that developments in doctrine threatened to undermine monotheism, he argued that Jesus was born human but given special powers at his baptism. According to **Eusebius of Caesarea**, amongst his followers were another Theodotus, a money-changer, and an Asclepiodotus.

THEOGNIS (fourth/third century BC)

According to **Clement of Alexandria**, Theognis was a daughter of **Diodorus Cronus** who studied with her father and became an accomplished philosopher.

THEOGNOSTUS (fifth/fourth century AD)

Theognostus was a pupil of **Democritus of Abdera**.

THEOMANDER OF CYRENE (fourth century BC)

According to **Athenaeus of Naucratis**, citing **Theophrastus of Eresus**, Theomander claimed to be able to teach happiness. He was probably an early member of the Cyrenaic school.

THEOMBROTUS [1] (fourth/third century BC)

A Cynic, Theombrotus was a pupil of **Crates of Thebes** and possibly of **Metrocles of Maronea**. He in turn was the teacher of **Demetrius of Alexandria**, and probably **Echecles of Ephesus** and **Menedemus of Lampsacus** as well.

THEOMBROTUS [2] see CLEOMBROTUS OF AMBRACIA

THEOMNESTUS [1]

Theomnestus was a Cynic.

THEOMNESTUS [2] (first century BC)

Theomnestus may have succeeded **Aristus of Ascalon** as head of the Platonist school in Athens. His lectures there were attended by **Brutus** after he had left Rome following the assassination of Julius **Caesar**. Some identify him with **Theomnestus of Naucratis**.

THEOMNESTUS OF NAUCRATIS (first century BC)

According to Flavius **Philostratus**, Theomnestus was a philosopher who delivered his lectures in such an extremely elaborate and artificial style that he was not always taken seriously.

THEON [1]

Theon was a pupil of a philosopher called Alexander, but it is not known which one.

THEON [2] (second century AD)

Theon was the author of a letter to **Heraclides** [4] in which he greeted him as a philosopher. The letter discussed some Stoic texts, but Theon may have been a Platonist like Heraclides.

THEON OF ALEXANDRIA (fourth century/fifth century AD)

Theon was a philosopher and mathematician who wrote on a variety of subjects and produced a series of commentaries on the works of **Ptolemy** [1]. He was the father of **Hypatia of Alexandria**.

THEON OF GAUL (fourth century AD)

Theon was one of the 'healing sophists' who appeared during the fourth century. According to **Eunapius**, he made a great name for himself in Gaul, presumably as a healer.

THEON OF SMYRNA (first century AD)

Theon was a mathematician and a Platonist. He likened progress in philosophy to going through stages of initiation into a mystery religion, and wrote a work setting out the order in which the works of **Plato** [1] should be studied to that end. He also wrote a commentary on the *Republic*.

THEON OF TITHOREA

According to **Diogenes Laertius**, Theon was a Stoic with a reputation for sleepwalking.

THEOPHEIDES (third century BC)

Theopheides was a friend of **Hermarchus of Mitylene**. Hermarchus wrote him a letter in which he attacked **Alexinus of Elis**. It seems likely Theopheides was an Epicurean.

THEOPHILUS OF ANTIOCH (second century AD)
Theophilus was a Christian philosopher and bishop of Antioch. He wrote a work for his friend Autolycus in which he set out the superiority of Christian philosophy to Greek myth and explained the nature of God in philosophical terms.
(*Ante-Nicene Fathers*, vol. II)

THEOPHRASTUS OF ERESUS (fourth/third century BC)
Theophrastus was originally called Tyrtamus, but acquired his nickname (Theophrastus means 'divine speaker') because of his eloquence. He first became acquainted with philosophy in his native Lesbos, and went on to study in Athens with **Plato** [1] and **Aristotle** [1]. Aristotle appointed him as his successor at the Lyceum, and left him his library in his will. He was a prolific author and a popular teacher, attracting large numbers to his lectures. Although he wrote on a wide range of topics, including hair and honey, he was most productive in the field of science. History, however, has looked with greater favour on his *Characters*, a series of sketches of unusual people designed to serve as moral lessons. When he died in 286 BC he was succeeded by **Strato of Lampsacus**.
(Theophrastus, Herodas, Cercidas and the Choliambic Poets, trans. J. Rusten, I.C. Cunningham and A.D. Knox, Loeb, 1993; Theophrastus, *Metaphysics*, trans. M. van Raalte, Leiden, Brill, 1993)
[W.W. Fortenbaugh, P.M. Huby and A.A. Long (eds), *Theophrastus of Eresus: on his life and works*, New Brunswick, Transaction, 1985]

THEOPHRIS OF CROTON (fifth century BC?)
Theophris was the father of **Philtys of Croton**. It is assumed that he, like she, was a Pythagorean.

THEOPOMPUS (fourth century AD)
Theopompus was a philosopher mentioned by **Libanius** [1].

THEOPOMPUS OF CHIOS (fourth century BC)
Theompompus was a sophist and historian who wrote a book claiming that the dialogues of **Plato** [1] were mainly plagiarised from the works of **Aristippus of Cyrene** and **Antisthenes of Athens**.

THEOPORUS (third century BC)
Chrysippus of Soli dedicated a book on moral theory to Theoporus, who was probably a Stoic.

THEORIDES OF METAPONTUM. (fifth century BC?)
According to **Iamblichus of Chalcis**, Theorides was a Pythagorean.

THEOSEBIUS (fifth century AD)
Theosebius was a pupil of **Hierocles of Alexandria**. His main interest was in moral philosophy, and he was a great admirer of **Epictetus**, but while he appreciated the moral teachings of Epictetus, he could not accept the principles

of Stoicism on which they were based. In areas other than ethics, he was more influenced by Platonism. However, he remained convinced that ethics was the most important part of philosophy and that a good character was more important than an accumulation of knowledge.

THEOTIMUS, POPILLIUS (first/second century AD)
Theotimus was the head of the Epicurean school in Athens. He was succeeded in this position by **Heliodorus** [2].

THEOXENUS (fourth century BC?)
Theoxenus may have written a book about **Anacharsis the Scythian** and been a Cynic.

THERAMENES OF STIRIA (fifth century BC)
Theramenes was best known as an Athenian politician and general. However, he had studied with **Prodicus of Ceos** and may himself have taught **Isocrates of Erchia**. He may also have been an acquaintance of **Socrates**. He was condemned to death in 404 BC and is said to have met his end philosophically.

THERIS (second century BC)
Theris was a Platonist and the teacher of **Dion of Thrace**.

THESMOPOLIS
According to **Lucian of Samosata**, Thesmopolis was a Stoic philosopher who became a Cynic. However, his historicity is questioned.

THESPIS (third/second century BC)
Thespis was an Epicurean and the teacher of **Philonides**.

THESSALUS (first century AD)
Thessalus was the pupil of **Themison of Laodicea**, and with his teacher established the Methodist school of medicine. He took an anti-determinist approach to medicine, arguing that there was no necessary link between signs presaging the onset of a disease and the disease itself. The name of Thessalus is also connected with astrology and Hermeticism, but it may not be the same person.

THESTOR OF POSIDONIA
Thestor was a Pythagorean who is said to have gone to the aid of **Thymarides of Paros** purely on the basis that he was another Pythagorean and in need of assistance. This is cited by **Iamblichus of Chalcis** as an example of the Pythagorean approach to friendship.

THEUDAS (second century AD)
Little is known about Theudas other than that he was a Sceptic.

THEUDIUS OF MAGNESIA (fourth century BC)
Theudius spent some time at the Academy and was one of the first to produce a systematic approach to geometry.

THOMAS (third/fourth century AD)
Thomas was a follower of **Mani** and taught in Egypt.

THRASEA PAETUS, PUBLIUS CLODIUS (first century AD)
Thrasea Paetus was a Roman politician of the Stoic persuasion. As a member of the Senate, he fearlessly followed an independent line, and in the process antagonised Nero, who eventually pressurised the Senate into condemning him to death in AD 66. He duly committed suicide by opening his veins in the presence of his son-in-law **Helvidius Priscus** and **Demetrius of Rome**. He was a great admirer of **Cato the Younger** and wrote a biography of him.

THRASEAS OF METAPONTUM (fifth century BC?)
According to **Iamblichus of Chalcis**, Thraseas was a Pythagorean.

THRASYALCES OF THASOS (sixth/fifth century BC?)
According to **Strabo of Amaseia**, Thrasyalces was an early natural philosopher who attributed the flooding of the Nile to summer rains in Ethiopia. He may have been influenced by **Thales of Miletus**.

THRASYDAMUS OF ARGOS
According to **Iamblichus of Chalcis**, Thrasydamus was a Pythagorean.

THRASYLLUS (first century BC/first century AD)
Thrasyllus is an enigmatic figure. He taught the future emperor **Tiberius** [1] during his stay on Rhodes. Although sometimes thought to have been a Pythagorean, his main interest appears to have lain in astrology and other branches of divination. A Thrasyllus from the same period edited and organised the works of both **Plato** [1] and **Democritus of Abdera** and he may be the same person. He believed that Plato had originally written his dialogues in groups of four, and that there were fourteen such groups of them (a figure he arrived at by counting each book of *Republic* and *Laws* as separate dialogues). He arranged the books of Democritus according to the same plan.

THRASYLLUS THE CYNIC (fourth century BC)
Thrasyllus is best known because of an anecdote concerning an encounter between himself and Antigonus, one of the successors of Alexander the Great. When Thrasyllus asked for a drachma he was told that such a small amount was not fitting for a king to give. But when he then asked for a talent (6,000 drachmas), Antigonus replied that such a large amount was not fitting for a Cynic to receive.

THRASYMACHUS OF CHALCEDON (fifth century BC)
Thrasymachus is best known for the role he plays in the *Republic* of **Plato** [1], where he seeks to defend the view that justice is what is in the interests of the strong and that therefore might is right. As he is generally regarded as a rhetorician, it is entirely possible that he did not actually believe this even if he said it. He also had some experience as a diplomat, first coming to Athens as a representative of his native Chalcedon. He may have died by hanging himself.

(Rosemary Kent Sprague (ed.) *The Older Sophists*, Indianapolis, Hackett, 2001) [Rachel Barney, 'Callicles and Thrasymachus', *The Stanford Encyclopedia of Philosophy (Fall 2004 Edition)*, Edward N. Zalta (ed.), plato.stanford.edu/archives/fall2004/entries/callicles-thrasymachus/ *Routledge Encyclopaedia of Philosophy*, vol. 9]

THRASYMACHUS OF CORINTH (fourth century BC)
Thrasymachus was probably a Megarian, a pupil of **Ichthyas**, and, according to **Diogenes Laertius**, a teacher of **Stilpo**.

THRASYMEDES OF METAPONTUM (fifth century BC?)
According to **Iamblichus of Chalcis**, Thrasymedes was a Pythagorean.

THRASYS (third century BC)
Thrasys was a pupil of **Lacydes of Cyrene**.

THYMARIDAS OF TARENTUM (sixth/fifth century BC?)
Thymaridas was a Pythagorean, mentioned in a work by **Androcydes** in which he is shown as a strong believer in divine providence. According to **Iamblichus of Chalcis**, a Thymaridas, possibly this one, was a pupil of **Pythagoras** himself.

THYMARIDES OF PAROS
Thymarides features in a story told by **Iamblichus of Chalcis** designed to illustrate the importance of friendship amongst Pythagoreans. He tells how **Thestor of Posidonia**, hearing that Thymarides had fallen on hard times, raised some money and took it to Paros in order to help him.

TIBERIANUS (fourth century AD)
Tiberius came from Baetica and was a follower of **Priscillian**, writing a number of works in defence of his views.

TIBERIUS [1] (42 BC - AD 37)
Tiberius was emperor of Rome from AD 14 until his death in AD 37. He took an interest in philosophical matters, and appears to have been particularly drawn to Scepticism. As a young man, he studied with **Theodorus of Gadara** and **Thrasyllus**.

TIBERIUS [2]
Tiberius was a sophist best known for his works on rhetoric, although he also wrote on historical and philosophical subjects.

TIMAEUS OF CROTON (fifth century BC?)
According to **Iamblichus of Chalcis**, Timaeus was a Pythagorean.

TIMAEUS OF CYZICUS (fourth century BC)
Timaeus is said to have been a pupil of **Plato** [1] with tyrannical tendencies.

TIMAEUS OF LOCRI (fifth century BC)
Timaeus appears as the lead character in a dialogue by **Plato** [1], which was named after him. He is described as rich, a sometime holder of high office, and

a philosopher of considerable accomplishment. According to **Cicero,** Plato had met Timaeus and studied with him. In the dialogue, he expounds a theory of how the natural world came into existence. It is impossible to know whether Timaeus himself espoused the views attributed to him, although it seems reasonable to assume at least some basis in fact. Cicero describes him as a Pythagorean, and Locri, situated in the far south-west of mainland Italy, was certainly within the Pythagorean sphere of influence. **Iamblichus of Chalcis** identifies two people called Timaeus as Pythagoreans, but neither is associated with Locri. Writings purporting to be by Timaeus are by a far later author who appropriated his name.

(David Fideler (ed.), *The Pythagorean Sourcebook*, Grand Rapids, Phanes, 1987)

TIMAEUS OF PAROS
According to **Iamblichus of Chalcis**, Timaeus was a Pythagorean.

TIMAEUS OF TAUROMENION (third century BC)
Timaeus was an historian, and a source used by **Diogenes Laertius** in his account of **Empedocles of Acragas.**

TIMAGORAS (first century BC)
Timagoras was an Epicurean mentioned by **Cicero.**

TIMAGORAS OF GELA (fourth/third century BC)
Timagoras was a student first of **Theophrastus of Eresus** and then of **Stilpo.**

TIMARATUS OF LOCRI (sixth/fifth century BC)
According to **Iamblichus of Chalcis**, Timaratus was a Pythagorean, and probably a student of **Pythagoras** himself, who achieved great eminence as a lawgiver in Locri. However, he says exactly the same thing about a **Timares of Locri**, which is either a remarkable coincidence or a mistake. The latter is perhaps more likely as on both occasions he links the name with another, that of **Zaleucus,** suggesting that Timaratus and Timares are one and the same person.

TIMARCHUS (third century BC)
Timarchus was a pupil of **Epicurus.**

TIMARCHUS OF ALEXANDRIA (third century BC)
Timarchus was a pupil of **Cleomenes** [1] and a Cynic.

TIMARES OF LOCRI (sixth/fifth century BC?)
Timares is described by **Iamblichus of Chalcis** as a Pythagorean and an important lawgiver in Locri. Some modern scholars think that Iamblichus or someone else has made a mistake and that 'Timares of Locri' should read 'Timaeus of Locri'. As **Plato** [1] nowhere describes Timaeus specifically as a lawgiver, the identification is at best inconclusive. However, Timares does seem to be the same person as **Timaratus of Locri.**

TIMASAGORAS see NICASICRATES

TIMASIUS OF SYBARIS (fifth century BC?)
According to **Iamblichus of Chalcis**, Timasius was a Pythagorean.

TIMESIANAX OF PAROS
According to **Iamblichus of Chalcis**, Timesianax was a Pythagorean.

TIMOCLES (second century BC)
Timocles was a pupil of **Panaetius of Rhodes**.

TIMOCRATES [1] (fourth/third century BC)
Timocrates was the brother of **Metrodorus of Lampsacus** [2]. At one time a
follower of Epicurus, he later turned against him, accusing him of eating far too
much and knowing far too little about philosophy.

TIMOCRATES [2] (fourth/third century BC)
Timocrates was one of the executors of the will of **Epicurus**, jointly entrusted
not only with the Garden, but also the responsibility for preserving its
distinctive way of life.

TIMOCRATES [3] (third century BC)
According to **Diogenes Laertius, Chrysippus of Soli** dedicated a set of essays
on logic to Timocrates and **Philomathes** in which their own works were
criticised. Timocrates was therefore evidently a logician and probably also a
Stoic.

TIMOCRATES OF HERACLEA (second century AD)
Timocrates was a well-versed individual who had studied medicine and the
philosophy of **Democritus of Abdera** before making the acquaintance of
Euphrates of Tyre and becoming more interested in oratory. He was renowned
for his bad temper. **Lepidus of Amastris** was one of his pupils.

TIMOLAUS OF CYZICUS (fourth century BC)
Timolaus was a student of **Plato** [1].

TIMOMACHUS (fourth century BC?)
Timomachus was the supposed recipient of a letter falsley attributed to
Diogenes of Sinope and is assumed to have been a Cynic.

TIMON OF PHLIUS (fourth/third century BC)
Timon was an important figure in the early history of Scepticism. After a career
as a dancer, he went on to study first with **Stilpo** and then with **Pyrrho of Elis**.
He moved to Chalcedon, where he made a lot of money as a teacher, before
finally settling in Athens where he died as a very old man in around 225 BC. He
was a prolific writer, composing poems and plays as well as philosophical
works that set out the fundamentals of Scepticism. He had a gift for satire and
took great pleasure in mocking the teachers and teachings of other schools.
Whereas he had the greatest respect and admiration for Pyrrho, he dismissed
most other eminent philosophers as wafflers, windbags, or worse.
[Richard Bett, *Pyrrho: his antecedents and his legacy*, Oxford, Oxford University

Press, 2000; R.J. Hankinson, *The Sceptics*, London, Routledge, 1995; Richard Bett, 'Timon of Phlius', *The Stanford Encyclopedia of Philosophy* (Fall 2002 Edition), Edward N. Zalta (ed.), plato.stanford.edu/archives/fall2002/entries/timon-phlius/]

TIMONAX (third century BC)
Chrysippus of Soli dedicated a book on the problem of knowledge to Timonax, suggesting he was either a colleague or a pupil.

TIMONIDES OF LEUCADIA (fourth century BC)
Timonides was a pupil of **Plato**.

TIMOSTHENES OF ARGOS
According to **Iamblichus of Chalcis**, Timosthenes was a Pythagorean.

TIMOSTRATUS (third century BC)
Chrysippus of Soli dedicated a book to Timostratus, suggesting he was either a colleague or a pupil.

TIMOTHEUS OF ATHENS
According to **Diogenes Laertius**, Timotheus wrote a book called *On Lives*, which seems to have included a number of biographical sketches including one of **Aristotle** [1].

TIMOTHEUS OF PERGAMUM
According to **Clement of Alexandria**, Timotheus wrote a book *On the Fortitude of Philosophers*.

TIMYCHA OF SPARTA (fourth century BC)
Timycha was a Pythagorean and the wife of **Myllias of Croton**. She was regarded as an exemplification of Pythagorean self-control and courage. When pregnant, she and her husband were captured and taken before Dionysius I of Syracuse who tried to extract Pythagorean secrets from them. When they refused, he commanded that she be tortured. In reply, she bit her own tongue off and spat it out at him. Her Spartan upbringing may have helped.

TISANDER OF APHIDNA (fifth/fourth century BC)
Tisander was one of a philosophical circle that also included **Andron of Gargettus**, **Callicles of Acahrnae** and **Nausicydes of Cholarges**. They agreed that while the study of philosophy was valuable, it should not be taken too far.

TISIAS (fifth century BC)
Tisias came from Syracuse. A pioneer of rhetoric, he emphasised the importance of appeals to probability in argument. He taught **Gorgias of Leontini**.

TORQUATUS, LUCIUS MANLIUS (first century BC)
Torquatus was an Epicurean, and was chosen by **Cicero** to represent his school in *On Moral Ends*. Whether fairly or not, his understanding of Epicureanism is

portrayed as somewhat crude and superficial. He was killed in 48 BC, during the civil war.

TREBATIUS TESTA, CAIUS (first century BC)
Trebatius was a lawyer and a friend of **Cicero**. When he converted to Epicureanism in 53 BC, Cicero wrote to him questioning whether being an Epicurean was compatible with belonging to the legal profession. Trebatius was also the author of some works on religion.

TREBIANUS (first century BC)
Trebianus was a friend of **Cicero** who took an interest in philosophy and may have been an Epicurean.

TRIBONIANUS (sixth century AD)
Sometimes known as 'the Younger' to distinguish him from the more famous legal scholar of the same name, Tribonianus came from Side and wrote a book about the life of **Theodotus** [3].

TRIBUNUS (sixth century AD)
Tribunus was both a physician and a philosopher. A Peripatetic, he wrote some widely admired commentaries on **Aristotle** [1] and found favour with **Chosroes I**, with whom he spent some time.

TRYPHON (third century AD)
According to **Porphyry**, Tryphon was both a Stoic and a Platonist. He told **Amelius Gentilianus** that people in Greece were accusing **Plotinus** of plagiarising the works of **Numenius of Apamea**, and Amelius duly published a refutation of these claims.

TUBERO, LUCIUS AELIUS (first century BC)
Tubero was a friend of **Cicero** and studied for a time in the Academy. **Aenesidemus of Cnossus** dedicated his *Pyrrhonist Discourses* to him.

TUBERO, QUINTUS AELIUS (second century BC)
Tubero was a Stoic and studied under **Panaetius of Rhodes**.

TUCCA, PLAUTIUS (first century BC)
Tucca was an Epicurean, a pupil of both **Philodemus of Gadara** and **Siro**. **Virgil** and **Horace** were amongst his friends and he edited the manuscript of Virgil's *Aeneid* when the poet died.

TYCONIUS (fourth century AD)
Tyconius was an African theologian who was particularly interested in the problem of understanding scripture. This led him to develop a number of rules of interpretation, and so to set out the foundations of an approach to hermeneutics. **Augustine** was sufficiently impressed by the rules to borrow them.

TYRANNIO (first century BC)
Tyrannio was primarily a grammarian. A friend of **Cicero**, he often taught in

his house. His importance in the history of philosophy is that he made copies of a number of works of **Aristotle** [1] that might otherwise have been lost.

TYRSENIS OF SYBARIS (fifth century BC?)
According to **Iamblichus of Chalcis**, Tyrsenis was one of the most famous Pythagorean women.

TYRSENUS OF SYBARIS (fifth century BC?)
According to **Iamblichus of Chalcis**, Tyrsenus was a Pythagorean.

❖ U ❖

ULPIAN OF GAZA (fifth century AD)
Ulpian studied in Alexandria under **Olympiodorus** [1]. While he was there he got to know **Proclus** [1]. When **Marinus of Neapolis** came to write his biography of Proclus, Ulpian was able to provide him with information about the Alexandrian period of his life.

URANIUS (sixth century AD)
Uranius originally came from Syria but spent many years in Constantinople. There he became a well-known figure, always ready to engage others in philosophical discussions. However, he was viewed by many with a degree of suspicion. Not only was he a dedicated social climber, but he also supposedly chose people less educated than himself for his discussions because they were easier to impress. However, sometime after AD 532 he travelled to Persia and there succeeded in impressing **Chosroes I**, who took a keen interest in philosophy. Chosroes treated him generously, and he returned from Persia a rich man.

❖ V ❖

VALENTINUS (second century AD)
Valentinus was originally from Alexandria, but lived in Rome for much of his life. He was the founder of a gnostic sect whose members believed themselves to be the only people able to attain the highest level of salvation. **Hippolytus** claimed Valentinus had been influenced by the ideas of both **Pythagoras** and **Plato** [1], although this is questionable. At the heart of the Valentinian philosophy was a complex account of the origins of the world.

(Arland J. Hultgren and Steven A. Haggmark (eds), *The Earliest Christian Heretics*, Minneapolis, Fortress Press, 1996)
[Hans Jonas, *The Gnostic Religion*, Boston, Beacon, 1963]

VALERIUS MAXIMUS (first century AD)
A person of little originality, and a notorious flatterer of **Tiberius** [1], Valerius is best known for producing his nine books of *Memorable Doings and Sayings*. The work was designed primarily as a resource for moral education by means of examples, showing how virtue is rewarded and vice punished. It preserves many otherwise lost snippets taken from a variety of sources. His books are not much regarded today, but they were popular throughout the medieval and renaissance periods.
(Valerius Maximus, *Memorable Doings and Sayings* (2 vols), trans. D.R. Shackleton Bailey, Loeb, 2000)
[Clive Skidmore, *Practical Ethics for Roman Gentlemen: the work of Valerius Maximus*, Exeter, University of Exeter Press, 1996]

VALERIUS, PUBLIUS AVIANIUS (second century AD)
Valerius was a philosopher who had a statue erected in his honour in his home town of Hadriani.

VARIUS RUFUS, LUCIUS (first century BC)
Varius Rufus was an Epicurean and a friend of **Philodemus of Gadara**. He was a poet and one of his works, *On Death*, was doubtless shaped by Epicurean thoughts on the subject. It is said to have had a significant influence on **Virgil**, but it has long been lost. He may have studied under **Siro**.

VARRO, MARCUS TERENTIUS (116-27 BC)
Varro led an active and sometimes risky political life. Although he backed the wrong side in the civil war, he survived to spend his later years in quiet retirement. He studied with **Posidonius of Apamea** for a short time when the latter visited Rome in 86 BC, but the most important philosophical influence on him was **Antiochus of Ascalon**. Varro wrote hundreds of works, most of which have since been lost. Amongst them was an extended series of fictional philosophical dialogues, the *Logistorici*, in which assorted Romans debated a variety of topics, illustrating their arguments with examples from history. **Tertullian** called him a 'Roman Cynic', perhaps because of some satires he wrote, but it is highly unlikely that he was one. Better attested is his interest in Pythagoreanism, and he is said to have been buried according to Pythagorean rites.

VATINIUS, PUBLIUS (first century BC)
Vatinius was a politician, a supporter of Julius **Caesar**, and a friend of **Cicero** who, at different times, both attacked and defended him. Vatinius apparently called himself a Pythagorean, although Cicero questioned his right to do so on account of his dubious behaviour.

VELLEIUS, CAIUS (second/first century BC)
Velleius was an Epicurean. He was used by **Cicero** as a representative of Epicurean views on religion in his *On the Nature of the Gods*. Although a senator, his philosophical views led him to steer clear of politics.

VERUS, LUCIUS (second century AD)
Like **Marcus Aurelius**, Verus was adopted by Antoninus Pius. They shared many of the same teachers including **Herodes Atticus**, Marcus Cornelius **Fronto, Apollonius of Chalcedon** and **Sextus of Chaeronea**. They both succeeded to the imperial throne when Antoninus died in AD 161, but Verus was always the junior partner and died relatively young in AD 169. After his death, Marcus had him deified.

VIGELLIUS, MARCUS (second century BC)
Vigellius was a Stoic, a friend and pupil of **Panaetius of Rhodes**.

VIRGIL [PUBLIUS VERGILIUS MARO] (70-19 BC)
Virgil spent some time as a young man in fellowship with an Epicurean community at Naples headed by **Siro**. He appears to have been a particular favourite of Siro, inheriting his villa on his death in 42 BC. The extent to which Epicurean ideas influenced his poetry has long been debated. It is sometimes argued that the influence is less marked in his later works as his attachment to Epicureanism weakened.
(Virgil, *The Aeneid*, trans. D. West, New York, Random House, 1983; and many other translations; classics.mit.edu/Browse/browse-Virgil.html)

VITRUVIUS POLLIO (first century BC)
Vitruvius produced one of the most famous works on architecture ever written. Broad in scope, it considers every aspect of the subject, such as materials, location and proportion. He regarded a knowledge of philosophy as important for architects as it made them more modest, more polite and more honest. Philosophical writings were also a source of knowledge about physics and geometry, both of which were indispensable. References to a wide range of philosophers are scattered throughout his text.
(Vitruvius, *The Ten Books of Architecture*, trans. M.H. Morgan, New York, Dover, 1960)

VOLUMNIUS EUTRAPELUS, PUBLIUS (first century BC)
Volumnius was a friend of **Cicero** and Marcus **Brutus**. According to **Plutarch of Chaeronea** he was also a philosopher, and it seems most likely that he was an Epicurean.

VOLUSIANUS (fourth/fifth century AD)
Volusianus was a man of great learning who became proconsul of Africa. He evidently had some knowledge of Platonism, and for a time exchanged views on philosophical and religious issues with **Augustine**.

VOPISCUS, PUBLIUS MANLIUS (first century AD)
Vopiscus was an Epicurean and patron of the poet Statius.

VRANIUS see URANIUS

XANTHIPPUS
There are references to a Cynic philosopher of this name, but nothing is known about him.

XENARCHUS OF SELEUCIA (first century BC)
Xenarchus was a Peripatetic, who rejected the idea of a fifth element in Aristotelian metaphysics. Originally from Seleucia, he taught in Alexandria and Rome and became a friend of **Arius Didymus** and Augustus. **Strabo of Amaseia** was one of his pupils.

XENEAS OF CAULONIA (fifth century BC?)
According to **Iamblichus of Chalcis**, Xeneas was a Pythagorean.

XENIADES (fourth century BC)
Xeniades is said to have bought **Diogenes of Sinope** as a slave in Crete and taken him back to Corinth. There he entrusted him with running his household and looking after his children. Xeniades came to develop a great admiration for Diogenes and may have become a Cynic himself.

XENIADES OF CORINTH (sixth/fifth century BC)
Xeniades believed that all the evidence of the senses and all opinions were false, and that everything that exists comes from and returns to the non-existent. According to **Sextus Empiricus**, the views he held were virtually identical with those of **Xenophanes of Colophon**.
(Rosemary Kent Sprague (ed.), *The Older Sophists*, Indianapolis, Hackett, 2001)

XENOCADES OF METAPONTUM (fifth century BC?)
According to **Iamblichus of Chalcis**, Xenocades was a Pythagorean.

XENOCRATES
According to **Diogenes Laertius**, Xenocrates was a philosopher and a rather bad poet.

XENOCRATES OF CHALCEDON (396-314 BC)
Xenocrates succeeded **Speusippus** as head of the Academy in 339 BC, having previously studied with both **Plato** [1] and **Aristotle** [1]. He was said by some to have been the first person to divide philosophy formally into the three different areas of physics, logic and ethics, although others believed that **Zeno**

of Citium was the first to do this. Along with his predecessor, he worked to make Plato's philosophy both more systematic and more dogmatic, and to that end worked on producing authoritative texts as well as developing conceptual schemes. He believed it was possible to deduce the nature of reality from first metaphysical principles, and his tendency to work with threefold divisions in doing so in some ways anticipated trends that were to become more noticeable in Neoplatonism. He was noted for his independence as an individual and had a reputation as a disciplinarian at the Academy.

[John Dillon, *The Heirs of Plato: a study of the Old Academy (347-274 BC)*, Oxford, Clarendon Press, 2003; Russell Dancy, 'Xenocrates', *The Stanford Encyclopedia of Philosophy* (Fall 2003 Edition), Edward N. Zalta (ed.), plato.stanford.edu/archives/fall2003/entries/xenocrates/]

XENOPHANES OF COLOPHON (sixth/fifth century BC)
Xenophanes is a colourful and puzzling character. He appears to have spent much of his life in exile, mainly in Sicily, and to have lived a rather nomadic existence. He was said to have been the teacher of **Parmenides of Elea**, but many doubt the reliability of this claim. His few surviving fragmentary writings are all in verse. It is difficult to extract any kind of systematic philosophy from them, although it is clear that he was interested in a number of important philosophical issues such as the nature of the world and the gods, and the limits of human knowledge.

He criticised the poets for portraying the gods as immoral, and believed human beings projected their own image onto their gods, observing that the Ethiopians had black gods, and that horses, if they could draw, would depict their gods as horses. He postulated instead one single supreme unchanging deity. He believed that everything came from earth and water, and that the stars were clouds on fire. He held that it was impossible for human beings to know everything, and if anyone did, they would not know that they knew!

(J.H. Lesher, *Xenophanes of Colophon: fragments*, Toronto, Toronto University Press, 1992; Jonathan Barnes, *Early Greek Philosophy*, Harmondsworth, Penguin, 1987)

[*Routledge Encyclopaedia of Philosophy*, vol. 9; James Lesher, 'Xenophanes', *The Stanford Encyclopedia of Philosophy* (Winter 2002 Edition), Edward N. Zalta (ed.), plato.stanford.edu/archives/win2002/entries/xenophanes/]

XENOPHANTES OF METAPONTUM (fifth century BC?)
According to **Iamblichus of Chalcis**, Xenophantes was a Pythagorean.

XENOPHILUS OF CHALCIS IN THRACE (fifth/fourth century BC?)
Xenophilus was a Pythagorean, said to have lived to a very old age. Music appears to have been his special interest, and he may have been a teacher of **Aristoxenus of Tarentum**.

XENOPHILUS OF CYZICUS
According to **Iamblichus of Chalcis**, Xenophilus was a Pythagorean.

XENOPHON OF ERCHIA (fifth/fourth century BC)

Xenophon would not trouble the historian of philosophy long were it not for his association with **Socrates** and the fact that he wrote about him. As it is, he is an important source. For many years he led a very active life, involving himself in military adventures. He wrote a number of books, but it is his *Memoirs* that is of most interest to philosophers. Unlike the stylised dialogues of **Plato** [1], it purports to be a straightforward recollection of things Socrates said and did. As such, some have believed it to be the best historical material available on the life of Socrates, although opinions differ on its reliability. It is unclear how long or how well Xenophon knew Socrates, or how much he understood his teachings. He clearly had philosophical pretensions of his own and wrote at least one dialogue, *The Symposium*, in his later years. Some have seen in the selection of a title identical to one used by Plato an indication of a rivalry between the two. The work of Xenophon is generally taken to be the later one. He also wrote an *Apology* on the trial of Socrates, but it is entirely based on the reports of others as he was away from Athens at the time.

(Xenophon, *Memoirs of Socrates* and *The Symposium*, trans. H. Tredennick, Harmondsworth: Penguin, 1970; classics.mit.edu/Browse/browse-Xenophon.html)

[*Routledge Encyclopaedia of Philosophy*, vol. 9]

XUTHUS (fifth century BC?)

Xuthus was a Pythagorean. He seems to have developed an argument, aimed at **Parmenides of Elea** and his followers, that if the universe is finite, then there must exist 'something' outside it, which is the void. Some have identified him with **Ion of Chios**.

❖ Z ❖

ZACHARIAS (fifth/sixth century AD)

Zacharias came from Gaza and studied philosophy in Alexandria under **Ammonius**. Later he became a lawyer in Constantinople and eventually bishop of Mitylene. He wrote a great deal but his only work to survive, *On the Creation of the World*, is an attack on Neoplatonism. He may have been the brother of **Procopius of Gaza**.

ZALEUCUS OF LOCRI (seventh century BC?)

Zaleucus achieved great repute and respect as a lawgiver in Locri, and had a reputation for being both humane and severe. He established fixed penalties for each offence, and two stories are told about the consequences of this. According to the first, the punishment for adultery was the loss of both eyes. When his own son was found guilty of it, he ordered that the punishment should be divided between them so that they lost one eye each. The second story tells how the penalty for entering a particular public building carrying arms was death. When Zaleucus inadvertently violated the law, he executed himself. **Diogenes Laertius** and **Iamblichus of Chalcis** both call him a student of **Pythagoras**, but his laws are usually dated to the middle of the seventh century BC, making that impossible.

ZALMOXIS (sixth century BC)
It is said that Zalmoxis was a slave of **Pythagoras**, and studied with him before being set free. He then returned to his native Thrace where he sought to civilise the Getae, a notably warlike tribe. He tried to convince them that there was life after death and sought to prove it by disappearing into an underground cavern for three years before returning to them, as if from the dead. However, the Getae also had a god called Zalmoxis, and he too was associated with life after death, so it is possible that the legends relating to the two may have become confused. There was also a legend that at some stage in his career Zalmoxis turned into a wolf. According to **Hippolytus**, Zalmoxis was responsible for introducing Pythagoreanism to the Celts.

ZARATAS (sixth/fifth century BC)
According to **Hippolytus**, Zaratas was a pupil of **Pythagoras**.

ZECHERIAH DIDYMUS (first century BC)
Zecheriah wrote on logic, and advanced the view that the ideas of **Antisthenes of Athens** in this field were borrowed from **Prodicus of Ceos**.

ZENO (fifth century AD)
Zeno was a Jew from Alexandria who renounced his religion for philosophy. He was not regarded particularly highly as a scholar and was prone to forgetfulness.

ZENO OF ALEXANDRIA (second century BC)
Zeno was a pupil of **Carneades of Cyrene**.

ZENO OF CITIUM (334-262 BC)
Zeno was the founder of Stoicism, which was named after the Painted Stoa in Athens in which he taught for many years. He was born in Cyprus although his family may have been Phoenician in origin. He is said to have arrived in Athens as the result of a shipwreck and only then to have become interested in philosophy. Although the exact sequence of his philosophical education is unclear, he is said at one time or another to have studied with **Crates of Thebes**, **Diodorus Cronus** and **Polemo of Athens**. Eventually he formulated his own philosophy which owed its debts to these and others as well.

From Crates, Zeno seems to have acquired the principle of life in accordance with nature, although he rejected the Cynics' anti-social interpretation of it. From others he realised the importance of having a systematic philosophy to back up and build on the principle. According to **Diogenes Laertius**, he was the first to divide philosophy into logic, physics and ethics, the first concerned with knowledge and argument, the second with the nature of the world, and the third with a way of life within the world. Although he wrote several books, none of them survive. As a result, little is known about Zeno's views on logic, apart from the fact that he clearly attached importance to it. With regard to physics, Stoicism always had a strong belief in both materialism and determinism, and this seems to go back to Zeno himself. For the Stoics, even the soul was nothing more than an extremely fine kind of matter that was able to occupy the spaces left by the coarser kind of matter that made up the body. The soul possessed reason, which was also a characteristic of the universe, or nature, as a whole. In a world governed by reason, determinism presents itself as the physical manifestation of logical necessity.

By identifying ethics as the third and last of his divisions of his philosophy, Zeno seems to have intended it to be regarded as its culmination. Life in accordance with nature was above all an ethical principle and represented the Stoic understanding of virtue. However, given the strong element of determinism running through it, Stoicism always had a very limited view of what an individual could actually achieve. It therefore developed an ethic of reaction rather than one of action since if events could not be controlled at least responses to them could. Consequently Stoicism attached considerable importance to the control, if not elimination, of the emotions, especially the stronger ones. There was also a pragmatic dimension to this because wanting the impossible could only bring unhappiness. Life in accordance with nature was therefore not only the virtuous life but also the happy one.

Zeno was both popular and admired in Athens, being given the freedom of the city and having a statue erected in his honour in his own lifetime. It is said he ended his life by his own hand, but this is uncertain. On his death, **Cleanthes of Assus** became head of the school.

[Brad Inwood (ed.), *The Cambridge Companion to the Stoics*, Cambridge, Cambridge University Press, 2003]

ZENO OF ELEA (fifth century BC)
Zeno was a friend of **Parmenides of Elea**, and is best known for some paradoxes he devised that have intrigued philosophers ever since. The paradoxes are designed to throw doubt on two apparently obvious beliefs. The first is that there are many things in the world (as opposed to just one), and the second is that things move. For example, he argues that if things are divisible, then they are either infinitely large or they do not exist! If things are infinitely divisible, then they have an infinite number of parts, each of which must be of some magnitude. But if that is the case, an infinite number of them will constitute something infinitely large. If, on the other hand, things are not infinitely divisible, because a stage is reached when nothing is left, then things are made up of finite numbers of nothings, in which case they are themselves nothings and do not exist.

More famous are his paradoxes of motion, especially the one that has come to be called that of Achilles and the tortoise. According to this, if Achilles gives the tortoise a head start, he can never catch him, because in the time it takes him to get to where the tortoise *was*, the tortoise has moved ahead again. Another well-known one, the Stadium, argues that motion is impossible because in order for a runner to cover any distance it is first necessary to cover half the distance. But before that can be done, it is necessary to cover half of that distance, and so on. The runner ends up confronted with the problem of achieving an infinite number of targets in a finite time.

Exactly what Zeno meant to achieve with these paradoxes is unclear, as they survive only as fragments and references in the works of others. It is generally assumed that they are intended to make the position of Parmenides, that everything is one, more coherent, or at least to make the positions of his rivals less coherent. The connection between the two kinds of paradox, those of multiplicity and those of motion, is presumably that if movement is of one thing relative to another, then movement is impossible if there is only one thing.

(H.D.P. Lee, *Zeno of Elea*, Cambridge, Cambridge University Press, 1936; Jonathan Barnes, *Early Greek Philosophy*, Harmondsworth, Penguin, 1987) [J.A. Faris, *The Paradoxes of Zeno*, Aldershot, Ashgate, 1996; *Routledge Encyclopaedia of Philosophy*, vol. 9; Nick Huggett, 'Zeno's Paradoxes', *The Stanford Encyclopedia of Philosophy* (Summer 2004 Edition), Edward N. Zalta (ed.), plato.stanford.edu/archives/sum2004/entries/paradox-zeno/]

ZENO OF PERGAMUM (fifth century AD)
Zeno was a philosopher from Pergamum who was a friend and pupil of **Proclus** [1].

ZENO OF SIDON [1] (fourth/third century BC)
Zeno studied under **Diodorus Cronus** and was sometimes known as Zeno the Younger to distinguish him from **Zeno of Citium**.

ZENO OF SIDON [2] (second/first century BC)
Zeno was an Epicurean and for a time led the school. His successor was **Phaedrus**. He was interested in problems of logic, scientific method and mathematics, and he wrote a book called *On Signs* that discussed some of them. He was much admired by his pupil **Philodemus of Gadara**, but **Cicero** took exception to both his behaviour and unflattering remarks he made about **Socrates** and **Chrysippus of Soli**.

ZENO OF TARSUS (third/second century BC)
Zeno was a Stoic and succeeded **Chrysippus of Soli** as head of the school. Apart from some of his views on the divisions of philosophy, little is known about his thought. It seems likely that he was the Zeno to whom Chrysippus dedicated or addressed several of his books.

ZENOBIA (third century AD)
Zenobia was a celebrated queen of Palmyra and a person of considerable

learning. She became the patron of Cassius **Longinus**, but it is unclear how far she shared his philosophical views. After her defeat at the hands of the Romans she was taken to Rome where she died in old age.

ZENOBIUS (second/third century AD?)
Zenobius was an Epicurean, the target of a lost book by **Alexander of Aphrodisias**.

ZENODORUS OF TYRE (second century BC)
Zenodorus was a pupil of **Carneades of Cyrene**.

ZENODOTUS [1] (third century BC)
Chrysippus of Soli dedicated a book on proverbs to Zenodotus, suggesting he was either a colleague or a pupil.

ZENODOTUS [2] (fifth century AD)
Zenodotus taught philosophy in Athens and **Damascius** was one of his pupils. He had himself been taught by **Proclus** [1] and became the head of the Neoplatonist school after the death of **Marinus of Neapolis**.

ZENODOTUS OF ALEXANDRIA (fourth/third century BC)
Zenodotus is best remembered for being the first head of the celebrated library of Alexandria, although he was an author of works on grammar, Homer and other Greek poets as well. Someone of the same name, also based in Alexandria, wrote works criticising the philosophy of **Plato** [1].

ZENODOTUS THE STOIC (second century BC)
Zenodotus was a pupil of **Diogenes of Babylon**, and wrote an epitaph for **Zeno of Citium**.

ZETHUS (third century AD)
Zethus was a student of **Plotinus** and married the daughter of **Ammonius Saccas**. However, most of his energies went into pursuing careers in public life and medicine.

ZEUXIPPUS OF CNOSSUS (first century BC?)
According to **Diogenes Laertius**, Zeuxippus was a Sceptic, the pupil of **Aenesidemus of Cnossus** and teacher of **Zeuxis**.

ZEUXIS (first century BC/first century AD?)
According to **Diogenes Laertius**, Zeuxis was a Sceptic. He was a friend of **Aenesidemus of Cnossus**, the pupil of **Zeuxippus**, and the teacher of **Antiochus of Laodicea**. He argued that we can trust our senses, but cannot trust any deductions we make on the basis of their evidence. He is not to be confused with a famous painter of the same name.

ZOILUS OF AMPHIPOLIS (fourth/third century BC)
Zoilus was best known for his attacks on Homer (earning him the nickname of Homeromastix, 'the scourge of Homer'). As a result of their savagery, his own

name was subsequently applied to any harsh critic. The poet was not his only target and he gave the same treatment to the works of **Plato** [1]. He was the teacher of **Anaximenes of Lampsacus**, and some, but not all, regarded him as a Cynic. He is said to have met an unpleasant end in one way or another.

ZOILUS OF PERGE (fourth century BC?)
Zoilus was a source used by **Diogenes Laertius** in his account of **Diogenes of Sinope**.

ZOPYRUS (fourth/third century BC)
Carneiscus dedicated a book about friendship to Zopyrus, suggesting he was probably an Epicurean.

ZOPYRUS OF COLOPHON (fourth/third century BC)
According to **Diogenes Laertius**, Zopyrus, in collaboration with **Dionysius of Colophon**, may have been the author of some of the works attributed to the Cynic **Menippus of Gadara**. He was a pupil of **Arcesilaus of Pitane**.

ZOPYRUS OF HERACLEA (fifth century BC?)
Zopyrus was the probable author of a number of mystical poems that **Plato** [1] may have drawn on for some of the myths and imagery in his dialogues. He was possibly a Pythagorean, and almost certainly was if he is to be identified with **Zopyrus of Tarentum**, as some believe.

ZOPYRUS OF TARENTUM (fifth century BC?)
According to **Iamblichus of Chalcis**, Zopyrus was a Pythagorean. He appears to have specialised in mechanical matters, and in particular the design and construction of weapons. His skills were evidently in demand and there are reports of him working in places as far apart as Miletus and Cumae. It is possible that he is to be identified with **Zopyrus of Heraclea**.

ZOSIMIANUS, JULIUS (second century AD)
Zosimianus was a leading Stoic in Athens.

ZOSIMUS (third/fourth century AD)
Often known as 'the Alchemist', Zosimus came from Egypt and spent many years in Alexandria. His philosophy comprised a potent mixture of a number of different elements. He drew on the works of **Iamblichus of Chalcis** and his views on metaphysics were taken from **Democritus of Abdera**, while his approach to moral philosophy showed the influence of both gnosticism and Stoicism, holding that spiritual salvation came through radical detachment from the world. He also borrowed from Hermeticism and Egyptian religious traditions to set alchemy on a new footing.

ZOSIMUS OF ATHENS (second century AD)
Zosimus was a Platonist honoured at Delphi at the same time as **Bacchius of Paphos**, **Nicostratus of Athens** and **Cornelianus of Mallus**.

ZOSTRIANUS (second/third century AD?)
According to **Porphyry**, a book by Zostrianus was in circulation in the time of **Plotinus**. That book may well be identical with a badly damaged text found at Nag Hammadi. From the fragments it is apparent that it was a gnostic text, but not a Christian one. The author would appear to have been a pagan philosopher.
(James M. Robinson (ed.), *The Nag Hammadi Library*, Leiden, Brill, 1977)

ZOTICUS (third century AD)
Zoticus was a poet and critic who was a follower and companion of **Plotinus**.

Bibliographical Essay

The aim of this essay is twofold, first to indicate the principal sources I have drawn on in producing this book and secondly to provide some guidance on further reading. Those familiar with the area will probably derive most benefit from the first, those newer to the area may find the second more useful.

The essay is divided into sections in order to facilitate use. I should point out that I have had to be selective and the omission of any particular book is not to be interpreted as an automatic criticism. There is far more good material to be found than can be fitted into a bibliographical essay of this size. Unless otherwise indicated, only the most recent editions of books are cited. I should also point out that although there is some overlap, the aim is not to reproduce information easily abstracted from the body of the text.

Reference

It is an interesting comment on the amount of work involved in producing substantial works of reference that two of those I have used in the production of this book have yet to be completed. The most useful by far has been *Dictionnaire des Philosophes Antiques* edited by Richard Goulet. Published by CNRS, Paris, the first volume (A) appeared in 1994. There have been two further volumes (B to D and E to J) and a supplement, but there is still a long way to go. For those able to read French, this work is indispensable for its breadth and depth of coverage. Those who can read Latin will find the second edition of *Prosopographia Imperii Romani saec. I, II, III* helpful. Published in Berlin by Walter de Gruyter, the first part (A to B) appeared in 1933 under the editorship of Edmund Groag and Arthur Stein. It is now under the collective editorship of the Academy of Sciences of Berlin and Brandenburg and part seven (Q to ?) is in progress. Readers of German have access to *Paulys Realencyclopädie der classischen Altertumswissenschaft* published in 83 volumes (including supplementary ones) between 1893 and 1978. A shortened and updated version, *Der neue Pauly*, was published in 15 volumes between 1996 and 2003. An English version, *Brill's New Pauly*, edited by Hubert Cancik, Helmuth Schneider and Manfred Landfester, is now being published by Brill of Leiden. The first volume came out in 2003 and others have appeared regularly since.

The *Routledge Encyclopaedia of Philosophy* edited by Edward Craig (London, Routledge, 1998) is valuable. Although the number of ancient philosophers with individual entries is relatively small, many others appear in its pages and can be tracked down through the efficient index. The *Oxford Classical Dictionary*, now in its third edition and edited by Simon Hornblower and

Antony Spawforth (Oxford, Oxford University Press, 1996) obviously covers a lot of relevant ground while for Christian thinkers the *Oxford Dictionary of the Christian Church* (3rd revised edition) edited by F.L. Cross and E.A. Livingstone (Oxford, Oxford University Press, 2005) performs a similar task. Approaching the subject matter of this book from a different direction is the *Prosopography of the Later Roman Empire* (Cambridge, Cambridge University Press). Vol. I (1971), edited by A.H.M. Jones, J.R. Martindale and J. Morris, covers AD 260-395. Vol. II (1980) covers AD 395-527, and vols IIIA/IIIB (1992), edited by J.R. Martindale alone, cover AD 527-641.

Three other books deserve a mention. *Who's Who in the Roman World* (London, Routledge, 2001) and *Who's Who in the Greek World* (London, Routledge, 2000), both by John Hazel, are useful, while *Lemprière's Classical Dictionary* (London, Bracken Books, 1984) is a mine of information even if it is not always reliable.

General

Surprisingly few books cover the whole of ancient philosophy. Historical approaches tend to begin or end with Plato or Aristotle. A useful exception is A.H. Armstrong's *An Introduction to Ancient Philosophy* (London, Methuen, 1965). The first volume of Frederick Copleston's *A History of Philosophy* (London, Continuum, 2003) covers most of the period, and is particularly good in its coverage of the smaller schools. The early chapters of the second volume cover some of the later thinkers. The six volumes of W.K.C. Guthrie's *A History of Greek Philosophy* (Cambridge, Cambridge University Press, 1962-81) are more detailed, but end with Aristotle. The only surviving substantial history of philosophy from antiquity, Diogenes Laertius' *Lives of Eminent Philosophers* (2 vols, trans. R.D. Hicks, Cambridge, Harvard University Press, 1931 and 1972) is also worth reading for all the extra information (and in particular the gossip) I have had to leave out. While not always reliable, it remains indispensable.

Four recent books deserve special mention. The first two volumes of *The Routledge History of Philosophy* (London, Routledge, 1997) are valuable. Vol. 1, *From the Beginning to Plato*, is edited by C.C.W. Taylor and vol. 2, *From Aristotle to Augustine*, by David Furley. They both contain much more bibliographical information than I have been able to include here. I have also been particularly impressed by *The Cambridge Companion to Greek and Roman Philosophy* edited by David Sedley (Cambridge, Cambridge University Press, 2003). Finally, *What is Ancient Philosophy?* by Pierre Hadot (Cambridge, Belknap Press, 2002) is a stimulating discussion of what ancient philosophy was meant to be about.

The Presocratics

In the text I have frequently cited Jonathan Barnes' *Early Greek Philosophy* (Harmondsworth, Penguin, 1987) because it is the most easily available source of translations of the earliest philosophical writings. Covering the same ground in greater depth are G.S. Kirk, J.E. Raven and M. Schofield's *The Presocratic*

Philosophers (Cambridge, Cambridge University Press, 1987), which gives the Greek texts along with the translations and commentary, and Richard D. McKirahan's *Philosophy Before Socrates* (Indianapolis, Hackett, 1994). For more descriptive treatments, Jonathan Barnes' *The Presocratic Philosophers* (London, Routledge, 1982) is useful, as is A.A. Long (ed.) *The Cambridge Companion to Early Greek Philosophy* (Cambridge, Cambridge University Press, 1999). There is still much to learn from John Burnet's *Early Greek Philosophy*, which has gone through many editions and publishers and is sometimes available online.

Pythagoras and Pythagoreans
Because, unlike the other Presocratics, Pythagoras founded a school that survived (or was revived), the literature is rather greater in this area and a few titles of interest may be mentioned. Walter Burkert's *Lore and Science in Ancient Pythagoreanism* (Cambridge, Harvard University Press, 1972) has become a classic. More recent and very useful is Charles H. Kahn, *Pythagoras and the Pythagoreans: a brief history* (Indianapolis, Hackett, 2001). Peter Kingsley's *Ancient Philosophy, Mystery and Magic* (Oxford, Clarendon Press, 1995) is fascinating and challenging. Dominic O'Meara's *Pythagoras Revived* (Oxford, Clarendon Press, 1989) is, as its title suggests, primarily concerned with the later history of the school. Of a different order altogether is Iamblichus' *On the Pythagorean Life* (trans. G. Clark, Liverpool, Liverpool University Press, 1989). It is the sole source of the names of many Pythagoreans otherwise unknown (and in some cases possibly nonexistent!). David Fideler (ed.), *The Pythagorean Sourcebook* (Grand Rapids, Phanes, 1987) contains a variety of texts ascribed to early Pythagorean authors.

The Sophists
G.B. Kerferd's *The Sophistic Movement* (Cambridge, Cambridge University Press, 1981) gives a useful overview of the topic while Rosemary Kent Sprague (ed.), *The Older Sophists* (Indianapolis, Hackett, 2001) is valuable for its collection of original fragments and extracts. Philostratus' *Lives of the Sophists* and Eunapius' *Lives of Philosophers*, found together in one volume of the Loeb library (trans. W.C. Wright, Cambridge, Harvard University Press, 1921) are a good source of information on the later sophists and a host of other characters.

Socrates
The problem with Socrates is that there are so many different interpretations of (or guesses at) his philosophy that different commentators sometimes seem to be talking about different people. Probably the most solid reputation in Socratic studies in recent decades has been that of Gregory Vlastos and anything with his name attached to it is a good starting point.

Plato and Platonism
There is no shortage of materials on Plato. A recent interesting addition to them

is *The People of Plato: a prosopography of Plato and the other Socratics* by Debra Nails (Indianapolis, Hackett, 2002) which contains a vast amount of information on the characters who wandered through Plato's dialogues and life. For Plato's immediate successors there is now the excellent *The Heirs of Plato: a study of the Old Academy (347-274 BC)* by John Dillon (Oxford, Clarendon Press, 2003) while his earlier *The Middle Platonists 80 BC to AD 220* (London, Duckworth, 1996) remains invaluable. J. Glucker's *Antiochus and the Late Academy* (Gottingen, Vandenhoeck and Ruprecht, 1978) contains a lot of material not easily found elsewhere.

Aristotle and the Peripatetics

The Cambridge Companion to Aristotle edited by Jonathan Barnes (Cambridge, Cambridge University Press, 1995) is useful. Volumes in the 'Ancient Commentators on Aristotle' series edited by Richard Sorabji and published by Duckworth continue to appear and constitute an increasingly important resource. J.P. Lynch's *Aristotle's School* (Berkeley, University of California Press, 1972) provides a helpful overview.

Hellenistic philosophy

There are two valuable collections of excerpts and fragments from the Stoics, Epicureans and Sceptics. A.A. Long and D.S. Sedley's *The Hellenistic Philosophers* (Cambridge, Cambridge University Press, 1987) comes in two volumes, but vol. 2 will be of interest only to those who can read the original Greek. Vol. 1 contains the translations and an informative commentary. There is less commentary but a lot of translated material in Brad Inwood and L.P. Gerson's *Hellenistic Philosophy: introductory readings* (Indianapolis, Hackett, 1997). Both books are arranged thematically and both are recommended. In terms of finding what specific philosophers said, the 'Index of Philosophers' in Long and Sedley gives it a clear edge. A.A. Long's *Hellenistic Philosophy* (Berkeley, University of California Press, 1986) is a good introduction to the main schools, as is R.W. Sharples' *Stoics, Epicureans and Sceptics: an introduction to Hellenistic Philosophy* (London, Routledge, 1986). A.H. Armstrong (ed.), *The Cambridge History of Later Greek and Early Medieval Philosophy* (Cambridge, Cambridge University Press, 1970) is, as its name suggests, particularly strong on the later part of the period, especially the Neoplatonists and the Christian theologians influenced by them. Very different in its approach is Gregory H. Snyder's *Teachers and Texts in the Ancient World: Philosophers, Jews and Christians* (London, Routledge, 2000) which focuses on *how* the schools taught rather than *what* they taught.

Stoicism

The Cambridge Companion to the Stoics edited by Brad Inwood (Cambridge, Cambridge University Press, 2003) provides a good thematic coverage of Stoicism although it is less helpful with its history. Still valuable are John Rist's

Stoic Philosophy (Cambridge, Cambridge University Press, 1969) and his edited volume *The Stoics* (Berkeley, University of California Press, 1978). Anything written about Stoicism by A.A. Long is worth reading. Although not without its faults, John Sellars' *The Art of Living: the Stoics on the nature and function of philosophy* (Aldershot, Ashgate, 2003) sheds some useful light.

Epicureanism

The Epicureans have not been particularly well served. Norman De Witt's *Epicurus and his Philosophy* (Minneapolis, University of Minnesota Press, 1954) contains a lot of material. Two more recent books are Howard Jones' *The Epicurean Tradition* (London, Routledge, 1992), which takes a very broad sweep, while Catherine J. Castner's *Prosopography of Roman Epicureans, from the second century BC to the second century AD* (Frankfurt, Peter Lang, 1991), as its title clearly suggests, has a narrower focus.

Cynics

Three books merit special mention. Donald R. Dudley's *A History of Cynicism from Diogenes to the Sixth Century AD* (Chicago, Aries Press, 1980; 2nd edn, London, Bristol Classical Press, 1998) is still valuable. A more recent coverage of much of the same territory is Luis E. Navia's *Classical Cynicism* (Westport, Greenwood Press, 1996). R. Bracht Branham and Marie-Odile Goulet-Cazé (eds), *The Cynics: the Cynic movement in antiquity and its legacy* (Berkeley, University of California Press, 1996) is a particularly good collection of essays with useful appendices.

Scepticism

R.J. Hankinson's *The Sceptics* (London, Routledge, 1995) provides good coverage of the history of scepticism. Richard Bett's *Pyrrho: his antecedents and his legacy* (Oxford, Oxford University Press, 2000) keeps its focus primarily on Pyrrho but within a context that includes many other thinkers. Miles Burnyeat's *The Skeptical Tradition* (Berkeley, University of California Press, 1983) is an interesting collection of essays.

Neoplatonism

A good introduction is R.T. Wallis, *Neoplatonism* (London, Bristol Classical Press, & Indianapolis, Hackett, 1992). Also valuable are A.C. Lloyd's *The Anatomy of Neoplatonism* (Oxford, Clarendon Press, 1990) and the essays in R. Baine Harris (ed.) *The Significance of Neoplatonism* (Norfolk, International Society for Neoplatonic Studies, 1976).

Minor Schools

The minor schools have attracted few monographs, but *The Epistemology of the Cyrenaic School* by Voula Tsouna-McKirahan (Cambridge, Cambridge University Press, 1998) is a relatively recent addition to the literature.

Gnosticism

Still worth reading on gnosticism is Hans Jonas' *The Gnostic Religion* (Boston, Beacon, 1963). Another good overview of the subject is Kurt Rudolph's *Gnosis* (Edinburgh, T & T Clark, 1983). Arland J. Hultgren and Steven A. Haggmark (eds), *The Earliest Christian Heretics* (Minneapolis, Fortress Press, 1996) contains some excerpts from some of the gnostic thinkers.

Christianity

Vol. 1 of Jaroslav Pelikan's *The Christian Tradition: a history of the development of doctrine* covers most of the ground covered here: *The Emergence of the Catholic Tradition 100-600* (Chicago, University of Chicago Press, 1971). J.N.D. Kelly's *Early Christian Doctrines* (A & C Black, London, 1977) is a helpful guide through the doctrinal maze. Extremely valuable as primary sources are the ten volumes of the *Ante-Nicene Fathers*, the fourteen volumes of the first series of *Nicene and Post-Nicene Fathers* and the further fourteen volumes of the second series. The earliest volumes appeared at the end of the nineteenth century and all have been published at one time or another by Eerdmans. They are now all available online at www.ccel.org/fathers2/

Several more early Christian thinkers can be found at the 'More Fathers' website: www.ccel.org/p/pearse/morefathers/home.html

Index of Places

This index refers to the maps on pp. ix-xviii.